WITHDRAWN
UTSA LIBRARIES

ELLIOTT CARTER

Collected Essays and Lectures, 1937–1995

RENEWALS 458-4574

DATE DUE

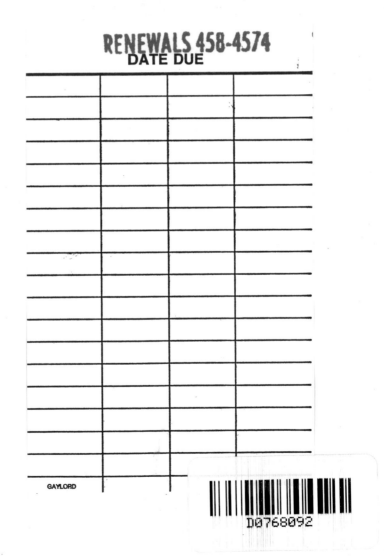

GAYLORD

D0768092

Eastman Studies in Music

ELLIOTT CARTER

Collected Essays and Lectures, 1937–1995

edited by

Jonathan W. Bernard

University of Texas

University of Rochester Press

Copyright © 1997 Jonathan W. Bernard

All Rights Reserved. Except as permitted under current legislation, no part of this work may be photocopied, stored in a retrieval system, published, performed in public, adapted, broadcast, transmitted, recorded or reproduced in any form or by any means, without the prior permission of the copyright owner.

First published 1997
Reprinted in paperback 1998

University of Rochester Press
668 Mt. Hope Avenue
Rochester, New York 14620, USA
and at PO Box 9, Woodbridge, Suffolk IP12 3DF, UK

Library of Congress Cataloging-in-Publication Data
Carter, Elliott, 1908–
    [Literary works.   Selections]
    Elliott Carter : collected essays and lectures, 1937–1995 / edited by Jonathan W. Bernard.
        p.   cm. — (Eastman studies in music, ISSN 1071-9989)
    Includes bibliographical references (p.   ) and index.
    ISBN 1-878822-70-5 (alk. paper)
    1. Music—20th century—history and criticism.   I. Bernard, Jonathan W., 1951–   II. Series.
    ML197.C3425   1996
    780'.9'04—dc20   96-26355
                                                          CIP
                                                          MN

British Library Cataloguing-in-Publication Data
A catalogue record for this book is available from the British Library.

Library
University of Texas
at San Antonio

Typesetting by Generic Compositors
This publication is printed on acid-free paper.
Printed in the United States of America

Contents

Introduction:
Essayist Despite Himself

Not long after his return to the United States in 1935, Elliott Carter wrote a letter to his former teacher, Walter Piston, a draft of which reads in part as follows:

> In looking for a job to carry me through the year I have swallowed my pride deciding to give a try as music critic, so that I can have a chance to hear many concerts. Of all the evils I have thought that for the present this would, if I could get a job in this capacity, solve my financial problem and at the same time give me a certain amount of leisure to compose.
>
> I know your opinion of this work at least as you voiced it to me in connection with [Theodore] Chanler. I dislike the whole idea of having to be both critical and political myself but in the present situation I do not see any other type of work . . .[1]

Evidently the critic's profession was held in no higher esteem among composers at that time than it is now. After six years at Harvard and three more with Nadia Boulanger in Paris, Carter could hardly have imagined that he would ever find himself writing music criticism for a living. But he had returned from abroad to an America deep in the throes of the Great Depression; teaching jobs were practically impossible to get; and his businessman father, displeased at his son's choice of career, had long since cut his financial support to a pittance. Few palatable alternatives presented themselves.

Soon thereafter, it would seem inauspiciously, began Carter's service as a music critic. Yet of all the positions he might conceivably have held, the one he was offered with Minna Lederman at *Modern Music* must have promised more stimulation for a young composer than most: he could write about the music he liked best, rather than the standard repertoire that he would have been obliged to cover for the popular press. Further, he brought to his job a wide acquaintance with the other arts—a distinct advantage in a profession often marked, then as now, with a certain parochialism—which meant that he could be sent occasionally to review the ballet, theatre, and films. Carter, who in college had divided his energies between an academic concentration in English, philosophy, and classics and an extracurricular study of the modernist arts, could not have felt that his talents were going entirely to waste at a journal where good writing and a progressive aesthetic stance were so well appreciated. From the beginning (1937), his prose was marked with a compact clarity and grace which gave ample evidence of the pains he had taken with it.

Carter gave up regular reviewing in the early 1940s in order to teach and to serve as Music Consultant to the Office of War Information; after that time

1. Elliott Carter, letter to Walter Piston, pencil draft; undated, probably early 1936; in Walter Piston Letters file, Carter Collection, Paul Sacher Foundation.

he wrote only occasionally for publication until, with the establishment of his international reputation as a composer in the early 1950s, the musical world began to find his views of contemporary music, and twentieth-century music in general, of particular interest, and presented him with more and more frequent opportunities to express them at length. His activity as a writer began to abate noticeably after 1970, probably owing to the steadily increasing demands placed on his time by compositional commissions, but has never entirely ceased.

It is thus an interesting irony of Carter's life that the composer who never wanted to be a critic has had what amounts to a parallel career, less spectacularly visible than his compositional one but scarcely less distinguished, as an essayist and lecturer. One might even point out that his career as a writer is the longer of the two—if only in the sense that his first publications were not scores but those early reviews in *Modern Music*. In a rather more important sense, it is also the broader. For although Carter has sometimes written (always with a certain reluctance) about his own music, and although a half-dozen or so of his articles in this vein have become classic texts for all students of his compositional oeuvre, more often his subject has been something else. His interests range from the state of new music in Europe and the United States, to the relations between music and the other arts, to such aspects of music as time and rhythm considered as abstract, even philosophical problems, to the work of individual composers both past and present.

Carter's life as a composer, it is fair to say, has provided him, as a writer, with a point of departure: he often seems to feel impelled, in the medium of prose, to generalize upon his own experience. For example, over the years he has devoted a good deal of attention to what it means to be an American composer: whether there is such a thing as an *American* music, with identifiable traits that set it apart from music written anywhere else; or whether, rather, composers in America are significant principally to the extent that they participate in the international musical community. This has led him to raise, in pointed fashion, certain issues that are not always comfortable to consider: the impact of the great numbers of émigré composers that the United States absorbed during the 1930s and '40s, especially on indigenous advanced-music movements; the seeming inability of rich America in the 1950s to lend more than token support to serious new music, while many European countries, devastated by the Second World War and still struggling to recover economically, were doing far more—and the way in which this circumstance has affected European views of American musical life; and the staggering odds against success faced by aspiring young composers who attempt to interest professional American symphony orchestras in playing their works. As trenchant, if at times rather opinionated observations of the contemporary musical scene, his essays are among the very best of their kind. Their value to readers today goes considerably beyond the historical—a value they would have in any case, since Carter has outlived most of his contemporaries. For the combination in Carter of enormous musical gifts and deep experience in the musical profession with a far-ranging, long established acquaintance with most of the other modern arts lends his opinions about music and its place in twentieth-century culture an unusually weighty authority. Furthermore, many of his expectations for what was then the future (hopes and fears both, perhaps especially the latter) have turned out to be remarkably prescient; and much of what he had to say, even in essays and lectures written fifty or more years ago, is if anything more relevant than ever to musicians who, in the waning years of the twentieth century, seek to understand how we have arrived at our present-day situation, and where we might go from here.

The predecessor of this book, *The Writings of Elliott Carter*, edited by Else and Kurt Stone and published by Indiana University Press in 1977, brought together almost everything ever published under Carter's name, from his very beginnings as a critic up to 1976, arranged in strict chronological order.[2] Not long after Mr. Carter asked me to take on the job of preparing a new collection of his prose, I began to feel that it would be better to take a different approach this time—and I was much relieved to find that Carter agreed with me. For the *Writings* ran to over 400 pages of fairly compact print, and it seemed unwise to tax the reader's endurance by assembling anything much longer—yet this limit had somehow to be reconciled with the need for space, not only for the relatively few articles that Carter had published since 1976 (as well as a couple of uncollected items dating from before 1976 that should perhaps have appeared in the earlier book), but also for certain of Carter's previously unpublished essays and lectures that are particularly significant to his life as composer and as thinker about music.

In March 1994, at the invitation of the Paul Sacher Foundation in Basel and at the request of Mr. Carter himself, I spent several weeks with the Carter Collection there, examining Carter's unpublished writings and transcribing all of them. There are about twenty-five substantial unpublished documents in widely varying states of completion, mostly from the 1950s and '60s, and many shorter ones; the present book includes about half of the former and a few of the latter—essentially, that is, everything of genuine interest that had already been brought close to publishable standard or that could be salvaged with a certain amount (in a few cases considerable amount) of revision on the author's part and further editorial work on my part.

The reader might well be curious as to why Carter has left so much that is worthwhile unpublished over the years. The circumstances vary from essay to essay, as the source notes in Appendix 1 will show, but they all come down to the same thing: Carter has always been a composer first and a writer second, and publication of his own prose, especially as his rise to prominence was boosted by the international *éclat* attendant on his First String Quartet in the early 1950s, has stood appreciably lower in his order of priorities. One gets the impression that unless some editor happened to ask for a written version of a lecture or paper, and kept after him until it was delivered, the text was likely to be shoved aside and eventually buried under the sketches for the next

2. A very few previously unpublished pieces, totaling about twenty pages, were collected in this edition.

composition. Most of the previously unpublished essays chosen for this collection, in fact, had been completely forgotten before Carter's papers and manuscripts were bought by the Sacher Foundation in 1986 and its staff had had the opportunity to sort through the immense accumulation which arrived over the next several years.[3] Some of these texts posed an additional challenge to their author, in that at the time of oral delivery they existed in several different forms, none completely satisfactory, and the not inconsiderable task of amalgamating them ended up being deferred indefinitely as more urgent (compositional) deadlines intruded.

Just as the present selection of previously unpublished texts represents our joint decisions, so does the exclusion of some of the contents of the *Writings*. Most of the previously collected articles that do not appear in this volume date from Carter's earliest years as a critic and consist largely of routine concert reportage; readers familiar with the *Writings* will also notice that a few other "occasional" pieces, as well as the shorter program notes that have accompanied Carter's published scores and the commercial recordings made of his music, have also disappeared. The undeniable historical value of Carter's reviews from the 1930s and early '40s remains, of course—and the reviews themselves remain available for consultation in research libraries, in the *Writings* or the original issues of *Modern Music*, the *Saturday Review*, and other periodicals—but their subject matter itself was, for the most part, never of more than topical, immediate interest. It must be said, too, that the intrinsic value of many of these articles is limited by the relative naiveté of their author at that time in his life. These *Collected Essays and Lectures* thus tend to emphasize the more extended pieces of writing that Carter has done, while by no means entirely eliminating the shorter ones. The resulting balance seems somehow appropriate for a composer who is best known for his musical works of larger scope—and who hardly ever tends to the aphoristic even in the briefer works clustered during his early career and over the past decade. (See Appendix 2 for a complete list of those of Carter's previously published articles that do not appear in the present collection.)

Those who know the *Writings* will find some other changes in the present collection as well. First of all, chronological arrangement of contents has been abandoned in favor of thematic grouping. One could certainly argue that for a less selective collection, especially one that contained so many reviews treating diverse topics, the chronological option was the most sensible. And of course the editors Stone were quite right to point out, in their Introductory

---

3. This process is by no means yet finished. For one thing, of course, Carter is still active as a composer, which means that the Foundation receives a sizable package of sketches and manuscripts from him every so often. For another, within the past couple of years there has been another, quite large influx, as the Carters sold their summer house in Waccabuc, New York and cleared out a considerable pile of material that had been previously overlooked. During my visit to the Foundation in 1994, I exhumed several essays myself from a still-unsorted carton. Thanks to the careful and thorough work of the staff, however—in particular Dr. Felix Meyer, curator of the Carter Collection—I am reasonably certain that I was able to locate and transcribe all extant unpublished texts.

Note to the *Writings*, that no single thematic arrangement could ever be ideal, since Carter typically treats many different subjects in the course of a single essay. But it is also true that each essay, despite its various digressions and asides, has a central focus which it is well to respect by setting it alongside other essays that are similar in focus—this for the sake both of making the collection as a whole more readable and of facilitating its use for reference (to which latter purpose the Index will serve as a useful complement). Each of the six categories ("Surveying the Compositional Scene"; "American Music"; "Charles Ives"; "Some Other Composers"; "Life and Work"; "Philosophy, Criticism, and the Other Arts") is sufficiently broad to encompass numerous different topics and types of prose pieces—with the obvious exception of "Charles Ives," the contents of which have been set apart in acknowledgment of the extensive and sustained attention that Ives in particular has received in Carter's critical writing over several decades. Organization within the sections defined by these categories varies: sometimes it is thematic as well—for example, "Surveying the Compositional Scene" begins with several general essays, continues with two critiques of specific compositional methods, and ends with a series of reports on European concerts and festivals; in other sections, such as "American Music" and "Charles Ives," chronological order seemed the most useful. The only section in which arrangement is essentially arbitrary (if, it is hoped, interestingly so) is "Some Other Composers," where the essays appear in the order determined by the composers' dates of birth.

This reordering of contents has also made it necessary to consider them as a whole, instead of simply as a compilation of pieces previously published separately. In any collection of this sort, no matter how organized, overlaps between essays are inevitable—and are in fact not necessarily bad, since the same point made in different ways may benefit from the extra dimensions it thereby acquires and may also reveal a progression in the author's thinking about important issues over time. This is certainly true, for example, of the essays on Ives. But the same point made too many times in the same way quickly makes for tedious reading, and in a number of cases some editorial intervention was clearly desirable. At all times I have attempted to tread lightly, and in all places (there are relatively few of them) where the wording of previously published prose has been adjusted I have changed no more than seemed absolutely necessary for the sake of readerly flow. There are a few changes of other sorts throughout as well, where the original editing was deficient in some obvious way; most such changes are extremely minor. I have also taken it upon myself to standardize such minutiae as punctuation, capitalization, and citation practice, and have in some cases modernized the last for the reader's convenience (one prominent instance of this is the suppression of all references to the original 1920 edition of Ives's *Essays Before a Sonata*, no longer widely available, in favor of Howard Boatwright's edition of 1962). The Stones' notes and explanatory headings, if carried over to this collection at all, have been consigned to the notes, where they bear the legend "[S]," or to the source notes in Appendix 1. My own notes, most of them supplied for the sake of bibliographic authentication where it was possible to track down quoted material previously unattributed, are identified by "[B]"; the few of the Stones' notes that I have added to or otherwise modified are identified by "[S,B]."

Despite the very different shape that these *Collected Essays and Lectures* have taken by comparison to the *Writings*, it goes (practically) without saying that I owe a substantial debt to Else and Kurt Stone for the work they did to gather together Carter's published writings through the 1970s. I would also like to express my thanks to the Paul Sacher Foundation for its generous support of my visit to Basel in March 1994, and to its staff, in particular Dr. Felix Meyer, curator of the Carter Collection, who was a veritable font of useful advice, and who could not have been more helpful in ensuring that I gained access to all relevant documents. I am grateful to the University of Washington for sabbatical leave during the 1994–95 academic year, which has made the completion of this project possible, and to Dr. Daniel Neuman, Director of the School of Music until June 1994, for letting me adjust my teaching and administrative schedules around a three-week trip to Basel in the middle of an academic year. I would also like to acknowledge the financial support provided by the Amphion Foundation (New York), which has been much appreciated. Special thanks for rendering invaluable bibliographic assistance and providing other important information go to Anton Vishio (Harvard University) and William Pastille (St. John's College). My heartfelt thanks as well to Ralph P. Locke, Senior Editor of Eastman Studies in Music at the University of Rochester Press, for his terrific enthusiasm about this project right from the time I first proposed it, and for the encouragement that has carried me through its various stages of development; and to Directors Robert Easton (past) and Sean M. Culhane (present) of the Press for their meticulous and efficient work toward its publication. Most of all, I would like to thank Elliott and Helen Carter for their unflagging encouragement and moral support as this collection has wended its way to publication—and, finally, Elliott himself, for the time he has taken out of a very demanding schedule to attend to the task of revision and to reply promptly and patiently to my many questions, and for composing the wonderful works that, ultimately, are what make this collection worthy of sustained attention from all who take music seriously.

August, 1996   J. W. B.

Acknowledgments

NOTE: Every effort has been made to contact the owners of copyright for the material reprinted in this book (previously published, previously collected, or not). In a few cases it proved impossible, either to ascertain who now holds copyright, or to establish communication with the apparent owners after repeated attempts. To all the others, listed below, the editor hereby expresses his gratitude. (Please see Appendix 1 for full bibliographical citations of previously published essays.)

The American Academy of Arts and Letters, for "Igor Stravinsky, 1882–1971" and "Roger Sessions, 1896–1985," and for quotations from the letters of Charles Ives that appear in "Documents of a Friendship with Ives." Courtesy of the American Academy of Arts and Letters, New York City.

Associated Music Publishers, Inc., for excerpts from works by Elliott Carter, Charles Ives, and Walter Piston. Piston, Symphony No. 2, copyright 1944 by Arrow Music Press; copyright renewed 1972 by Associated Music Publishers, Inc. (BMI); all rights reserved; used by permission. Piston, String Quartet No. 1, copyright 1934 by Arrow Music Press; copyright renewed 1967 by Associated Music Publishers, Inc. (BMI); all rights reserved; used by permission. Piston, Sonata for Violin and Piano, copyright 1939 by Arrow Music Press; copyright renewed 1967 by Associated Music Publishers, Inc. (BMI); all rights reserved; used by permission. Ives, Symphony No. 4, copyright 1965 (renewed) by Associated Music Publishers, Inc. (BMI); all rights reserved; used by permission. Carter, String Quartet No. 1, copyright 1955, 1956 (renewed) by Associated Music Publishers, Inc. (BMI); all rights reserved; used by permission. Carter, Variations for Orchestra, copyright 1958 (renewed) by Associated Music Publishers, Inc. (BMI); all rights reserved; used by permission. Carter, *Eight Etudes and a Fantasy for Woodwind Quartet*, copyright 1959 (renewed) by Associated Music Publishers, Inc. (BMI); all rights reserved; used by permission. Carter, String Quartet No. 2, copyright 1961 (renewed) by Associated Music Publishers, Inc. (BMI); all rights reserved; used by permission. Carter, Double Concerto, copyright 1962 (renewed) by Associated Music Publishers, Inc. (BMI); all rights reserved; used by permission. Carter, Piano Concerto, copyright 1967 (renewed) by Associated Music Publishers, Inc. (BMI): all rights reserved; used by permission. Carter, *Eight Pieces for Four Timpani*, copyright 1968 by Associated Music Publishers, Inc. (BMI); all rights reserved; used by permission.

Elliott Carter, for "An American Destiny," "Introduction to a Poetry Reading by W. H. Auden," "Brass Quintet," "The Composer's Choices," "Gabriel Fauré," "A Further Step," "Charles Ives Remembered," "Music Criticism,"

"The Genial Sage," "For Pierre Boulez on His Sixtieth," "Reminiscence of Italy," "Some Reflections on *Tre per sette*," "'La musique sérielle aujour-d'hui.'"

The College Music Society, for "'The Composer Is a University Commodity.'"

Doubleday & Company, Inc., a division of Bantam Doubleday Dell Publishing Group, Inc., for Carter's reminiscence of Balanchine included in *I Remember Balanchine*, ed. Francis Mason.

ECS Publishing, for excerpts from Walter Piston's Suite for Oboe and Piano included in "Walter Piston." Copyright 1934 by E. C. Schirmer Music Co., renewed 1961. Copyright assigned 1964 to Ione Press, Inc. Sole selling agent: ECS Publishing, Boston, Mass. Reprinted with permission.

European-American Music, for excerpts from Pierre Boulez's *Improvisation sur Mallarmé II* and Bo Nilsson's *Ein irrender Sohn* included in "ISCM Festival, Rome." Used by permission of European American Music Distributors Corporation, sole U.S. and Canadian agent for Universal Edition (London) Ltd., London. Boulez, *Improvisation sur Mallarmé II* © Copyright 1958 by Universal Edition (London) Ltd., London. Copyright renewed; all rights reserved. Nilsson, *Ein irrender Sohn* © Copyright 1959 by Universal Edition (London) Ltd., London. Copyright renewed; all rights reserved.

G. Schirmer, Inc., for excerpts from works by Walter Piston. Symphony No. 1, copyright 1945 (renewed) by G. Schirmer, Inc. (ASCAP); international copyright secured; all rights reserved; reprinted by permission. String Quartet No. 2, copyright 1946 (renewed) by G. Schirmer, Inc. (ASCAP); international copyright secured; all rights reserved; reprinted by permission.

Institute for Studies in American Music at Brooklyn College (CUNY), for "On Edgard Varèse."

League of Composers/ISCM, for all articles originally published in *Modern Music*: "Fallacy of the Mechanistic Approach," "Once Again Swing; also 'American Music,'" "American Music in the New York Scene," "The Case of Mr. Ives," "Ives Today: His Vision and Challenge," "American Figure, with Landscape," "Stravinsky in 1940," "More about Balanchine," "With the Dancers," "Theatre and Films," "Music as a Liberal Art."

Oxford University Press, for all articles originally published in *The Musical Quarterly*: "ISCM Festival, Rome," "*Rasputin's End* and *Lady Macbeth of Mtsensk*," "Edward Steuermann," "Walter Piston," "Roger Sessions: Violin Concerto," "Shop Talk by an American Composer."

The Paul Sacher Foundation, for quotations from Elliott Carter's correspondence, and for the following previously unpublished essays and lectures of Carter: "The Challenge of the New," "ISCM Festival, Amsterdam," "The Agony of Modern Music in America, 1955," "The European Roots of American Musical Culture," "The Three Late Sonatas of Debussy," "The Recent Works of Goffredo Petrassi," "To Be a Composer in America," "On Saint-John Perse and the Concerto for Orchestra," "'Elle est la musique en personne': A Reminiscence of Nadia Boulanger," "Time Lecture," "The *Gesamtkunstwerk*," "Soviet Music."

Perspectives of New Music, for "Letter from Europe," "Expressionism and American Music," "Igor Stravinsky, 1882–1971," "In Memoriam: Stefan Wolpe, 1902–1972," "To Think of Milton Babbitt," "Roger Sessions Admired."

The Poetry in Review Foundation, for "Documents of a Friendship with Ives."

Theodore Presser Co., for excerpts from works by Charles Ives and Conlon Nancarrow. Ives, *Calcium Light*, copyright 1953 by New Music Edition; used by permission of the publisher, Theodore Presser Co. Nancarrow, *Rhythm Study No. 1*, copyright 1952 by New Music Edition; used by permission of the publisher, Theodore Presser Co.

The University of Oklahoma Press, for "The Orchestral Composer's Point of View."

The University of Texas Press, for "Music and the Time Screen."

A Carter Chronology

1908   Born 11 December, New York.

1926–30   Following graduation from the Horace Mann School (New York), attends Harvard University, majoring in English literature (A.B. 1930), while studying music at the Longy School.

1930–32   Pursues graduate studies at Harvard (A.M., Music, 1932): harmony and counterpoint with Walter Piston, composition with Gustav Holst.

1932–35   Study at Ecole Normale de Musique, Paris (*Licence de contrepoint*, 1935); private instruction with Nadia Boulanger.

1937   Begins writing music criticism for the periodical *Modern Music* in New York; his articles appear there until 1946. Music director of Lincoln Kirstein's Ballet Caravan (until 1939).

1939   Marries Helen Frost-Jones, sculptor and art critic.

1940–45   Instructor in music, Greek, and mathematics at St. John's College, Annapolis, Md. (through 1944). Serves as music consultant to the Office of War Information (1943–45).

1945–46   Awarded Guggenheim Fellowship; completes Piano Sonata.

1946–48   Professor of Composition, Peabody Conservatory, Baltimore. Cello Sonata commissioned by Bernard Greenhouse.

1948–50   Professor of Composition, Columbia University.

1950–51   Second Guggenheim Fellowship spent composing First String Quartet, which in 1953 wins first prize at the Concours International de Quatuors à Cordes, Liège, Belgium.

1953–55   Awarded Prix de Rome and spends year (1953–54) as Fellow of the American Academy in Rome, working on the Variations for Orchestra, commissioned by the Louisville Orchestra through the Rockefeller Foundation.

1955–56   Professor of Composition, Queens College, New York.

1956   Elected to National Institute of Arts and Letters. Variations for Orchestra premiered by the Louisville Orchestra under Robert Whitney, 21 April.

1958   Instructor at the Salzburg Seminars.

1960   The Second String Quartet, premiered by the Juilliard Quartet in New York 25 March, wins the Pulitzer Prize and the New York Critics' Circle Award that year, and the UNESCO Prize the following year.

1960–62   Professor of Composition, Yale University.

1961   The Double Concerto for Harpsichord and Piano with Two Chamber Orchestras, commissioned by the Fromm Foundation and premiered in New York 6 September, wins the New York Critics' Circle Award. Receives the Sibelius Medal for Music and an honorary doctorate from New England Conservatory.

1963   Begins work on Piano Concerto while composer-in-residence at the American Academy in Rome. Elected to American Academy of Arts and Sciences, Boston.

1964   Composer-in-residence, Berlin, under the auspices of the Ford Foundation. Professor of Composition, Juilliard School of Music (through 1984).

1965   Receives honorary doctorate from Swarthmore College and the Creative Arts Award from Brandeis University. Begins work on the Concerto for Orchestra.

1967   Piano Concerto, commissioned by Jacob Lateiner and the Ford Foundation, premiered by Lateiner and the Boston Symphony Orchestra under Erich Leinsdorf in Boston, 6 January. Honorary doctorate from Princeton University; Professor of Composition at the Massachusetts Institute of Technology.

1967–68 Andrew D. White Professor-at-Large, Cornell University.

1968   Composer-in-residence, American Academy, Rome.

1969   Receives the Premio delle Muse, "Polimnia," awarded by the Associazione Artistico Letteraria Internazionale, Florence. Elected to American Academy of Arts and Letters.

1970   Concerto for Orchestra, commissioned by the New York Philharmonic for its 125th anniversary year, premiered by the Philharmonic under Leonard Bernstein, 5 February. Honorary doctorates from Harvard University, Yale University, Oberlin College, and Boston University.

1971   Gold Medal for Eminence in Music awarded by Aaron Copland for the National Institute of Arts and Letters.

1973   The Third String Quartet, commissioned by the Juilliard School of Music for the Juilliard Quartet and premiered 23 January, wins Carter his second Pulitzer Prize. In honor of his sixty-fifth birthday, the Library and Museum of the Performing Arts of the New York Public Library at Lincoln Center mounts an exhibition of his sketches and scores in manuscript.

1974   Brass Quintet, commissioned by the American Brass Quintet, premiered on the air at the BBC, 20 October.

1975   Duo for Violin and Piano, commissioned by the Library of Congress, premiered in Washington by Paul Zukofsky and Gilbert Kalish, 21 March.

1976   *A Mirror on Which to Dwell*, commissioned by Speculum Musicae, premiered 24 February.

1977   *A Symphony of Three Orchestras*, commissioned by the New York Philharmonic and the National Endowment for the Arts, premiered by the Philharmonic under Pierre Boulez, 17 February. Performances of several chamber works at the opening of IRCAM/Centre George Pompidou, Paris.

1978   *Syringa*, commissioned through the National Endowment for the

Arts, premiered by Speculum Musicae on December 10, the eve of Carter's seventieth birthday.

1980   *Night Fantasies*, commissioned jointly by Paul Jacobs, Gilbert Kalish, Ursula Oppens, and Charles Rosen, premiered by Oppens at the Bath Festival, England, 2 June.

1981   Performances at Venice Biennale. Awarded the Ernst von Siemens Music Prize (Munich).

1982   *In Sleep, in Thunder*, commissioned by the London Sinfonietta, premiered 26 October. Performances at the Holland Festival (fourteen works) and at the Badenweiler Festival, Germany.

1983   *Triple Duo*, commissioned by the BBC for the Fires of London, premiered in New York, 23 April. Seventy-fifth birthday concerts at the Library of Congress and at the Arnold Schoenberg Institute in Los Angeles. Honorary doctorate from Cambridge University.

1985   *Esprit rude/esprit doux*, commissioned by the Southwest German Radio (Baden-Baden), premiered on the air, 31 March. *Penthode*, commissioned by Pierre Boulez and the Ensemble InterContemporain, premiered in London, 26 July. National Medal of the Arts (US).

1986   Fourth String Quartet commissioned by the Composers Quartet, who give the premiere 17 September in Miami as part of a complete cycle of the Carter quartets.

1987   *A Celebration of Some 100 x 150 Notes*, commissioned by the Houston Symphony, premiered 10 April. Performances at the Holland Festival. Awarded the rank of Commandeur dans l'Ordre des Arts et des Lettres by the French Government.

1988   Oboe Concerto, commissioned by Paul Sacher for Heinz Holliger, premiered in Zurich, 17 June. Performances at Pontino Festival, Rome. Eightieth birthday tributes at Tanglewood and the Bath Festival, and in New York, San Francisco, Cincinnati, Hartford, and Buffalo. *Remembrance*, commissioned by the Fromm Foundation, premiered at Tanglewood, 10 August.

1989   Performances at Settembre Musica, Turin. *Anniversary*, commissioned by the British Broadcasting Corporation, premiered by the BBC Orchestra under Oliver Knussen, 5 October.

1990   Violin Concerto, commissioned by Ole Böhn and the San Francisco Symphony, premiered 2 May. *Con leggerezza pensosa*, dedicated to Italo Calvino, premiered in Latina, Italy, 29 September. Performances at Royal Academy of Music, London (some nineteen works), at Aldeburgh Festival, and at Wien Modern (thirteen works).

1991   "Compositeur invité" at the Centre Acanthes, Avignon Festival (July), a two-week session featuring lectures and master classes focused on his music, and performances by Charles Rosen, the Arditti Quartet, and Pierre Boulez with the Ensemble InterContemporain.

Other performances at London's South Bank Centre; in Brussels, Hannover, and Moscow; at the Getty Center in Santa Monica; and in New York, where the Juilliard Quartet performs all four string quartets. Awarded rank of Commendatore in the Order of Merit of the Republic of Italy.

1992   *Trilogy*, commissioned by Heinz Holliger, premiered at the Pontino Festival, 30 June. Quintet for Piano and Winds, commissioned by Heinz Holliger and KölnMusik, premiered in Cologne, 13 September. Composer-in-residence, Getty Center. Performances in Geneva, Lisbon, Royaumont, and Oslo.

1993   Performances in Rotterdam, San Francisco, and Paris. *Gra*, commissioned by the Pontino Festival for Witold Lutoslawski's eightieth birthday, premiered at Pontino, 4 June. Eighty-fifth birthday concerts given by Speculum Musicae (New York) and Boston Musica Viva.

1994   Composer-in-residence, Getty Center. *Partita*, commissioned by the Chicago Symphony, premiered 17 February under Daniel Barenboim. *90+*, written in honor of Goffredo Petrassi's ninetieth birthday, premiered at Pontino Festival, 12 June. Recording of Violin Concerto on Virgin Classics wins Gramophone Award for Best Contemporary Composition.

1995   *Esprit rude/esprit doux II*, written for Boulez's seventieth birthday, premiered in Chicago, 31 March. *Figment*, for solo 'cello, commissioned by Thomas Demenga, premiered in New York, 8 May. *Of Challenge and of Love*, five songs on poems of John Hollander for soprano and piano, premiered at Aldeburgh Festival, 19 June. *Adagio Tenebroso*, commissioned by the BBC for the 100th anniversary of the Proms, premiered 13 September by the BBC Symphony under Andrew Davis. Fifth String Quartet, commissioned by the Arditti Quartet, premiered by the Arditti in Antwerp, 19 September. Future compositional plans include an orchestral work to complete the trilogy begun with *Partita* and *Adagio Tenebroso*, and a Clarinet Concerto commissioned by the Ensemble InterContemporain.

ELLIOTT CARTER

Collected Essays and Lectures, 1937–1995

I

Surveying the Compositional Scene

The Composer's Viewpoint
(1946)

It seems that everything is a problem to the composer. We always seem to be trouble-shooting, trying to explain ourselves to ourselves and to others. We bother our families with such talk and we get together in meetings to see what can be done to help things, sitting around tables as if we were highly paid executives with big problems of organization on our shoulders. Each of us has already said so much that by now it is hard to know where to begin.

There is, however, just one simple fact, I think, on which all the problems of serious composers hinge. What almost any composer worth his salt would like to write, what all performers and publishers would like to find, what teachers, critics, and audiences agree is what they want to hear, is interesting and durable music. I mean by this, music that stands on its own feet and says what it has to say so well that it can be heard many times with constantly growing interest and understanding. Some cynics have claimed that this cannot be written in our time, that we have lost the knack. But just the same we all seem hopeful, for our clamor about American music and about new music in general really betrays the desire to find and to nurture such durable music.

It is obvious that the world of serious music needs a considerable amount of this music to exist at all. Its public appeal depends on this music and all its operations revolve around it. If we once forget this fact and give the short-lived, the so-called "novelty music" a central position, performers will begin to lose their skill for want of mature compositions to call out their best abilities, and audiences will begin to get bored. The whole profession will run downhill, losing its direction and prestige along the way.

The kind of music I am talking about does not grow in a desert. It needs encouragement, and the right kind of encouragement. We composers think our desire to write durable music a far-sighted one, though to our performing and publishing friends it often seems very stubborn of us to take things so seriously, turning out sonatas and symphonies that have few chances of performances and fewer of sales. Some of us like to think, perhaps naively, that we could turn out the kind of work that would be immediately successful at once if we wanted to. But many of us feel that a little of this goes a long way. Sometimes what we think is our best work catches on with the public, to our own surprise and delight, though in a way this is disturbing too. We have all seen the public go wrong so often in matters of serious music. We think of all those

3

great works, now a part of our repertory, that were complete failures when they were first played. That thought makes us suspicious, especially here in America, where practically none of our great writers and other creative artists were successful during their lifetimes. You can see what I mean when I say that everything is a problem to a composer.

What composers do in this situation is to surround themselves with like-minded people in the hope that if one does not have what it takes to write such music, at least he can help another do so by providing the encouragement and understanding which one should be able to find among those more in touch with commercial enterprises. Part of the development of a composer comes when he gets the chance to hear his music played before an audience. So, to help each other out, some turn concert managers, publishers, writers, and lecturers—generally, of course, on a non-profit basis, like the poverty-stricken philanthropists they very often are. They start such organizations as the League of Composers, the New Music Editions, the American Music Center, the Eastman Festival of American Music, and the rest, in the hope that durable music will be able to develop unhampered by the disturbing distractions that come with our present economic setup. They don't want a quick success that results in quick collapse. The results of such organizations prove that composers know their job. For most of our important contemporaries have developed in close contact with such groups.

Composers, as you know, are often people of vision. They are willing to make long-term investments of their own time and their creative effort, believing that only in this way will anything good ever be accomplished. But they are surrounded by a society that insists on quick returns for its money, and in the process is continually meeting with the disappointing fact that successes fostered in this way are transient. When you think of how profitable the durable classics of music have been to everybody concerned, how much more profitable than any passing novelty, then you cannot understand why more performers, publishers, and teachers are not out to foster new music of this level.

Just the opposite is only too often the result of their efforts. Most performers, for instance, treat all works of new music as novelty items, clamoring for first performances as if they did not believe the work could stand a second hearing. Composers are put on the spot by this and have to keep writing music, often more than they should, in order to remain before the public. With the kind of system for publicity that we have set up in this country, it often seems more important to keep a name, rather than a work, in the limelight because revivals of older works by new composers are among the rarer events in this wasteful quest for novelty.

The destructiveness of this foolish attitude is immediately apparent. It is not confined to performers alone. Publishers are always looking for short, appealing, and easy works, real novelty merchandise, that is intended to sell for a short time and be forgotten for good. In fact they heave long sighs and shake their heads if the misguided music writer shows up at their offices with longer, more important works.

It is silly to take a top-lofty attitude in these matters, for novelties are indeed often the spice of life, if not its meat and drink. But what we composers are worried about is that our musical meat and drink seem so severely rationed at the present time. For its production and distribution are being discouraged by the very individuals who stand to make a profit if really good music were uncovered. We tend to see an analogy to the harmful practices of lumberjacks who cut down all the trees in a forest without replanting for another year's harvest. Certainly there are only too few evidences of a long view, a view that would stimulate the best of our talents to mature and be productive.

And so I would urge everyone connected with music to consider his responsibility in helping to develop this durable music here in this country. For if a long view is not taken, the short-term stress on novelty may very well crush more lasting efforts and result in a sense of frustration all around. Publishers should be willing to take more risks on works that aim in the right direction, and performers and teachers should be on the lookout for good works, whether they have ever been performed or not.

We must stress and stress again musical quality, looking behind the facade of prestige, of publicity, often such deceptive indications of lasting worth. For it is the achievement of high musical quality that rouses the enthusiasm of each of us, and gives our profession its distinction and power. We must jealously guard it.

A Further Step
(1958)

At present a new situation seems to be taking shape in the field of musical composition. Many young and a few older composers are being driven by what appears to be an imperious need to find a new principle of musical structure. Up to now, twentieth-century composers have explored new domains of harmony and their implications and have tried experiments with rhythm, timbre, and sonority; but for the most part they have employed these new materials in familiar contexts, and often produced expressive or formal effects similar to those found in older music. But today—as befits an art whose formative dimension is time—the technique of continuity and contrast, of qualities and types of motion, of the formation and development of a musical idea or event, and in general the various kinds of cause and effect patterns that can be suggested in musical flow, occupy the attention of composers more than harmony or other matters, all of which now become simply details in a larger kind of concern.

In this view, no item, no unifying principle or method of continuity is self-evident or considered a given part of musical process, but all are considered in light of the whole and included or worked over so as to be able to fit the general scheme. Such a reexamination of musical discourse seems inevitable now, and a necessary culmination of all the different efforts of composers in our century. The intention is somewhat similar to the emancipation of musical discourse that took place during the time of Bach's sons and the Mannheim school, although today's is much more thoroughgoing. As in the products of that period, there have been many foreglimpses of change preceding the present transformation.

Perhaps the first clear indication of this new direction was enunciated by Debussy in his letters and articles, in which he made it plain that he was seeking a new and fresher musical psychology that did not use such classical devices as development and sequence. His ideas are, of course, wonderfully carried out in the later works, although within a limited frame. The influence of his point of view was widespread, leaving its effect on Stravinsky, particularly in the work dedicated to Debussy's memory, the *Symphonies of Wind Instruments*, and in the remarkable *Symphony in Three Movements*, a work that gives a first impression of being a loose construction of short condensed ideas but with familiarity reveals a tight organization of inner relationships that provides an entirely new solution for the problem of large-scale continuity.

In Vienna the influence of Debussy's ideas fell on fertile ground, as shown particularly in the works written there before the adoption of the twelve-tone method, such as Schoenberg's *Five Pieces for Orchestra* and *Pierrot lunaire*, Alban Berg's *Four Pieces for Clarinet and Piano* and *Three Pieces for Orchestra*, and Webern's *Bagatelles*. These and other works of the time give a glimpse of a new universe of emancipated discourse, unfortunately quickly abandoned when Schoenberg returned to the classical musical shapes upon adopting the twelve-tone system.

Similar explorations can be found in some of the music of Sibelius and Janáček, in the early works of Chávez and Arthur Lourié, and to a lesser extent in Charles Ives and Roy Harris, as well as in a number of scarcely remembered Americans and in some Russians from before the time of Stalin. This trend remained secondary, emerging only from time to time, as in Schoenberg's String Trio, op. 45 (1946), a work that is significant for its combination of the twelve-tone method with the emancipated discourse of his earlier period. Even today, this development is not clearly discerned by critics, who confound it with stylistic trends that have at times come to grips with the challenges of this kind of discourse, such as "serial technique," "pointillism," or "expressionism." Clearly, none of these is necessarily associated with the other, nor are they mutually exclusive since each comes from a different category of description.

While it is not the point of this article to maintain the very dubious notion that artistic quality appears only in the musically advanced works, still it must be pointed out that new directions and ideas in art exercise in our day an increasing influence, even on conservatives. One of the present problems among musicians is that of keeping abreast of the time, since the musical world, like any other professional world of today, is in a state of very rapid change. The purpose here is simply to try to establish a general description of the direction which many different trends seem to be taking today, to consider a few of the many reasons for this, and to speculate on the problems of artistic quality and intelligibility that these new departures seem to raise. One of the most interesting and perplexing of these problems is that of the extent to which our judgment of "musicality," or of the possibility of important communication that a work contains, depends on the carrying over of preestablished patterns, both of attitude and of method, from familiar works that unquestionably have these qualities.

When listening to the recent works of Stravinsky, such as *Agon* or the *Canticum sacrum*, or Copland's new *Piano Fantasy*, there can be no doubt in the mind of the listener accustomed to the new music that these works make a kind of impression that more immediately accessible music never can. They may now be perplexing to many of the musical public because of their unusual sound and unfamiliar ideas and procedures; but to those listeners for whom modernity holds no terrors, they are on the same high level as many works of the older concert repertory. Hence they will, sooner or later, unquestionably become accessible to the larger public. At first hearing, we are struck by their artistic power and unity of vision, all the more remarkable for having been achieved by integrating very conflicting currents of feeling, thought, and technique, and by using this integration in a positive way to communicate a musical experience of commanding importance. Just as in the classics of the repertory, there are many levels of different preestablished techniques in these works. There is first of all the personal vision of the composer and his high standards of integration and of musical interest, which in turn are part of his sense of professional responsibility. There is the personal musical point of view that involves using a musical commentary on other styles as a feature of one's own expression. Then there are the many stylistic and formal features, small and large, that have become part of the composer's vocabulary over the years—a mixture of digested techniques drawn from other music, with predilections and inventions of his own. Lastly, in these particular works there is the use of twelve-tone technique (comparatively new in both composers), which Stravinsky and Copland have turned to their own uses. As in the case of the classics, a new work is made out of the materials of all these preestablished elements, each of them the result of slow, painstaking musical evolution.

A more trivial example may illustrate one of kind of improvisation, at least, and its relation to preestablished techniques. Many of the older generation of French organists have developed an extraordinary ability to improvise on a given theme and occasionally give public demonstrations of their prowess, asking the public for the notes of a theme. At one of these sessions a particularly tortuous twelve-tone series was presented by a group of music students. With hardly a moment's hesitation the organist pulled out his stops and embarked on a half hour of variations, a passacaglia and fugue with many incidental canons; all quite audibly connected to the given theme, but all in the standard post-Franckian style with its Romantic altered chords, its modulating sequences—and winding up, of course, with an apotheosis of the theme against a background of rapid arpeggiation. The power of this highly developed, scholastic, preestablished world of musical devices was so great that it could meet any musical problem with a ready-made solution of great intricacy and refinement. There was, of course, no pretense that this was great music; it was intended simply as a demonstration of skill—much the same kind of skill (but with an added element of genius) that Bach must have revealed to Frederick the Great. But while in Bach's time, and especially in his later life, many elements of general technique and of his own were "given" as part of his musical vocabulary, fifty years ago such was not the case, and it was unlikely that an improviser could do more than astonish his listeners with a display of remarkable musical ingenuity based on a whole group of academic or commercial routines. In fact, one might almost say that improvisation itself, if it is to be interesting to the listener, must have a whole set of pat, standardized, prearranged techniques, even though devised by the performer. Thus in improvisation as we know it today, especially in much popular music, the weight of preestablished routine is often great enough to carry the music forward like a well-oiled machine without reacting to any communication from the outside.

These two examples of different uses of preestablished compositional methods—the recent works of Stravinsky and Copland, which reveal a living and meaningful sensitivity to the mutual interaction of details and whole and to differences of qualities and styles based on a thorough reworking of the inherited musical language; and the improvisation of the French organist, which ticks away like a complicated clock, insensitive to the human meaning of its minutes and hours—should serve to clarify the new direction away from preestablished techniques that this article is attempting to describe. This new direction may be labeled "emancipated musical discourse" after the "emancipation of dissonance," which Schoenberg coined for the new trends in harmony.

One cannot escape the feeling that this new direction is a reaction to the extraordinary increase of interest in the past and the remote, bringing to what was once a product of Romantic nostalgia (and still is, perhaps) modern scientific precision and modern techniques. The bewildering wealth of all history and of all cultures has suddenly been made easily available through phonograph recordings and publications, and our temperaments do not permit us to discuss older styles as most of the composers of earlier periods would have done. On the contrary, as everyone knows, the present-day interest in older music even of rather obscure and not too interesting composers is on the whole greater than in that of our contemporaries—a situation that would have profoundly shocked any of the older composers whose music is now being exhumed.

This vast array of information, of methods and ideas, increases composers' range of possibilities so enormously that one of their problems now is to make choices, to decide what to discard and what to keep for their own use. Even the most erudite composers of the past did not have so much to learn and so much to choose from. Therefore it becomes imperative for composers to limit their range so that they can concentrate their efforts. This need for choice explains why young composers have relied on one dominating figure after another—following Stravinsky and others in neoclassicism, or Schoenberg in expressionism. In this matter the twelve-tone system has been particularly helpful, since it allows considerable latitude while limiting the composer's choices and giving these choices a kind of hierarchy of relationships. Once one has chosen the twelve-tone row, one has chosen a method of harmony and a collection of motives that are all interrelated. This is an enormous advantage, for it helps to put the composer in that situation of focused freedom that finds its counterpart in all species of musical training, from learning to play an instrument to writing an opera.

The resurrection of this vast world of forgotten music and the bringing into the living room of music from all parts of the world as it sounds is such a recent development that it is still intellectually and artistically undigested—quite unlike the situation in literature and the fine arts, where the opening up of the horizons of the past and of the remote took place some time ago, allowing several generations of critics and historians sufficient time to discover stimulating facts and to elaborate valuable ideas. Musicology has hardly passed the cataloguing stage, and so far has provided very little intellectual or aesthetic stimulus. However, the activity of musicology which has, in America and elsewhere, raised music to a university discipline brings with it scientific attitudes—among them the analogy of the composer to a scientist in a laboratory who works for years on some piece of obscure research which will be brought to light only when explained by a professional popularizer, or when some imaginative scientist uses his data as part of a comprehensive theory of large application. Whether this attitude is healthy, when applied to the public art of music, remains to be proved. Likewise the amassing of vast amounts of information about all branches of this art tends also to draw it away from the general public, since there is so much to know that the public simply becomes discouraged.

For the composer, in spite of all, does write for a public. One might very well wonder *what* public, if it were not for the fact that the public is constantly changing, and one of the forces exerted upon it is that of the very works of music themselves. For now we can see that strong, commanding works of art, no matter how strange they seem on their first appearance, sooner or later reach the public. Their intrinsic quality acts as a centripetal force that first educates the musical profession and finally the public to understand. In the context of this article, the question to be asked at this point is whether the familiar, delayed public acceptance that has greeted so many contemporary works will be delayed forever if works in the new advanced style eliminate too many of the preestablished techniques in their efforts to obtain complete consistency and very close coordination of all their elements. The effort of striking out along the new path, which was described at the beginning of this article, could result in complete hermeticism. We may well wonder today how far along this road toward hermeticism it is possible to go, when we see the poems of Mallarmé and Valéry in our children's high school French book.

It is not an easy or a comfortable thing for a musician trained in the traditional techniques to break away from them—particularly from those discussed here which are so fundamental. One might suppose that a person without traditional training might be able to approach the problem more freshly. Yet in spite of the fact that musical training is still not at all adapted to deal even with the most familiar modern techniques, experience so far has shown that the work of practically all untrained musicians is either so chaotic or so pedestrian as to be without interest. Usually such people, like many listeners with little musical experience, are overwhelmed by the sheerly physical qualities of sound and can do little more than make a display of surprising sound effects like a display of fireworks, which pay slight attention to organization, since this seems meaningless to them. A knowledge and feeling for the high standards of coherence and meaning which the musical tradition has brought to great subtlety is probably much more important than many musicians of advanced tendencies have thought. What is needed is a restudying of existing music and the elaboration of a more significant kind of music theory that is more widely applicable. This inevitably goes with the point of view discussed here and is found reflected likewise in many places. The musicians of the United States have produced a number of important books, articles, and teachings in this field, which are revolutionizing the thinking of the present student generation of composers.

In Europe, the search for emancipated musical discourse has been much more closely associated with the twelve-tone system than in the United States. There it has taken its departure from Webern's pointillist works and has applied serial methods to other dimensions besides that of pitch. As a method of discovering new possibilities of momentary and unexpected sound effects, this exercise is useful. At its best it resembles the turning of a musical kaleidoscope that shuffles at random fragments of sound which may or may not fall into interesting patterns—the burden of reading meaning and of finding interest in these rests with the listener and not the composer. The real problem of such music-puzzles is illustrated simply by the verbal palindrome ("able was I ere I saw Elba"), which has to obey both a strict patterning of letters and has to make sense into the bargain. A palindrome of random letters is a bit pointless in itself. Although musical meaning is not quite so easy to establish, still up to the end of Webern's life this dual standard of order and of meaning applied to all such types of musical ingenuity, with the exception perhaps of certain Medieval and early Renaissance works. But the recent European school seems to have become occupied with pattern alone, hoping somehow that interest and meaning would emerge. Even on their own admission, this has not always been the case. This ordering according to the random application of number systems seems wasteful because it produces so many useless possibilities, like the monkeys at typewriters.

In the United States, the tendency has been to start with a coordinating principle having to do with techniques of listening or to begin with our experience of time and not some arbitrary numerological formula. Examples of emancipated discourse in America are beginning to be more numerous. Some of the abstract works of Copland and especially the recent works of Roger Sessions, such as his Third Symphony, and those of the writer of this article, strive for this principle using any system or musical procedure that seems suitable. Others, like Milton Babbitt, use the twelve-tone system emphasizing coordinative possibilities rather than its disintegrative ones as the Europeans do. Certainly, audible musical order that can be distinguished, remembered, and followed is a necessary condition for this new adventure.

The Challenge of the New
(1960–62/94)

Interest in music, if we take account of its social and commercial as well as its aesthetic aspects, has become so many-sided a phenomenon in our time that it sometimes seems that those objects which are the very center of the musical world, *compositions*, are being forgotten. Yet it is obvious, or should be, that compositions are of prime importance to the profession; for it is these assemblages of dots, lines, Italian words, and metronome markings which furnish a livelihood for solo performers, orchestras, copyists, engravers, and recording engineers. They are the stuff that makes all business and management operations connected with music potentially profitable. Indeed, it is for their sake that concert halls and opera houses are built, so that the public can hear performances of these scores under acoustically flattering conditions—we hope.

Today in America, however, it seems that more attention, publicity, and monetary expenditure is lavished on the building of new halls and opera houses, or on the refurbishing of old ones, than on the development of a vital repertory to be played in them. "Save Carnegie Hall" was a *cause célèbre*; to have made more effort to save Bartók back in 1942 would have been more to the point. As matters now stand, there is greater preoccupation in and out of public print with the number of cubic feet of lobby space per customer planned for Lincoln Center's New Philharmonic Hall than genuine concern for the role to be played by the Philharmonic's repertory in contributing to the lifeblood of the musical community. This is alarming, for in the absence of any effort to maintain composers' interest in writing for the orchestra, more and more of them will turn to chamber music and electronic music, as they are doing even now. Compositions are not merely fundamental to the profession—they are one of the most important agents of change. Composers, by creating new repertories of compositions, bring new instruments and new combinations into acceptance; they also send old instruments and combinations into decline by ceasing to write for them.

Throughout musical history, of course, new instruments have continually made their appearance. Sometimes they have been modifications of extant instruments, designed to extend the range of qualities, to increase the sensitivity, volume, or dexterity already available. Or, sometimes, new instruments have been developed—such as the piano—to make possible the expression of ideas for which existing instruments were simply inadequate. The electronic studio responds to both needs in its ability to produce any conceivable sound or combinations of sounds. It is not at all surprising that most of our more adventurous young composers are excited by the prospect and consequently take this new medium quite seriously. To their credit, they are not much concerned with the mere generation of sound effects—such as the eerie whistlings that have furnished tension to science-fiction movies—but rather with compositional problems. These machines are capable of practically unlimited tricks and novelties of sound, but it should be readily apparent that such things quickly become silly and tedious, as hackneyed as the trick of playing the violin upside down. Tricks do attract momentary attention, as Franz Clement, with his upside-down violin playing, knew full well; but this musician is still remembered for one program on which he did more than his usual stunt—he also gave the first performance of an almost impossibly hard violin concerto, the one Beethoven had written for him. It is this score, which Clement took such pains to help Beethoven alter so as to be most effective for the solo instrument, that has stimulated so many violinists to conquer the most difficult problems of their instrument—and it is this score and others of equal stature that have acted as a powerful persuasion to the public to value our profession, after all the antics and publicity stunts have been forgotten.

No matter from what point of view one considers the musical profession, one always comes back (and especially if one is a composer) to the question of compositions—what the nature of these is, what steps can be taken to insure the production of new good works to supplant those that fall out of the repertory. One year the tone poems, concerti, and symphonies of Saint-Saëns fade away, another year those of Sibelius, next perhaps it is the turn of Weber or Schumann. In order to keep this repertory from shrinking to a few overworked pieces, one would have thought that drastic steps would be taken to find replacements. Yet what has been done so far seems ineffectual. The durable orchestral repertory has shrunk markedly in America during this century; whether the consequent impoverishment will not reduce the orchestras first to being museums for a narrow band of musical history and finally to closing shop altogether for lack of anything new to display is open to question.

There are three important advantages that the electronic medium offers the composer, to which orchestras must somehow respond if younger members of the profession are to remain interested in writing for them. The first is that electronic music makes it possible to do without the intermediary of the performer. In so doing, it permits boundless technical and imaginative freedom and eliminates a very costly element of music making. The electronic medium has arrived at an opportune time for those composers who need only a fellowship to give them the time they need to develop their ideas concretely, without the vast sums required to work out new problems at orchestral rehearsals.

A second advantage is that electronic composers can deal with the actual sound of their compositions as they are working and can develop as composers always in direct contact with the world of sound. Theirs is analogous to the happy position of Haydn and his bell-pull, with which he could at any time summon the Eszterházy orchestra to try out something new. Perhaps one of the most severe problems for orchestral composers of any adventurous bent nowadays is how to deal in a truly fresh way with the exceedingly subtle and complex medium that the modern symphony orchestra has become. Occasionally we hear performances of orchestral music that has not been well assimilated by conductor and players; sometimes this happens because the music has not been put into properly playable shape by the composer. No matter how skilled a composer is, no matter how clearly he may hear his music in his head, he must still get it down on paper so that performers will be able to produce the effect he wants. Therefore, to have profitable experiences of their own works, to correct details so that scores come out exactly as they imagined them, composers must hear many different and carefully prepared performances, with different orchestras and under varied acoustical conditions. It was on the basis of such experience that such skilled composers as Debussy, Puccini, and Mahler made innumerable changes in their scores, even after publication from engraved plates. The high cost of orchestra rehearsals today makes it more difficult than ever for the young composer to gain this necessary experience; and when composers cannot have the opportunity of a complete and satisfactory testing of their newly written scores, they then have no choice but to fall back upon the standard routines of orchestral writing. Largely because of this frustrating situation, many good composers are becoming hesitant to devote the time and effort to the kind of writing that the modern orchestra requires. Why should they bother, when they can gain much more experience in chamber music and electronic music than they can in orchestral music these days?

The third advantage of electronic music has to do with its prospects for public acceptance. Here we come to the ever-widening schism between the public for recorded music and the concert-going public, measured in terms of knowledge and acceptance of new music. It is a difference of which student composers quickly become aware. They avidly study recordings and scores of important works of contemporary music, learn to love and respect them, and, as students do, take them as a point of departure for their own works. However, when their music is played by our orchestras, they encounter perplexed musicians and public. Sometimes the young composer is hailed as original when he himself knows that his own music is derived from sources entirely familiar to record collectors, or condemned as unintelligible when he is only building upon things that have been done by many others for the past thirty or forty years. Such experiences are frustrating indeed, especially if composers end up feeling that anything new and important that they might have expended considerable effort to say has been completely lost on everyone else. For the fact is that our orchestras have not made their public familiar with the important contemporary works, instead discharging what little educational responsibility they feel by playing new pieces chosen for other than their intrinsic musical merits. By contrast, when a composer's work is recorded, it is usually received far more intelligently because it reaches an audience that has developed appreciation and discrimination by contact with the important new works. The electronic studio, designed to deal with recorded sound directly and to bypass the concert audience with its conservative tastes, is proving irresistible in its attraction to younger composers.

Up to now, I have been talking about the advantages of electronic music from a rather idealistic standpoint. It is easy for us to spin fantasies about our profession and to imagine all sorts of vain things, but it is the condensation of these ideas into actual works of enduring interest, such as the profession lives by and the public enjoys, that is most important. This is no easy task to accomplish at present, for it is not merely the effort of the composer that is involved, but also an effort on the part of the musical society in which the composer lives. We know that our repertory was developed under the most sophisticated of conditions. The musical education and taste of the small population of aristocrats and wealthy bourgeois that nurtured it has left its mark on all the works in this repertory—works which set a standard of "seriousness" even in their most light-hearted moments. Without this standard, serious art music ("concert music") would become dissipated in the wider worlds of semi-classical and popular music, each quite valid in itself but also very different in aim. Serious music is to be listened to attentively. Its qualities have always been difficult for the beginner to grasp. Yet as a reward for the effort of being perceptive, listeners are given wonderfully beautiful experiences about the passing of time, very real to us as humans but impossible to translate into words. With such a special kind of communication, one cannot tinker too much. To those of us accustomed to traditional instruments, electronic music seems to be in a pioneering stage, even if filled with an infinite array of possibilities, and its raw materials in need of being brought into order before anything but crude communication is possible. In any case, it is not always possible for a composer to switch from one medium to another very unlike it.

Since I am talking to musicians whose lives revolve primarily around orchestras, I would like to return to the question of the experience and knowledge it takes to write for this medium. It is not only a matter of the difficulty with which such experience and knowledge are acquired, but also that writing a score and checking the parts is an unbelievably laborious and cumbersome task. I do not wish to complain about the fact that the copyist of an orchestral score usually gets more per page than its composer does for a commission, but the very great effort entailed by this kind of composition makes any composer think twice before undertaking it. And in addition to the physical effort required, there is the imaginative effort involved in the planning and execution of all the details. Yet composers are often treated as though they were being done a favor simply by virtue of having their works played. One is always surprised to see orchestras handling new compositions so cavalierly, as if there were such a wealth of good ones. After all, one way to make an audience dislike any kind of music is to perform poorly chosen, artistically weak examples of it. Not even the music of the eighteenth and nineteenth centuries would have survived such treatment.

If the need for good, durable, new American works is as great as we sometimes hear, then drastic steps have to be taken to develop a climate in which they can thrive. The selection of works for performance must be done by members of the profession who know enough about new music to distinguish between the outstanding and the mediocre, and an audience able to appreciate their qualities must be cultivated through repeated exposure. Without such efforts at development, the wholesale playing of American orchestral music can be nothing but a philanthropic project, tacitly implying the belief that American music will always be poor, but that it is a worthy act to help the poor.

Fallacy of the Mechanistic Approach
(1946)

The Schillinger System of Musical Composition will most likely arouse considerable feeling, especially among those who have not seen this type of book before. The point of view comes straight out of Middle Europe in the early 1920s, when the application of a mechanistically conceived scientific method to the arts was all the rage. In this respect Schillinger's work closely resembles the Bauhaus books and the prose writings of Eisenstein on the movies. An elaborate show of scientific language, of schematic exposition that apes mathematical texts, plenty of graphs and pseudo-algebraic formulas, all do about as much to confuse as to clarify.

For this form of exposition is really a rhetorical method not particularly aimed at careful scientific rigor but at a kind of surprise and shock effect. Violent invective, dogmatic assertion, repetition of ideas and phrases, and a certain megalomania are combined with apparently dispassionate and rigorous analysis. Old-fashioned, "intuitive" methods are ridiculed, mistakes of the great composers are shown up in the light of the "new, objective, and scientific methodology." Any of the subtler forms of persuasion, like those found in real scientific treatises, which substantiate generalizations with verifiable facts, are omitted; the reader is browbeaten. Schillinger's book even has a rather hermetic and cultlike quality because of its lack of regard for the reader. The terminology is unfamiliar: musical terms are referred to by letter symbols which even a generous glossary at the back does not always clarify, because their significance changes from chapter to chapter.

But this is all a bitter coating for a book that makes many interesting contributions. The system aims at the all-inclusive, under the one aspect of mathematical patterning. Within the covers of these two volumes one finds the most comprehensive tabulation of musical elements, devices, and procedures that probably has ever been made, certainly within the limits of such a relatively short work. For a book that is to include a systematization of rhythm, scales, melody, harmony, counterpoint, fugue, composition, orchestration, and musical expression must necessarily be brief on many scores. Although it is presented as comprehensive and self-explanatory, the book seems really a manual to supplement actual lessons in which principles are more elaborately and convincingly expounded. Thus the huge number of tabulations, which Schillinger does not derive from already composed works, but primarily from the permutation, combination, and serial arrangement of the divisions of time and pitch. And he is rarely content to mention possible permutations, even of numbers, without listing them all. This takes up space but, as the editor points out, helps save time for hurried arrangers.

Again, if the book is more than a supplementary manual, how can one account for the rather surprising omissions which occur in almost every chapter? In the first one on rhythm, for instance, the function of the barline in relation to upbeats and downbeats, and the existence of the additive madrigal type of rhythm (which starts with a unit or a foot as a basis and combines these units in changing meters) are never mentioned. But he does hit on the novel idea of deriving temporal divisions and irregularities by combining two regular patterns, such as three notes against four, into one line. The whole chapter is systematized on the claim that all rhythms are portions and groupings of such "resultants" of the "interference" of one set of regular beats by another. This conception of "resultants" of "interference" creeps into every part of the book like a Pythagorean refrain, with not too musical results.

Another chapter shows how to construct melodies after the rise and fall of graphs of various kinds of motion and rhythms of growth. One finds that Beethoven did not always balance things "scientifically" because he relied so much on intuition. But the principles of resistance and climax as presented are quite helpful in classifying melodies. The "Special Theory of Harmony" treats triadic harmonies and their sequences in an unusual way, tabulating at tremendous length each type of bass motion and each possible type of combination. The "General Theory of Harmony (Strata Harmony)" constitutes perhaps the most elaborate treatment of modern dissonant harmony to appear in this country so far, with its list of different chords and their progressions.

All this material is presented with no particular regard for when to use what, for whether it sounds good or bad. It is here that Schillinger's system falls down. The composer is not shown how to use the facts or to select from them. Rigid adherence to the mathematical, which here results in rather uninteresting examples, could in fact very well diminish the young composer's ability to discriminate; this would produce a result just the opposite of the best kind of more "intuitive," less "scientific" teaching. However, for musicians interested in filling up radio time or in writing descriptive background music of a not too original character this system will save a lot of trouble and thought. It is curious that a method which gives such a high place to abstract art (art is classified in terms of its abstractness, the highest place being given to the non-representative or non-symbolic) should be followed by practitioners mostly occupied with the most functional aspect of music.

The basic philosophic fallacy of the Schillinger point of view is of course the assumption that the "correspondences" between patterns of art and patterns of the natural world can be mechanically translated from one to the other by the use of geometry or numbers. When this conception is carried to even greater lengths in the belief that music will stimulate reactions if it follows the graphic projection of geometric patterns of "mechanical and biomechanical trajectories," one can only feel that the whole idea is arbitrary in the extreme. It comes from a Pythagoreanism that is quite out of place as a primary consideration in art music. Wherever this system has been successfully used, it has been by composers who were already well trained enough to distinguish the musical results from the nonmusical ones.

"La Musique sérielle aujourd'hui"[1]
(1965/94)

Composers since 1945 have been increasingly concerned with mathematical patterning, with improvisational immediacy, and with "open form." Continuing the previous neoclassic attack on the "masterpiece," which either deliberately avoided or else parodied the "grand manner," the new direction has been concerned with experimentation within the musical work itself and with the musical event in its relation to its environment, which encompasses concert halls, performers, audiences, and even newspaper coverage. Thus it seems that the idea of composing works of definite, fixed character, of high conceptual focus and of enduring interest, has become secondary to the mere exploration of possibilities. This trend probably owes much of its vigor to the hidebound conservatism of the music profession after the Second World War. In Europe, where this traditionalism has seemed even more oppressive and deadening than in America, the reaction to it, in the form of the general movement of "musique sérielle," has been especially intense.

Most commentary about artistic movements, and in particular about this one, leads easily to a confusion between the general style and the individual works which implement it and give it artistic importance, in the classical sense of the term (not necessarily in the "experimental" sense). Today, such individual works seem paradoxical to the extent to which they aspire, more or less, to the old criteria of "masterpiece." For example, such a masterpiece, as it seems to many, is Luigi Nono's *Il canto sospeso*, in which, perhaps, the violence done to familiar musical procedures by the application of the Fibonacci series to all the parameters (except—so I am told—tempi, octave location of pitches, instrumentation, and linearity), reflects the heartbreaking violations of human beings expressed in the texts. In the context of present-day developments, such works are atypical, for the typical product of today is the "experimental" work, which does not need to be heard more than once, since its experimental intentions must be obvious and since its sole justification for existence resides in just these intentions. Repeated performances are of little interest except to new listeners or under new interpretive conditions that allow the experiment to produce new results. Whether the work relies on a definitively written out score or on aleatoric procedures, the experimental intention remains the same. Yet in spite of this circumstance, experimental music continues to assume the existence of conventional relationships between public, performers, and composers; a listener more thoroughly aware of experimental techniques would interpret the results very differently.

In truth, the development of "musique sérielle," whatever may be claimed

---

1. See Notes on Sources (Appendix 1). The French of the title, and the reference throughout this essay to "musique sérielle" rather than to its literal English equivalent, is meant by Carter to signal his reference to the special kind of compositional practice, sometimes called "integral serialism" or "total serialism" in the United States, that originated with Olivier Messiaen and his pupils shortly after the end of the Second World War and that was taken up by many composers in other countries thereafter. [B]

about it, does not proceed at all in continuation of Schoenberg, Berg, and Webern but rather as a function of one limited angle on their work, as viewed through Messiaen's aesthetic and technical preoccupations in one relatively brief compositional period. The Viennese were always concerned with music in the familiar expressive and artistically ordered way; by contrast, the application of schematic devices of the serializing type as an idea of interest in itself (more in Berg than in Webern) began to pervade pre-Stalinist Soviet music, as we see both among the Scriabinists and in the work of Joseph Schillinger, who brought such ideas to the United States where many, such as Ives, Varèse, Riegger, Cowell, and Crawford, were already working in this direction.

This approach has its analogue in modern painting, with one major difference. Modern painting appeals to those special collector-traits which music cannot, since a work of music cannot be owned exclusively in a physical sense and, for the most part, is difficult to own intellectually since it is not easily remembered. Nevertheless, certain composers today have made their works prodigious collections of "special sounds" and special procedures, "geometric" or aleatoric, as painters have with their materials, and as writers have with words and techniques of thought recognition. This aspect is pursued by many with the avidity of stamp collectors. Furthermore, as in the other arts, many such works of music are intended, at least in part, as critiques of other music and of traditional musical institutions. What, for instance, could more effectively ridicule orchestra managers' thirst for premieres than an aleatoric work whose every performance is a premiere since it is never to be played the same way twice—and what a time-saving effort for the composer!

Alongside the push toward freedom there is the other trend in recent music, toward greater inner organization, inspired perhaps by literary works such as those of James Joyce, Marcel Proust, Michel Butor, Alain Robbe-Grillet, and William S. Burroughs. These works have encouraged musicians to find new ways of dealing with perception, recognition, understanding, experience, and memory. Only certain aspects of dodecaphonic systems have been helpful in this search. For in developing dodecaphony, the Viennese were taking a retrogressive step in view of their earlier works, and both the mechanical, musically arbitrary routines of "musique sérielle" and the ostensibly antithetical aleatoric methods have even more limited potential. They have dealt with tiny musical microstructures, the basic material of music, but very little with the potential of their interconnection for musical thought and expression. Some of us have been interested in these more fundamental principles—principles which concern the operations of the human mind when listening to music—and in the manifold types of communication they suggest.

ISCM Festival, Rome
(1959)

The Italian Section of the International Society for Contemporary Music and the RAI-Radiotelevisione Italiana were hosts this 10–16 June in Rome to the ISCM delegates and to the unusually interesting festival for which their jury had chosen six programs. Two more concerts of prize-winning works in a contest sponsored by the Italian Section, the Radio, and several Italian publishers made up the generous number that formed the thirty-third festival held annually except during the war and the fifth given in Italy. Since the Society was founded in 1922 by a few far-sighted composers and musicologists, with the late Edward Dent as its active president for many years, the question of its continuation has come up repeatedly. For it has been beset by great political and artistic troubles, and many believe that the increasing public acceptance of new music and its more frequent and widespread performance have robbed the Society of one of its main reasons for existence. Yet it survives and seems likely to go on, for unlike many similar organizations, this one has laid its main emphasis on live performance—performance of new, forward-looking works that were judged imaginative and talented and that would engage the attention of cultivated musicians—and not on the manufacturing of propaganda. Occasionally some of the works on the programs have been disappointing, yet at each festival enough were important or remarkable and enough more contained moments of special musical interest—sometimes combined with instructive miscalculations—to make the majority of delegates feel that the effort was worthwhile. Of course, besides offering this important professional experience to musicians, the Society has repeatedly brought to light new scores of merit that were later presented to a larger public. The opportunity for sympathetic performance before intelligent audiences and the possibility of arousing knowing enthusiasm and encouragement—familiar features of these festivals—have helped many a young composer over the trying period between finding himself and finding his public. It is hard to imagine how modern music could have become what it is without the Society's activity.

During each festival, delegates from the sections discuss, among other things, questions of policy that invariably arise from the stresses of the double commitment of the Society, "international" and "contemporary." When it was founded, there was no question about what kind of music it was committed to encourage. As its influence spread in the late 1920s and early '30s, "advanced" young composers flocked to its performances—and have stayed to run it in their middle age. Therefore, the problem of whether to continue as champion of the older, now accepted styles of many of its composer-members, indeed whether to perform older, established composers at all or instead to keep up with the more advanced trends of the young, has become a matter of controversy. Its present president, Dr. Heinrich Strobel, and one of its vice presidents, the young French critic Claude Rostand, are definitely in favor of rejuvenation, to a return, really, to the basic reason for existence of the Society. There are members of the German, Italian, English, Swedish, and Japanese sections who are of this opinion.

But to list these five sections is to imply the opposition or wish for compromise of others; and at once the problem of the second commitment, international representation, arises. This problem has been much complicated by the large number of composers like Ernst Krenek and Roberto Gerhard who changed citizenship after establishing their reputations. For not falling clearly into a national group, they tend to be neglected, although in 1955 the English submitted a score by the former Spaniard, Gerhard, and the Swiss one by a former Russian, Wladimir Vogel. Obviously the reason sections have joined this society is to present the new music written in their respective countries before an international audience, to learn what is being done elsewhere, and to join in an exchange of music, experiences, musical judgments, and aesthetics. To keep this exchange on a certain high level of quality and contemporaneity, the delegates screen quite carefully new applications for admission and watch over the progress of each section especially when there are drastic changes of personnel. Each section wants to be represented as often as possible on the festival programs, and considerable dissatisfaction is felt when its country's name is omitted for several years. Since the festivals have a maximum length in terms of both the interest of the audiences and financial outlay, various rules have been tried to assure fairness; the most recent, adopted shortly after the war, gave to each section in good standing the right to at least one performance every three years. The United States, under this plan, has figured as one of the favored nations, having had two or three works played each year, though this time but one.[1]

As a former international juror, this reviewer had it clearly brought home to him that the modern styles he was familiar with in America were prevalent in almost every country. To realize that each, whether a centrally located European country or one halfway around the world, had its representatives of the old-fashioned Romantic, the "motoric" neoclassic, the folkloristic (whether polymodal or polytonal), and the expressionistic schools, and that the "advanced" of each country were adopting twelve-tone techniques and even, in some scattered places, the Darmstadt methods described in *Die Reihe*, gives one the impression that the ISCM has succeeded too well in exporting all the styles of Europe to the ends of the earth. But as a juror, one sees that what all jurors of this festival must have sought from the beginning was liveliness of imagination, avoiding the grey neutrality that infests these styles as they travel from country to country. One also realizes that the styles themselves have been enriched by ideas brought from elsewhere to these and similar concerts—ideas that, perhaps because of the incoherent cultural conditions in the places where they originated, were scarcely noticed, not developed, and seldom given the striking embodiment supported by cultural propaganda that they receive in the more unified and intellectually alert milieu of Europe. Cases of this are the contributions of such very diverse American musicians as Ives, Varèse, Babbitt, and Cage to the thinking of many younger Europeans, ideas that will become known in the world—even finally in the

1. Brazil, Czechoslovakia, Chile, Korea, Mexico, New Zealand, Norway, South Africa, Spain, and Switzerland were not represented at the regular concerts in Rome. Germany and Sweden had three works apiece; Austria, France, Italy, and Poland two each; Argentina, Denmark, Finland, Great Britain, Holland, Japan, U.S.A., and Yugoslavia one each. To these the jury added five works not submitted by the sections (and not to be counted as national representations). The two prize-contest concerts added two more American and two more German works, and one each of England, Italy, Sweden, and Switzerland. Of the sections not performed, some were being penalized for not paying their dues, others did not submit scores, while the rest had not submitted works of sufficient interest to the international jury, and did not have to be played this year.

United States—through the works now being written abroad. Outside of Europe, few countries submit works of unusual character, it seems, with the possible exceptions of the U.S.A. and Japan. Often, as in the case of this festival, Japan has supplied a very striking work, such as the *Samai* (for orchestra, 1957) of Yoritsune Matsudaira—a compelling combination of total serialization and antique Japanese court dance music. The score provided a striking musical experience of the type that helps to make the festivals a success by offering relief from the rather routine quality of so many scores that have to be played because of the three-year rule. Also Milton Babbitt's *Two Sonnets*, although much milder in impact, owing to a restrained instrumentation, was a moment of highly organized music unusual in approach. Both helped the programs on which they appeared and yet both certainly are not characteristic of the mainstream of their native music as many at home must see it. For choosing a series of interesting and varied programs out of the bundles of six scores submitted by the juries of each section leaves a great deal to chance. One year four violin concertos of similar style were submitted by four different countries, for instance. Therefore, it is not surprising that this year's jury included Stravinsky's *Agon*, Dallapiccola's *Tartiniana II*, Boulez's *Improvisations sur Mallarmé*, Messiaen's *Oiseaux exotiques*, and Nono's *Incontri*, although not submitted by the sections, "in the general interest of the programs."

The review of each section's past year, usually given orally by each delegate, was dispensed with at Rome, and written reports were allowed to suffice. By far the most impressive was the 153-page *Neue Musik in der Bundesrepublik Deutschland 1958/59*, edited by the German Section, printed by Schott, and prepared, perhaps, to help persuade the delegates (who did not need such persuasion) to accept the German invitation of next spring's festival to Cologne. The booklet listed some 150 live concerts, fifty of them orchestral, entirely of contemporary music; also innumerable new works played on programs of old music and even more on radio programs during this past season. The quality was, on the whole, both high and challenging, and all schools were generously represented. Acknowledged masters like Stravinsky and Bartók led in number of performances. Schoenberg had about thirty-six, which included several operas and numerous orchestral and chamber works. Advanced young composers were also abundantly in evidence. Luigi Nono, for instance, had eleven performances, more than half of which were large choral works. Of music recently composed, Stravinsky's *Threni* received six, as did two works on the ISCM festival: Fortner's excellent twelve-tone *Impromptus* and Henze's highly romantic *Nachtstücke und Arien*. Pitifully few American works were played.

The Swedish report gave the programs of seven chamber music concerts, one of which was presented by John Cage and David Tudor along the lines familiar to their New York audiences. As a novel experiment the Swedish radio gave six live concerts of new music coordinated with the appearance of each of six issues of the new modern music magazine *Nutida Musik* in which was discussed the music about to be played at the concert.

The United States Section had no report to submit. Since the spring of

1955 it has given no concerts in New York, confining its activities to award-
ing commissions, paying its annual international dues and the costs of engaging soloists for the American works played at the festivals, electing a delegate
to the central assembly, and choosing and sending its allotment of six scores
annually to the festival jury.[2] Even in its most active years, the United States
Section was never able to operate on the scale of those sections supported
partly or wholly by state cultural funds or state radio taxes. Its fight for con-
tinuance during concert seasons was so demanding that it could never expand
enough to be able to include foreign works in reciprocation for American
works played abroad. All it could do was to give badly needed hearings to
local composers and to works acknowledged elsewhere to be of prime importance and not known here, such as the all-Webern concert given in 1952 at
New York.

The necessities involved in developing a contemporary musical culture
seem to be fairly clear to the important European countries, necessities that
are more difficult to satisfy in our widely spread-out country, perhaps, than in
the close confines of a European one. Only frequent, widespread performance
of the best, most interesting of American and other contemporary music before professionals and public can remedy this situation. At least, then, many
would have a similar basis of experience and, one hopes, understanding. For
discussions, congresses, reports, articles, and reviews, no matter how numerous, will never do much good unless they refer to the common musical experience of the speaker and reader. From what has been said above, it should be
obvious that the Europeans have begun to accomplish this since the war and
that Europe is fast becoming again the source of our musical culture. The fact
that money can be found to print an English version of *Die Reihe* and none to
print a contemporary music magazine of our own is a sign of our sad plight.

The difficulty the United States Section has of operating on a small scale
becomes paralyzing whenever it has considered inviting the festival here. It is
true that during the war the section gave two festivals, without, of course, the
sanction of the central committee, which had ceased to exist. Now it is especially to be wished for, since we have been treated so generously at festivals
and by the sections of many countries. Some of the directors of the United
States Section thought it might be appropriate to give such a festival around
the time of the opening of the Lincoln Center in New York City. But to find
people familiar with the festival's problems who could also spend the vast
amount of time and effort it would take to convince those who would have
either to pay or play, and to do all this several years in advance of the event
(bids for festivals in 1961 and '62 have already been made) was considered
impossible. Indeed, in view of the far from brilliant record of performances in

2. The few regional chapters that continue to give concerts have lost contact with the central
section in New York, neither submitting scores for the U.S. jury to choose from for the festival, nor contributing funds to help pay the annual international dues, nor sending their programs to indicate whether the nature of their activities justifies their continued use of the
ISCM name.

America of important new European scores, the delegates from other sections would need a lot of convincing that we would be able to meet the standards of performance common to most recent festivals. Because the international delegates must long ago have given up expecting either kind of reciprocation from the United States, one has a rather strange mixture of pride and embarrassment that so much American music has been played by the ISCM.

This reviewer does not feel that he can dismiss with a brief phrase the many fine, imaginative, and conscientiously composed scores heard in Rome—many of which need several hearings to be judged seriously. Quite a number certainly deserve the extended discussions frequently given in these pages to works that interest their critics, but because of the abundance at the festival, all must be penalized for lack of space.

Reflecting what seems to be an almost universal movement outside the Soviet Union and a few other countries not in contact with the mainstream of new music, practically none of the scores, even those by composers who once wrote differently, could have been written without the precedent of the Viennese Three. Their influence has registered, sometimes directly through their compositions, sometimes through the twelve-tone method by which these composers revealed the typical earlier twentieth-century concern with musical design, and sometimes indirectly through techniques derived from this method without concern for its original intentions, stressing instead "sound." As in impressionism, here tone color, register, attack, texture, perhaps dynamics, and "time"—the physical materials assume prime importance—are the subject mater of the composition, as "space," the physical materials of painting and their types of application, has become the subject matter of the abstract-expressionist painter. In the music that depends on design, the colorist elements are used to emphasize or more completely characterize interval structure, motive, rhythm, and their combinations into musical "ideas," themes, chords. This kind of music assumes an experienced listener who can grasp and remember the initial groupings of these "ideas" and "follow" their uses and transformations. From this, musical meaning emerges. With the adoption of "sound" as the primary concept, the elements of design tend to be reduced to vagueness, to unobtrusive amorphousness; and so, in appealing to the ear's ability to distinguish contrasts of all kinds of physical sound qualities, this procedure makes very little demand on the listener's memory and for this reason has frequently attracted with its striking sounds a musically inexperienced public that would be completely at sea in front of music that depended more on design.

In this festival more than ever before, this division was very pronounced. Almost all the works of the talented young European composers were written deeply under the influence of the "sound" concept, particularly as it has been developed in Darmstadt. One cannot fail to realize how much more fruitful in possibilities and more challenging to the imagination these new ideas are than were the neoclassic ones the young subscribed to twenty years ago. Of course, just as then, there are a lot of unimportant taboos and formularized "musts" that the less individual composers faithfully reproduce. Yet when one hears works of the young like *Prolation for Orchestra* by the Englishman Peter Maxwell Davies, or *Tre studi* by the Italian Aldo Clementi, or the *Canticum psalmi resurrectionis* of the German Dieter Schönbach, the vast new domain of musical thought that is opening up offers an exciting prospect that gives their music much freshness.

The more completely realized works of the festival can be put fairly clearly into the two categories distinguished above. All three of the American works depended clearly on design. In Milton Babbitt's *Two Sonnets* and George Rochberg's *Cheltenham Concerto* (one of the prize winners) tone color was soberly used; in Babbitt's work the expressive vocal line was allowed to be the main feature, in Ramiro Cortes's String Quartet (another prize winner) the lyrical quality came from linear design. Europeans were not so ascetic in the use of color to emphasize design. Wolfgang Fortner's *Impromptus* for orchestra have a bold, strong shape helped along by clear-colored orchestration; relying much more on intervals and rhythmic motives than on "themes," the work produces a striking impression. Don Banks's elegantly written and very changeable *Three Studies* for cello and piano made much of the instruments, while Michael Gielen's highly effective, clearly articulated setting of *Vier Gedichte von Stefan George* for mixed chorus, six assorted clarinets, and some other instruments was perhaps the most memorable of the works directly derived from the Viennese compositions but nevertheless full of personal intensity. Of a somewhat freer type, depending on design, were Tadeusz Baird's unusual *Quatre essais* for an orchestra that included two pianos, two harps, and harpsichord with the usual instruments, and Ingvar Lidholm's highly dramatic and declamatory *Skaldens Natt* for chorus and orchestra (a prize-winning work), filled with astonishing, abrupt changes of character. Displaying even greater freedom was Hans Werner Henze's *Nachtstücke und Arien*, three of the former alternating with two of the latter, for soprano and orchestra, which depended for their unity on intensity of poetic feeling and taste, since the variety of styles, textures, melodic shapes, and degrees of dissonance is so great that the listener might be reminded of certain not well integrated but extravagant moving picture scores if the music were not so imaginatively constructed and so unified in mood.

A few works fall between the two categories, like Goffredo Petrassi's *Serenata* and, perhaps, Messiaen's fantastic *Oiseaux exotiques*, a counterpoint of bird calls scored for piano and winds, in that they depend on design as well as sound for their effect. Those that feature the concern with "sound" were Yoritsune Matsudaira's *Samai*, Nono's *Incontri*, Bernd Alois Zimmermann's *Omnia tempus habent*, Boulez's *Improvisations sur Mallarmé*, and finally, the work that many thought was the best on the programs, *Ein irrender Sohn* by the youngest composer to be played, the Swedish Bo Nilsson.

This reviewer found great pleasure in Petrassi's fantastic little *Serenata* (1958) for harpsichord, flute, viola, contrabass, and percussion because of its great freedom of movement, which at times sounded like very advanced serial music while at the same time appealing to the listener's sense of audible order (see Ex. 2, pp. 192–93). It begins with a flute solo of the demanding nature that many advanced Europeans now write encouraged by their champion, Severino Gazzelloni, the first flutist of the RAI orchestra, who delights in overcoming every difficulty (including double stops) on his instrument.

Especially interesting, because of its unusual use of sonorities, was the second of two *Improvisations sur Mallarmé*, by Pierre Boulez, setting the poem *Une Dentelle s'abolit* (Ex. 1). It treats piano, harp, vibraphone, bells, and celesta as ringing instruments, using percussion largely for producing upbeat crescendos leading to ictuses of the bell sounds. Against this a voice sings the text in elaborate expressionistic vocalises. At first hearing, one is struck by the constant use of unisons to prolong notes in ever-varying arpeggiation, and the slow introduction of one note after another into the ringing chords and their arpeggiation in the voice. The prolongation of chords and their slow shifting

Example 1. Pierre Boulez, *Improvisation II sur Mallarmé*, mm. 17–18.

around common tones was, of course, characteristic of impressionistic composers (whom, perhaps because of the Mallarmé text, Boulez is evoking) and
has been uncommon until recently. The groups of grace notes (as in Chopin)
are to be played *ad libitum* before or within a beat, wherever they are placed
visually.

This *ad libitum* playing, a feature given the approval of "new" at Darmstadt a few years ago (formerly used, of course, by composers to suggest to
the performer a style of playing found in the improvisations of folk or popular performers, and for similar reasons in our time by Ives, who encouraged
great latitude of interpretation in his prefaces and even in the notation of his
scores), found an extreme demonstration in Bo Nilsson's twenty-six-measure
piece *Ein irrender Sohn* for alto voice, alto flute, and eighteen other players,[3]
all distributed, as in some works of Henry Brant, around the concert hall, according to a seating plan given in the score, with only the conductor on the
stage. In Rome, the more conventional alternative of seating the performers
on the stage was used with a good deal of reason, since some parts have many
groups of grace notes and others are notated with even more rhythmic freedom—dots being placed in various parts of a measure without indicating time
values—and if the instrumentalists were spread out, it might be difficult to
achieve an ensemble, especially if the exceptional places, indicated by vertical
connecting lines, where notes are attacked together, are to be accurate. This
work actually has a simple continuity established by a free-sounding improvisation of the alto flute for the first fourteen measures, continued at the fif-
teenth by the voice in the same style; later the two alternate until the end.
Against this constant core of sound, all sorts of sudden high, low, loud, soft
sounds are played in a highly irregular way, sometimes in groups, sometimes
alone—all quite unpredictably. This surrounds the core with a hazy, uncertain, and agreeable dust of sound, which might perhaps be much the same,
given the instruments and the above description, no matter what notes were
played. Having heard several works of Nilsson, this reviewer finds them
gifted and intriguing. One of the less complicated measures of the work will
illustrate the notational method (Ex. 2; all notes sound as written).

A number of other Americans, besides the three composers, contributed to
the success of this festival. Gloria Davy's marvelous performance of the two
arias in the Henze work, Herbert Handt's expressive and accurate singing of
the difficult vocal part of Klaus Huber's cantata *Des Engels Anredung an die
Seele*, and finally Francis Travis's conducting of the Bo Nilsson (which gives
the conductor complete freedom as to tempos) showed that there are Americans perfectly able to deal with the most difficult problems of contemporary
music. In the lavish program booklet designed and edited by the Society's

---

3. The instrumentation of Nilsson's work is interesting: alto voice, alto flute, viola and double
bass (both played only pizzicato), piano, harp, electric mandolin, electric guitar, xylorimba,
celesta, keyed glockenspiel, vibraphone, bells, timpani, very high and high maracas, medium
and low *Schellenbäume*, high, medium, and low suspended cymbals, low and very low
gongs, four Korean woodblocks from high to low, high and medium snare drums, low and
very low tambourines, very high and medium bongos, low and very low congas, very high
and high castanets, and very high, medium, and low triangles.

Example 2. Bo Nilsson, *Ein irrender Sohn*, m. 4.

general secretary, Robert W. Mann, the bobolink, the wood-thrush, the mockingbird, the Baltimore oriole, and many other American birds were credited with calls used in Messiaen's *Oiseaux exotiques*. For readers of these pages, perhaps the most interesting and concealed American contribution, in view particularly of his outspoken lack of artistic sympathy for it, is that of Everett Helm, who as U.S. Army Theatre and Music Officer in Wiesbaden helped to establish the Darmstadt School after the war and at various times since has saved it from being overwhelmed by numerous situations that have threatened its existence.[4] By this he has earned the gratitude of a whole generation of young European musicians.

Rasputin's End and *Lady Macbeth of Mtsensk*
(1960)

The almost simultaneous German premieres of two operas about Russia, *Der Tod des Grigori Rasputin (Rasputin's End)* by Nicolas Nabokov at Cologne and *Lady Macbeth of Mtsensk* by Dmitri Shostakovitch at the Düsseldorf opera, had an unexpected interest to the American observer unconnected with the German scene. It was the enthusiastic, lavish, interested productions given these works in two medium-sized Rhenish cities, on a par with Broadway at its most artistic and elaborate in direction, acting, and stage designing and with the Metropolitan Opera in musical performance. The ability to achieve such results suggests an unusual unanimity among supporters, managers, and directors as well as among all the collaborators about the importance of giving new works the most convincing and effective productions possible. The stage designers of both had created settings of high artistic originality that added very markedly to the effect of each and had solved problems of change of scene, lighting, and action from different points of view, each fascinating in its own way—a way far removed from the stiff world of painted flats and old-fashioned lighting common in most American opera productions. The remarkable, moody sets by Teo Otto for *Lady Macbeth* were outdone by the elaborateness and mobility of those by Caspar Neher for *Rasputin*. The stage direction of Bohumil Herlischka for the Shostakovitch and of Oscar Fritz Schuh for the Nabokov were on a level with the best of Harold Clurman or Tyrone Guthrie. These efforts, combined with imaginative and well-trained musical performances, avoided any of the sense of fatigue or tedium arising from lack of conviction that makes performances of older operas intolerable but that, in new works, is complacently overlooked because they are expected to be tiresome anyway. If contemporary opera is to be done, it is clear that it must be done with a conviction that kindles the enthusiasm and imagination of everyone concerned, including the supporters, who must feel that the enterprise is so important that enough money is allotted to allow for the proper fruition of commanding conceptions. Certain opera houses in Germany seem

---

4. Described in Antoine Goléa, *Rencontres avec Pierre Boulez* (Paris: Julliard, 1958), 72–75.

willing enough to do this occasionally, even with works, such as these, by non-Germans.

Shostakovitch's *Lady Macbeth* in its first and only version so far, the version performed in Cleveland and New York in 1936, was withdrawn from circulation after the composer was reprimanded officially before the war. Still taboo in Russia, its present production, forbidden in vain by the composer, was possible because a copy of the score nobody thought existed was discovered. Since the composer is said to be rewriting the work, he will certainly try to prevent further performances.

As an indication of the cultural condition of Russia of the 1920s and '30s by a child of the time, the score presents a terrifying example of musical genius, vitality, and skill put to purely opportunistic uses with total disregard for musical unity, taste, and coherence. In its lack of concern for any consistent point of view, moral, political, or even artistic, it resembles a "comic" book, particularly since it is the expression of a temperament that only gives evidence of a craving for grim physical excitement, but does not always succeed in expressing even this, because of an inability to clarify intentions and consequently to be self-critical. Styles of Alban Berg, Hindemith, Mahler, Tchaikovsky, Mussorgsky, and Offenbach confront each other without transition. Genuinely inventive passages follow others of extreme mechanical dullness. The timing is haphazard. A long scene of wrong-note operetta music pokes fun endlessly at the ineffectuality of the local police, while one of the culminating scenes—that in which the heroine mixes rat poison, feeds it to her father-in-law (who has just horsewhipped her lover), and watches his death agonies impassively—is dismissed briefly and weakly. The relation of the music to the action is unaccountable, ranging from opposition, as in the scene in which the heroine and her lover strangle her husband on a large stage-sized four-poster bed to a lively dance tune, to the more familiar underlining of action and mood. Today, the makeshift and callous quality of all this recalls poignantly the description of those years in Russia in Boris Pasternak's novel *Dr. Zhivago*, when values that had always given human meaning to the individual's life were ridiculed and rejected. The gusto and very real musical talent with which the composer expresses his sense of physical excitement, of rowdy comedy, and of disgust make the opera worth hearing, no matter how disturbing it is as an example of an artist looking coldly on a society of passionate people living violently and brutally, and giving no sign of sympathy or of understanding in his music. The very possibility of human understanding itself seems banished along with any ideological point of view that at least might have helped to give the work some serious justification.

Nicolas Nabokov's *Rasputin's End*, with a libretto by Stephen Spender, in almost complete antithesis to this, is a sympathetic and convincing portrayal of human characters and situations with a comparatively unified musical vocabulary which is affecting not because of its surprises, brutality, and brashness but because of its aptness and explicitness and warm, human lyricism. A revision of the composer's earlier *The Holy Devil*, commissioned, performed, and recorded by the Kentucky Opera Company as part of the Louisville

commissioning project, the new version is definitely grand opera in that it requires elaborate staging, good voices, a big orchestra, and many rehearsals.
The action is a series of flashbacks occurring like a nightmare during the moments after Rasputin has been given the poison by the conspirators in the first
scene and before he awakes in the last scene to the realization of the plot
against his life, attempts to escape, and is shot. All this takes place behind a
scrim curtain, scenes fading in and out noiselessly with the flexibility of a
moving picture and without pauses or musical interludes, except for the inter-
missions. Thus the music is always directly connected with the persons on the
stage, the lurid and violent aspects of the action are played down, and the
human traits and feelings of the characters emphasized. The composer never
overwhelms his listeners with an orchestral comment of any length, but like a
very sensitive dramatist brings into vivid focus the moods and feelings of his
characters, their conflicts, and their relation to the general character of the
scene. Yet, theatrically effective as this score is, it is also, as that of any good
opera must be, interesting in its own right. The skill with which arias, ensembles, and other "numbers" are made to take shape and conclude is unusual
since one is hardly aware of these musical events apart from their function
within the stage action itself.

The scene of Rasputin's "cure" of the young Czarevitch's haemophilia is
most memorable because in it are kept distinct many different strands of
human attitudes and each is given convincing musical expression—the Countess Marina's disapproval of Rasputin, the Czarina's fanatic faith, and
Rasputin's intense, personal, spellbinding quality as he tells the boy a childlike bedtime story and finally induces him to get out of bed and walk. This
many-faceted scene is convincingly presented as one complicated ensemble
piece, and each situation is played off against another with a very strong sense
of theater, yet all is worked out in a beautiful musical form that makes sense
in itself. The same is true of the scene in which the Countess Marina, as a
nurse sitting in a little cubicle in the middle of the provisional military hospi-
tal that has been made out of her ballroom, writes to her husband at the
front, recalling their past happiness, and describing her anxiety for the future,
against a background of bedridden, wounded soldiers calling for water, cry-
ing out in nightmares, or singing love songs. Against this same background,
the conspirators enter, discuss the reasons and plans for the assassination of
Rasputin, and argue with the Countess, who is against taking this step. Another such complex ensemble scene is that of Rasputin's dream during his
visit to the gypsy's house, in the course of which each of the principal women
in the opera appears singing important themes of the opera while a chorus of
monks accuses Rasputin and he tries to placate them. Such scenes, especially
when produced as effectively as they were in Cologne, make the opera memorable both as theater and as music.

To integrate many "characteristic" styles such as those of Russian folksongs, soldiers' songs, religious chanting, gypsy music, and a French chanson in the popular style of the period (played on a scratchy phonograph
record) into a score featuring the elaborate and cultivated vocal, ensemble,

and orchestral techniques that are an accepted part of this medium, is difficult without destroying the immediacy and directness of reference of the "characteristic" music. This muting of character is very noticeable in *Wozzeck*, for instance, where, because of Berg's obliqueness of reference, the meaning of the whole opera loses its sense of particular locale, becomes more generalized and fantastic and probably more inaccessible to the larger musical audience that must now be appealed to, it seems, in order to justify the great expense of effort and money opera requires. The Nabokov work, unlike the Shostakovitch, reveals an awareness of this problem, a new one, since certainly many older operas encompass a great variety of musical styles that nobody is bothered by. But today the importance of stylistic unity as an indication of the composer's integration of outlook, personality, and artistic approach is thought by many to be so fundamental that any stylistic mixture is unacceptable, no matter how skillfully the composer manages transitions or has tried to establish an all-encompassing musical frame that makes all stylistic divergences related, as Nabokov has. This type of criticism of the score overlooks its effect in the theater, where it makes a stirring impression. Indeed the recall of various styles of music helps to set the stage by evoking the special "feel" of the place and time, as must happen in such a realistic story. In other places, when the composer speaks with his own voice, the work is most convincing, and worth all the effort and imagination spent on it at Cologne.

Letter from Europe
(1963)

The proliferation of European festivals and conferences focusing on contemporary music is becoming so great that any of the group of musicians regularly invited who accepted all invitations would be kept busy for almost all year simply in traveling from one country to another. For there is a small nucleus that meets over and over again, once even in Tokyo (as happened in 1961) but most often at the annual festivals, such as the Biennale in Venice in April, the Zagreb Festival in May, the ISCM Festival at the beginning of June—last year (1962) in London, this year in Amsterdam—and, during the summer, in the courses at Darmstadt, Dartington Hall, Cheltenham, and elsewhere; then again in September in Warsaw, in early October either at Palermo or Berlin, and at Donaueschingen in late October. Although each of these festivals has its local supporters, performers, composers, and a special public that has grown rapidly in recent years, there is an increasingly large itinerant group of young enthusiasts that goes from one place to the other. To everyone's amazement (but to the delight of only some), modern music festivals are becoming increasingly successful. This year the size of the audiences for the third annual Palermo festival (about 2,500 for each event) has stimulated other, less thriving Italian music festivals of other types to rethink their plans for next year in an attempt to attract some of this modernistic public, even though modern music festivals are notoriously expensive to give, requiring sometimes extravagant numbers of rehearsals and sometimes the assistance of one of the special group of conductors and performers accustomed to the problems of new music.

The main artistic orientation of these festivals has become more and more that of the Darmstadt school, not so much because its members have made a concerted effort to control the programs, but because increasing amounts of music of an interesting nature have their source there. By now it is clear that the members of this school have become the arbiters of what it is to be "modern" in Europe, for the novelty of their music and their ideas has been intensively and quite intelligently promoted by many different agencies. Sometimes it seems that the very fact of such musical activity within a limited sphere, brilliant and fascinating as it sometimes is, will lead quickly to surfeit, but right now this is the lively school and its influences are felt everywhere in Europe where young composers try to strike out for themselves against the older generation and find recognition among their younger colleagues. Although apparently all of a piece, sometimes subsumed under the general critical heading of "post-Webernism," there is really quite a large number of different concepts and methods distinguishable at Darmstadt. Many of the important composers of the school alternate between "total serial" and "aleatoric" compositions, between compositions using, as sound sources, ordinary musical instruments, percussion instruments, or electronic instruments, as well as myriad combinations of all of these. Yet, for all their seeming variety, all these various methods and sound materials coincide in revealing an acceptance of the same few aspects of some works of the Viennese school, of Debussy, and of Varèse as almost the sole models of procedure from the past, and the ideas of theorists like Cowell, Hába, Hauer, Schillinger, and others who participated in the avant-garde movements of the 1910s and 1920s. In continuing the trends initiated in that lively time, atonalism, bruitism, dadaism, microtones, polyrhythms, and the imposition of rather arbitrary arithmetical patterns such as those discussed by Schillinger, they have been faced with all the problems and contradictions which contributed to the decline of that earlier period. Like the old avant-garde, the neo-avant-garde has a very great preoccupation with the physical materials of music—sounds, their instrumental and mechanical sources, their projection in halls, and finally their method of notation. The presentation of these in time concentrates at present on producing varied or kaleidoscopic alternations such as are inevitably achieved by either total serialization or the use of aleatoric devices. There seems to be very little concern with the perception of these sounds, the possibilities of their intellectual interrelation by the listener, and, therefore, their possibilities for communication on a high level. Most of the time the possibility of communication is denied, or, if admitted, kept on the primitive level of any music that has only a sensuous effect. The most talented works, by very definition, communicate, apparently almost unintentionally, while many of the others consist in an auditorily random display of unpredictable groupings of sound, rather violently opposed in pitch, speed, intensity, and color. The fundamental frustrations resulting from this apparent refusal to deal with the matter of communication, and even the denial of its possibility, explains a great deal about the various directions this school has taken. Yet many of these have considerable interest, and since they are approached from such an untraditional point of view have an important effect on aesthetic and philosophical ideas about music; perhaps they could even become useful if given direction by equally "advanced" concepts arising from an awareness of the listener's psychology. But without such direction, even in the most stimulating sound combinations, there is usually a stultifying intellectual poverty that no amount of arithmetic patterning will overcome; for either such a pattern can be heard by the listener, in which case it is usually far too simple to be of any interest, or it cannot, in which case an impression of pointless confusion results. For the most part, the Darmstadt music seems to waver between these two extremes—that is, when it is heard in large amounts—for there is no denying that on first impression some of the works are quite striking.

It is interesting to try to classify the various methods, in order to formulate a position about them, and to sift out what seems significant from all the welter of publicity, propaganda, and articles. First of all, as noted, this is a neo-avant-garde school and as such its direction has, up to now, been away from the "traditional" and the "conventional" toward the "future." The judgment of how "advanced" a work can be, since this is still considered a virtue, is a very relative matter; to those familiar with musical history of the 1920s very little that happens today seems really "advanced," although the present movement occasionally has more sophistication and interest than the often foolish experiments of previous times. Thus it is misleading to establish categories and trends based on "advancement," but perhaps one can find degrees of difference from the Viennese school from which this movement claims to have taken its start.

The furthest away (from this school) is, of course, the neo-dadaist school, of which there are several small "anti-music" groups in various places that operate on a more primitive level than John Cage and Dieter Schnebel (whose "Visible Music" amused many at Palermo this year). The best that can be said of them is that they test the audience-performer-composer relationship and violate the faith that underlies the conventional acceptance of the pattern. Certainly the poverty of communication and often its complete dissolution in the tedious routine of many concerts of by now familiar format become more infuriating to musicians each year, since their art is based on the quality of commanding experience that can be communicated to the audience through important works. The familiar efforts to arouse listeners from their apathy today rely on publicity. The kind usually employed stresses all the superficial aspects of musical life—personalities, buildings, and so forth—and is really not so far from the dadaist assault, which also results in publicity. Both assault the naive faith in the possibility of important communication and draw attention to the peripheral at the expense of the central. Both interest the news reporter in an effort to attract audiences not primarily interested in or able to grasp serious music. It could be that the neo-dadaists are more honest in their attack on the concert ritual; certainly they are more interesting and amusing, if not actually to witness, at least to think and talk about.

The usual complaint, that the musical iconoclasts are heaping opprobrium and ridicule on the musical profession and if allowed to go too far in the use of musical facilities will finally destroy themselves and the profession too, was made a number of times at the UNESCO conference on Music and Its Public, which took place in Rome (27 September–3 October 1962). Although the counterpart of this idea, that the traditional methods of musical dissemination were becoming less and less effective and were all leading in the same direction, was never stated, the conference gave the impression that all its participants—educators, critics, directors of radio stations, concert managers, and a few performers and composers—felt that the growth of serious music was keeping pace with almost no other field of public artistic and intellectual endeavor today. All seemed to share a sense that music was declining rapidly in widespread cultural importance. However, as often happens at such conferences, no clear idea of why this was or what could be done to remedy the situation could be agreed upon. In this predicament, the ambivalent comic anger, the mystifications and absurdities of the neo-dadaist are sympathetic, if scarcely helpful, and perhaps less destructive than the big-time publicity efforts which have still less relevance to the problem.

To take all this seriously is no doubt foolish, and maybe the interest in the neo-dadaist can be laid to the deplorable decline in circus and vaudeville, where the musical clown once was a staple feature. Harpo Marx, Grock, and, in motion pictures, the concert given by Buster Keaton and Charlie Chaplin in *Limelight,* or Laurel and Hardy in an upper berth with a cello, accomplished such feats as we see today, using the physical material of music to ridicule pretentiousness and giving a glimpse of the musician's battle to communicate amid the recalcitrant apathy of instruments and public. Anyone who witnessed such remarkable performances as that of the clown who tore the piano to pieces playing a pseudo-Saint-Saëns concerto and was swept away with the debris (and did this six times a day) can never find these new musical "happenings" really entertaining.

On the other hand, the Darmstadt group which deals directly with the organization of music is a little nearer to the familiar situation, although when pushed to extremes its results are indistinguishable from those of the neo-dadaist. One type of this, less characteristic now than before, is "total serialization"; another is "aleatory." By turns, each of these concepts has captured the imaginations of many composers, first in Darmstadt and then elsewhere, just as for a moment similar ideas captured the fancy of many earlier composers (such as the *Musikalisches Würfelspiel*). For instance, a number of less advanced Polish composers like Witold Lutoslawski in his *Jeux vénitiens* and Tadeusz Baird in his *Etiuda* have written aleatoric scores. The degree to which chance is controlled or directed, how much is left up to the performer, allows for a very great variety of types. At one extreme are the blank pieces of paper with the direction to the performer at the foot: "Play anything you like but be sure to put the title and my name as composer on the program"; at the other is the figured-bass, or the "ossia," which gives alternatives that are easier, or harder, than the version in the text. As one progresses in degree of control from the latter to the former, the question of authorship becomes more acute (one could imagine, on the analogy of Bach-Busoni, such attributions as Tudor-Cage, or Fortuna-Bussotti), and a host of dadaist problems arise, not the least of which are the matters of predictability of result and the effects of repeated hearings. The decision to play such and such a work to the public—and the relationship of these predictions of what is going to happen to what actually does happen—involves a complex, many-sided responsibility, and finally again brings into play the peripheral concern with what can be expected from the performer and the composers and not with what the actual work will be. In a way such works receive many first performances and have to be conceived in a very different way from other music: since to be worthwhile they must be immediately intelligible and effective, the methods must be very simple and definite although in a different but equally effective way at each performance. As the amount of carry-over from one repeated hearing to another is sometimes slight, the listener cannot get to know the work better and grasp the relevance of more of its facets. From the example of this that I have heard played in many different ways by the same pianist, Stockhausen's *Klavierstück XI*, the aleatoric principle has come to seem grafted onto the work from without, since there are really only a few effective orders of performance.

This aleatoric method has its direct counterpart in our educational training today, which encourages us to classify artistic works by trends, similar procedures, concepts, and so forth (as I am doing here), rather than to look at specific works and recognize their special qualities in all their uniqueness. Aleatoric pieces with any degree of free choice are simply demonstrations of certain general styles or methods of composition without ever becoming concrete individual works in which every detail, and aspect of order, contributes in some way or other to the total effect. In considering this kind of music, one cannot help thinking that for some composers it might very well have become a matter of indifference just what shape the small details of a work would take, so long as a certain general effect is produced, and they came to think that it might be reasonable to let the performer choose how he wanted to make this effect—especially since so many listeners could not tell the difference anyway.

The other prevalent way of organizing music, "total serialization," is actually quite similar to the aleatoric methods except here the elements of random choice come in at the compositional rather than the performance level. For, while the music is written out, giving fairly precise directions to performers, the methods of relating a pattern of pitches to durations, intensities, tone colors, and so on are highly arbitrary because intervallic relationships (such as the motion from E to F) have a perceptual meaning entirely different from that of intervallic relationships in durations or intensities (such as following a duration of eight sixteenth notes with one of nine sixteenths, or of getting slightly louder—from *mf* to *f*). Each of the "parameters" has a different way of being perceived and hence cannot be organized according to the same system of serialization and have any similar effect. Yet, as in all periods of art where "conceits" of this sort were practiced, it is possible to derive an artistic result from such an apparently arbitrary patterning, but it takes a musician with a strong sense of artistic value to produce something of any quality at all.

The more fundamental matters of textural organization, of musical flow, and the combination of a large repertory of sounds to produce these have been a less explicit but more important concern in the Darmstadt school than the above, and have been the real factors controlling many of the "total serialist" and aleatoric choices made. As is often pointed out, one of the main tendencies of this school has been the persistent avoidance of the usual notion of theme or melody as the basic factor in musical organization and also of the shaping effects of regular rhythmic patterns and pulses. This avoidance has led to a focusing of musical invention on many other aspects not previously of so much concern. One of the concepts of textural organization, supplanting previous "pointillist" methods, was, perhaps, first developed in compositions such as *Pithoprakta*, by the Greek composer Iannis Xenakis, and carried further by Penderecki, Gorecki, Ligeti, and a host of others. This technique uses many striking contrasts of thin and thick textures of many different qualities and draws continuities from their evolving and changing progress, making previous "one-note-at-a-time" textures seem a little faded and thin. For the isolation of single notes by pitch, dynamics, timbre, and their brief or prolonged overlapping, once used so delicately and effectively by Webern and further developed with more dramatic intensity by Luigi Nono, as in his *Canto sospeso* (1956), is a device that no longer seems to stimulate the writing of interesting music, while the thick, packed, dissonant textures and vivid juxtapositions of whole clusters or constellations of notes seem to lead, these days, to livelier results. Xenakis, using terms borrowed from probability theory in the impenetrable explanations of his works in program notes, calls his music "stochastic." Actually his point of view has evidently led him to think about the behavior of large groups of notes, rather than single ones, and from this to the development of complex and strangely organized textures, usually without reference to counterpoint.

With the new textural development naturally goes an exploration of new possibilities of sound, an increasing interest in percussion and in novel ways of playing the more familiar instruments. Penderecki's most impressive score, *To the Victims of Hiroshima: Threnody*, for fifty-two strings, calls for a host of new methods of playing these instruments aside from using all the effects found in the Viennese scores. It asks for "highest sound without pitch, play between the bridge and the tailpiece, arpeggio on four strings behind the bridge, play on the tailpiece," as well as quarter-tones and vibrati of several different speeds and widths. This exploitation of some of the cruder and more uncharacteristic sounds of the instruments borders on the dadaist, in some cases; in others, as here, the extremely violent, almost "anti-artistic" expression of the music justifies the means.

Such searching into the physical aspects of musical production also leads to considerable interest in new, more graphic ways of notation, which sometimes result in a clearer depiction of the composer's intention than conventional notation affords, but often puts up an enigmatic barrier between his imagination and the possibility of physical, sonic realization. The highly skilled and costly efforts of some publishers, particularly those in Poland, to follow composers in this direction is amazing in view of the very limited number of such scores that can be sold.

It is important to realize that this entire school of music, with its great preoccupation with physical sound, can have a wide appeal on a simple sensuous level, and often attracts those not trained to expect and grasp the higher types of order found in older music. In this it parallels, on another level, the return to the more fundamental and primitive elements of music characteristic of "folkloric" tendencies; interestingly, *Le Sacre* seems to point in both directions at once. The fact that this new music can have a strong appeal was particularly evident at the recent Warsaw Festival, where it was repeatedly hailed with great enthusiasm by large audiences.

This, the most elaborate of annual festivals, celebrated its sixth anniversary between 15 and 23 September 1962. Extensive as it is, it forms only part of the still larger Warsaw Autumn, held to commemorate the gradual resurrection of the city since its almost total destruction during the war. Each year some new section is rebuilt, and each year's festival features a new step in Poland's artistic post-war renaissance. In a few years, the grand old opera house, reconstructed with one façade in its old neoclassic style, will reopen with entirely new equipment; plans for a huge commissioning project of new operas and new productions of leading contemporary operas are already at an advanced stage. In general, the festival seems to act as a safety valve for all the somewhat submerged advanced tendencies in iron-curtain countries. Since the Polish government provides lavish financial support and allows artists and composers themselves to decide freely what they want to present, the programs and exhibits attract the more progressive from East Germany, Hungary, Czechoslovakia, Rumania, Bulgaria, and the Soviet Union to a reunion where they can discuss their ideas with one another and where their works can be presented before a sympathetic public.

Last September there were eight symphonic concerts, one ballet evening, one electronic and nine chamber orchestra or chamber music programs, each containing from two to two and a half hours of music, all contemporary. Besides this intensive listening, there was much social activity, for "observers" had been invited from everywhere, and those countries where there is state support for musicians' traveling expenses (the Polish government paid expenses within Poland) were well represented. There were, it seemed, twenty observers from the Soviet Union as well as several busloads of Moscow Conservatory students, who reacted vivaciously to the advanced scores, both pro and con. Also in attendance were quite a number from Bulgaria and other iron-curtain countries, a few from Western Europe, and, from our hemisphere, a woman from Cuba and myself. There were no East Asians or

Africans present. Each morning a polylingual (Polish, Russian, French, German) discussion took place, called a "press conference" but in reality a good-natured social gathering in which the composers and performers, or conductors of the previous day's concerts, were questioned and their works discussed. All were very attentive, particularly the Russians, who took elaborate notes on what was said. In private talks with them it was impossible to fathom what motivated their special interest, since like everyone else they seemed well versed in the Viennese school and in the schools of music presented and were eager, as we all were, to hear the new works. To my amusement one of the Russian musicologists criticized my *Eight Etudes and a Fantasy*, brilliantly played at the festival by the Dorian Wind Quintet, as not being advanced enough. The Russians I met, in fact, seemed unexpectedly knowledgeable and aware, were familiar with some American scores, and were especially enthusiastic about those of Sessions. Wishing to know more, they, like many Western Europeans, regretted that it was so difficult to learn about our music without being overwhelmed with scores and information about works that did not interest them. I pointed out that we had to suffer under the same kind of unselective representation from the Soviet Union. The same problem bothered the festival directors, who were much interested in American music but had a hard time finding the kind of scores that would fit into the rather advanced yet highly developed context of their festival. Varèse's *Arcana* was played, and I arranged to send a number of scores of some older Americans like Ives, Ruggles, Riegger, and Cowell that did not seem to be known. The interest in the United States was very genuine, and the two concerts played by Americans, those of the La Salle Quartet and the Dorian Quintet, were packed with standees.

This year, more than ever, the festival favored the advanced school of Polish composers: Penderecki, Gorecki, Kotoński, Serocki, Schäffer, and the conductor Jan Krenz. Of these the first three seemed to be the most effective. The young Polish student of Nadia Boulanger, Wojciech Kilar, provided one of the "wows" of the festival, *Riff, "62"* for orchestra, which combined the tone-cluster technique of Penderecki with remote suggestions of very rowdy jazz. The packed hall gave the work such an ovation that it had to be repeated. Other interesting scores were *Aprèsludes* by the Italian Niccolò Castiglioni, *Lyrische Gesänge* by the German Dieter Schönbach, two violin-piano sonatas by the Soviet composers Halina Oustvolska and Boris Klouzner, and works by the Rumanian Aurel Stroe and the Bulgarian Lazar Nicolov. Unusual works by Bartók, Stravinsky, Schoenberg, and Webern were played, but only two works of the older neoclassic tendency, one by a Pole, the other Shostakovitch's Eighth Symphony.

It is clear that in Poland, as in most countries where there is considerable state support of serious music, subsidy came as a continuation of the types of support possible under aristocratic patronage, which comprehended all the important aspects of professional activity, and with it plans for educating more professionals and audiences to keep the whole enterprise alive. It was, therefore, only natural that when the state took over its almost total subsidy,

contemporary composers, performers, orchestras, as well as educational institutions, the public, and those invited from the outside to observe and
comment, should be included. There is even a far-sighted policy in the importation of foreign performing talent and foreign compositions, for it is by
such contact with the international musical world that the local activity can
maintain an important standard and avoid the provincialism that isolation
invariably produces. The Polish Composers' Union is allotted a fairly large
sum annually to distribute as commissions to its members by the government.
Composers themselves make applications for a commission to an annually
elected board of composer-directors, presenting a project for the size and kind
of work they intend to write. The board decides how much to allot, taking
into account not only the dimensions of the projected work but the composer's importance and reputation and the total sum to be distributed. The
composer usually receives enough to live on reasonably during the writing of
the work. This plan applies to composers of all schools. The completed works
are usually printed by the state Polskie Wydawnictwo Muzyczne or by other
publishers, performances are found for them, they are put on tapes distributed to radio stations abroad, and they are often recorded by the state
recording company, Polskie Nagrania.

Obviously the amount of effort, thought, planning, and expenditure incurred by such a festival is tremendous, but the results were indeed remarkable. Every important orchestra in Poland—the two in Warsaw, the Cracow
Philharmonic, the Silesian Philharmonic, the Pomerian Philharmonic of Byd-
goszcz—presented a program or two, and at each of these concerts at least
one or two of the advanced works were played with remarkable seriousness
and care for the total effect. One reason that could be perceived for spreading
the work over many orchestras is that the players and their local audiences
are thereby kept in touch with present-day tendencies.

Besides providing the observers with much to discuss, the festival revealed
to us how many similar attitudes and experiences we shared about new music.
Strangely, most of what was expressed, especially by those not specifically involved in the Darmstadt movement, was discussed in the preface to the
printed program taken from an article written in 1926 by Szymanowski,
Poland's most revered recent composer:

The intellectual atmosphere of the most cultivated strata of contemporary life, the
stage on which is acted out the fierce struggle for a new form, for a new expression
of reality, becomes more and more complicated, bringing into play ever more specialized and subtle concepts. This process, by the nature of things, has brought the
artist into the very heart of ideological conflicts, opposing his intuitive and instinc-
tive method of work to the effect of the concept of art as an objective aesthetic
problem. Already with Wagner, theoretical considerations on the nature of the musical drama preceded in large measure the artistic concretion of the idea essential to
many of his most remarkable works. This excellent example is an irrefutable argument against the (conservative) type of critical thought which (apparently) wishes
to see the checkmate of contemporary art in its excess of intellectualism, in its abstraction, which results, so it is said, from theories made *a priori*. In reality, there is

in this a clearly elementary misunderstanding which consists in confusing (more or less consciously) the notions of form and content in art, and in ignoring their organic interrelationship. . . .

One cannot describe the spirit of the contemporary European musical world today without mentioning Hans Rosbaud, whose death was a great loss to the entire contemporary music movement. The level of this man's cultivation, even aside from musical gifts, was extraordinary: he spoke English, French, Italian, and, of course, German perfectly, and up to the end of his life took daily lessons in Russian, Greek, and advanced mathematics. He had a phenomenal power of concentration, was able, after the first reading of a complicated orchestral score, to grasp all its details—as I was able to observe at the ISCM Festival in London—and to deal with orchestral matters with a sure sense of the totality, as well as explain patiently to the performers how this was to be achieved—even at a time when obviously he had very little physical energy left. His quiet humor, his extraordinarily cultivated knowledge of literature and art, as well as his adventurousness in tackling any score, no matter how problematic, in which he found something valuable, made him one of the truly remarkable human beings of our time. It is to the credit of the Southwest German Radio, the Zürich Tonhalle, and the Chicago Symphony, among others, that he was so frequently engaged to present, in his inimitable way, the masterpieces of the twentieth century and other works he believed in so deeply. These scores he conducted with enormous care and precision, bringing out their innermost musical qualities and beauties, unbelievably and almost effortlessly, it seemed, without show, without extravagant gestures, but as a truly cultivated and civilized man would, by persuasion and not by force.

ISCM Festival, Amsterdam
(1963/94)

The annual festival of the International Society for Contemporary Music (ISCM) is of much smaller dimensions than many new music festivals that take place these days (it is dwarfed, for example, by Warsaw Autumn), but it is the one with by far the longest history. In recent years, I have been involved with ISCM events in several ways. I was appointed the American delegate to the Thirty-sixth ISCM Festival in London, 31 May through 6 June 1962, at which my Double Concerto was performed under the direction of Hans Rosbaud. This was the third time that this annual festival had taken place in London since its inception in 1922. The 1962 festival was supported in part by the British Arts Council and a formidable list of guarantors and presented excellent performances of Schoenberg's Variations for Orchestra, Stravinsky's *A Sermon, a Narrative, and a Prayer*, and a very impressive cantata, *Cuius legibus rotantur poli*, by the young Swiss, Klaus Huber. In all, four concerts were presented of music chosen by the ISCM jury from among all the sections—two orchestral and two of chamber music—and also performances of

British music: Michael Tippett's *King Priam,* and a program of chamber music presenting many of the younger British composers.

At this festival I was elected by the delegates to the international jury for the Thirty-seventh ISCM Festival, to take place in Amsterdam on 8 through 15 June 1963, as were Conrad Beck (Switzerland), Marcel Mihailovici (France), Guillaume Landré (Holland), and Jan Maegaard (Denmark). We met in the early part of January 1963 to consider the approximately 130 scores submitted by the various sections. We had a number of new problems which bothered us, especially Mihailovici, Landré, and myself, who had served in 1960 on the jury in Cologne. The new style of writing scores, and particularly the influence of the music of Stockhausen and Penderecki, has become increasingly widespread among the young, and the challenges of judging the effectiveness of music written in such unusual notation, while at the same time encouraging advanced efforts of music in countries where such efforts are exceptional or unrecognized, made responsible choices difficult. Most of the jury members had heard Penderecki's work, *To the Victims of Hiroshima: Threnody,* on the radio, but almost none of us could have imagined how it would sound from the score alone. There was the additional problem of presenting this work with a Dutch orchestra (which would have been the same with any American orchestra), in which the string players were required to make unexpected and brutal effects with the instruments; this raised fears that the orchestra players would refuse to play the work, even if they knew that the final result would be as effective as it had already proved to be. The mood on the jury, after having faced Penderecki's score and many other, far more perplexing kinds of notation—and especially after having heard quite a number of uninteresting works using such notation—was that the effort required to decipher such scores was more trouble than it was worth.

The difficulty of maintaining a broadly inclusive artistic representation always becomes more and more formidable as the jurors look through the scores. By and large, the more conservative (who today perpetuate the neoclassic style), the middle of the road (followers either of twelve-tone Schoenberg or of Messiaen), and the advanced (like Penderecki) fall into a hierarchy, with central Europe and Poland, the most advanced, at the center, and other countries less advanced in proportion to their cultural and geographical distance from this center. (Only Japan, an outpost of the advanced, is really an exception to this pattern.) Where does the United States fit in? Our most extreme music from earlier in the twentieth century—Varèse, Ruggles, Crawford, and Ives—was always of a different type from the European and, since it has almost no propagandists abroad, has rarely been heard and has seldom been successful, owing either to bad performances or to the total incomprehension of audiences. Ironically, in the past Varèse's scores were often submitted by the United States section, invariably to be rejected by the international jury—yet now Varèse is considered one of the leaders of the new European school and is played everywhere.

It is interesting that in a place like Poland, with its special musical economics, works of rather extreme experimental nature can be written and rehearsed in considerable detail, in some cases even greater detail than is possible in Western countries with state-sponsored radio orchestras or other forms of subsidy—and certainly in far greater detail than is possible in countries like the United States, where private patronage can afford neither the expense of the careful, lengthy rehearsal requisite to the success of such new music nor the risk of ultimate audience disapproval. Thus it appears that for the foreseeable future the course of new orchestral music is going to depend on the many trials and errors, experiments successful and unsuccessful that take place in Europe. This is, of course, musical experimentation on a very high level. In America, experimentation assumes other forms. We do have a group of musically untrained performers who give demonstrations of anti-music; we also have the various musical counterparts of present-day literary and graphic art movements, who simply produce sonic realizations of long-familiar philosophical ideas—which back in the days when most people had more vivid imaginations would not have required a night at the concert hall to make their musical deficiencies obvious.

At Amsterdam, the jury thought to render a significant service to contemporary music by presenting an important score which has rarely been played and remains scarcely known, not being available in printed form: Schoenberg's *Vier Orchesterlieder*, op. 22, a work written almost fifty years ago and frequently referred to as one of Schoenberg's most remarkable compositions. The fact that there are quite a few works of such importance still lying on shelves (scores by Ives, Crawford, Ruggles, and even Varèse, to mention American examples) while so much effort and money is spent on presenting the latest efforts of young and inexperienced composers is one of the disturbing paradoxes of the profession. At the American Academy in Rome, for instance, an annual orchestral concert is donated by the RAI at which the latest works of the Fellows are played each year. Since there are generally but three Rome Fellows, each of whom stays about three years, each spends most of the year getting a new work ready for the annual concert by the radio orchestra, one of the world's outstanding orchestras for such scores. Perhaps never again in his life will the composer holding this fellowship have such an excellent orchestra at his disposal as for these three consecutive years, during which he can write anything he likes within reason and get it played. The contrast between this remarkable opportunity and the kind of opportunities available to almost all other American and European composers, even composers of universal reputation like those mentioned above, is disheartening—although of course one would not wish things to be otherwise for the Rome Fellows.

No matter how much one has heard about it, the extent of subsidy for music in Europe always catches one by surprise. In Italy, for instance, I found that a very elaborate concert series (one of the best in the world) of thirty-six annual concerts of everything from fourteenth-century music to Vivaldi operas to Stockhausen is subsidized to the tune of fifty to seventy percent by the government—the rest covered by the sale of subscriptions and individual tickets. This is, of course, only one of several concert series in Rome alone that receive important subsidies—and then there are many other such festivals and musical events all over Italy.

Along with the great advantage accruing to those who benefit from the kind of patronage which supports national groups or age groups, rather than individuals or individual works, goes the danger of boring the well-disposed public with a lot of music that is being presented to them for reasons other than its intrinsic interest. It falls to the jury, as it did to the ISCM jury for the festival at Amsterdam to which I was elected, to guard against such problems. Here we were faced with the complicated challenge of representing as many different countries as possible, and as many different styles as we could, and at the same time trying to find interesting pieces that would provide effective contrasts among themselves on programs. Given the fact that the bulk of the works must be chosen from the selections sent in by national juries, one is often at one's wits' end. Very often the best or most interesting composers of the country are not represented that year among the submissions, or the best works of these composers are not submitted, or works of only a single style are represented that do not contrast well with those sent by other countries, and so forth. For these reasons, it is hardly surprising that festivals organized according to a particular point of view—such as those in Poland—have often turned out to be the best.

Due to a long history of frustration in this respect, the United States has tried over the years to submit a large variety of works in every style. Since the membership of the European jury changes from year to year, and since the submissions from the various countries themselves vary enormously in terms of outlook and quality, it is very hard to predict what will prove appealing. The jury this year, as it has in each of the other two times I have served, was predisposed toward finding interesting, novel, and original works—although because the directors of the festival refused to accept any works that required electronic equipment (due to the cost of renting and installing it), a large range of possible choices was eliminated automatically. Numerous interesting submissions of this type were made by countries that had failed to read the list of limitations accepted previously by the delegates at London. Nowadays, substantial numbers of works combine prerecorded tapes in many different ways with live performance; at least two works of this type looked very interesting and under other conditions would have been played.

The use of percussion also was a great stumbling block, since the cost of renting and transporting elaborate ensembles of such instruments is so high in Holland. We heard distressing stories about how much it had cost to have some special bells cast for the new version of Boulez's *Pli selon pli* and how the performances of the work had worn out a number of the expensive percussion instruments because the composer insisted on their being hit so hard. One work, by the Swede Sven-Erik Bäck, *Favola*, for clarinet solo "e batteria grande," interested us a good deal—but like many works it too had too large a percussion outlay.

II

American Music

Once Again Swing;
Also "American Music"
(1939)

Swing. Most everything has already been said about swing. A good many people get more thrills out of swing than out of "classical music," though some say it is a kind of dope—lots of kick that puts your mind to sleep. Some call it non-indigenous and African, though it was really invented by whites. Others call it entertainment music having no emotional or intellectual appeal, with the same relation to "art music" that *Saturday Evening Post* illustrations or comic strips have to works by Pavel Tchelitchew or Dali. Some say the future of American music lies here. Still others, hating its illiteracy and routine formulas, predict it will shortly die of emotional and intellectual starvation. Foreigners recall that gypsy orchestras used to play with the same kind of abandoned improvisation, and historians report that the "polka mania" was just the same sort of craze in the last century. All our lives we have been hearing this astonishing and vigorous music develop. It makes the money, it gets the performances, its popularity exceeds the wildest dreams of serious composers. It has set the feet of the whole world stamping in 4/4 time.

At Carnegie Hall, during the holidays, the intellectuals of swing organized a fascinating historical concert. Starting with African records, they traced its development through the spiritual, jazz, and boogie-woogie on up to Count Basie. Performers from little churches in the deep South who had never traveled before were brought out on Carnegie Hall stage, and in this spacious and, perhaps, specious atmosphere attempted to project the charm they exhibited back home. Negroes, probably because of their social history, have always been a race of entertainers like the gypsies in Europe. Theatrically their tradition is outside that of serious music. But this concert, since it was given in Carnegie Hall, challenged comparisons. Certainly the main factor is the hall itself. A concert hall performance of the usual kind takes place as a ritual in which public and performer are ultimately subservient to the ideas of a composer who has put his notes on paper. Swing, on the other hand, is the glorification of the performer. All the adulatory swing slang—"a killerdiller beating his chops," "gut-bucket licks," "in the groove," "boogie-woogie," "jitterbug," "a solid sender doin' some tall rug cuttin'"—refer to the performer, to the type of performance, or to the audience, but never to the actual, composed "paper" or music. It is, as we well know, a performance that stresses the intensity of nervous excitement "sent out" by the performer rather than the stuffed-shirt feeling of the concert hall. In order to make serious music palatable to the swing audience, composers like Bach and Debussy have to be arranged, to eliminate everything but the tune; rhythms, developments, and harmonies which might confound the jitterbug must be straightened out. When played in the appropriate jam style (for the "paper men," or men who can read music, do not play the notes in the classical time values but have a tradition which, from the point of view of the serious musician, distorts or "swings" eighths and quarters into rhythms impossible to notate) this becomes the genuine article and loses its original flavor. By the same token, swing tends to lose *its* character and take on another when appropriated by serious composers for the concert hall. In that setting the music will never interest audiences until a serious composer with artistic perspective is able to stylize and make it express his personal, creative attitude toward American life. Up to now swing still remains, except for a few isolated instances, in the stage of Russian folk song or gypsy music before Glinka, Mussorgsky, Liszt, or Brahms.

"The American composer should. . . ." Here we are back in the middle of a fight with the exponents of American music talking through their hats. The *New York Sunday Times* has, in the last months, published letters and critical articles revealing not only how wide a variety of opinions exists on this subject but also how little real information its steamy exponents have about what has been and is being done by American composers. The question was not whether Samuel Barber's *Adagio for Strings* (so typical of Toscanini's choice in contemporary music) was good or bad in its reactionary style, or whether it was better, say, than Barber's *Symphony in One Movement* or Roy Harris's Third Symphony and if so why; no, the question was, rather, whether *all* American music should be "reactionary" or *all* should be "modern." This furor disregards the fact that a composer is good not because he is reactionary (like Brahms) or advanced (like Beethoven), but because he has imagination, vitality, and other qualities which are always encountered regardless of school or nationality. In fact, I believe, none would be more disappointed than these critics and correspondents who so glibly tell the composers what to do, if musicians followed them and wrote scores in strict accord with their ideas. Certainly neither Henry James nor Walt Whitman ever fulfilled a previous "should," and no important composer past, present, or future may be expected to do the same.

The critics are not well informed about American music. How could they be? They do not cover concerts devoted to it, such as, for example, the WPA Composers' Forum Laboratory, or that of the Musical Art Quartet, which this month presented four American quartets by Daniel Gregory Mason, Quincy Porter, Mark Wessel, and Rudolph Forst. Two of these men have considerable reputations and yet only the *Times* and *Herald Tribune* bothered to send even their second-string reviewers, who were perfunctory enough to come late or leave early. Other papers made the kind of passing mention accorded to third-rate artists.[1]

The four first performances by the Musical Art Quartet were chosen to give a picture of the studious and serious side of American chamber music. Mason's *Intermezzo* for string quartet is one of the best pieces by this academic composer from the point of view of musical interest, though it lacked the personal quality of his *A Lincoln Symphony* played here last year. Quincy Porter's Sixth Quartet is one more Porter quartet with his usual smoothness, excellence of string writing, and transparency. There is a lighter touch here than in some of his others, but nothing is told that we don't already know about his music. Rudolph Forst's Quartet, as might be expected from an NBC award, was a fireworks piece, all the tricks of impressionist quartet writing, form stunts from Brahms and Strauss, ideas having no stylistic or emotional relation to each other, and a lack of musical conviction. Mark Wessel's Quartet was the surprise of the evening. It was not altogether easy flowing or free from reminiscences of Hindemith, but it had a kind of suffused passion and excitement which left one anxious to know his other music.

When Aaron Copland has two premieres in one short month, it is an event of considerable musical importance. Again the critics revealed their lack of information and interest. In reviewing Koussevitzky's excellent performance of *El Salón México*, these probers gave no evidence of ever having heard works by Copland before and hence failed completely to discuss the important changes in style made evident in this piece. *El Salón México* is clearly a milestone in the composer's development, for it represents a change from the introspective attitude shown in its immediate predecessor, *Statements for Orchestra*, and in almost all his previous works. Beginning with the Mexican piece, Copland's music has become more relaxed and free, more ascetic in texture, more tonal, more consonant, and much more straightforward and melodic. He has discovered a kind of beautiful simplicity which bears a definite spiritual relationship to the simple, direct, and honest people of this continent. Characteristically, *El Salón México* is a musical description of the liveliness of a Mexican "hot spot," and it is done with gaiety and abandon. The clear orchestration—no trick doublings and messy textures, strong and free—is very typical of its composer. The style is much more accessible to the average public than that of his earlier work, yet it is marked at every point with Copland's personality. In the Symphonic Ode there are the same breathless rhythms, insistence on brilliant triads, and crescendi of excitement, but here there is a jubilance that is new.

If the critics did not do justice to this work, they scarcely even mentioned Copland's most recent *An Outdoor Overture*, sensibly written for high school orchestra, commissioned and performed by the New York City High School of Music and Art. These orchestras, far less bound by tradition than our more

---

1. Paul Henry Lang describes the critical situation brilliantly in his penetrating article, "Ecce Criticus," *The American Scholar* 7 (1938):478–95.

impressive institutions, will unquestionably play a very great role in developing the appreciation of American music. The score is cleverly suited to the needs of young musical performers and serves them especially well as it makes them sound like an orchestra of professionals. Since *El Salón México*, Copland's music has become clearer and more sharply defined in feeling and character. *An Outdoor Overture* is a more impressive piece than the high-school opera, *The Second Hurricane*, for it contains some of his finest and most personal music. Its opening is as lofty and beautiful as any passage that has been written by a contemporary. It is Copland in his "prophetic" vein, a vein which runs through all his work, the slow pages of *Vitebsk*, the opening of the *Ode*, the conclusion of the *Piano Variations*, the "prophetic" movement of the *Statements*, and the beginning and end of his new ballet, *Billy the Kid*. Never before, though, has he expressed it so simply and directly. The rest of the overture with its changes of pace, like the *Music for Radio*, develops very naturally with lots of charm and variety. Each new work of Copland only goes further to prove that he is one of the most important, original, and inspiring figures in contemporary music either here or in Europe. But it is useless to expect the critics to hail him so, for they do not bother to hear or study his works.

American Music in the New York Scene
(1940)

Critics, performers, and public are making an unprecedented effort these days to evaluate American music. The difficulties of this job have recently been aggravated by bringing, into an already acrimonious debate, allusions to other arts more productive and successful here. Although perhaps natural enough, such comparisons lead easily to confusion. Obvious and important distinctions between the arts and their various developments are not kept clearly enough in mind. In America, painting and literature, for instance, have had a good head start over music and are already in the midst of a kind of golden age. Music has been handicapped by certain physical and economic factors: not only must a work be written, it must be performed before it can be heard. The hazards of the field naturally act as a deterrent to the entries; they limit the number of creations. Moreover, in speaking of an obviously American music, the abstract nature of the art should not be overlooked: it is harder to associate music than painting or literature with the external facts of locale.

America, it is frequently pointed out, has as yet developed no composer of the importance of writers like Whitman or Poe, or indeed of many contemporary painters. But how many other countries have? Germany certainly; perhaps also Italy. The plain facts elsewhere are that now, as in the past, composers have less importance than painters or writers. This concession, however, does not deny the virtues of men like Mussorgsky, Purcell, Couperin, Berlioz, or Debussy—all composers in countries where music is generally overshadowed by the other arts.

Nor do parallels between the cultures of other nations and of America come to much either, for it grows steadily clearer that America cannot and will not follow in Europe's footsteps. We won't have an American Beethoven or an American Mussorgsky, even though we may have composers who work toward the same high musical standards Europe has raised.

Nevertheless, important composers are already with us in America. Ours is a varied musical scene: the music-makers, few as they are in comparison with other artists, write in every kind of style, whether or not it derives from Europe, whether it is boldly original, extreme, conservative, crude, or highly polished. They make up a complex, interesting picture, much more individual than many a European scene and just as interesting. Their quality, competence, and seriousness is on a generally high level. Indeed, the variety of current aesthetic attitudes is proof that the question of musical competence is no longer the problem it once was. One might almost say that American music was born when these differences began to take convincing shape in works. That happened not so long ago, but it has happened, and all-American concerts like the ones given by Koussevitzky and the Boston Symphony (whatever the arguments for or against them) show how much life there is in our music today.

Of all the new pieces played at these Koussevitzky concerts, Roy Harris's Third Symphony stands out as the most striking and thoroughly unusual score. A rehearing of this has overcome many of my previous objections.[1] It now seems to me to be his best orchestral work. Its inspiration is remarkably sustained and eloquent, and that grand expansiveness so often sought by Harris has never been achieved so well as here. Harris's work reveals several important tendencies that deserve consideration at this moment—chiefly the apparent deliberate effort to write "American" music. Toward this end his procedures seem intelligibly recognizable. First of all, he has given musical expression to the challenging, vigorous, "strong-arm" movement already well known in our indigenous art and literature. The emphasis is prevailingly on qualities of American pioneer life, physical strength, unflinching courage, strong conviction, and the grand, lonely bleakness of certain stretches of the natural scene. The work is of the school of Dreiser, Benton, ultimately of Whitman. Sharing this attitude, Harris has not, however, fallen into the naiveté of previous American musical folklorists. He has invented a whole new style to give his point fresh meaning. The themes are not actual quotations of folksongs or hymns, although some of his melodic turns are reminiscent of these genres. The rhythms are closer to various types of American speech and voice inflection than to native dance forms. It is much the most sophisticated and intelligent approach yet made to an American treatment of folklore.

Musically, Harris's Third Symphony represents a step toward simplification,

1. See, for instance, "Season of Hindemith and Americans," *Modern Music* 16, no. 4 (May–June 1939): 249–54; repr. in *The Writings of Elliott Carter*, ed. Else and Kurt Stone (Bloomington: Indiana University Press, 1977), 60–63. [B]

so that only the most typical and fundamental characteristics are expressed. It is in five block-like sections, each one with a dominating idea so definite that its character can be grasped at once; within each section very little happens that goes against it. Each of the five is built on clearly stated themes, often of considerable length. The articulation of phrase and of section is always clearly marked; transitional material is almost completely eliminated. Voice leading is arranged to give a contrapuntal impression even in places where harmony predominates; counterpoint with one part well emphasized dominates the entire piece. Themes return formally in different sections but surrounded by such a changed atmosphere that little sense of musical position results. This has always been one of the curious qualities of Harris's work. Here such constant change is saved from giving a sense of wandering by the emphasis each theme receives when it first appears. As a folkloric work with literary overtones, it reminds me of the Borodin symphonies but, of course, it is in an entirely new idiom.

The other major event of this season was the all-Sessions concert at the Composers' Forum Laboratory. By comparison to Harris, Roger Sessions is, obviously, more austere. His devotion to the purest tradition of his art is such as to eliminate all non-musical, literary elements. Among the latter he would probably include the trivialities of folklore and the cultivation of personality by the indulgence in formulae that give a trademark to music. This concert, which included his Piano Sonata [No. 1 (1930)], String Quartet [No. 1 (1936)], two songs (*On the Beach at Fontana* and *Romualdo's Song*), and two short new piano pieces, was a clear demonstration that Sessions, during his whole life as a composer, has shunned the easy effect and the immediate appeal, has fought to keep his music honest, serious, conscientious to the limit of his power. Slowly over the years he has developed his own style. Though every work has always had great musical qualities, not all have been as original as the more recent ones. His development has been by conquest and mastery of the whole art rather than by the cultivation of personal manner. While not so insular as the later works of Bartók, Schoenberg, and Berg, Sessions's recent music resembles theirs in thoroughgoing point of view; like theirs also it is open to the criticism of over-intellectualization. Certainly his music is not easy, even for the musician. But no one can fail to be impressed by the strong, stubborn conviction and the musicianship, which have produced this highly developed music. It takes a lot of concentration to penetrate the musical structures of Sessions, and yet one is, I think, amply repaid by the severe, orderly completeness of their expression. Sessions is unique in American music, and yet his intransigent rigor is certainly familiar to us as a native quality: his devotion to high standards and ideals is typical of our best. Along with the older works on this concert, there were the two new short piano pieces, *Pages from a Musical Diary*,[2] which are the kind of music he should bring to light more frequently as preparation for his longer works. In these few but concentrated measures he has packed an extraordinary amount of meat. The slow

2. Later called *From My Diary*, suite for piano. [S]

piece based on ninths is particularly fine in its sudden, violent rise to an abrupt climax. It presents in small form all the power and impressiveness that is Sessions.

Many other figures appeared on the American landscape this month. The Koussevitzky concerts did not stop with the Harris work, nor did the Composers' Forum with the Sessions evening. The former gave us Walter Piston's elegant Concertino for Piano and Orchestra, which has been reviewed here before, and William Schuman's new *American Festival Overture*, written for the occasion. Schuman's work is frankly in a lighter vein than his better Second Symphony, but it has vitality and conviction behind it. Unfortunately he begins here with his weakest foot—a long "motivic" introduction based on the minor third "wee-awk-ee" street cry that supplies a certain amount of material for the ensuing fugue. This first section, which returns again later, has not the character of an introduction, being too long and too emphatic and closing with a big "collapse," nor is it integrated as a section in its own right. But when the fugue starts up in the strings, there is, in spite of a redundant repetition of the exposition in the woodwinds, a considerable amount of real musical interest. The overture follows the constant accelerando pattern so familiar among the disciples of Harris, and in the end winds up with lots of good spirits and gaiety. Schuman's gift is undeniable, though so far his musical material has shown a tendency to be slight.

It is always a pleasure to rehear Carpenter's *Skyscrapers*, his best score to date. It was superbly performed at the Boston concert and I mention it now only to say that here is as directly pictorial a work as any critic might want for comparison with other arts in America. In spirit close to the Reginald Marsh and Dos Passos pictures of the American 1920s, it evokes just as keenly as they do that boisterous, brutal era of the mechanical heart.

Among the reactionary pieces played by the Boston orchestra, Howard Hanson's Third Symphony proved once again how skillful, fine, and ambitious a composer he is. It rightly won acclaim for its clear, excellent writing and seriousness of mood. While not so advanced as *Pan and the Priest*, it has many a place where the somber atmosphere reminds one of Sibelius. To me this work compares more than favorably with the best works of the Finnish composer (the Fourth and Seventh Symphonies and *Tapiola*); it has many more interesting musical events and more meaty material.

The Violin Concerto by Edward Burlingame Hill, although its slow movement is sensitive, was not on the level of his more significant works. Randall Thompson's Second Symphony, with its charming attempt to bring back the kind of American folklore practiced in the 1890s, does not bear up under frequent hearings. The conventionality of development undermines the buoyancy of this very lighthearted work, and it is not saved by the suavity and beauty of scoring from growing a little pedestrian. *Americana* and the *Peaceable Kingdom* are much more successful.

David Diamond's Cello Sonata received a performance at the Composers' Forum Laboratory which was the subject of considerable debate then and there between the composer and the program arrangers. To me there seemed some justification for Diamond's complaint; everyone knows that it is hard to tell how accurately a new work is being played; composers have suffered, and probably always will, from bad performances. Nevertheless many pages of the Cello Sonata did come across very well, the opening of the first movement and the closing of the last; the slow movement seemed particularly effective. In the hands of five Juilliard students his Quintet for Flute, String Trio, and Piano were excellently done; its gaiety, strength, and great musical invention were apparent, as they were not in a previous performance reviewed here. Each work of Diamond's (and there are many) seems to have a new point of departure. While there are sensitive musical qualities in most of them and much originality of technique, there does not always seem to be a clear individuality behind the music. However, his *Elegy in Memory of Maurice Ravel*, originally composed for brass, harps, and percussion and played last month in a version for strings and percussion by the Orchestrette Classique under Frederique Petrides, is a sincerely touching and moving work, its appeal more direct in the strings than in the brass. In these slow, expressive works, Diamond's originality seems to be most in evidence. Since they are in the dissonant style that conductors and audiences seem to shy away from we do not often hear them.

Lazare Saminsky also had a concert devoted entirely to his music. It suffered from both poor performances and a poor choice of pieces. These were all short, mostly slight compositions, which made it hard to form a definite picture of the various sides of the composer. It was clear, however, that Jewish themes such as in the *Two Chorales*, adapted from ancient chants, and the *Violin Pieces*, adapted from old Eastern melodies, had awakened in Saminsky the most beautiful and delicate treatments. In fact, the whole evening of music demonstrated that a sensitiveness of ear and refinement of sonority seem to be Saminsky's greatest attributes. There was no chance here to judge his more extended works.

When Ralph Kirkpatrick announced a program of twentieth-century music for the harpsichord, no one could fail to wonder what music he would play. Most of it, not surprisingly, was written for the occasion. Otto Luening's Sonata for Flute and Harpsichord was the best-conceived work for the instruments; it had a delicate, wistful simplicity, an elegance skillfully "more made for sweetness than for violence." By comparison with Florent Schmitt's Trio for Harpsichord, Flute, and Clarinet it seemed more suitable; it avoided the heavy chords and soggy sonorities that filled the latter, mildly humorous work. Other works, by Robert McBride and Ernst Lévy, were equally suited for piano.

The New York Philharmonic goes on quietly, unobtrusively selecting new pieces that never offend or surprise. Occasionally they delight, as did Ibert's Concertino, already reviewed in *Modern Music*. Little pleasure was to be derived from Arthur Bliss's *Suite for "Checkmate,"* a well-composed, brilliant score in a style which no longer entertains except when used by its originators—Ravel, Strauss, and the Stravinsky of *Petrouchka*. Weinberger, it seems, is a permanent fixture at these concerts; now we have an appropriate *Christmas*, far less amusing than *Schwanda* or even the *Chestnut Tree*.

Like all other music, that intended for the masses can be good or bad. Effectiveness in putting across a message is no criterion of artistic value. Both Eisler and Blitzstein have shown that real musical imagination and originality can be of great service to their political points by adding character and incisiveness. But such music on the recent Theatre Arts Committee evening, gallery-funny pieces like Henry Brant's *Marx Brothers* or Morton Gould's Sonatina or *Child Prodigy*, or gallery-serious cantatas like Kleinsinger's *I Hear America Singing* or Earl Robinson's fresher *Ballad for Americans*, begin to sound thin and the attitude of the composers condescending. Their apparent assumption is that the masses don't know anything about music and never will. I wouldn't be a bit surprised if works like the Sessions Quartet or the Harris Symphony were to become more popular than these self-conscious and restricted compositions ever will be.

The Agony of Modern Music in America, 1955
(1955/94)

This year the situation of contemporary music has been particularly difficult in the United States. In New York City the director of the New York Philharmonic, Dimitri Mitropoulos, has continued his policy of not programming any controversial contemporary works. This is a result of vigorous pressure applied by the board of directors of the orchestra several years ago, when numerous works of Schoenberg, Webern, and Berg were performed and the size of the audience diminished. Ironically, many of these performances were commercially recorded and continue to be released by Columbia Records: works such as Berg's *Wozzeck* and Schoenberg's *Erwartung* and Violin Concerto. In fact, the sales of these recordings have apparently been sufficient to encourage Columbia to release the recording made by the Nordwestdeutscher Rundfunk of Schoenberg's *Moses und Aron*. But this growing interest in contemporary recordings does not seem to affect the attitudes of the concertgoing public. Even the Boston Symphony and the Philadelphia Orchestra have become more cautious in their programming, and this is typical of orchestras throughout the United States.

One symptom of the apparently growing conservatism of concert life is the recent appearance of a stupid but rhetorically very effective book by Henry Pleasants, *The Agony of Modern Music*.[1] The publisher sent pre-publication copies to well-known musicians all over the United States and asked for their comments. Most of the composers (some of whom were misquoted in the book) were indignant and wrote angry letters to the publisher. After the book came out last month, the publishers arranged for a radio and television debate between the author and a music critic in the intermission of

---

1. Henry Pleasants, *The Agony of Modern Music* (New York: Simon and Schuster, 1955).

the Sunday Philharmonic broadcast. Unfortunately, the critic did not rebut Mr. Pleasants's points very effectively. The subsequent letters to the broadcasting company ran ten to one against modern music. Later, Aaron Copland wrote an article against the book and appeared on television with Mr. Pleasants (who brought along the conductor Erich Leinsdorf to help him) and tried to argue him down. In general the reviews of the book in the newspapers have been by musicians who have dismissed it as illogical, unsound, based on a misrepresentation of the facts, but without explaining their opinions in detail.

The argument of the book is simply that music died around 1920—that in no matter what style, all concert music since has been written for a small intellectual audience and has no popular appeal; that the only living music is American jazz, which is very popular with audiences and even with serious composers; and that this popularity is proof of its value, while the lack of popularity of "modern music" reveals its lack of vitality. Mr. Pleasants claims that all the great music of the past was written for large audiences and was immediately appreciated by the public, and that the misunderstood composer is a fiction and never existed except at present.

This book is, of course, a polemic, intended to appeal to the very large audience of partially educated music lovers. But Mr. Pleasants conveniently overlooks the fact that there always has been a larger public for popular dance music than for concert music. In the nineteenth century, there is no doubt that more people loved the waltzes of Johann Strauss and Joseph Lanner than ever liked the music of any one of the serious composers. By that test of popularity, all concert music would inevitably fall by the wayside. It would be just as true to say that the waltzes of Lanner and Strauss are the only living music of the time of Schumann, Mendelssohn, Wagner, and Brahms because the public did not support them as much as it did the waltz kings, and that this music is therefore dead. Every music student knows that Brahms was considered difficult and obscure in his time; in fact, it is only since the Second World War that his music and that of Tchaikovsky has been comparatively widely appreciated in France and Italy.

Composers in all periods have been in contact with the popular music of the time. Bach wrote suites of dances—even if the dance rhythms are at times so distorted as to be nearly unrecognizable. Mozart, Haydn, Beethoven, and Brahms all used contemporary dance music of their period in some (though not all) of their own music, just as many more recent composers have done. The conducting career of Berlioz was not very different from the conducting career of Stravinsky, except that Stravinsky has many more engagements and seems on the whole more successful with the public.

It would be hard for Mr. Pleasants to prove that works like the symphonies of Shostakovich, Ravel's piano concerti and *Bolero*, Stravinsky's *Symphonie de psaumes*, Hindemith's *Mathis der Maler*, Honegger's *Jeanne d'Arc au bûcher*, Bartók's Concerto for Orchestra, or Vaughan Williams's Fourth Symphony have not been more frequently performed, more widely known and appreciated than any of the works of Beethoven, Bach, Schubert, Schumann, Mozart, or Haydn were when they were "modern." The sales of recordings alone of any of these twentieth-century works indicate that more people have heard them and liked them than heard and liked the music of earlier composers during their lifetimes.

The interesting thing about Mr. Pleasants's point of view is that it is actually nothing new: throughout the history of Western music, new works have often been greeted with a certain hostility. Bellini's *Norma* and Puccini's *La Bohème* were hissed off the stage of La Scala; people accustomed to the orchestra of Mozart and Haydn found Beethoven's works noisy and complex to the point of unintelligibility—and what a fearful rumpus was caused by the works of Wagner and early Richard Strauss!

As yet the book has not been out long enough to have made any general impression. Most musicians think it is so poor that its effect will be negligible. Others feel that it may help the cause of modern music by focusing attention on it. And of course others are worried, since at present our musical life is very much influenced by the mass mind. More money and effort has been spent in publicizing this book than was ever spent on a piece of modern music—a circumstance which is all the more appalling in light of the fact that, with attendance at concerts everywhere in this country on the decline, the last thing people need is a book that provides them with specious reasons for further discouragement. Some prominent individuals, at least, are taking the opposite tack. Mr. Judson, the head of Columbia Concerts, a very large agency which has always had the reputation for being against contemporary music, has recently come out in favor of attempting to attract more concert-goers through the performance of new works—this, however, only as a stopgap measure, until such time as some new "star" performers, recently in short supply, can be developed.

In the affairs of the League of Composers/ISCM, the situation has been very tense. In New York, we have tried to give concerts that would reveal what is new in music today and to live up to the concert exchange program by playing works written by an Italian, a Brazilian, and a Norwegian, some Americans (Sessions, Copland, Ives, Wallingford Riegger, and Karol Rathaus), and a few of the Europeans unknown here, such as Giselher Klebe, Mátyás Seiber, and Edward Steuermann; Stravinsky's Shakespeare songs were also included. Although our concerts were sold out (we gave only three), we will lose money on them. And what is worse, we have been subjected to scathing criticism for being too esoteric, for appealing too much to a special audience. No doubt there will be a great deal more trouble before the season ends. The choice of Erich Itor Kahn's *Actus Tragicus* and my Cello Sonata for the Baden-Baden Festival has been vehemently attacked as unrepresentative of American music. Each year the jury sends works representative of all trends in American music, and usually only the more extreme ones are chosen. There will no doubt be an effort made to form another kind of American jury, now that the League of Composers, which is the more conservative organization, is joined with the ISCM. And it could happen that in the future only conservative works—which it is true are more representative of what goes on here—will be sent. But this problem is no doubt typical of most ISCM sections.

The basic problem here is one of leadership. At one time Aaron Copland was able to reconcile all these conflicting points of view and get the League of Composers to function properly. Roger Sessions does not seem to be interested enough to do this, and Copland refuses to be president of the new organization, since he feels he has devoted a great part of his life to this work already and wants to spend more time composing. There are no younger composers who are capable of persuading this society to forget its differences and join in a common effort; instead, among the younger men there is an unfortunate tendency toward factionalism.

In merging with the League of Composers, the ISCM lost a great many of its American-based central European supporters, who were also the performers of much atonal music, and in fact has angered most of those interested in twelve-tone music (and who were the best performers) because this year it performed several works that were perhaps more significant historically than musically. The League of Composers group, more inclined to neoclassicism and the Stravinsky and Copland influence, are angry that more such music was not played, feeling that this is more typically American and more important for the future than the other. Such differences of opinion spill over into other areas too. When Stefan Wolpe recently received a commission of one thousand dollars from the League/ISCM, for his Symphony, there was a great outcry from the more conservative elements of the organization—which they made quite publicly—because they consider his work so extreme. It looks as if it may be impossible to give concerts next year because most of the members are so dissatisfied with those of this year. The organization will then become simply an agency for propaganda by mail.

Many chapters of the ISCM throughout the United States are active, some of them giving more interesting concerts than is possible in New York because of the costs of such enterprises in this city and also because, being formed of fewer individuals, they tend to greater unanimity of viewpoint. The prominent Swedish composer Karl-Birger Blomdahl visited the United States this year and saw more of it than most of us do. He felt that quite a lot of good music is written here, but that little of it gets performed. Why much of it is not performed ought to be quite clear from the foregoing. In our particular situation, most of the less conservative composers have looked to the ISCM as a way of joining together in an attempt to have our music performed and known. If the old US Section of the ISCM loses its character because of the merger with the League of Composers, many of us will be forced to resign and start another organization. In the end, this is the same problem that must be faced in many countries, and it seems to me that the attempt to make the whole ISCM a big organization representative of all trends in each country is a very unfortunate one, in view of its original mission. In the United States, right now, it would be tragic if there were no group to continue to present both here and abroad the most advanced and competent works. This is a weak and powerless group in relation to American society, but many of our best composers, such as Sessions, Ives, Varèse, Kahn, and Leon Kirchner, belong to it.

It is truly puzzling that the sale here of great numbers of recordings of contemporary works, including those of Varèse and other extreme composers, seems to have little effect on concert life. In the past, the US Section of the ISCM and the League of Composers gave first American performances of many of Bartók's, Hindemith's, Stravinsky's, and others' chamber music works to small audiences. Now recordings from these performances are all being bought up by discophiles, who apparently have no interest in going to concerts. Perhaps recordings will take the place of concerts in this huge and culturally so variegated country.

The Rhythmic Basis of American Music
(1955)

It would be convenient if one could say—as so many have done—that the distinguishing mark of serious American music is its employment (or reworking) of the rhythms of our native folk or popular music, particularly jazz. Yet the attempt to reduce national characteristics to a few simple traits is a game that quickly wears thin in the artistic world, as in life itself. In earlier years, when American music was just beginning to take shape, such an attempt may have been useful; but now that a substantial number of works has accumulated, neither critics nor composers feel it any longer necessary to emphasize national characteristics. On the contrary, instead of insisting that American music stands apart from that of Europe, it becomes interesting to consider the many foreign influences by which it has been nourished.

During the 1920s, jazz had a great influence on European music as well as on ours. Its impact in Europe was strong precisely because its techniques had already been anticipated by various composers. Bartók, Stravinsky, and even Schoenberg (in the first of his *Five Pieces for Orchestra*, written in 1909) had all been using irregular rhythmic patterns, and the appearance of jazz stimulated further interest in this rhythmic procedure. Indeed, European composers adopted only those aspects of jazz that had already been tried to some extent before its arrival. These very same aspects influenced the young American modernists of the time; but through greater familiarity with the source they had a different feeling for rhythm. As a result, jazz had far more effect abroad than in many quarters at home.

The American composer's relationship to jazz is in fact quite different from what one might expect. Heard constantly from every corner, this music has lost its original freshness; the techniques have become shopworn, the performances routine and dull. It is perhaps for these reasons that most composers have avoided using the jazz idiom in their concert music; and also because orchestral musicians often do not play jazz well, and cannot under the conditions of concert life be afforded the rehearsals needed for good jazz. Today in out-of-the-way places one can still find fresh, lively jazz performances, and the improvisatory character of what is played is impossible to imitate with concert musicians. There are Marc Blitzstein, Leonard Bernstein, and Morton Gould, who, writing in the jazz idiom for popular consumption, have tried to place it (as Kurt Weill did) on a more meaningful and artistic level. But the majority of composers interested in this trend have drawn only on certain characteristics of popular music, combining them with other folk sources or neoclassic ones to produce works of larger scope, more interesting formal possibilities, and more variety.

There were four composers who helped to establish these techniques in the early stages of the contemporary movement in America. Roy Harris, Aaron Copland, and Roger Sessions followed the lead given them by contemporary European music and jazz and embodied a new feeling for rhythm in their music. The fourth, Charles Ives, living in seclusion, followed a different and more curious path, and his achievements are not yet well enough known to be properly judged.

Early in his career, Harris made a remark that has often been quoted: "Our rhythmic sense is less symmetrical than the European rhythmic sense. European musicians are trained to think of rhythm in its largest common denominator, while we are born with a feeling for its smallest units."[1] Although this appeared after a number of outstanding works by Stravinsky, and after Bartók had revealed the possibilities of irregular groupings of small units— which is what Harris is talking about—there is no doubt that he had a point in mind which becomes clear in the context of his own music and of jazz practice. For in spite of their irregular rhythmic patterns, written with constantly changing meters, Stravinsky and Bartók do often treat their irregular accents as displacements of regular ones by marking them with the same kind of vigor that was reserved in older music for syncopations. The quality of these accents is quite different from those used in jazz and in much new American music. In jazz, especially of the 1920s and '30s, the melodic line frequently has an independent rhythmic life; the metrical units are grouped into irregular (or regular) patterns, in melodic motives whose rhythm runs against the underlying 1, 2, 3, 4 of dance rhythm. Roy Harris carried this technique further by writing long, continuously developing melodies in which groups of two, three, four, or five units (such as eighth notes) are joined together to produce irregular stresses, but with the underlying regular beat of jazz omitted. Several such lines when sounded together produce interesting textures of "cross-accented counterpoint," which is not unlike such counterpoint found in the English madrigal school, although stressed more intensely and associated with very different types of melody. A characteristic example of this is to be found in the canonic last movement of his First Piano Sonata, op. 1 (1929).

Aaron Copland has been outspoken about his relationship with popular music both in his writings and in his composition. He drew from the jazz of the 1920s a principle of polyrhythm in which the melody is accented in regular groups of three quarter notes while the bass plays its conventional 4/4. In

1. Roy Harris, "Problems of American Composers," in *American Composers on American Music: A Symposium*, ed. Henry Cowell (1933; repr. ed. with a new introd. by Cowell, New York: F. Ungar, 1962), 151. [B]

works closely concerned with the jazz idiom, like his Piano Concerto (1926), we find this polyrhythmic method extended to groupings such as 5/8, 7/8, and 5/4. In many sections of these works Copland followed jazz in sounding the regular beat but, as in Harris, there were places where the beat was not expressed. In works written a little later, such as the *Symphonic Ode* (1929) and the *Short Symphony* (1933), he dispensed with the regular beat altogether. Unlike Harris, Copland maintains a direct relationship with jazz or other kinds of American dance music, especially in his fast movements. For instance, in *El Salón México* (1936), he applied his rhythmic method to Mexican popular dances in which alternations of 6/8 (two groups of three eighth notes) and 3/4 (three groups of two eighth notes) are characteristic. Great portions of this work are made of the irregular rhythms that result from sounding these groups of two and three in such patterns as two, three, three, two, two, three. Similar patterns may be found in the faster parts of his Piano Sonata, Clarinet Concerto, and Piano Quartet. His style, far more incisive than that of Harris, has the variety of quality of accent characteristic of its American sources. But although he mentions the fact that jazz performers often play their improvisations with great rhythmic freedom, sounding their notes a bit before or after the beat, Copland has never incorporated this into his own music.

Roger Sessions carried the technique of irregular grouping to much greater extremes—particularly in contrapuntal textures—in the first movement of his First Symphony (1927), which is one of the most extensive essays in cross-accented counterpoint yet attempted. Although this work clearly derives from the European neoclassic school, its remarkable rhythmic shifts give it an American sound, and for this reason it exercised (together with Sessions's First Piano Sonata) a considerable influence on composers of the 1930s.

But this particular technique is only one of the many rhythmic devices to be found in jazz. It is well known, for instance, that in the actual interpretation of written notation a tradition of making slight distortions of note values in the interests of rhythmic and expressive freedom has been handed down from one performer to another in the jazz world. It is a tradition surprisingly similar to that of the Baroque "notes inégales." In both, equal eighth notes are played in dotted fashion or as triplets of quarter note and eighth note. But jazz performers not only take liberties with notation, they also improvise so freely that their parts have an expressive rubato, slowing down and speeding up while the rhythm section keeps its steady beat. It is in this domain that Charles Ives worked, although much of his music was written before the technique became a common practice in jazz bands. It may already have been present, however, in the ragtime of Ives's day, as it is a tendency which is noticeable in any long-continued tradition of dance music, being occasionally found in the late periods of the waltz as well as in South and Central American popular music.

Ives went one step further than the composers mentioned above by exploring the realm of "artificial divisions"—triplets, quintuplets, and the like—to produce such complex polyrhythmic combinations that they seem to defy adequate performance or even audibility. His was usually a literary point of view in which fairly literal quotations of familiar patriotic, religious, or dance tunes are presented simultaneously with an expressive commentary in another remotely related or unrelated speed. For instance, in the second movement of *Three Places in New England*, a boy dreams of two groups of soldiers marching at different speeds, one disappearing as the other appears; in *The Unanswered Question*, the question is posed ever more insistently and rapidly by the winds while the strings play a quiet, meditative background, impassively unrelated in speed and harmony and requiring a separate conductor. This combination of different rhythmic planes involved Ives in complex problems of notation, especially in his later works, written between 1910 and 1920.

He uses three main procedures. The first consists in the superposition of different speeds that can be expressed in notation with a common unit, as in the second movement of his Fourth Symphony, written in 1916 and revised and published in 1929 (Ex. 1). Later in the work he shows a greater freedom of rhythm. In Example 2 the second, third, and fourth lines are the rhythms of the brass and winds playing a dissonant harmonization of a national anthem, with the violas and cellos helping out in the line above the bottom. The sixth and bottom lines contain the rhythms of piano, bells, and basses playing a hymn tune in another system of dissonant harmony. The other lines are rhythms of various figurations, those of the quintuplets and septuplets belonging to the strings.[2]

A second type of rhythmic device used by Ives consists in notated rubati on one level and strict time on another, as in *Calcium Light* (Ex. 3). In a third

2. It should be noted that in Examples 1 and 2 Carter has been somewhat selective in depicting the polyrhythms, notating only what he regards as the principal components of the texture. Some minor errors that had crept into the transcription of Example 3 as it was originally published in 1955 and reprinted in 1977 have been corrected in this edition. [B]

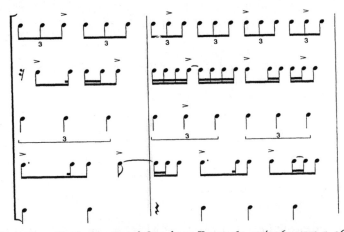

Example 1. Charles Ives, Fourth Symphony, II, mm. 69–70 (1965 score, p. 36: second and third measures before rehearsal no. 13), rhythmic notation.

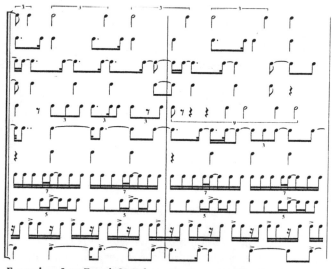

Example 2. Ives, Fourth Symphony, II, mm. 137–38 (1965 score, p. 52: third and fourth measures before rehearsal no. 21), rhythmic notation.

type, two unrelated levels are heard simultaneously. In both *The Unanswered Question* and *Central Park in the Dark*, a quiet ostinato of strings directed by one conductor forms the background for faster, louder music directed by another conductor and played fragmentarily, allowing the soft background to be heard in the silences. Similar unrelated planes of music requiring the services of several conductors occur in the Fourth Symphony and others of Ives's later works.

These various procedures, so novel and occasionally of remarkable effectiveness, were described in Henry Cowell's book *New Musical Resources*,[3] but have gained little currency because the great difficulties of performance that they involve have proved a real deterrent to a number of composers interested in continuing Ives's methods. A striking resolution of this problem has been made by Conlon Nancarrow, a composer who patiently measures and perforates his compositions on player-piano rolls. Not having to be concerned with performance, he has composed a number of interesting works, including three *Rhythm Studies* derived from the jazz idiom and employing unusual polyrhythms. In the most elaborate measures of his *Rhythm Study No.* 1 four

3. Henry Cowell, *New Musical Resources* (New York: Knopf, 1930).

Example 3. Ives, *Calcium Light,* mm. 1–7, rhythmic notation.

Example 4. Conlon Nancarrow, *Rhythm Study No. 1,* mm. 50–51.

distinct planes of rhythm are combined, as will be seen in Example 4. Since the player piano cannot accent individual notes, the third line of chords in this example marks the accents of the groups of seven of the notes on the first staff. The polyrhythmic combinations are: first and second staves—three against two, grouped in figures of seven and three, respectively; first and fifth staves—five against two; second and fourth—eight against three; second and fifth—five against three; fourth and fifth—five against eight. The whole produces a most novel sound.

The works of Ives and Nancarrow are scarcely known even in America, but they attest to a continuing interest in rhythm which seems a part of the American scene. A few, such as Henry Brant and the author, have worked in this field. Brant has followed Ives in using a technique of unrelated or "uncoordinated" rhythm, as he calls it. The author's approach is discussed elsewhere in this issue.[4]

It must be said, however, that only a few American composers are seriously concerned with rhythmic problems. Owing to the influence of Copland, Harris, and Sessions, many seem to have an innate rhythmic sense that is different from that of European composers. But there has been little temptation to explore the field, since each of these has lately become much more conservative in this respect, and performances of their rhythmically difficult works have been rare.

The European Roots of American Musical Culture
(1961/94)

Concert music and opera in the United States, like numerous other American pursuits, were imported almost entirely from Europe at first, and even now, after many years of development, still remain closely allied to their origins. In important ways, our art music is another branch of European music, and like

4. William Glock, "A Note on Elliott Carter," *The Score and I.M.A. Magazine* 12 (June 1955): 47–52. [S]

the French or Swedish branches, for instance, is influenced by ideas originating in other branches and in turn affects the others itself—as in the case of our contemporary, the Franco-American Edgard Varèse, whose music has had such an influence abroad. Just as American spoken language is almost identical with that of England and has preserved many of the same patterns of thought and feeling, so our art music has not only made use of grammatical and syntactical structures of a type familiar to Western listeners but has also sought to maintain the highest standards of artistic, expressive, intellectual, and auditory interest, along with the aesthetic and moral concepts that they imply. Indeed, such frequently discussed questions as the relation of the composer to his performers and public, the relation of art music to popular or folk music, and, more abstractly, the relation of human feelings and thoughts to music have found answers in the works of the classical repertory—answers which cannot be overlooked by any professional in this field—that are as thoroughly convincing to American musicians as to their European colleagues. And paralleling the experiences of many Europeans, Americans have recently come to feel that this musical heritage does not furnish answers to many important new questions, necessitating a search for new answers outside the traditional approach.

In a very important sense, the world of Western art music forms a single large professional community with commonly shared standards based on a repertory of significant works, the presentation of which to the public is its chief reason for existence. Professions, by their very nature, tend to be self-perpetuating, and the musical profession is no exception: another of its aims is to insure its own future by fostering the creation of new, similarly important and valuable works to refresh the repertory. Most musicians involved in this tradition, whether German, Peruvian, Australian, Japanese, or American, live their lives as members of the international professional community as much as they live as citizens of their own countries. This is true, with certain well-known restrictions, even of musicians in the Soviet Union and its more submissive satellites. Such a specialized profession really has more in common with that of medicine or law than it does with those of the other arts, depending as it does on a wide variety of highly specialized skills so demanding that few musicians can do effective work in other directions. It is perhaps for this reason that most of them are not well informed in detail about the relationships between their art and the communities and countries that it serves. Curiously enough, very little significant thinking has been done along this line by professionals; the few non-professionals who venture into it betray a lack of understanding of fundamental matters and, naturally, make mistakes. For this reason, I, as a professional, beg your pardon if I seem superficial or misinformed in what I say about Europeans and their musical tradition. I am not so much attempting accurately to represent the facts as to portray as faithfully as I can the American consciousness of Europe and to show how this has guided and affected our profession, even though much of this consciousness may be built on illusions. I hope that this portrayal will be interesting even to those who do not share such illusions, if only because the idea of Europe plays such an important role in the culture of the United States.

The main differences between European and American culture owe their origins, not to heritage, but to development within a different political, social, and historical environment. While many people came to live here bringing with them music from almost all Western cultures and social strata, few members of the aristocratic and cultivated bourgeois classes who supported art music in Europe left home. Those who did found themselves no longer in a position to be arbiters of taste here. Thus many different cultural heritages confronted one another with no generally acccepted hierarchy of aesthetic values that might give one artistic trend precedence over another. For this reason, there has been and still is a very confused situation which must seem to Europeans, accustomed to more unified conditions, anarchic. Coming as it did in the wake of a revolution of colonists in a comparatively undeveloped land, this confusion resulted in a total break in the continuity of almost all cultural institutions connected with music.

From an American musician's point of view, all European societies have had a continuous history of musical culture, which is reflected in their institutions. Opera houses, concert halls, and conservatories were supported financially by religious, aristocratic, or bourgeois patrons, and when this became difficult or undesirable the government continued their support out of taxes. No matter whether there were wars, revolutions, changes of boundaries or of social structure, most European societies persisted in a very strong desire to keep musical institutions going. This has given great power to musical tradition and has insured a continuity of musical development, not just for the short span of an individual musician's life, but over the long periods necessary for development of the high skills and standards of taste that reflect the regard for and love of music in these societies.

With the continuity of tradition broken in America, certain very serious problems arose as the highly developed professionalism of art music began to be more widely appreciated. This music came first, of course, as a product that might be called imported were it not for the fact that cultivated Americans had been interested in such music long before good performers of it could be brought across the Atlantic and before musicians could be well trained here. The dilemma in which American society found itself, possessing an interest and appreciation for such music but lacking institutions that would allow the needed skills to flourish, was acute and is still somewhat so today. It cannot be said that the problem has arisen simply because we are a young country. In many ways, we are just as old as the societies from which our citizens came—and from another point of view, it could be that the problem of dealing with a broken cultural continuity and of keeping institutions going under these conditions will become an increasingly pressing one in many places in the world, perhaps even in Europe itself, once the benevolent authoritarianism of previous times has diminished.

Consider, for instance, the Metropolitan Opera House in New York City. To the surprise of many in the business world, this institution cannot support itself; instead, with each successive year it loses more money even though the tickets increase in price and the performances are always sold out. Once, these losses were made up by a few patrons who could agree to follow the lead of such progressive directors as Gustav Mahler. But, as our socioeconomic conditions changed, more patrons were needed to pay these deficits, resulting in an ever more conservative policy chosen to appeal to as many as possible. Even those who would like to see the opera supported by the government admit that the problem of convincing a large number of taxpayers that it was worth doing would be next to insuperable. And those who think that it could be done are not convinced that an opera house could be run effectively by the government, since there is no common understanding of what constitutes art music. For government support of the arts presupposes agreement, if only by custom, that such arts are a valuable contribution to the society and not just entertainments for a minority group that can no longer afford to pay for them. It also presupposes experts who can be trusted to distinguish accurately between good art music that deserves to be supported and entertainment that ought to be able to support itself. These experts must be given free rein even when the projects they select for support seem inimical to the immediate public interest, as in the case of unusual new music. Every state-supported project in art music has to face these problems, but Europeans are better equipped to deal with them: by virtue of their cultural continuity and fund of experience, their societies are able to understand that this art is very demanding and that success in it can come only through a vast amount of trial and error by both performers and composers.

Just as there are but few good performers among a large number of mediocre (if well-trained) ones, so are there only a few really good compositions among a large number of weak ones. Indeed, the challenge of promoting a public situation in which even second-rate efforts get a hearing needs to be addressed, since it is only against the background of a many-sided and flourishing profession producing generally high-quality work that the first-rate efforts can emerge. On every level, the musical profession is formidably demanding and expensive to operate, and if there is not a very widespread and firm belief in its value and a general willingness to support it, its efforts will not amount to much. Misguided efforts to persuade Americans to take music more seriously because it will give our country more prestige abroad, or for other extraneous reasons, will not change anything—for it is an unflattering idea that we cannot be expected to like and support art music for what it is but only for its effect on others.

Europeans' high regard for music, and their willingness to pay for it, derive from a long cultural continuity which has never existed in America. Our musicians have faced an enormous variety of difficulties, and this has led them to rethink and reinvestigate aesthetic, artistic, and cultural questions, the answers to which are largely taken for granted in Europe. First of all, the actual value of art music as an educational experience for the individual has never been agreed on here as it has abroad—and without such agreement, there will seem hardly any sense to a musician's expending such great effort to meet professional standards. This state of permanent uncertainty, which no doubt seems absurd to Europeans, has been a powerful stimulus to American musicians' efforts to perfect themselves in their art and to make it so compelling that its value will have to be recognized. Composition tends to be an act of faith in the power and value of music, just because it defies the limitations of this situation.

Since it has always been a problem in America to decide whether music is just another entertainment or whether it does play a more educational role, the question of support of our native talents has remained troublesome. It is intensified by the dominance of our English cultural heritage, since England during the nineteenth century, when its ideas were influencing us most, had a weak internal musical life, and like America imported its music largely from the Continent. Indeed, we must have gotten from them that special high regard for imported music which at times has led to a greater appreciation of it here than it has earned in the countries of its origin. The two countries are similar, too, in that native work has had to struggle against the prestige of Continental art, and consequently has had trouble finding itself—even if this situation has changed markedly in both places since the beginning of the twentieth century.

On the other hand, in large part because of the heterogeneous character of their country's heritage, American composers over the past fifty years have studied one European school of composition after another with great care, in their desire to express themselves truly and effectively. As a result, there can be no simply defined American tradition or style, and it is entirely possible that there never will be one. It is interesting to realize that almost the reverse relationship exists between Europe and America in the field of popular music. In its style, method of performance, and use of a set of formulae, as well as its broad public appeal and commercial success, this music is an export from America, and might never have existed or developed abroad without continual revitalization from new American influences. Only slowly has European popular music of the modern era acquired an identity of its own, just as American art music has begun to do.

A consideration of how the influences of various European schools have been felt may give some hint of this identity. In general, for Americans, the interest of German music lies in its organic logic and its great variety of expansive expression. French music, on the other hand, interests us principally for its capacity for definite characterization, delicacy of inflection, color, and ability to suggest dance and human gestures. In the early period of American music, during the nineteenth century, the German school was dominant here and resulted in an artificial attitude or posture for us, an imitation of German Romanticism. To this earliest generation of American musicians, German music was a stimulus to sentimentality and grandiosity, on the one hand, or to dry academicism on the other, both of which stultified the composer and aggravated his already difficult position.

But when our composers, under the influence of nationalist ideas prevalent at the end of the last century, began to be interested in their own folklore and in jazz, they went to study in France, since French music was so skillful in evoking exotic milieux and had furnished through Berlioz, Lalo, and Bizet various techniques which were then successfully applied by the Russians to their own folklore as a way of appealing to the concert audience. The Brahms-Liszt treatment of Hungarian music and the Smetana-Dvořák handling of Bohemian music came a little too early in our development and had little influence, except on Edward MacDowell's treatment of American Indian themes. Coming at the turn of the century, French music acted as a liberating influence, somewhat in the same way that influences of French literary realism and impressionistic painting did in the other arts. The French, who pride themselves on being wide-awake, unsentimental, up-to-date, and on the look-out for fresh approaches, provided a frame of reference that allowed our composers to find a style of their own within the field of art music yet related to popular and folk music. This occurred, interestingly enough, at a time when two major orchestras, those of Boston and Philadelphia, engaged many French instrumentalists to replace departing Germans and Italians, as well as conductors of French, Russian, and Polish origin. Later on, this influence expanded when many Americans went to Paris in the 1920s and '30s to study with Mlle. Nadia Boulanger, one of the few teachers at that time who took new music seriously.

But the liberation that came with the French influence was only partial. As long as interest in music, for Americans, was related to the sentimental evocation of European culture without real understanding of it, and as long as American folk music could only be seen in the light of a European exoticism, it was impossible for our music to be itself. The mood of nostalgic longing for contact with an imaginary European age of refinement and luxury surrounds many of our musical institutions, such as the Metropolitan Opera House, which, to judge by its repertory, is going through an artistic ritual devoted to evoking and prolonging the dream of high culture through performances that make little attempt to be convincing in modern terms, instead suggesting, ineffectively, productions of a quarter-century ago. Hence its performances appeal to a portion of the public that would be apathetic toward or angered by anything that disturbed this ritual with a display of real vitality. In concerts, there is a similar tendency to confuse true artistic understanding with the magical evocation of this chimerical golden age, and this has made the problem of introducing new music, particularly new music that suggests modern life, difficult. Ironically, the very idea of using popular and folkloric elements as well as the techniques for doing so were taken directly from European models, to which, often, little was added except an American tune—but it was this connection with European models that helped in the eventual public acceptance of such music.

By contrast to the Franco-Russian influence, which succeeded the first wave of the German, Italian musical art played almost no role in our musical history until recently, when composers have looked to Verdi and Puccini as models for operas that would be suitable for modest university performances. More advanced recent composers, following a general trend of post-War interest in Italy, have been much influenced by study with Luigi Dallapiccola and Goffredo Petrassi. English music has had little influence, except for that of the sixteenth and seventeenth centuries, which with its interesting irregular rhythms derived from English speech helped our composers find a characteristic irregular scansion which their contact with jazz had suggested. In fact, these along with the music of Stravinsky and Bartók are the sources of one of the most striking features of most new American music: its polyrhythmic structure.

Today it now seems, especially when we consider other arts less involved in the requirements of professional presentation, that styles which allow for intensity of expression and free, rather Baroque fantasy, such as characterizes certain periods of German art, are closer to us than more formal and symmetrical styles. Now we are turning to art and literature that is concerned with the inner life of human beings as individuals away from a concern with social relationships and their delineation. For this reason, the French ability for characterization, at first so useful to us, has become now less valuable than the German concern for inner psychological states and the search for an organic order in them—paralleling, perhaps, the paths opened by Freud and Jung earlier in this century.

This and other aspects of German thinking became particularly important after 1935, when so many central Europeans, among them composers, came to practice their arts and teach in America. Contact with Arnold Schoenberg, Paul Hindemith, Ernst Krenek, Ernst Toch, and others helped our composers to mature and crystallize their individuality. For by 1935, American musicians had begun to develop opinions about each of the various schools these composers represented. At that time, visiting foreign composers could vastly improve the technical command of their students but no longer Europeanize them. The German influence from about 1935 to about 1950 was especially valuable in bringing a whole generation of composers to a vivid awareness of the importance and beauty of organic design and order and their contribution to the meaning of musical composition, thus changing the direction of American music away from the concern of the previous generation with style, timbre, and dramatic gesture derived from the French influence.

Once the French and Russians had enabled us to look at ourselves from the outside and find our outward physiognomy and style, we then felt the need, as I have said, to find an expression in music for our inner life. Here the question of folklore became crucial, for while it served to give an outward character to our music, it now became a question whether folklore could also give our music an inward, more serious one. Certainly the professional composer of art music and his audience seldom had any real experience of folk music except through those who had transformed it into a form of entertainment lacking in any but a weak sentimental meaning, or through recordings made by ethnologists. The drive toward political freedom, as in the case of the Bohemian nationalist movement during the nineteenth century, or toward the freeing of the serfs in Russia at the same time, gave the folklorist movements of that time a powerful emotional and political meaning, a kind of meaning lacking among the American groups occupied with art music, since in their world such political problems were already solved or were in the process of being solved. Therefore, after the period of early jazz influence, folklore ceased to have much significance and meanwhile was rapidly being debased into a meaningless routine by its popularity as an entertainment for the mass public.

Europeans have often expressed impatience with Americans for trying to write art music at all, wondering why they do not devote all their energies to music directly derived from jazz; indeed, many Americans have expressed similar sentiments. This is a question that nobody would have seriously thought of asking a composer of art music in the past. Just as some Europeans wish that American music would specialize in purveying its native, jazzy flavor, so some American tourists are disappointed when they find Europeans living in houses with electricity, not wearing the peasant costumes they expected to see. Each culture wishes, I suppose, that the others would remain in their earlier, more primitive and individual state of development—although the drawbacks of such a state are obvious; every country is still trying to overcome them. The desire to encounter a foreign culture different in many ways from our own is understandable, as it is natural to wish for the greatest amount of cultural variety in the world. But true, meaningful variety cannot be obtained in a simple and childish fashion, as, for instance, by depriving one culture of the benefits of another, but must be won on a level of greater maturity. Such variety must reflect the valuable differences that exist today, not the differences we recollect with a certain nostalgia for more backward conditions.

The constant desire of American composers to find a music that will have a real connection with the life we lead today, both as members of our society and of our profession, has led in a great many directions, but since about 1940 these have all converged on the university. American education is very much better endowed, because its role in our lives is generally accepted, than are the serious arts, and it was therefore natural for the arts to seek a more hospitable and more culturally unified situation within the frame of education. This is particularly true of contemporary composition, since the position of new, advanced music in this country differs greatly from that of painting or literature of similar direction. Outside the university, such music is rarely played. Public concerts favor, as they do in many places in Europe, the standard repertory of eighteenth- and nineteenth-century classics, with a few of the works of the early twentieth century thrown in. Universities, by contrast, with the limited means at their disposal, are far more open-minded in their concert series. Also, one finds at many universities a population of students who are avid collectors of recordings of new music and are thus very familiar with the most advanced and unusual works in this way, many of which have seldom or never had public performances in America. It is entirely possible that because of this ferment of interest in educational circles, music will develop very differently in the next fifty years here.

Actually, general public interest in the more challenging contemporary music is not very different from what it is in Europe, although in Europe there still seems to be a substantial group of music critics and music lovers whose opinions are respected enough by the public to instill a certain sense of obligation to try to understand the new. The position of new music in contemporary society is much discussed and has been explained in many different ways, but the one thing that differentiates the situations in Europe and America is the point of view within the profession itself from which the meaning and direction of new developments are seen. To an American musician, the post-War European trends seem to have been directed toward the disintegration of the routines and formulae that characterized the highly accomplished techniques of all previous, great European composers. To us, this appears to have been undertaken in a spirit that is very thoroughgoing, even to the point of denying the fundamental reasons traditionally put forth for writing music. A definite break with the past on every level seemed urgent to the younger European composers. This attitude led to the application of various arithmetical plans or methods of random which take no account of the special order related to the human ear and, through it, the human abilities to discriminate, organize, and remember patterns of sound. Their position, to us, represents an unwillingness to admit the possibility of highly purposeful communication.

Such a view is nearly impossible to hold seriously in America, where the musical tradition and its accompanying danger of academicism do not count for so much. Indeed, in our country, almost all new techniques, including the serial and electronic, have been thought of as ways to broaden the communicative possibilities of music through the human perceptions. Even the most anarchic tendencies in our music cannot be considered purely destructive because audiences here are too concerned with the novelty of hearing music in a concert, too interested in trying to understand what kind of an experience this is, to be willing to accept a nihilistic attitude as the motivation of some of the strange theatrical events that such concerts occasionally turn out to be. In defense of these events, such explorations of the relations of the composer, the performers, the public to the environment of a concert hall may be somewhat fruitful, in the sense of making the matter of musical communication more vivid to those who have not given the matter much thought and who find that music of a more highly specialized nature, one dependent on experienced listeners, eludes them.

But such experiments in the musico-theatrical situation are few and do not represent the general attitude of the most advanced—and of course not that of the more conservative. Here there is a fundamental belief in the development of music that reaches the human feelings and brain through the ear. Unlike many Europeans, apparently, Americans believe that such communication is possible. This carries on a similar belief implicit in the older tradition of music.

The American composer, having to face the continual uncertainty which surrounds his small, financially unprofitable, and but slightly respected artistic efforts, is almost forced into a position of affirmation if he is to compose at all. Destructive efforts are scarcely meaningful in this situation, although exasperation with the poor quality of much of our mass entertainment is widespread and sometimes leads to great pessimism and rebellion. Indeed, the tendency to adopt positions counter to those accepted in the society in which they live is characteristic of many contemporary artists and intellectuals, especially when faced with the low grade of mass culture. And this position in America leads the artist to reaffirm the traditions of Europe as a gesture of reaction against his society. A person with this point of view has, therefore, no inclination to turn to the almost nihilistic defiance so understandable among advanced thinkers and artists in Europe today. Nor does the American composer need to deny the value of experiment by holding to an equally nihilistic cultivation of naiveté. It is by carrying on the European tradition and by following the methods of some of its experiments in the context of his own experiences that our composer affirms his identity and the identity of American music.

Thus in America a composer of art music comes face to face with many of the most urgent problems of modern civilization. Living in a situation where routine, custom, and habit no longer insure the continuity of culture but where such culture needs to be continually retested and reaffirmed before a mass public apathetic to these interests, he fights a special kind of adventurous battle. The fact, for instance, that compositional skills of the sort that form the basis of a professional approach are only laboriously mastered well enough to promote the imaginative conceptions of the composer, and the fact that these skills are still being learned at a time when they can seem unimportant to a profession which has, under public pressure, been forced to devote its abilities to the performance of works of the past, makes the composer's struggle seem quixotic. Yet this struggle is entered into by more and more young people every year, and this small fraction of a small minority group, the musical profession, whose importance is not generally accepted by a large enough part of our citizens to provide adequate support, forces the profession to meet the very difficult challenge of constantly proving its worth. The fact that our universities have lent more and more protection to this struggle does pose the danger that music may be assimilated to the historical, semantic, acoustical, or psychological branches of musical research and thus be weakened as a public artistic communication. Once compositions are treated as illustrations or examples of general principles rather than for what they are in themselves, they lose a large measure of their significance. On the other hand, so many people are becoming involved with this field that certainly some will constitute part of the future musical public and influence those with less training. In any case, the random development of music here, without imposition of the authority of custom in attitudes and tastes, will be the prime factor in molding our music into something of its own, with a freshness, it is to be hoped, drawn from these very circumstances and with a quality, not necessarily simpler or more naive—perhaps the very reverse of this—that affords a vivid sense of what it is to communicate through the sound medium itself.

Art music in America has been like a plant, transplanted to a new place that provides a very different environment from the one in which it developed. In this new situation, hitherto unrealized qualities inherent in its nature began to appear and the special challenge of trying to live and develop under new circumstances may produce a considerable mutation. The plant is sturdy, the environment strange to it, the desire for adaptation great, and the process of adaptation filled with difficulties which at times seem insurmountable and threatening to the life of the plant, yet the wish to live and develop is very strong.

Expressionism and American Music
(1965/72)

The tendency for each generation in America to wipe away the memory of the previous one, and the general neglect of our own recent past, which we treat as a curiosity useful for young scholars in exercising their research techniques—so characteristic of American treatment of the work of its important artists—is partly responsible for the general neglect of the rather sizable number of composers who in their day were called "ultramodern," and who wrote in this country during the early decades of our century. And it is also part of this unfortunate pattern that interest in these composers is being awakened now because their music fits into a new frame of reference imported from Europe since the war, thus confirming the disturbing fact that the world of serious music here is still thought of as an outpost of that European world which Americans have so often found more attractive than the reality of what they have at home. In fact, it often seems as if we have no genuine interest in looking at our own situation realistically—at least in music—and developing ourselves for what we really are, but are always trying to gain admission into the European musical world (which, at present, is rapidly losing its inner impetus and is fading into a lifeless shadow of what it was).

When interest in Schoenberg and his circle began to be imported into America some years after the war and various of our agencies sent Americans abroad to learn what Europeans were doing and invited Europeans over here to reveal their secrets to us, those who had been close to this music all along began to be treated with a little more respect, while previously their efforts (including those of Schoenberg and his followers living in this country) had been dismissed as meaningless. Thus with the introduction of the post-Webern music and aesthetic here, it was only natural that we should begin to take more interest in our early ultramoderns, whose techniques and outlook had much in common with the Viennese school of about the same time.

The long neglect of these American composers has resulted in a lack of information about them, unfamiliarity with their ideas and music, and often a falsification of facts, so that it now is important to reconsider our attitude about them in the light of actual information in order to understand our own musical situation more clearly. The purpose of the series of articles which *Perspectives of New Music* is devoting to various composers of that time is not a nationalistic one in the European sense at all. It is undertaken in the attempt to clarify the special attitudes these creators developed in relation to the unusual musical situation of America, which gave an entirely different direction to this group than that of its counterparts in Europe. For they came at a time when ideas that were to change the face of each of the arts were widespread, and the same sort of thinking which formed the background of the Central European expressionist movement also informed the thinking of artists both in Russia (which does not concern us here) and in the United States.

Because of many similarities of outlook, the great amount of analytical and philosophical thought which has recently been lavished on German expressionism by European and even American scholars can perhaps be helpful in filling the large empty gap of serious criticism which surrounds the works under consideration, and can be helpful in understanding what went on in this country almost independently. The works produced at that time here, some of clearly great interest, others simply curiosities, have the special traits of the artistic milieu out of which they came, which has not changed much in the intervening years. Very little serious thought and criticism is devoted to our music even today except by composers themselves, and this can be laid partially to the conflict between the American reality and the American dream of Europe which patrons of music try to perpetuate in our musical institutions.

During the period with which we are concerned, a great deal of contemporary music was performed in New York, Chicago, Boston, and San Francisco. The Metropolitan Opera House kept *Petrouchka*, *Le Rossignol*, de Falla's *Vida Breve*, Gruenberg's *Emperor Jones*, and Carpenter's *Skyscrapers* in its repertory. The International Composers' Guild and the League of Composers organized many important performances, including *Wozzeck*, Schoenberg's *Glückliche Hand*, and Ives's Prelude and second movement from his Fourth Symphony. There was an interest in microtonal music,[1] and besides the concert of Hans Barth and Ives discussed by Howard Boatwright,[2] the League of Composers presented a *Sonata casi Fantasia* in quarter, eighth, and sixteenth tones by the Mexican composer Julián Carrillo for guitar, octavina, arpacitera, and a French horn made in New York that could play sixteen tones, in 1926, on the same program as the first U.S. performance of Schoenberg's Wind Quintet. In the next year Carrillo appeared with a larger ensemble of microtonal instruments and recorded his *Preludio a Cristóbal Colón* for Columbia Records. But the two important rivals in presenting modern music to the large musical public were Leopold Stokowski—an irrepressible experimenter, in those days, who played Schoenberg, Varèse, and Ruggles, and was

---

1. Ferruccio Busoni, *Entwurf einer neuen Aesthetik der Tonkunst* (Leipzig, 1907), trans. Theodore Baker in *Three Classics in the Aesthetic of Music* (New York: Dover, 1962), 73–102. On 93–95 Busoni makes out a case for the division of the whole tone into sixths and refers to an American acoustician, Thaddeus Cahill, whose Dynamophone could produce any division of pitch required of it. Also see Dane Rudhyar, "The Relativity of Our Musical Conceptions," *Musical Quarterly* 8, no. 1 (January 1922): 108–18, for a discussion of microtones.

2. Howard Boatwright, "Ives's Quarter-Tone Impressions," *Perspectives of New Music* 3, no. 2 (Spring–Summer 1965):22–31.

a supporter of the more extreme "ultramodernists"—and Serge Koussevitzky, also dedicated to the new, but really most interested in the Franco-Russian schools and launching the (then) younger generation of American composers, giving them the kind of enthusiastic support he had previously given to young Russians in Europe. At that time these institutions felt it their obligation to keep their audience abreast of new developments—especially those coming from abroad—and, in the case of Koussevitzky, of the American composers he sponsored, just as art museums still do today. Few good scores (allowing, of course, for the particular tastes of the conductors) had to wait for any length of time to be heard. Each new work of Stravinsky, for instance, was heard within a year after it was composed, performed with serious devotion by one of the outstanding orchestras, quite contrary to the situation today. In the end Koussevitzky's energy and persistence won a larger audience for the new American neoclassical, folkloric, and populist school and adherents of other aesthetics were more and more bypassed and forgotten.[3]

It was in the early, more advanced stages of this period that the American ultramodern school was especially active, but when the Boston Symphony composers began to dominate the scene in the mid-1930s most of this activity came to a standstill. If there had not been such a drastic change, it is possible that Ives, Varèse, Ruggles, Cowell, Riegger, Leo Ornstein, Dane Rudhyar, John J. Becker, George Tremblay, and those a bit younger, like Ruth Crawford, Gerald Strang, and Adolph Weiss, among many others who are beginning to be heard again, would have had an entirely different development. In any case, Cowell's *New Music Edition* carried on valiantly from 1927 to the present, keeping the scores of this group in circulation and thus enlivening the sometimes very pessimistic outlook for the "ultras."

It is at first surprising that the American group seems to have been but dimly aware of its counterparts in Vienna and Russia, but on closer familiarity with the period it becomes clear that the general opinion here of the Viennese school, particularly as regards Schoenberg and Webern, was of a kind that would lead few to become deeply involved in their music. Paul Rosenfeld, for instance, whose enthusiastic and sympathetic criticism was influential even among musicians in the 1920s, found that Schoenberg's works "baffle with their apparently willful ugliness, and bewilder with their geometric cruelty and coldness. . . . It is only in regarding him as primarily an experimenter that the later Schoenberg loses his incomprehensibility."[4] When one realizes that Rosenfeld knew the early tonal works and opp. 11, 16, and 19 when he wrote this, it is easy to see how the appearance of twelve-tone works must have

3. Ives was a subscriber to a box at the Saturday afternoon concerts of the Boston Symphony at Carnegie Hall, and this author remembers being invited to join him and Mrs. Ives at concerts where Scriabin's *Poème de l'Extase* and *Prométhée*, Stravinsky's *Le Sacre*, and Ravel's *Daphnis et Chloé* were performed.

4. Paul Rosenfeld, *Musical Portraits* (New York: Harcourt, Brace, & Co., 1920), 233 ff.; but compare his praise a few years later, in *Musical Chronicle* (New York: Harcourt, Brace, & Co., 1923), 300–14.

strengthened this opinion, which is still widely held in America, despite the evident fact, revealed by a number of recordings, that quite the opposite is true. This attitude persisted to the very end of Schoenberg's life in this country and succeeded in restricting his influence to a much smaller circle than he deserved, and kept most of the composers discussed from coming to grips with his music. Cowell, however, did publish the second of Webern's *Drei Volkstexte*, op. 17, in 1930 (in a slightly different version from the one now published by Universal Edition) and Schoenberg's op. 33b in 1932 in *New Music Edition*, yet in his book *New Musical Resources*,[5] he mentions a new system of tonal organization used by Schoenberg but shows no understanding of it, perhaps because the book had been written, so the author explains in a preface, in 1919. Until around 1930, and even after, it is hard to escape the impression that the Viennese music left very little impact on most of the ultra-moderns. Riegger, it is true, did start to use a very simplified version of the twelve-tone system then and wrote his *Dichotomy* (published 1932) incorporating this method but in a way utterly different from the Viennese.

The reverse influence is interesting to speculate about. We do know that Webern directed works of Cowell, Ruggles, and Ives in Vienna in 1932, that Slonimsky conducted works of this school in various places in Europe, and that Schoenberg left among his posthumous papers an oft-quoted statement about Ives. Certainly an American is tempted to be reminded of the tone-cluster writings of Ives and Cowell when it appears so baldly on the piano in Berg's *Lulu* (mm. 16, 79, and in a number of other places, particularly during the recitative by Rodrigo, the athlete, mm. 722–768—perhaps to characterize and develop the idea of "Das wahre Tier," which is introduced by the tone-cluster in the Prologue. There may even be a reminiscence of Henry Cowell's *Tiger* here).

To clarify certain aesthetic, artistic, and technical matters central to this group, it is useful to compare them with those central to the composers associated with German expressionism. A number of papers presented at the Convegno Internazionale di Studi sull'Espressionismo of the Maggio Fiorentino of 1964 are particularly relevant.[6] The problem of trying to define and delineate the special features of this movement is troublesome, naturally, and there has been a tendency by German musical scholars and Luigi Rognoni to insist that it be limited only to the works of the Viennese—and to all of their works, although the paper of Dr. Stuckenschmidt was inclined to include some Russian and a few of the American composers to be discussed in the present *Perspectives* series. In any case, the basic manifesto of the movement, *Der blaue Reiter*,[7] was the first attempt to clarify its aims. In this pamphlet, music holds a

5. Henry Cowell, *New Musical Resources* (New York: Knopf, 1930).

6. Luigi Rognoni, "Il Significato dell'Espressionismo come Fenomenologia del Linguaggio Musicale"; Josef Rufer, "Das Erbe des Expressionismus in der Zwölftonmusik"; H.H. Stuckenschmidt, "Expressionismus in der Musik"; L. Mittner, "L'Espressionismo fra l'Impressionismo e la Neue Sachlichkeit: Fratture e Continuità."

7. *Der blaue Reiter*, a German collection of articles, reproductions of arts works, and music,

central position since by its very nature music is not a representational art but an expressive art[8] (a point of view derived from the type of thinking that put music at the top of the hierarchy of the arts, as in Walter Pater, in Busoni, and in Ives). *Der blaue Reiter* contained four important articles on music: Schoenberg's "Das Verhältnis zum Text"; Leonid Sabaneyev's "'Prometheus' von Skrjabin"; Thomas von Hartmann's "Über die Anarchie in der Musik"; and N. Kulbin's "Die freie Musik." Other statements about expressionism and music are to be found in Kandinsky's *Über das Geistige in der Kunst*, in Schoenberg's *Aphorismen* and his *Harmonielehre*, and more peripherally in Busoni's *Entwurf einer neuen Aesthetik der Tonkunst.*[9] Comparison with the general tenor of statements in these works and those made in Ives's *Essays Before a Sonata,*[10] as well as the critical writings of James Huneker and Paul Rosenfeld, reveals many similarities.

The main difference, as always, is that the state of American musical life was so inchoate that a revolutionary movement in this art would necessarily be less well thought out, less focused, and more of an affair of individuals only agreeing in a general way, hence less corrosive of the fundamental aspects of what seemed to all a moribund musical tradition, since the situation was not seen with any clarity—and for that reason tended to dissipate itself in superficialities and absurdities, as so often happens even today.

The basic point of agreement is Hegel's statement (quoted in part by Ives) that "The universal need for expression in art lies, therefore, in man's rational impulse to exalt the inner and outer world into a spiritual consciousness for himself, as an object in which he recognizes his own self."[11] This statement as quoted by Ives omits the words "and outer" and the last phrase "as an object . . .". Both of these omissions are very significant, for they reveal how close Ives's thinking was to that of the expressionists, for whom the inner world was of prime importance, and for whom art was not an object but a means of embodying his own spiritual vision, for himself, and, in view

---

among other things, of the avant-garde of the early 1900s, ed. Wassily Kandinsky and Franz Marc (Munich, 1912); repr. ed. with extensive commentary (Munich: R. Piper Verlag, 1965). Included is Schoenberg's "Das Verhältnis zum Text," an English version of which—"The Relationship to the Text"—appears in Schoenberg's *Style and Idea* (New York: Philosophical Library, 1950), 3–12.

8. Walter Sokel, in *The Writer in Extremis: Expressionism in German Literature* (Stanford: Stanford University Press, 1959), devotes a whole chapter, "Music and Existence," to this subject.

9. Wassily Kandinsky, *Über das Geistige in der Kunst* (Munich, 1911), trans. as *Concerning the Spiritual in Art* (New York, 1947); Arnold Schoenberg, "Aphorismen," *Die Musik* (Berlin, 1909–1910), Italian trans. in Rognoni, *Espressionismo e Dodecafonia* (Milan, 1954); Schoenberg, *Harmonielehre*, 3rd ed. (Vienna, 1922).

10. Charles Ives, *Essays Before a Sonata, The Majority, and Other Writings*, ed. Howard Boatwright (New York: W. W. Norton & Company, 1962).

11. Ives, *Essays Before a Sonata*, 81; and editor's note, 141.

of other statements, for others to share through what was later called an "intersubjective relationship."[12]

Rufer's excellent paper attempts to give a general definition:

There too (in painting and music) is an eruption into chaos, a state of total unrelatedness (which, however, manifests itself in formlessness!), intoxication, ecstasy, the undermining of the very foundation of representative art. "There are no 'objects' or 'colors' in art; only expression." (Franz Marc, 1911). . . . Music of intensely romantic—one might as well say expressionistic—character, with an increasingly pronounced tendency toward breaking the bounds of tonality, toward apparent destruction of musical coherence and traditional formal schemata. Everything was called into question and always seemed to lead into chaos. Today, in retrospect, it seems self-evident that so many fine talents were destroyed in this atmosphere. Only a chosen few, through the force of their genius and the strengthening effect of constant trials, found themselves again. And here I can do no better than quote Gottfried Benn: "The expressionists in particular experienced the profound, objective necessities demanded by craftsmanship in art: the ethos of professionalism, the morality of form."[13]

The actual texts of the period stress truthfulness of expression and the inner necessity of the artist to express his transcendent experiences, as Kandinsky writes:

[This] inner beauty arises from the pressure of subjective necessity and the renunciation of the conventional forms of the beautiful. To those unaccustomed to it, it appears as ugliness. Humanity, in general, is drawn to external things, today more than ever, and does not willingly recognize subjective necessity. The refusal to employ the habitual form of the beautiful leads one to hold as sacred all the procedures which permit the artist to manifest his personality. The Viennese composer Arnold Schoenberg follows this direction alone, scarcely recognized by a few rare and enthusiastic admirers.[14]

Schoenberg himself writes:

Beauty begins to appear at that moment when the noncreative become aware of its absence. It does not exist earlier because the artist has no need of it. For him, truth suffices. It is enough for him to have expressed himself, to say what had to be said according to the laws of his nature. The laws of the nature of men of genius, however, are the laws of future humanity. . . . Nevertheless, beauty gives itself to the artist even though he did not seek it, having striven only toward truthfulness.[15]

12. Rognoni, "Il Significato." "Just as expression is only possible in spoken language if an 'intersubjective relationship' is established, so it is in an ever more direct and immediate way in musical language." (My translation.)

13. Rufer, "Das Erbe des Expressionismus."

14. Kandinsky, *Über das Geistige in der Kunst*, 31–32 (my translation).

15. Schoenberg, *Harmonielehre*, 393.

Ives, in an elaborate discussion of form versus content and manner versus substance—a discussion which identifies form and manner with the generally accepted traditional forms and styles of music language, and content and substance with the artist's feelings and vision seeking expression:

> Beauty in its common conception has nothing to do with it [substance] . . . substance can be expressed in music, and that is the only valuable thing in it; and, moreover, that in two separate pieces of music in which the notes are almost identical, one can be of substance with little manner and the other can be of manner with little substance. . . . The substance of a tune comes from somewhere near the soul, and the manner comes from—God knows where.[16]

Curiously enough, although the expressionists were very aware in their writings that an inner vision was the driving force behind their search for new artistic means, Ives and Cowell, who were the only ones who wrote extensively about this music, did not state this idea directly in words. It must also be pointed out that the influence of mysticism—in Kandinsky the theosophy of Blavatsky (which is also partially evident in certain ideas of the Viennese composers), and in Ives the transcendentalism of Emerson—formed the basis for this sense of the importance of the inner vision and the disdain for the "material" world.[17] Ruggles, to judge by the titles of his works, and Rudhyar also were deeply influenced by mystical thought. The power of the inner experience to force these composers to find a new means of expression led in two apparently opposite directions, called by Benn "chaos and geometry" (recalling, oddly, Pascal's *l'esprit de sagesse et l'esprit de géometrie*). The former was the direction toward the basic, elemental aspects of human experience (and the elemental materials of art): Whitman's "barbaric yawp"—the baby's first cry at birth—what was sometimes called the *Urschrei* or the *Urlaut* (Busoni also discusses, in another sense, *Urmusik*)—the primeval, immediate expression of basic human emotion.[18] Mittner's paper is valuable on this point:

> The two main artistic procedures of expressionism are the primordial utterance (*Urschrei*, or in the terminology of Edschmid, *geballter Schrei*, almost "compressed cry") and the imposition of an abstract structure, often specifically geometric, on reality. These two procedures seem, and often are, diametrically opposed, since the "cry" arises in the soul of the seer who envisions or witnesses the destruction of his world, while "abstraction" is, primarily, the work of an ideal architect who strives to reconstruct the world or construct a completely new one. The relationship, however, is reversible, since geometry can deform and even disintegrate, while the "cry" can turn into an ecstatic shout of jubilation which invokes or creates a new world, an ideal world. . . . The *Urschrei* of German expressionism almost never realizes the "We," and thus reveals the tragic position of uncertainty of the bewildered bour-

16. Ives, *Essays Before a Sonata*, 76, 77.

17. Kandinsky, *Über das Geistige in der Kunst*; Ives, 36.

18. Busoni, *Sketch of a New Aesthetic*, 79.

geoisie. It is rarely the vaunted shout of rebellion and liberation, but primarily a cry of anguish and horror. The parallel with atonal music is significant. The *Urschrei* is most tellingly evoked in the monodrama *Erwartung*, which records with the precision of a psychograph the various moments of spasmodic expectation indicated by the title, followed by a series of cries of horror and desperation.[19]

Mittner also points out the relation of the *Urschrei* to silence:

In contrast to this concern for the lacerating, primordial "cry," a new power is found in *silence* which, paradoxically, is considered its metamorphosis, since a tragic occurrence is presaged or experienced in a silence analogous to an internal "cry" of the soul.[20]

Among the American ultramoderns, the urge for such intensification of expression is particularly in evidence in Ruggles, in Rudhyar, and to a certain extent in Ives. Certainly his song *Walt Whitman*, which has something of a caricature about it, perhaps, strikes a character of expressionistic intensity in its first measures, that is similar to the opening pages of the "Emerson" movement of the *Concord Sonata* and to the first movement of Ruggles's *Men and Mountains*.

The opposing expressionist tendency, as Mittner points out, is that of constructivism, familiar to Americans as an attitude through the aesthetic comments of Poe. In the American period under consideration many kinds of "geometrical" schemata were applied to music, as they were also in Europe and Russia. The rhythmic experiments of Ives partly come out of this thinking, as do those of Varèse, while Ruggles, Ives, and Varèse seem to have experimented with pitch organization in comparative isolation. Ruth Crawford, in particular, developed all kinds of patterns of this sort. Her *Piano Study in Mixed Accents* (1930) uses variable meters and a retrograde pitch plan that reminds one of similar methods of Boris Blacher, while her String Quartet (1931), especially the last movement, juggles with quite a number of different "geometric" systems, one governing pitch, another dynamics, and still another the number of consecutive notes before a rest in any given passage. Besides, the whole movement is divided into two parts, the second a retrograde of the first a semitone higher. Cowell's book *New Musical Resources* has a chapter dealing with the association of pitch-interval ratios with speed ratios after the manner "discovered" later by certain Europeans.[21] During the late 1920s and '30s, Joseph Schillinger, who had come to America from Russia, bringing with him the fruits of similar thinking there, taught here. After his

---

19. Mittner, "L'Espressionismo fra l'Impressionismo." On this point the author has a footnote referring to another interpretation of the dichotomy by Sokel, in *The Writer in Extremis*, who traces, as he calls it, "pure form and pure formlessness" back through German literary history to show that it is a special product of the German cultural situation.

20. Mittner, "L'Expressionismo fra l'Impressionismo."

21. Cowell, *New Musical Resources*, Part II, "Rhythm," 45–108.

death, his *The Schillinger System of Musical Composition* was published (1946) with an introduction by Cowell; although it attempts to be an all-embracing method of explaining the technique of music of all types, it is, ultimately, simply another example of this aspect of expressionist "geometry" in that it applies "extrinsic" patterns derived from other fields of systematization and theoretical description to music, often without sufficiently taking into account the "intrinsic" patterns of musical discourse. As Mittner points out in this connection, "geometry" can be a way of building an entirely new world or a way of deforming or dissolving the old. It is possible that an illogical, disorganized geometry or a totally irrelevant one can be just as much of a deforming or even constructive pattern as one more obviously relevant and logical (although the chances are obviously higher that the latter will be more fruitful) in the hands of an imaginative composer. The history of the canon in all its phases is a clear demonstration of this.

To get down to actual musical practice, the most obvious similarity is that of the "emancipation of dissonance." Just when this began has not yet been explored and hence it is difficult to say, as is often said, that Ives worked independently and before Schoenberg at this, since there many have been a prior obscure source, as there is to microtonal music. Certainly René Lenormand's *Étude sur l'harmonie moderne* gives examples from Ernest Fanelli's *Tableaux Symphoniques* of 1883 containing whole-tone progressions, Eric Satie's chords constructed on fourths in 1891, and a twelve-tone chord used by Jean Huré in 1910.[22] It is true that Ives seems to have tried a tremendous variety of harmonic methods from about 1900 on. He composed passages of consistent harmonic structure (such as is common in Scriabin) in works such as the songs *Evening, Two Little Flowers, Harpalus, Walking,* and *Soliloquy,* and with very great diversity of harmonic structure, as in *Majority* and *Lincoln,* as well as with polyphonic textures derived from these opposing attitudes toward harmony. Ruggles, Ornstein, and Rudhyar maintained a very much more consistent harmonic approach. Ruggles, in particular, shows a great sensitivity to the handling of major sevenths and minor ninths and their interrelationships with other intervals. The fourth *Evocation* is a particularly fine example of this. Tone-clusters, which might be considered a reduction of harmony to its most primitive and undifferentiated state, may have been first used by Ives in his First Piano Sonata of 1902 and then by Cowell in 1917. By 1912, Ives was writing large tone-clusters for divided strings in his orchestral music, especially in the *Fourth of July,* in which several streams of tone-clusters rush up and down scales in contrary motion simultaneously. Berg uses clusters in the men's chorus in the first tavern scene in *Wozzeck.* Indeed both tavern scenes in this opera have a strikingly similar character to those works of Ives that suggest crowd scenes, like the one mentioned above, and the second movement of the Fourth Symphony. The strings divided into tone-clusters, which seems to have been one of Ives's discoveries, did not come into wide usage until very recently in the works of Xenakis, Ligeti, Penderecki, and Cerha. Ives's attitude toward dissonance is summed up in the following:

22. René Lenormand, *Étude sur l'harmonie moderne* (Paris, 1912).

Many sounds we are used to do not bother us, and for that reason we are inclined to call them beautiful. . . . Possibly the fondness for individual utterance may throw out a skin-deep arrangement which is readily accepted as beautiful—formulae that weaken rather than toughen up the musical muscles.[23]

Although Cowell wrote a number of piano works exploring polyrhythms (and using a notation devised by him for the purpose) and Ornstein used irregular bar lengths—and Rudhyar and Ruggles used irrational note divisions in order to give the impression of rubato and rhythmic freedom—it was again Ives who explored the field of rhythm most extensively, using precompositional patterns of note-values and all types of polyrhythms, of approximately coordinated instrumental groups, of passages more or less improvised rhythmically, carrying such exploration much further than any composer of his time. In a desire to make the performance situation vivid, Ives sometimes wrote remarks in the score directed to the performer to encourage him to give free rein to his fantasy. His remark "Perhaps music is the art of speaking extravagantly" gives some clue to his general approach and links him once again to the expressionists.[24]

One of Ives's most puzzling aspects is his extreme heterogeneity, a characteristic of some of Cowell and Ornstein too, but not shared by the other Americans, whose attitude resembles much more closely that of Schoenberg as stated in "The Relationship to the Text." Here Schoenberg indicates the kind of thinking which would eventually lead him to adopt the twelve-tone method:

Inspired by the sound of the first words of the text, I had composed many of my songs straight through to the end. . . . It then turned out . . . , to my greatest astonishment, that I had never done greater justice to the poet than when, guided by my first direct contact with the sound of the beginning, I divined everything that obviously had to follow this first sound with inevitability.

Thence it became clear to me that the work of art is like every other complete organism. It is so homogeneous in its composition that in every little detail it reveals its truest, inmost essence.[25]

Such a sense of inner cohesion is closely allied with the general tendency among expressionists toward "reduction" in technique, to finding the basic material of any given work. This method became acutely important to musicians as the form-building function of tonality was eliminated, obviously, and also as various familiar methods of beginning, stating, developing, and ending began to seem outworn because they weakened the intensity and vibrant immediacy of individual musical moments. As in literature, much concern and invention was lavished on new methods of fragmentary presentation, such as starting *in medias res* or ending with an uncompleted phrase. Closely allied

23. Ives, 97, 98.

24. Ibid., 52.

25. Schoenberg, "The Relationship to the Text," in *Style and Idea*, 4.

with this was the tendency toward very short, concentrated totalities after the analogy of a Chinese character or a hieroglyph. The works of Schoenberg and Webern of this type are well known. It is interesting that among the Americans only Ives attempted this in works such as the songs *Anne Street, Maple Leaves, 1,2,3*, and *Soliloquy*.

Besides this type of fragmentation, the expressionists tended as well to a fragmentation of the materials of the work. In this respect the music of Varèse is particularly significant in that its material is made up of small fragments for the most part and these fragments are generally reduced to very basic, elemental shapes—melodic material made of repeated notes, repeated chordal sounds depending for their telling effect on their instrumentation, vertical spacing, and timing. Varèse's music corresponds very closely to Mittner's delineation of several stages in the development of the expressionistic vision as seen in poetry and painting:

> The visionary power of expressionism did not result in a sudden turning away from the observation of reality, but reached this goal through a series of steps. The first was a reduction of sense data. [Ernst] Barlach, in his sculptures, took a most important step in this direction in 1901 . . . he began to reduce methodically the lines of his figures to those which seemed to him the most important, and so achieved a new, vigorous, and very plastic presentation of the essence of his subjects. The second step consisted of the extraction and separate use of each aspect of the total sense perception as a thing in itself, detaching it from the object to which it belongs, with the consequent deformation of reality as an entity. Such a procedure evolved also in poetry through means specifically derived from painting, where it had caused a revolution in the field of color. . . . Color was no longer added to figure, but figure to color. From such an unnaturalistic coupling of color and figure it is but a short step to the unnaturalistic coupling of any of the other elements of reality.[26]

The dissociation of the various elements of reality and their reassembling in new ways, isolating, as Kandinsky did, color from shape, and so forth, is paralleled by the dissociation, first, of the various so-called "elements" of music—melody, harmony, rhythm. The next step was the more subtle one of dissociating certain qualities from others, such as tone color from the above three, and finally the dissociation of all the "parameters" (as they are called at present) from each other. All of these tendencies along with the "reductive" method are evident in Varèse.

In passing it is interesting to point out that the development of the resources of instrumental techniques, which was not so common in Europe until recently, had during this period an important exponent in America. Carlos Salzedo's *Modern Study of the Harp* (New York, 1921) presents a whole new repertory of effects for that instrument that are still not incorporated into our composers' vocabulary, as are the latest tapping and scraping of the violin from France and Poland.

26. Mittner, "L'Expressionismo fra l'Impressionismo."

Perhaps the other striking feature of resemblance between these two groups is the avoidance of repetition and the sense of continuous variation. Ives's statements about this are very indicative:

> Unity is too generally conceived of, or too easily accepted, as analogous to form, and form as analogous to custom, and custom to habit.[27]
>
> Coherence, to a certain extent, must bear some relation to the listener's subconscious perspective. But is this its only function? Has it not another of bringing outer or new things into wider coherence?[28]
>
> There may be an analogy—and on first sight there seems to be—between the state and power of artistic perceptions and the law of perpetual change, that ever-flowing stream, partly biological, partly cosmic, ever going on in ourselves, in nature, in all life . . . perhaps this is why conformity in art (a conformity which we seem naturally to look for) appears so unrealizable, if not impossible.[29]

"The Composer Is a University Commodity"
(1970)

The effect of teaching in universities by young composers, on them and their works and on the public and music profession, will have to go through many stages and be reconsidered many times before it can be evaluated, if it ever can. Certainly between 1959, when Stravinsky wrote his advice, and 1969, when I write this, so much has happened in American society and its relation to education and so much within the field of music that one hesitates to give any general answer at all—music is not what it was in 1959, and neither are universities.

One can, now as then, list the goods and bads only and not predict. But there is one fundamental question—the one of education itself as a pattern which indicates that it could be an unhealthy situation for composers to be too much involved with education, especially in a university. For the age level of students, and their level of preparation, is always the same in each new class, from year to year, while the composer changes and develops and naturally grows older—and more experienced in the ways of his own generation (often thought nowadays to be irrelevant to the next generation). This constant rebeginning for the sake of the young is not always the best atmosphere for a composer to develop in.

Also the fact that the university is a passing stage, a preparation (?), a training (?) for life outside of the university for students, means that the academic society itself should have this as its goal and not become too much involved with itself—which it very often tends to do, and therefore a composer living in this atmosphere could lose the sense of writing for the outer society which he should be helping to develop. One could imagine students today

27. Ives, 98.

28. Ibid.

29. Ibid., 71.

being very critical of many of the more recondite activities of American graduate schools, including music schools.

To come down to more precise matters:

BAD: The American composer, like his colleagues on university faculties,
tends to be treated as a commodity with these tangible assets: *reputation* (the
kind formed by American publicity, or taken up by American publicity from
foreign cultural propaganda), which the university does little to help him to
increase once engaged, and hence which often deteriorates during the teaching years; *verbal articulateness* (not characteristic of composers *qua* composers, although sometimes found even in good ones); *new ideas* about music
techniques, analysis, theory, and teaching techniques (preferably those that
will provoke publicity—now computer methods, etc.); *closeness to the "new"
trends*, as defined, of course, by the news media.

While one can have no objection to having all of these taught in a university (except on the basis of the quick obsolescence of most of the "new" in
art), the emphasis on these is hardly conducive to the composer's own development. For the composer's own work becomes of small importance to his
department (which explains the American Society of University Composers)
unless it can get important write-ups in the news, or unless the composer is
willing to tear his own pieces apart, explain them in detail, and show his students how to do it in a few easy lessons. Thus his work is of little importance,
so it often seems, unless it can be transformed into the tangible assets of "reputation" or "articulateness."

BAD: Since composers seem to be regarded as immediate (and often dispens-
able) commodities both by university management, by most of their students,
and even by their departmental colleagues (for the most part), they become
part of a competitive market. Since universities usually tend to downgrade
composers' reputations once they hire them, they are constantly on the lookout for those not previously associated with American universities—composers whose reputations are made and sustained by effective cultural propaganda from the country of their origin, not available to American composers.
Many of these from other countries continue to profit by the cultural propaganda of their country even while employed here, thus putting their American
colleagues in the shade.

Naturally, one would not want to eliminate the important thought and
contribution of non-Americans to our culture; it is simply that in terms of acquiring the particular asset of "reputation" they have a much better opportunity to do so than any American composer—and have often been inflated far
beyond their intrinsic value.

BAD: The effort to develop in his own way is met, for a composer, with constant frustration by the very demands of the situation. What appears to be an
utter lack of responsibility toward the needs of its compositional faculty
seems to be characteristic of most university music departments today. To

make matters worse, departments are often willing to pay high prices for those who have profited by the culturally more responsible situations that exist outside the United States. This is profoundly disturbing to all involved in it and should be to all American graduate students. For the latter cannot fail to realize that, if things keep up this way, they will be done out of jobs by young professionals trained elsewhere under more culturally responsible situations, when they graduate. We don't even approve of the results of our own education, so it seems (perhaps because education itself is not a commodity, only the act of educating is). In fact, in music one cannot help but feel that in composition, education is a training in obsolescence and is likely to be a hindrance in future teaching—for only thus can the presence of certain individuals on university faculties be explained today.

BAD: In 1969 (as not in 1959) the question of what can be useful to the next generation and how it can be presented has reached crisis proportions. If this continues to be the (what seems to me healthy) situation of universities, teaching should be done by those who can constantly be concerned with the young and their attitudes, and not by composers who can only hope to interest the next generation by their honest work.

GOOD: In 1959 it used to be said that the university in America was the home of the arts—a place where they could be taught, studied, discussed, enjoyed, and developed outside of the mercantile pressures that link our society together. It is possible and much to be hoped that this continues and will continue to be true until the time when our society can find the kind of cultural consensus which will allow a large enough community of citizens to encourage musical composition outside of the university.

III

Charles Ives

The Case of Mr. Ives
(1939)

To tell the full story of the first and second New York performances of Charles E. Ives's *Concord Sonata* at Town Hall, 20 January and 24 February 1939, is not my purpose here, for that deserves a whole article. In tabloid form, however, it would read as follows:

First performance: very small house.

In the next ten days: enthusiastic reviews cribbed from Ives's prefaces by critics most of whom had not been at the concert.

Second performance: packed house and disappointment of critics on hearing work, obviously for the first time.

For a good long while now many of us have been puzzled about the musical merits of the *Concord Sonata* and others of Ives's longer pieces. I came to know the sonata in the years when Stravinsky first scandalized America in person and Whiteman gave the Carnegie premiere of the *Rhapsody in Blue*. A keen time with lots of enthusiasm and lots of performances of new music to which I sometimes went with Ives himself. Sunday afternoons, after these concerts, a few of us would go down to Gramercy Park, where Ives then lived, or later uptown when he had moved to East 74th Street, to discuss the music in the calm atmosphere of his living-room, a Henry James, old New York interior. They were lively talks; new music was new and very "modern" and Ives was much interested. Often he would poke fun, sit down at the piano to play from memory bits of a piece just heard, like *Daphnis et Chloé* or *Le Sacre*, taking off the Ravel major seventh chords and obvious rhythms, or the primitive repeated dissonances of Stravinsky, and calling them "too easy." "Anybody can do that," he would exclaim, playing "My Country 'Tis of Thee," the right hand in one key and the left in another. His main love, however, was for Bach, Brahms, and Franck, for he found in them spiritual elevation and nobility, which, like many a critic of his generation, he felt contemporary music had simplified away. To start the day fresh, he would often play a fugue from the *Well-Tempered Clavier* before breakfast and long hours at the office. Not that he needed much cheering up, for, being a good sturdy Yankee with plenty of vitality, he poured lots of pep, salty humor, and good spirits into everything he did.

During these afternoons we would coax him to try some of his own music, and as he saw we were sincere and not merely polite he would jump to the piano and play. Then the respectable, quiet, Puritan atmosphere was oddly disturbed, a gleam would come into his eyes as fiery excitement seized him, and he would smash out a fragment of "Emerson," singing loudly and exclaiming with burning enthusiasm. Once the captain of the football team at Yale, he put the same punch into his music. It was a dynamic, staggering experience, which is hard even now to think of clearly. He hated composers who played their works objectively "as if they didn't like them." This strong, wiry Yankee vitality, humor, and transcendental seriousness were very much to our taste and we always came away from Ives full of life's glad new wine and a thousand projects for the future.

In those days Ives was practically never played. Once, in 1927 at a Pro Musica concert, two movements of his Fourth Symphony were given under the direction of Eugene Goossens, who sat up all one night with a towel around his head trying to figure out how to keep the orchestra together in the places where the barlines do not coincide. Ives had the percussion to his house to teach them the rhythms. It is no wonder the work didn't go any too well, for the score of the "lively movement," later published by *New Music*, has complexities well nigh insurmountable. At the time we asked why he didn't write his work more practically, so that performers could play it more accurately. He would reply that it was written as simply as possible, and then would play over precisely what was written indicating that it was not as hard as all that. We remarked that certain very complicated textures would never sound, but he countered that he had already tried them out when he conducted a theatre orchestra at Yale. Then we asked why the notation of the *Concord Sonata* was so vague, why every time he played it he did something different, sometimes changing the harmonies, the dynamic scheme, the degree of dissonance, the pace. He even made a transcription of "Emerson" with many notes changed and the dynamic plan completely altered. He said that he intended to give only a general indication to the pianist, who should, in his turn, recreate the work for himself. In a footnote to "Hawthorne," he writes: "If the score itself, the preface, or an interest in Hawthorne suggest nothing, marks (of tempo, expression, etc.) will only make things worse."

This improvisational attitude toward music, so familiar in swing, affects all of Ives's more mature work. It affects his conception of performance and of composing. Unlike Chopin and Liszt, who wrote out very accurately in note values what they improvised, Ives leaves a great deal to the mercy of the performer. In his compositions, the notation of a work is only the basis for further improvisation, and the notation itself, frequently of music first conceived many years before, is a kind of snapshot of the way he played it at a certain period in his life.

The improvisation often consists in adding dissonances, harmonies, and complicated rhythms to a fundamentally simple work. This is obvious in many songs, and especially in a comparison of "Hawthorne" with the scherzo of the Fourth Symphony, which contain much identical material, greatly overladen with extra harmonies and complicated rhythms. The fuss that critics make about Ives's innovations is, I think, greatly exaggerated, for he has rewritten his works so many times, adding dissonances and polyrhythms, that it is probably impossible to tell just at what date the works assumed the surprising form we now know. The accepted dates of publication are most likely those of the compositions in their final state. Anyhow, the question is not important. Ives himself has said that he prefers people to judge his music not for when it was written but for what it is.

Up to the time John Kirkpatrick gave his performances no one had heard the *Concord Sonata* in its entirety in a concert hall. Some of us came wanting to see in the whole work what we saw in fragments. We found ourselves sadly disappointed. Kirkpatrick's extraordinary feat of interpretation did make a great deal of the music assume a shape through clever dynamic planning. But all the ingenious interpreting in the world could not dispel the fact that the sonata is formally weak. Kirkpatrick played the work with more finesse and less breadth and grandeur than Ives does, but this is understandable as Ives rarely ever played the whole work through but stuck to little fragments which he particularly loved; the whole work as a piece seemed to interest him less.

To turn to the music itself. In form and aesthetic it is basically conventional, not unlike the Liszt Sonata, full of the paraphernalia of the overdressy sonata school, cyclical themes, contrapuntal development sections that lead nowhere, constant harmonic movement which does not clarify the form, and dramatic rather than rhythmical effects. Because of the impressionistic intent of most of the music, the conventional form seems to hamper rather than aid, resulting in unnecessary, redundant repetitions of themes, mechanical transitions uncertain in their direction; unconvincing entrances of material; dynamics which have no relation to the progress of the piece. Behind all this confused texture there is a lack of logic which repeated hearings can never clarify, as they do for instance in the works of Bartók or Berg. The rhythms are vague and give no relief to the more expressive sections, and the much touted dissonant harmonies are helter-skelter, without great musical sense or definite progression. The aesthetic is naive, often too naive to express serious thoughts, frequently depending on quotation of well-known American tunes, with little comment, possibly charming, but certainly trivial. As a whole, the work cannot be said to fill out the broad, elevated design forecast in the composer's prefaces.

However, there is also much good in the sonata. Usually the statement of themes is beautiful: in "Emerson," the beginning, the first "verse" section, the allegro, and the coda; in "Hawthorne," pages 27 to 32, which lead up to the "pilgrim's song" and the funny parody of "Hail, Columbia"; though less characteristic of Ives's best, "The Alcotts" maintains a consistent level; and "Thoreau," with its lovely beginning and its beautiful "walking theme," is in the best Ives manner, though it too has a long redundant section which might be relieved by cutting pages 65 and 66.

While his music is more often original than good, the good is really very personal and beautiful. Unlike that of Charles Griffes, here is a fresh and touching impressionism, different from anyone else's. With Griffes, Ives shares many formal weaknesses as well as a similar sensitivity to curious chord formations, but though he has more scope, he is less able to realize his musical purpose. Despite all the problems of music and American culture which form the interesting context of the Ives case, it is not possible on the basis of the music we know to rank him among the great originals of American art, with, for instance, Albert P. Ryder and Whitman. Unlike theirs his work, though original, falls short of his intentions. In any case, it is not until we have had a much greater opportunity to examine and hear his music that Ives's position as a composer can be determined. The present canonization is a little premature.

Ives Today: His Vision and Challenge
(1944)

No matter how sincere and confidential men are in trying to know or assuming that they do know each other's mood and habits of thought, the net result leaves a feeling that all is left unsaid; for the reason of their incapacity to know each other, though they use the same words. They go on from one explanation to another, but things seem to stand about as they did in the beginning, because of that vicious assumption. But we would rather believe that music is beyond any analogy to word language and that the time is coming, but not in our lifetime, when it will develop possibilities inconceivable now,—a language, so transcendent, that its heights and depths will be common to all mankind.[1]

Few composers in our time have come to grips with the basic problem of musical expression, and certainly few have taken so definite a stand as does Charles Ives in his interesting *Essays Before a Sonata* (1920, now out of print).[2] Reading them, one cannot help feeling that such a man with such ideas *must* be capable of writing exceptional music. The tone is elevated, the wit brilliant. Here, as in his music, Ives reveals himself a devout believer in transcendental philosophy, in the immanence of God in nature, in the glorious mission of music, which is to be achieved only when freed from the pedestrian ideas of professional musicians, in the ability of man to grasp the divinity behind nature through feeling and not through artificialities of logic. Of American music he says that a composer who believes in the American ideal cannot fail to be American whether he uses folklore or not. Of performing musicians he says that the composer must lead the way, the performer must figure out how to play the music. The book is a little masterpiece; it should be known to all musicians.

1. Charles Ives, *Essays Before a Sonata, The Majority, and Other Writings*, ed. Howard Boatwright (New York: W. W. Norton & Co., 1962), 8.

2. The 1920 edition was published by The Knickerbocker Press, New York. *Essays Before a Sonata* is now more generally available in Howard Boatwright's edition (see note 1); therefore, throughout the present essay, as well as elsewhere in this collection, all of Carter's references to this work of Ives have been converted to the pagination of Boatwright's edition.
[B]

The difference between Ives and other mystical composers, Scriabin, for instance, is that he believes neither in ritual nor in the methodical training of the intuition which raises man from one level of consciousness to another, leading to a denial of the physical world. Ives follows Emerson. For him the natural world reflects the spiritual, and so is of great concern. Hence the divergence between the patterned music of the Russian and the free, almost random music of Ives.

Ives's dissonance differs from that of most other composers who use it to express physical excitement, sensations of pleasure and pain, or effects of distortion in the manner of the modern painters, or to reflect spiritual conflict, as in the works of Baudelaire. Ives is always in quest of the transcendental. On the surface of his work, the infinite complexity of nature, the rapidly changing moods of forest and plain, the web of counterbalancing forces appear confused and dissociated. But Ives's involved texture, while mirroring this superficial confusion, at the same time attempts to show the larger harmony of rhythm behind the natural process. Faith in the purpose and goodness of nature rather than concern over its savage conflicts and hostility determines his choice of moods. In his essays he says that Debussy, in works like *La Mer*, appears interested only in the physical aspects and never sees beyond them.[3]

Ives, with his exalted goal for musical expression, believes that composers should be free always to follow their highest instincts. Difficulty of performance is the performer's problem, not his. The quest for performances, for payment for music, for success, are beside the point. Ives himself makes his money in business and so has been free in his pursuit of music as one of his instrumental parts, whose barlines, rhythms, notes, and speed do not tally with the rest of the orchestra. He is as difficult to assimilate into the pattern of the organized musical world as such a part is into an orchestral texture. (He has persistently refused royalties, prefers not to have his music copyrighted so that performers may feel free to take liberties, and usually insists on paying for publication. Thus he strictly preserves his amateur status, while his reputation—based rather on what has been written about him than on the few performances of his music—constitutes a threat to the professional world.)

All who have written about his music, and their number is legion, are convinced that if performed it would meet the expectations aroused by his famous ideals. It probably would—provided that listeners made several allowances. They must be ready to grant that the quotation of familiar tunes, with which the music is studded, is a device sufficiently powerful to evoke the particular feelings apostrophized. Then there is also the amount of detail left to the interpreter's discretion. The polyrhythms, which appear to be precisely written, obviously call for an improvisatory technique hard to achieve in ordinary rehearsals. Bernard Herrmann and Nicolas Slonimsky have faced this problem most squarely. Herrmann claims that with the proper rehearsal, everything in Ives is playable. A few years ago he boldly gave an Ives series over C.B.S. and brought to the air several highly effective pieces, among them the

3. Ives, *Essays Before a Sonata*, 82.

Largo for Strings and the very affecting first and third movements of the Fourth Symphony. Taking advantage of Ives's suggestions that performers should "interpret" the works to suit themselves, Herrmann reorchestrated part of the first movement and ironed out some of its rhythmic complexities. But such a procedure, followed without great understanding of the music, could easily rob it of characteristic qualities.

Another artist, John Kirkpatrick, whose performance of the *Concord Sonata* is well known, also following Ives's expressed intentions, takes certain liberties with the polyrhythms. With great care and devotion he molds the music into a very moving auditory experience. That Kirkpatrick's conception can be found in the notes in unquestionably true, but it is also true that a good but unsympathetic musician might give a chaotic and unintelligible account of the same score. It is all a question of whether one can enter into the spirit of this music and then recreate it. Such a challenge is good for the profession: it demands a vision that goes beyond the notes.

A quick glance at Ives's total output—which can now be studied in print or in photostat (eleven volumes of chamber music and six of orchestral scores) in the Library of Congress, the Fleisher Collection, and the American Music Center—reveals many interesting facts.[4] The music shows a rather spasmodic development, from the product of a youthful organist with a classical background playing in a Presbyterian church, to the elaborate works most of us are familiar with. There has been, from the start, a preoccupation with hymns, marches, and other native American music. The First Symphony, written in the 1890s, has a fetching, naive quality; it shows influences of Mozart, Bach, and Beethoven and at the same time some strange harmonic progressions that resemble early Shostakovitch. The Second Symphony, following almost immediately, reveals chromatic influences, Franck, Brahms, and Dvořák. It is made up of arrangements of earlier organ works and an older overture. The Third, for small orchestra, although written only a little later, is a new departure. It has slow first and last movements and a folksy middle one that is gentle and full of charm. The first is made up of unusual progressions and the last is quite Franckian. Then comes a complete break: the Fourth Symphony, written about the time of the last war. It is full of surprising effects most musicians associate with Ives, which were not noticeable in his earlier works.

There are two other symphonies, *Holidays in a Connecticut Country Town* ("Washington's Birthday," a very solemn and beautiful "Decoration Day," an

---

4. John Kirkpatrick, Ives specialist and compiler, among other Ives items, of the monumental catalogue of Ives's works (New Haven, 1960), has kindly supplied the following note: "These photostat volumes of chamber music and orchestral scores, together with the printings available in 1944, hardly represent 'Ives's total output,' but do contain all of what he would have considered his most important work. At the time of his death he had given all such volumes away, keeping none. Consequently the Ives Collection at Yale University has only the two that happened to be in the possession of the curator [Mr. Kirkpatrick]. But the Collection has all the negative photostats from which these volumes were assembled (unless some set may possibly come to light containing the missing *Clarinet Trio* or the *Autumn Landscape from Pine Mountain*)." [S]

extremely elaborate and wild "Fourth of July," and a dithyrambic "Forefathers' and Thanksgiving Day") and a *Universal Symphony*, which has remained a rough sketch for the last ten years. *Holidays*, like the Fourth Symphony, is in his most advanced style and shows all the facets of Ives's music, as do also the *Second Orchestral Set*, the *Theatre Set*, *Three Places in New England*, and a few works in the chamber music volumes. In these latter there are, besides, what at least to this writer appear to be parodies of modern music, like his satirical songs about modern life.

The orchestral scores of his later period make use of several devices which deserve more comment than they have received so far. Ives is fond of using a separate instrumental group, playing some kind of ostinato figure and maintaining its own tempo behind a fast movement and even behind a slow one, but in different rhythm. This seems designed to give the natural setting of trees and sky against which he places human events. The transcendental background of faint sounds usually starts and ends a movement which may depict, in rather literal fashion by quotation of themes and in other ways, the noisy or religious or patriotic episodes of everyday life. This latter music is often naively pictorial, while his style verges on impressionism and takes on the most advanced dissonance when it represents the transcendental.

Ives's range is remarkably broad. He offers us the rural, homely qualities of Whittier, the severity of Emerson, the fancy of Hawthorne, and the meditation of Thoreau. These moods return again and again in all his later works. The contrast between the transcendental polyrhythm and polytonality, and the human music of hymns, dance, and march, is always present.

This year, on 20 October, Ives will celebrate his seventieth birthday. Yet real consideration of his music still lies in the future. However fascinating it may be to speculate about, its actual sound will be more enthralling. Let us hope, for our sake as well as for his, that performances will not be too long in coming. He has waited now for many years. The musical public has known all about him for more than ten. It is about time for a real demonstration.

An American Destiny
(1946)

Charles Edward Ives is one of those outstanding individuals whose personalities leave their mark on whatever they do. And whatever he does seems to emerge naturally from his own character rather than from some artificially invented plan forced on him from the outside. The bold pattern of his life, evolving in a highly unorthodox manner, reflects a personal logic that assessed the American musical scene of his time and his own capabilities and went its own way regardless of what other composers were doing. And the result is surprising: to be at the same time a highly successful businessman, the senior partner in the outstanding New York insurance firm of Ives and Myrick, built up by the two from scratch, and also the composer of a large body of music, much of it not only years ahead of its time but vital and important enough to be hailed by critics here and abroad as an outstanding contribution to the art of music, is certainly the achievement of an extraordinary man.

In many ways Ives stands apart from his time. In our age of specialization, the combination of executive and artistic ability, of originality and personal discipline, of shrewdness and moral integrity, and, above all, of relentless energy coupled with religious convictions, fervent patriotism, and a good sense of humor, seems typical of an earlier time. Few men of today can be talked of in superlatives in two different capacities. Ives is probably one of the few. He seems to have floated above the egomania, the pragmatism, and the doubts about the future of Democracy rampant before and after the First World War. Indeed, his reaction against these as against the modern music of that time, his heyday, was violent. In his *Essays Before a Sonata*, and in his political tract advocating a World People's Union (a United States of the World) sent to President Roosevelt and members of the Congress, he is scornful of many trends of the modern era, while firmly believing that out of the chaos there will be a spiritual affirmation that will sweep away the present troubles.[1] Being the kind of man he is, he could not fail to assert and to exemplify in his life and his art the noble ideals inherited from his New England background. And these older principles, voiced mainly by the Concord Transcendentalists, form the core around which all the parts of his life are joined.

This typically lean and wiry Yankee is of an exceedingly modest and retiring character. Not unlike many another New Englander, it is hard to get much biographical material from him. Yet before he withdrew from business and finally even from the exertion of receiving any but occasional visitors because of grave ill health which began to overtake him in 1930, Ives was not averse to telling jokes on himself. For instance, after a concert conducted in 1927 by Eugene Goossens, on which Debussy shared the program with two movements of Ives's dissonant and complex Fourth Symphony, Ives overheard two men talking outside Town Hall. One asked the other if the music was all by contemporaries. On learning that Debussy was no longer alive, he asked if Ives were dead. The answer being, "No," he remarked, Well, he ought to be."

Ives is against being photographed. One of the few pictures ever taken and the only one ever reproduced shows him sitting outside his house in West Redding in rough summer clothes. It is very much in contrast to the clean-shaven Ives who went to business daily for thirty years looking like any other commercial New Englander, inconspicuously dressed.

With this retiring disposition go many attitudes and opinions typical of one with his background. Often he would express scorn of the cheap and frivolous, of the decadent or lazy, in a sharp, witty phrase. I remember his humorous disgust at hearing of an American composer living in Paris who lay all morning in bed composing. Such behavior would be impossible in the

---

1. Ives, "Letter to Franklin D. Roosevelt" and "A People's World Nation," in *Essays Before a Sonata, the Majority, and Other Writings*, ed. Howard Boatwright (New York: W. W. Norton & Co., 1962), 215–31. [S, B]

respectable conventionality of *his* home. He deplored the excessive eroticism of late nineteenth-century music in his book as being like "the sad thoughts of a bathtub with the water running out." The one text of Whitman he has used in his songs represents a violent contrast to the generally conventional texts from newspaper poets and standard authors. "Who goes there? hankering, gross, mystical, nude" is the opening of the song which epitomizes the yawpingly physical aspects of the poet—to Ives justifiable, perhaps, as a strongly characterized human picture. But from his point of view, Whitman was hardly to be countenanced as furnishing an outlook on life, which the poet did for so many in the country during the very period when Ives was active.

Rather, the composer inclined to the lofty aspirations of Emerson, the nature moods of Thoreau, the fantastic in Hawthorne, the homely New England cheer of Whittier. His music and his writings reflect this optimistic tone, in their religious, patriotic, or gay moments. The bitter brooding of Melville or the searchings of the conscience of Hawthorne never seem to have moved him to music. And this, too, is characteristic of one aspect of New England Puritanism.

But along with this adherence to many attitudes typical of a slightly older generation than his own, there is a strong streak of originality, which, of course, finds its fullest expression in his music. It also found its way into his business affairs. At the office, he avoided formality; he liked clients to feel that they could come and see him whenever they wished without appointments. He refused to have a secretary and insisted on answering the phone himself. Having a clear mind and a good memory, he followed a personal method of ordering his papers, which meant that his desk usually looked messy. (His curious sense of order is also noticeable in the volume of *114 Songs*, which are, as far as any plan is perceptible, partially in reverse chronological order. Certainly it is not by chance that the song "The Masses," with its huge tone-clusters, opens the collection.) He apparently made an important innovation which drew customers by offering, at a time when businesses concealed their inner workings, to let his clients have free access to the books.

In his musical dealings he has persisted since about 1902 in maintaining an "amateur" status, almost consistently refusing any payment for performances or publication. In fact, he has been reluctant to allow his music to be published except at his own expense, and generally will not have it copyrighted unless the publisher insists. On the other hand, he has never paid for performances of his works, letting performers and performing organizations treat him in this respect as they would any other composer, always, however, waiting to be asked for his music. When able to get about he had to be persuaded to go to concerts where his music was played, and he never would take a bow.

This unusual attitude is the application of his idea that music is something more important and more spiritual than the commodities and professional services bought with money. It is the point of view of many non-artists. There is an element of truth in it insofar as we do demand of all artistic products that they seem to proceed from some other kind of love than the love of money. Ives also shunned any attempt to court artistic success, even when it started to come his way, because all of these worldly things probably seemed out of place in the domain of art. But in the end, Ives's life has amply justified adherence to high ideals not only by his business success but, more important, by the unusual quality of his music. Here is one case where pure high-mindedness won out.

This, however, is not to say that Ives always remains on a lofty pinnacle of abstract speculation in his music. On the contrary, all sides of life find their way there as they used to into his insurance office. There is a great love of the concrete—the mistakes townspeople made singing hymns, the way children used to cut up at religious camp meetings in Danbury, the national anthems played by conflicting bands on the Fourth of July, soupy theatre music, the confused sounds of the city heard at night in Central Park. These furnish part of the background of material closely related to the average man he so respected in his office. Continual contact with people prevented him from losing himself in the recondite. The intent of his compositions is usually easy to grasp on first hearing no matter how original and complex the tonal garb. Not only does the deep seriousness of his mature life come through, but so also do the charming reminiscences of the Danbury of his childhood, of the humor like that of the "Danbury Newsman," who set America to laughing over local cranks and eccentrics, and of the gay holidays.

For Charles Ives was born in that Connecticut country town (now the "Hat City") on 20 October 1874, of a father who was the center of musical activity. George Ives had been a bandleader at sixteen in the Civil War, and his son took after him in musical precocity. He learned harmony, counterpoint, and fugue thoroughly from his father. Along with these subjects went contact with the novel experiments in acoustics worked out in the household. George Ives—like a few other Americans stimulated by such new developments as Karl Rudolph Koenig's tonometric apparatus, shown at the Philadelphia Exposition of 1876, that divided four octaves into 670 parts—built instruments that produced quarter and other fractional tones. The effects of acoustical perspective made by placing instruments and even whole bands in antiphonal, opposing position on the village green were also tried. Sometimes one band performing one piece marched in the opposite direction from that performing another piece, and the Iveses enjoyed the fading in and out and the clashing of harmonies and rhythms. This led them to think up many new, dissonant chords. That all this was followed with intense interest by the son is clear, for he made liberal use of these experiments in his own music while inventing many more. What is still shocking conductors today was worked out in the 1880s in Danbury.

Seeing how musically gifted his son was, George Ives set him to learning organ playing. By the age of fourteen, young Ives was so good that became a regular church organist at a salary. To play in his father's band, he picked up drumming from the local barber. Working under his father, who taught him the works of Bach, Beethoven, and Stephen Foster, his talents grew abundantly. Soon he composed a march, which his father decided to play. This touched off another side of Ives, for feeling a certain shyness over his musical activities, he refused to participate. Indeed, at that time, when asked what he played, he would answer, "shortstop"—naming his position on the local baseball team.

In New Haven, at the Hopkins Grammar School and later at Yale, Ives kept up his professional musical activities side by side with a healthy athletic career. He was always an important member of a baseball or football team, even while conducting the Hyperion Theatre Orchestra and furnishing music for the services of the Center Church, one of the beautiful old structures standing on the Green. With his orchestra, he tried many new ideas and gained the practical knowledge of how to attain the unusual effects which appear in his later scores. At the same time he studied with Horatio Parker, an important composer of the period, for whom he wrote a considerable number of conventional works. However, there were glimmerings of what was to come even in his First Symphony, which Parker found had too many rapid changes of key.

Coming to New York after graduating from Yale in 1898, Ives had to decide whether to remain a professional musician or to take up a more lucrative activity. His views on the musical profession, expressed in his *Essays Before a Sonata*, suggest that he may have felt that it offered too limited a contact with life and was too narrow for a composer with new ideas. To get a good job in music meant "playing the game," writing music that would enhance his prestige. But he was not the man for expedient maneuvers of this kind. He wanted to lead the life of an ordinary citizen with a wife and child raised in a pleasant home, but saw that much of this might have to be sacrificed if he followed music, and that in turn his compositions would have to be limited by the enforced narrowness of a musician's life. So Ives boldly decided to go into business. Being from Connecticut, whose capital, Hartford, was the insurance city, Ives very naturally got into insurance.

He did not relinquish his performing activities at once. His last position was that of organist at the Central Presbyterian Church in New York (1900–1902). While there he wrote parts of the Third Symphony. In business, he first became a clerk for the Mutual Life Insurance Company of New York, where he stayed until 1906. Then, after starting an agency of his own in 1909 with Julian S. Myrick, he formed the firm which later became one of the largest of its kind in the country, Ives and Myrick, managers for the Mutual Life Insurance Company of New York. He retired in 1930 on account of ill health. After 1902, he had retired from the active musical scene, devoting himself quietly at home to composing before and after business hours.

A great body of manuscripts began to accumulate, most of them hastily scribbled, corrected, and revised frequently, which Ives got into shape from time to time. At his own expense, in 1922 and '23, he published a volume of 114 songs and the *Concord Sonata* for piano, which were sent around to the musical profession, leaving most of them scandalized—except a few who have been instrumental in getting Ives's music before the public since the composer made no effort of his own. But his musical ideas were too many to keep pace with his ability to make clear copies, and today, with his eyesight too bad to do much proofreading, there are many scores which still require patient deciphering before they can be performed. Around 1934, he had eleven volumes of chamber music brought out in photostat, some still in a very unclear state.[2] But since that time poor health has prevented him from doing any but a very little work on his music, a thing which would have been unthinkable in his active days.

To have combined such different activities in one life and to have done both so well and with such conviction was to Ives perfectly natural and satisfying in a way that would hardly be so to any other musician. In an interview with Henry Bellamann on the subject, Ives said:

> My business experience revealed life to me in many aspects that I might otherwise have missed. In it one sees tragedy, nobility, meanness, high aims, low aims, brave hopes, faint hopes, great ideals, no ideals, and one is able to watch these work inevitable destiny. And it has seemed to me that the finer sides of these traits were not only in the majority but in the ascendancy. I have seen men fight honorably and to a finish, solely for a matter of conviction or of principle—and where expediency, probable loss of business, prestige, or position had no part and threats no effect. It is my impression that there is more open-mindedness and willingness to examine carefully the premises underlying a new and unfamiliar thing, before condemning it, in the world of business than in the world of music. It is not even uncommon in business intercourse to sense a reflection of philosophy—a depth of something fine—akin to a strong beauty in art. To assume that business is a material process, and only that, is to undervalue the average mind and heart. To an insurance man there *is* an "average man" and he is humanity. I have experienced a great fullness of life in business. The fabric of existence weaves itself whole. You cannot set an art off in the corner and hope for it to have vitality, reality and substance. There can be nothing "exclusive" about a substantial art. It comes directly out of the heart of experience of life and thinking about life and living life. My work in music helped my business and my work in business helped my music.[3]

Charles Ives Remembered
(1974)

In 1924, when I was a student at Horace Mann School in New York City, my music teacher, Clifton Furness, who knew Ives, showed me some of his music. Furness was interested in contemporary arts of all kinds—not only Ives's music, but also various performers of new music like Katherine Ruth Heyman, and artists like the Russian refugees David Burliuk and Nikolai Roerich. Also, through Eugene O'Neill, Jr., a fellow high school student, we followed the lively productions of the Provincetown Playhouse on MacDougal Street in New York. It was an exciting time for the arts: *The Dial*[1] was in full swing:

2. See note by John Kirkpatrick, 92. [S]

3. Henry Bellamann, "Charles Ives: The Man and His Music," *Musical Quarterly* 19, no. 1 (January 1933): 45–58.

---

1. *The Dial*, monthly published in Chicago, 1880–1929. [S]

Ulysses, which we all read, was banned; and O'Neill wrote one remarkable play after another, stirring up a great deal of controversy.

Miss Heyman, a very progressive pianist for those days, had been a friend of Ezra Pound in London before the First World War, had befriended the much neglected Charles Griffes here, and was regarded by her circle as a spokesman for the avant-garde "great" from the immediately previous period, both as a musician and a conversationalist. It was at her weekend afternoons, in a loft apartment on 15th Street and Third Avenue, in a little triangular building (since razed), that I first heard parts of the *Concord Sonata* around 1924 or '25. She played much other new music for her friends then, particularly Griffes, Emerson Whithorne, Dane Rudhyar, Ravel, Debussy, Schoenberg's op. 11 no. 2, and especially Scriabin. The group that came to these dimly lit gatherings admired Scriabin in particular very much. I myself, enthusiastic, soon acquired all the late works at considerable effort and practiced the polyrhythms in works like *Vers la flamme* and the Eighth Etude of op. 42. Ives used to appear occasionally at these private recitals, but whether I met him there for the first time or elsewhere, I really couldn't say.

Both Furness and Miss Heyman, along with a few habitués who came to these séances, were involved with what might be called extramusical ideas. She was committed to mysticism, having been a member of the Annie Besant theosophical circle in her London days, while Furness was drawn to Rudolf Steiner's anthroposophy. I myself read quite a number of Steiner's works with great interest in those days. Therefore, the mystical, transcendental aspect of Ives's music had a particular appeal to the group. There was, however, a strong feeling among this group against Schoenberg's music, which was considered a kind of dangerous black art (the "Satanic" side of Liszt and Scriabin, on the other hand, seemed perfectly OK). From this point of view, Ives was considered a kind of white god and much reverenced. The mystical bias in all of this appealed to an adolescent, though it was not long before I began to feel these judgments unreliable when it came to artistic matters. In retrospect I would have thought that Ives would not have liked this kind of thing.

My impression, then, however, was that Ives had a rather restricted world of musical contacts, limited to the few who really admired his music, and it was understandable that he would be drawn to interested musicians, no matter what their other views, in a desire for human talk about contemporary music.

Ives was certainly involved and interested in music of his time and didn't remain aloof from it: as much as he could be, he was part of it. He was very generous to *New Music Edition,* publisher of modern scores quarterly for years, of which Henry Cowell was editor. Later, when I succeeded Cowell, for a while we continued to receive an annual contribution from Ives of a thousand dollars, which in those days went far to printing modern scores. Besides this help to other composers, Ives subsidized the printing of many of his own scores and his *Essays Before a Sonata* and sent these around to libraries all over the country, including, to my surprise, the library of the American Academy in Rome, where I found copies a few years ago. He was not a recluse in the sense that he didn't want his music to be known to the music profession, even though he looked on that profession with some suspicion; on the contrary, I think he was making a distinct effort to take his place among the composers of his time.

When Ives expressed opinions about the music profession as it existed in his time in America, there was much anger at its timidity and its secondhand cultural attitudes. He expressed himself in the *Essays*, verbally, but also in the many marginal comments in his music manuscripts. Some of the music itself is a direct reflection of his scorn and anger—poking fun at the music profession and sometimes, I think, punishing it with intentionally peculiar cacophony or vulgarity. No American composer can help but understand this attitude. During Ives's lifetime, Dvořák was brought over here to explain and demonstrate what American music should be, and now we subsidize Stockhausen and others as if they could show us the way.

Like many composers of his time, Ives was sensitive about the criticism that the modern composer really didn't know how to write "music." Once in talking about this he told me that in order to prove that he could write in a conventional style, he had written his Third Violin Sonata. He then played this, interjecting comments for my benefit, on a privately made recording by a violinist who had played all four sonatas the previous year, I think, at Aeolian Hall. It was at this same meeting, I believe, that he showed me the score of his First Symphony, written as a student of Horatio Parker, and pointed out details Parker had objected to, particularly modulations that did not follow the then accepted sonata-form formulas. How scornful he was of the latter—saying, as has often been said more recently (and also at that time by Debussy), that the great sonata writers had never followed the rules.

One of the most vivid memories I have of Ives is of an afternoon when he lived on East 22nd Street, near Gramercy Park. It may have been our first meeting, where we were invited after a concert on a Sunday afternoon, which I described in an article in *Modern Music* when my memory was fresher.[2] It was perhaps in the years 1924–25, when I was occasionally invited to sit in the Ives box at the Saturday afternoon Boston Symphony series at Carnegie Hall (to which he subscribed), and I remember returning with him to excited discussions of the new music at his house. I was then very surprised about his attitudes and so remember quite distinctly what he thought. He invariably felt that new pieces like, I think, Ravel's *Daphnis et Chloé* or Stravinsky's *Le Sacre* (although I am not sure about the latter), revealed extremely simple-minded ways of dealing with new harmonies and rhythms. I remember vividly his "take-off" at the piano of the Ravel chord and of the repetitiousness of Stravinsky. Ives was very literate and sharp about this—he seemed to remember quite clearly bits of what he had heard and could parody them surprisingly well. His point was that almost all contemporary composers of the time had chosen the easy way out. Perhaps out of deference to our interests at that time, I don't remember his taking off on Scriabin, although both *Le Poème de*

2. See Elliott Carter, "The Case of Mr. Ives," 87–90 in the present collection. [B]

l'extase and *Prométhée* were heard occasionally then. Scriabin's music might well have been criticized for the same reasons as the others—excessive repetition, mechanical formalism, and the isolation of some small formula in an unwillingness to deal with a large body of musical material. Ives's *Essays*, too, which contain rather pointed asides about Stravinsky and especially Debussy, express some disagreement with his musical contemporaries. But, in spite of what he said, I think Ives had a genuine interest in new music. I remember seeing, to my surprise, the score of Prokofiev's *Love of Three Oranges* lying on a desk in his house in Redding. I couldn't believe he could be interested in Prokofiev at that time, although it was right after the opera, commissioned by the Chicago Opera, had been performed. One of the myths that has grown up about Ives is that he never knew about and never heard contemporary music. This may have been true in his early years, but by the time I met him it was not. By then surely he had heard some of the piano pieces of Schoenberg[3] and Scriabin, and works of Stravinsky and others, and had read about all of these and others in the pages of the *Pro Musica Quarterly*,[4] copies of which he must have received as one of its sponsors, and also the scores of *New Music Edition*, which printed many new works besides his own.

I seem to remember—it's hard for me to believe now—that it used to be said among us that after a few social evenings early in their married life, at which Ives's excited, enthusiastic outbursts had overpowered the gathering, Mrs. Ives had considered it more prudent not to accept such invitations any more, as her husband could not be counted on to take a social situation into account. He was, as is well known, secretive with his business associates about his music. He would tell how he had gone up in the elevator to his office with someone who said, "Ives, you know, yesterday I heard *Parsifal* at the opera. It's a fine thing. You should go to the opera sometimes." He seemed ruefully proud that he kept all of this from the people in the office, but the other side of the story, apparently, was that they all knew of his music but played the game.

He was a complicated, quick, intelligent man with, obviously, an enormous love and wide knowledge of music, and with a determination to follow his own direction, believing in it deeply. Yet he seemed to have been almost unwilling to witness the imperfections of the performances his music received and reluctant to face and solve them. It may have been too disturbing for his excitable nature to discover his works did not come out as he wanted, either because they were not carefully or practically enough marked with dynamic indications—the score of the second movement of the Fourth Symphony,

---

3. After having made this statement, I read in Ives's *Memos*, ed. John Kirkpatrick (New York: W. W. Norton & Co., 1972, 27) that Ives wrote E. Robert Schmitz in 1931 that he had never heard a note of Schoenberg's music, and I realized that he must have been absent on each of the infrequent occasions when Miss Heyman played the Schoenberg piece (op. 11 no. 2). [Supplied by Vivian Perlis for the original publication of this remembrance.]

4. *Pro Musica Quarterly*, periodical published by the Pro Musica (formerly Franco-American) Society, 1920–32. [S]

printed after the 1927 performance, shows an elaboration of dynamic markings seldom found in others—or else because the musicians had not rehearsed sufficiently. So he seems to have avoided concerts where his own music was played, although attending the rehearsals, as he did with the performance of the Fourth Symphony movement. The suspense and excitement of public performance and the ensuing reaction were said to be too much for him to bear. I remember a dismaying demonstration of this overexcitability which occurred when he was playing parts of *Emerson* for me at Redding. A vein on the side of his neck began to bulge as if it were going to burst with the tremendous energy and excitement he was putting into the performance. Apparently accustomed to this, he stopped playing, pinched the vein as if to stop the flow of blood, and went to lie down on a sofa to recover, his wife bringing him a glass of milk. Perhaps he had been warned by a doctor that he must avoid excitement, and it's possible that for this reason he did not go to concerts.

In any case it seems in retrospect he had already begun to withdraw from active life by the time I met him, although this tendency, perhaps, had always existed. But it seemed clear even at that time that there had been a great disillusionment with America as it emerged from the First World War, a crass, materialistic society that no longer lived up to the ideals he so worshiped. I suppose his reputed refusal to read the New York newspapers, subscribing instead to the London *Times*, was a symptom of this. For in talk about contemporary politics, he seemed profoundly disturbed by the bungling and compromising that had gone on with the peace settlement and the postwar negotiations which had destroyed the illusion that the war had been fought for a noble cause.

Yet being the idealistic man he was, such things were not in the foreground of his thought. It was part of his attractiveness that he was so lively, so full of enthusiasm, and, except in the instances mentioned above, not given (at least at any time I saw him) to bitterness and pessimism. In fact, he was so uncritically enthusiastic about the things he cared for that there seemed to be little counterbalancing cool judgment or cynicism, which might have helped him to be more realistic about the notation of his more intricate scores.

A matter which puzzles me still is the question of Ives's revisions of his own scores. I can remember vividly a visit on a late afternoon to his house on East 74th Street, when I was directed to a little top-floor room where Ives sat at a little upright piano with score pages strewn around on the floor and on tables—this must have been around 1929. He was working on, I think, *Three Places in New England*, getting the score ready for performance. A new score was being derived from the older one to which he was adding and changing, turning octaves into sevenths and ninths, and adding dissonant notes.[5] Since

5. *Three Places in New England* was being prepared by Ives and Nicolas Slonimsky for the premiere of the work (1931) by Slonimsky's Boston Chamber Orchestra. (Since the work had originally been scored for full orchestra, it became necessary for Ives to rescore it to accommodate Slonimsky's small orchestra.) [Supplied by Vivian Perlis for the original publication of this remembrance.]

then, I have often wondered at exactly what date a lot of the music written early in his life received its last shot of dissonance and polyrhythm. In this case he showed me quite simply how he was improving the score. I got the impression that he might have frequently jacked up the level of dissonance of many works as his tastes changed. While the question no longer seems important, one could wonder whether he was as early a precursor of "modern" music as is sometimes made out. A study of the manuscripts would probably make this clear. It's obvious to me both from his music and his prose that Ives was really familiar with Debussy, for there are many piano figurations and conceptions of music that seem derived from the French composer, although, of course, he transformed them in a most original and personal way. Ives, although he was not aware of it, probably belonged to the 1890–1920 period with a strong retrospective view of the transcendental–Civil War period. This was brought home to me very intensely at our last meeting.

When my father and mother were living in Westport, Connecticut, I remember driving their car over to Redding with some music, showing it to Ives, and spending a whole day with him talking and walking around in the woods behind his house. My family was so upset about my becoming a musician that I thought I ought to get the advice of respected people before I really broke away and became the rebel I had to be. This was in 1928 or '29, during my college years. Ives was certainly not enthusiastic about the neoclassic music I was then writing. My memory is that he had seen other music of mine before I went to college which he thought more promising and had on the basis of that encouraged me to go on. (Just before Henry Cowell died, he returned one of my boyish compositions submitted to *New Music Edition* in the 1920s that had gotten lost in his files. It wasn't much good, I must say. It's a wonder Ives or anyone else could have seen anything in it.) That day was the last I saw Ives, except for occasional times when I used to take the morning train from Westport to New York during the summer, which stopped at South Norwalk and picked up passengers from the Danbury spur, among whom occasionally was Ives on his way to his office. When I saw him get on, I usually would wait until the last stop before New York before going to talk to him.

Ives's influence on my music has varied greatly from 1924 to now. It was very important before I actually decided to become a musician. But when I began to study music formally at college in 1926, its value for me diminished a great deal, because I was anxious to learn how to write music step by step, not only by traditional methods but from the new music that was within my grasp to imagine auditively and to formulate clear ideas about. From that time there was a mounting sense of frustration when I returned to Ives's music, which I have done frequently, because much of it then seemed so disordered and even disorganized that, given the point of view I held then, it was nearly impossible to understand how or why much of it was put together as it was. This experience, coupled with a growing anti-Romantic outlook characteristic of most young composers of the 1930s and '40s, led me to try to cultivate clarity and sharp definition of musical material, qualities antithetical to Ives's work.

Out of this attitude, a distressing dilemma arose, for when John Kirkpatrick finally gave the first performance of the complete *Concord Sonata* at Town Hall in 1939, I was disappointed in the piece that had previously meant so much to me. Unfortunately, being the critic for the magazine *Modern Music* and being quite knowledgeable about the sonata and about Ives, I felt I had to write a long review of the work expressing my views.[6] The critic's obligation to speak his thoughts frankly, painful as it was to me as one who wanted to admire Ives, made me very sad. After what I wrote then, I never had the heart to see Ives again.

Later, in the mid-1940s, I began to think I had been wrong about the *Concord Sonata*, that I should go back and reconsider all of Ives's works more closely.[7] I plowed patiently through the eleven-volume photostat collection of his unpublished works that Ives had deposited at the American Music Center.[8] As I did, frequently surprised and delighted, I began to list pages out of order, hardly legible, or apparently missing. It became clear to me that a great deal of work needed to be done to get some of the manuscripts in shape for performance, and it would help if Ives could be consulted, even in his sickness, before he died. I got in touch with Mrs. Ives to propose such a project, asking if Ives would cooperate. They agreed, so I began to work on one piece after another, raising questions, planning for copying. Unfortunately I found very quickly that I was temperamentally unsuited to unscramble the confusion of many of the manuscript sketches. Not only would they take inordinate amounts of time (with no certainly that an actual piece would emerge), but I could not make the rough decisions necessary, for only too frequently there was a palimpsest of three or four alternatives. The mounting sense of confusion with which his music has at times overwhelmed me was at this juncture too much for me to take, and I stopped, but not before finding others, in particular Lou Harrison and Henry Cowell, who were devoted to the project and more able to face its problems.

As I scanned the Ives manuscripts, the Fourth Symphony looked the largest and the most important. However, unlike the other three movements, the last was scribbled in pencil with many perplexing alternatives sketched in the margins. I remember a few measures for six trombones, a number never called for again. I began to wonder whether this movement could ever be gotten into playable shape. The second movement was printed after a concert performance in 1927 (Ives had invited the New York Philharmonic percussionists to his house and beaten out the complicated rhythms on the dining room table until they learned them). Its markings, as I have said, are much more elaborate and more carefully done than in any other Ives scores—which usually content themselves with very vague indications that

---

6. Carter, "The Case of Mr. Ives." [Supplied by Vivian Perlis for the original publication of this remembrance.]

7. See two articles that Carter wrote in the 1940s, "Ives Today: His Vision and Challenge" and "An American Destiny," 90–93 and 93–98 respectively in the present collection. [B]

8. See note by John Kirkpatrick, 92. [S]

force the performer, often, to invent his own. Perhaps if Ives had had more and better performances during his life, the other scores would have been similarly marked.

The first and third movements of the Fourth Symphony have been printed very much as they appeared in the photostatted volumes. The third, which is about seventy-five percent the same as the first movement of the First String Quartet, has a few irregular bar lengths, polyrhythms, and dissonances added especially at the expanded climax near the end. Comparison between these two shows, in small, how Ives revised his works to suit the changes brought about by his musical development, as do, in a much more problematic way, the incorporation of parts of the "Hawthorne" movement of the *Concord Sonata* into the piano part of the second movement of the Fourth Symphony.

It is most mysterious that it took musicians and public so long to catch on to the fact of Ives's music, once the contemporary movement began to take hold in the United States during the 1920s. Quite late, perhaps during the Second World War, I can remember talking Ives over with Goddard Lieberson,[9] who in turn arranged a lunch with Stokowski to try to convince him that there were a lot of remarkable pieces that ought to be played. The latter was very cautious, saying that the works were complicated, hard to rehearse, and would take much more time to prepare than could be arranged for.

With this and similar scenes in mind, I attended the ISCM festival in Baden-Baden in 1955, the year after Ives died, being one of the members of the Central Committee and having my Cello Sonata played there. I was immediately impressed by what was, to me, extraordinary, for I witnessed what was said to be the fiftieth (or so) rehearsal of Boulez's *Marteau sans maître*, at which the conductor, Hans Rosbaud, was still picking apart little details, patiently getting an instrument to play the part exactly as written and with the right dynamics, and so on. I immediately went to the director of the Südwestfunk (SWF), Dr. Heinrich Strobel, and told him, "You know, there's a very wonderful work of Ives, the Fourth Symphony, that the SWF Orchestra should play. It is probably the only orchestra that could afford the rehearsals of such a complicated piece, and with its conductor who is so interested in new music and so painstaking with it, you would be helping the cause of new music by presenting this important work in a fine, well-rehearsed performance." Strobel got in touch with the various people in the United States who had custody of the score, as I suggested. This led to those in the United States being disturbed by the possibility that the German radio might get the first performance of the work, and so they busied themselves with getting the score, especially the last movement, in shape, copying the parts, and finally convincing Stokowski to do it. It took a request by the German radio to get the ball rolling, which ended in the typically American "big-time publicity" given to Ives's music.[10]

9. See Goddard Lieberson's recollections in Vivian Perlis, *Charles Ives Remembered: An Oral History* (New Haven: Yale University Press, 1974), 206–9. [Supplied by Vivian Perlis for the original publication of this remembrance.]

10. During the preparation of the score and parts of the Fourth Symphony for its first completed

Many another remarkable piece, like the *Robert Browning Overture*, had to wait until the publicity had sifted down and done its work, while prior to this, efforts to get the orchestral works played in America by the major orchestras met with the kind of rebuff I described (except during the 1930s when Nicolas Slonimsky conducted a few, as did Bernard Herrmann).

In spite of the efforts of some of us to get Ives's scores in shape, the declining health of Ives and his consequent inability to check the orchestra parts of some of his available works meant that some of these were very badly, at times unprofessionally, copied. I know this, because when I was on another jury in Italy, I happened to have with me the old printed score of *The Fourth of July*, which I'd owned for a long time. When I presented this score to the music director of the Italian Radio (who had never seen it), he burst with enthusiasm and said, "We've got to play this—it's one of the most interesting pieces I've ever seen." (Quite different from the reactions one used to get from musicians in important positions in the United States.) So the Italian Radio sent for the parts, which turned out to be so mixed up and confusing that the radio librarian had to have them copied all over again. The director of the radio station was quite angry and almost canceled the performance because of the mess in the original parts, which, I believe, Ives had had extracted for *New Music*. Now the work has been brought out by another publisher, and there are probably better parts.

Each work has its difficulties because of Ives's inability in his later years to cope with musical situations. I remember that after I had looked through the volumes of photostatted manuscripts, two of the works which intrigued me a great deal were *The Unanswered Question* and *Central Park in the Dark*. As I was then teaching at Columbia University and there was an annual Ditson Festival, I persuaded the festival committee to include premieres of these two works on the program of 11 May 1946. I wrote to Mrs. Ives to ask if these were in fact first performances, and for other program information. She wrote back a very charming letter quoting her ill husband, that they would not want to say those works were having their premieres—Mr. Ives wanted to be fair to those "old fellers" who had played them in between the acts of a theatrical performance around 1907 or 1908.

I don't think Ives had much influence on other composers until the Fourth Symphony publicity after his death; for Ives's music is, for the most part, very programmatic, and during the period of his life most composers of concert music were interested in writing "abstract" music, that is, music that depends on its design for its expression. Movie scores are another matter, and

performance by the American Symphony Orchestra under Leopold Stokowski (26 April 1965), it was discovered that a few pages from the fourth movement were missing from the American Music Center's collection of photostats of Ives's music. A search was made and these pages were found. It was claimed that the fourth movement had been lost and was recovered as a result of the first performance preparations. Actually, all of the manuscript pages were complete and safe in West Redding, and it was only a few pages of negative photostats which had been temporarily mislaid. [Supplied by Vivian Perlis for the original publication of this remembrance.]

certainly those of Bernard Herrmann, who performed a lot of Ives's music with the CBS Symphony in the late 1930s and '40s, were much influenced, particularly the one for *The Red Badge of Courage*, which sounds very much like Ives, I think.

As for myself, I have always been fascinated by the polyrhythmic aspect of Ives's music, as well as its multiple layering, but perplexed at times by the disturbing lack of musical and stylistic continuity, caused largely by the constant use of musical quotations in many works. To me a composer develops his own personal language, suitable to express his field of experience and thought. When he borrows music from another style and thought than his own, he is admitting that he did not really experience what he is presenting but has to borrow from someone else who did. In the case of early music, like masses on *L'homme armé*, or cantatas on Lutheran chorales, the original melody has a deep religious meaning so that, understandably, a very devout composer feels he needs to borrow it as a basis, since its expression transcends his own religious experience. These old tunes both united the composer to his listener and were very close in style to the music for which they formed a basis. At the other extreme of borrowing are the endless variations on popular or famous tunes in the nineteenth century, a very few of which produced great music, not really because of the tunes. Then there were the entertaining potpourris or medleys of patriotic airs, sometimes arranged humorously for band concerts; these have no artistic pretensions and reveal little fundamental musical imagination. Some of Ives's works belong close to this latter category, except for his daring "take-off" technique that often makes these pieces resemble "realistic" sound pictures of festive scenes. It is, to me, disappointing that Ives too frequently was unable or unwilling to invent musical material that expressed his own vision authentically, instead of relying on the material of others. But what is striking and remarkable in his work, like much of the First and Second Piano Sonatas, is an extraordinary musical achievement.

Documents of a Friendship with Ives
(1975)

These letters and sketches of letters which the curator of the Ives Collection at Yale University, Mr. John Kirkpatrick, has been kind enough to allow us to copy give the history of a warm and inspiring friendship with Charles Ives. It started around 1924, when Clifton Furness, my music teacher at the Horace Mann School, introduced me to him. From what I can remember, we went to Ives's house by Gramercy Park on a dark, rainy Sunday and stepped into a cheery, old-fashioned interior, where we excitedly discussed modern music all afternoon. After this, I met Ives occasionally, sometimes when he invited me to join Mrs. Ives and him in their box at the Saturday afternoon Boston Symphony concerts at Carnegie Hall, or at Katherine Ruth Heyman's loft in a building that no longer exists, on Third Avenue and 10th Street huddling under the El, or later at his house on East 74th Street opposite the Mannes School.

To assist my entrance into Harvard in 1926, Ives graciously allowed me to use his name as a reference in my application for admission as a freshman. The typescript copy, which has scrawled across the top in his handwriting, "letter to Harvard Dean in re Elliot [sic] Carter," has this to say:

> Carter strikes me as rather an exceptional boy. He has an instinctive interest in literature and especially music that is somewhat unusual. He writes well—an essay in his school paper—"Symbolism in Art"—shows an interesting mind. I don't know him intimately, but his teacher in Horace Mann School, Mr. Clifton J. Furness, and a friend of mine, always speaks well of him—that he's a boy of good character and does well in his studies. I am sure his reliability, industry, and sense of honour are what they should be—also his sense of humour which you do not ask me about.

After going to live in Cambridge, I was to return fairly often to New York either by hitchhiking or by train, especially for concerts of contemporary music, and kept in touch with Ives, as the next two letters show. The first was written just after the first performance of the second movement of Ives's Fourth Symphony, given in New York at a Pro Musica concert under the direction of Eugene Goossens. This Pro Musica Society, which listed Ives as a sponsor on all its programs and periodicals, gave many seasons of concerts of contemporary music in New York, as did its chapters around the country, and published an important magazine, *Pro Musica Quarterly*. It also sponsored the first tours of Bartók and Prokofiev around the U.S. At the time of this letter, the organization was sponsoring a tour of Darius Milhaud.

C–22 George Smith Hall
Cambridge Mass.
Feb. 19, 1927.

Dear Mr. Ives,
    I am sorry that I was unable to come to see you that Sunday afternoon nor later to hear your symphony. As I am interested very much in your music I would like to *hear* it once instead of having to *work* over it to make it sound at all.
    I wonder if it would be possible to have a few more records of your violin sonata. Or is the stamp lost? Recently I have been greatly interested in recordings. I have eight records of 'Pelleas and Melisande', 'Pacific 231', Stravinsky's 'Petrouchka', 'Firebird', 'Ragtime', as well as Scriabine's 'Poem of Ecstasy'—only to mention moderns. I find the victrola a great help in studying Beethoven and Brahms. Unfortunately very little good Bach has been done.
    I am sending you a very interesting magazine dealing with recordings entirely. In it, this month, has appeared an account of private recordings. I wonder if Pro-Musica could not have a department for recording its more popular modern works. 'Pierrot Lunaire' and other things are waiting to be done as well as some Scriabine.
    The subscription record idea seems a very good one (at least to me) and would help in the understanding of modern music. I wish it were possible to start a modern music group here in Boston—it has never been done though we hear a great deal from Koussewitsky.

I am coming to Miss Heyman's concert Sunday evening Feb. 27. I hope I shall see you there.

Sincerely yours,
(Signed) Elliott C. Carter, Jr.[1]

The violin sonata referred to in this letter was the Third, privately recorded by Jerome Goldstein, I think. Miss Katherine Ruth Heyman, another friend of Ives, was an American pianist who had lived during the Bloomsbury days in London (Ezra Pound dedicated "Scriptor Ignotus" in *A Lume Spento* to her) but at this time was New York's principal exponent of Scriabin's music, as well as that of other moderns—Ravel, Schoenberg, and Americans like Emerson Whithorne, Charles Griffes, and Ives. Her book, *The Relation of Ultra-Modern to Archaic Music*, along with Claude Bragdon's *Dynamic Symmetry* and Ouspensky's *Tertium Organum*, was almost required reading for this somewhat Blavatskian circle.

The above letter reveals a concern for the presentation of contemporary music to the public, an activity which was to absorb almost all of my time in the late 1930s, '40s, and '50s, what with writing reviews and organizing concert seasons of modern music for the League of Composers and the International Society for Contemporary Music.

The next letter to Ives from Cambridge, with date and address left off, revealing no doubt the progress of my education, can be dated by the mention of Rudhyar's *Paeans*, published in January 1928. All the music of mine it refers to has been lost except a setting of Joyce in 5/8 time submitted to *New Music Quarterly* around the period of this letter and neither published nor returned until a few years ago when Henry Cowell turned it up among his old papers. *New Music Quarterly* (later called *New Music Edition*) was devoted to the publication of "modern" scores no other publisher would print. It was run single-handed by Cowell from October 1927 (its inaugural issue was the score of Ruggles's *Men and Mountains* discussed in this letter) to around 1942, when Cowell tried to retire and encouraged a number of us, including myself, to run it. We shortly turned the entire catalogue of music over to a commercial publisher. *New Music*, I presume, was partially subsidized by Ives from its inception. When I was its president we received a contribution of a thousand dollars from him annually. It was said among us that he had subsidized the publication of his own large orchestral scores and perhaps those of Ruggles and Cowell.

New Music fulfilled the same role in music that the old *Dial* or *transition* did in literature. It made known the work of North Americans primarily, some Central and South Americans, some radical Soviet composers, and assorted others, including the first publications anywhere of Schoenberg's *Klavierstück*, op. 33b, and Webern's *Drei Volkstexte*, op. 17 no. 2.

Among its steadies were, of course, Ives, Ruggles, Ruth Crawford, Carlos

---

1. A facsimile reproduction of this letter appears in Vivian Perlis, *Charles Ives Remembered: An Oral History* (New Haven: Yale University Press, 1974), 132. [S]

Chávez, and Dane Rudhyar. Enthusiasm for the music of the last-named, discussed below (who, besides being a composer, is an astrologer—his real name
is Daniel Chennevière), has grown since I have come to know more of his
music.

The following letter seems to be a thank-you note for scores Ives sent me.
The *New Music* scores (Ruggles's *Men and Mountains* and Rudhyar's
Paeans), being among the *Quarterly*'s first publications, were probably sent as
an inducement to subscribe. The Ives Violin Sonata (the First, of which I still
have the photostat copy) apparently was also included, as, perhaps, were the
Three Transcriptions from Emerson in photostat (which I later heard Ives
play at Redding) drawn from the "Emerson" movement of the *Concord
Sonata*. Several years before this, Ives had given me a printed version of the
latter with quite a number of notational changes in his hand, which I have
treasured for years.

> Dear Mr. Ives,
>   These examinations are something of a waste of time and they have taken me
> away from my music. Before they began I wrote two more songs and planned
> partly another movement of that string quartet.
>   I am getting together some fellows up here to play it and also that violin sonata
> of yours. I have not had time to look it over but it looks very good so far. I have not
> tried to fit the Emerson movement together yet. But the violin sonata seems to me
> to have the quiet emotionality which is the real inspiration of music. Music should
> be admitted to have an effect on people and more that has a good effect should be
> played.
>   Your violin sonata seems to make ideals and serenity sprout out of one as
> Brahms and Bach do. Mr. Furness has played Emerson for me and I think it is won-
> derful too. I have always wanted to hear you play these and possibly learn some
> one of them (as much as my poor technique would allow.)
>   And then too those. . . . *New Music*. That is really a great thing. Henry Cowell
> deserves much praise. I can hear some of 'Men and Mountains' but Rhudyar's [sic]
> 'Paeans' are good but they seem a little too majestic, too much of his own greatness
> taken for granted.
>   Anyhow, thank you very much for all these, they will last long and mean much.
> More, now, than I can say and certainly more than I have as yet discovered.
>
> (Signed) Elliott C. Carter, Jr.

My meetings with Ives stopped when, like many others who must have felt
as I did, I left the conservative teaching I had been receiving in America for
that of a more progressive Europe. In the United States, at that time, contemporary music was generally brushed aside by most musicians as the work of
lunatics. I had complained to Ives that most of my teachers, except for Walter
Piston, seemed to hold this opinion. I was particularly disgusted by and
scornful of those who raged, appalled, against Ives's work after having
thumbed through the privately printed scores he had sent to many college libraries. Understanding my attitude, Walter Piston advised me to study with

someone who took contemporary music seriously: Mlle. Nadia Boulanger, and this took me to Paris. I returned to the U.S. of the Depression in 1935, but remained out of touch with Ives until our paths crossed in what was for me, at least, a disastrously traumatic way.

For, as a sometime-critic (for the magazine *Modern Music*) I was put into the personally very dismaying situation—routine, probably, for professionals (else how to explain their callousness)—of having to give an unfavorable review of a work which I had once loved and whose composer, Ives, I counted as one of my great friends. I had to review the world premiere of his *Concord Sonata* given by John Kirkpatrick at Town Hall, New York, on 20 January 1939. This was the first of two performances, because hardly any critics except for Lawrence Gilman and myself, indeed hardly anyone, showed up. At Gilman's suggestion it was decided to repeat the concert about a month later after a concentrated publicity campaign had been undertaken—which did succeed in bringing in public and critics—proving what should have been obvious: that most music critics do not review, nor does the public applaud, the music *per se*, but rather the publicity that surrounds it—the present explosion of interest in Ives unfortunately being no exception.

By the time this premiere took place my taste in contemporary music had changed considerably from my college days. With the extravagant, bawling, impassioned demagoguery we witnessed on newsreels and heard on the radio emanating from Italy and Germany, it was hard to be taken in by or even be sympathetic to Romantic flamboyant gestures of any kind as we once were (sometimes in a joking way) and were to be again. At that particular time Ives's *Concord Sonata*, for all its qualities, seemed, at least to me, to have a strong element of extravagant Romantic gestures, however sincere, and it was impossible for me not to express my genuine antipathy to them, even though by doing so I was violating something I treasured a great deal. I don't know how much Ives was hurt by what I wrote. I know that I was deeply, so much so that I never had the heart to see him again.

From that time the distress caused by my own review, coupled with a growing sense of how remarkable the man and his music were, as I recaptured my early point of view, led me to take practical actions to further Ives's cause. My new thoughts were expressed in two articles published during the 1940s.[2] Replying to me about the first of these, Ives, as was his habit during these years, wrote out a rough first sketch and then a second, more finished one, in pencil in his irregular, nervous handwriting. Oddly, these were written from the point of view of Mrs. Ives, who then would transcribe and sign the letter. Here is the final version sent to me by Mrs. Ives—12 June 1944.

Dear Mr. Carter—
I am writing for Mr. Ives who, as you know is not well and it is difficult for him to do so.

2. See "Charles Ives: His Vision and Challenge" and "An American Destiny," 90–93 and 93–98 in the present collection. [B]

He appreciates very much your interest in his music and your kindness in writing the article in Modern Music Review. You have put things in a most interesting way. He feels there are some things not quite accurately referred to—though it is hardly your fault.

For instance, the 2nd Symphony was for the most part completed before Mr. Ives' father died fifty years ago (tho' it was fully scored a few years later) & Mr. Ives had not then heard or seen any of Dvorak's music which you assumed influenced this symphony. He says the themes in this were a kind of reflection of—or at least a hope to express in some way—the spirit of Stephen Foster, even if occasionally some of the old barn dance tunes were strewn over it—also themes from the old Camp Meeting hymn tunes, and in the last movement the stirring excitement the boys felt when the Danbury Cornet band of the '80s was marching down Main St. playing "The Red, White & Blue."

The 3rd Symphony, particularly the 1st & 3rd Movements he played as organ pieces and so not as fully as in the score in church services over 40 years ago and before he had heard or known any of Caesar [sic] Franck's music which it is inferred influenced it.

The last movement of the Holiday Symphony "Forefather's Day" Mr. Ives feels strongly is not dithyrambic—at least he hopes it reflects in no way the sallies of a crowd of revellers of Bacchus—no more than does that great solemn old hymn which a chorus sings towards the end of the Movement "O God, beneath Thy guiding hand Our exiled Fathers crossed the Sea."

In his chamber music there may be, he says, a poor joke or two but no parody of modern music was intended.

We hope that the inference in the last paragraph that no real consideration has ever been given to his music will not be misunderstood, that is, taken too literally nor seem unfair to those who have played, sung, conducted some of his music, written about it & "stood up for it" even when, as he says, some of them felt that in so doing they would probably get in wrong with some of "the powers that be"— & be not for that matter.

However, most of the above matters are secondary and rather unimportant. He feels that your thoughts as to the fundamentals of music are "thoughtfully and beautifully expressed" and that they seem to suggest something that may be seen in a "scenic landscape of an Art-Philosophy"—

He is deeply grateful for what you have done on behalf of his music & sends you his sincere thanks.

We were so glad to see that your Symphonies are being played & hope they were well performed & fully appreciated.

Mr. Ives hopes when he is better to have the pleasure of seeing you again.

With kindest remembrances from both of us I am

Sincerely yours
Harmony Ives

I cannot resist, however, making a few comments on the changes that occurred between the three versions of this letter. Ives's first sketch is far more friendly then either the second sketch or Mrs. Ives's copy.[3] The first version

3. A facsimile reproduction of the first page of the second sketch appears in Perlis, *Charles Ives Remembered*, 140. [S]

remarked in the first paragraph "a very well-written article," which recurred in the second but was crossed out. The short paragraph about the chamber music did not appear until the second sketch, nor did the sentence about being unfair to those who have performed the music. Evidently Ives read my article several times and became more and more severe about it. This caused him to eliminate the touching references to their cat, occurring only in the first sketch, with which it concludes:

> . . . and sends you his sincere thanks. He hopes to have the pleasure of seeing you again—and we won't let that old cat crawl on your shoulder again and try to take your coat off—You remember that happy day—She is now nearly 20 years old and now so polite and sedate. With kindest remembrance, Yours —————.

This last is a reference to what was an embarrassing moment for me as a youth at the Iveses' house, when their kitten crawled into the sleeve of my jacket and wandered around inside it behind my back, while I was trying to appear calm and collected. We had often laughed over this. It is entirely possible that if I had received the first version of this at the time, instead of seeing it for the first time now, I would have immediately gone to see him. Then, I received the version above addressed "Dear Mr. Carter," while all other letters were addressed "Dear Elliott."

Continuing my active efforts for Ives's music, I decided to start an Ives Society with the primary aim of getting some of his more muddled manuscripts into playable shape, with clear copies of score and practical parts, while he was still around to help with advice. This project was to be a special one connected with the American Music Center.

The following letter is self-explanatory.

Chairman of the Board: Otto Luening—Executive Secretary: Harrison Kerr—
Assistant Secretary: Shirley Brandt—Treasurer: Marion Bauer—
Assistant Treasurers: Aaron Copland, Douglas Moore, Quincy Porter

AMERICAN MUSIC CENTER, Inc.
250 West 57th Street, New York 19, N.Y.
For the Distribution of Published and Recorded American Music

Board of Directors: Marion Bauer—Aaron Copland—
Howard Hanson—Philip James—Harrison Kerr—Otto Luening—
Douglas Moore—Quincy Porter—Oscar Wagner
October 20th, 1944

Mr. Charles E. Ives
West Redding, Connecticut

Dear Mr. Ives:

In recognition of your outstanding achievement as a composer, and in acknowledgment of the many contributions you have made to the cause of American music, the Charles Ives Society wishes to send you greetings on your 70th birthday.

Representing a group of creative people to be known as the Charles Ives Society, I wish to tell you that it is our intention to assist in familiarizing the people with your works, feeling that they are entitled to the widest possible understanding.

Sincerely yours,
(Signed) Elliott Carter

This provoked the following reply, which exists in the Yale archives only in Ives's first and second pencil sketches, which differ primarily in that the first is warmer in tone while the second is more coherent—I give the second here. The words in parentheses are inserts, sometimes substituting for and sometimes adding to the text:

Mr. Ives was deeply affected by your kind letter and says he cannot find words to express his great appreciation of all you, Henry, and other kind friends are doing on his behalf but he feels that he doesn't deserve it all—and to form a society named after him is not fair to many other American composers and also that it will bring you all too much trouble and take too much (of your) time.

Just now he is so overcome and so embarrassed that he doesn't know what he ought to do about it all. When Henry wrote that an informal committee has been formed he felt somewhat embarrassed about that—but a Charles Ives Society of new composers[4] that's too much he says unless not only his name but the names of all American composers your committee approves of, can be nailed all over it.

He is not at all well as you may know, and can't do many things he would like to, or take an active part in any work (he couldn't go to meetings) and so he feels he should not let his generous friends put themselves so much out for his sake, he says. There are other composers (he says) who need your help too—among them Carl Ruggles, and in the next generation Henry Cowell and a younger friend of his, Elliott Carter, whom you probably know (may have met) and also others whose music should be widely known and often played.

But he does thank you all from the bottom of his heart.

He doesn't feel quite right about having a society named after him (he says it makes him feel like "sort of like a Hog") some of his friends (on the high way) may infer as has happened before that there is an old friend he doesn't stand up for enough—that one "is his music."

However, later on when he is better able to attend to things—and hears whatever you do, Henry, and other friends think ought to be done, he will try to do.

But he does thank you from the bottom of his heart all for your generous friendship and interest.

The Ives Society project continued for a number of years and involved the devoted activities of Henry Cowell and Lou Harrison, who prepared the scores of the *Robert Browning Overture*, the Second and Third Symphonies, and the First Piano Sonata, among other things, for performance

---

4. The previous three words have been crossed out in the original; "new" is a conjecture—only the "n" is legible.

and publication. I remember working on the Trio for violin, cello, and piano. This effort, which was mainly concerned with scores of which Ives had never had the occasion to make a fair copy, consisted not only in deciding which of the many palimpsest version of the MSS were usable but sometimes in composing little connecting passages, submitted, of course, for Ives's approval. In all of this, I found myself becoming more and more aloof, for the confusion found in many of the manuscripts began to keep me awake nights trying to decide how to make Ives's highly personal music emerge from his incomplete and often jumbled sketches.

During these years, I met quite regularly with Paul Rosenfeld, the most intelligent and hospitable critic American music has had the good fortune to have, to plan a book on Ives—he taking care of the biography and I the music. This was cut short by his death in 1946.[5]

In the spring of 1946, Columbia University, which had inaugurated an annual series of festivals of contemporary American music, was persuaded to present some of Ives's works. At first, it was uncertain whether *The Unanswered Question* and *Central Park in the Dark*, which I was particularly anxious to have performed since no one had heard them and few even knew of their existence, would be part of a concert of Ives's works or not, and so a series of communications about other possible works took place to gather information, as the following answers by Mrs. Ives to my various requests show:

164 East 74th Street
March 14, 1946

Dear Elliott—
    Mr. Ives thinks the enclosed may do as programme notes to the 3rd Symphony. He had some notes years ago but they are not around any more now. We think Herrmann's article nicely expressed.[6]
    If it is too long the sentences marked may be omitted.
    Hoping this will answer—Mr. Ives greatly appreciates all you are doing and hopes someday he may do something for you—
    Mr. Ives will be glad to have Mr. Pagano make a copy of the Symphony and says it must be done only at his expense—As he remembers there were 2 or 3 measures in the 1st violin and flute parts in which a note or two were not as they were in the old sketch. The last time he played it over several years ago the first way seemed better. However he says they were unimportant, and this page could be made over easily later after the score is copied. Also at the very end a kind of ad lib. chords for bells off stage were to represent distant church bells—but they can be left out until the sketch copy can be found—
    Of course Mr. Pagano will understand that the clarinet and horn parts are in the actual notes and not transposed as they should be in the score and also the viola part is not always in the viola clef—As I said to you over the phone the other day,

5. See Carter, "The Genial Sage," 306–307 in the present collection. [B]

6. Bernard Herrmann, "Four Symphonies by Charles Ives," *Modern Music* 22, no. 4 (May–June 1945): 215–22. [S]

the key signatures sometimes left out are throughout in the 1st movement B♭ and in the 2nd E♭ and in the 3rd B♭.

Mr. Ives says he hates to give you all this trouble—he feels it is an imposition and is very sorry!

With our best wishes

Sincerely yours
Harmony T. Ives

Mr. Carl Pagano, who for many years has been a great help to contemporary American composers through his patient and careful efforts as a copyist of their scores, had become quite an expert in dealing with Ives's scores. Part of the activity of the Ives Society of that time was meeting with Mrs. Ives to ask her to find out which scores Mr. Ives wanted to have worked on, then "editing" them when necessary, giving them to Mr. Pagano to copy and extract parts, and then proofreading these. Henry Cowell also became active at this time in persuading publishers to accept these works for publication. There had been a parallel effort by Bernard Herrmann, the conductor of the Columbia Broadcasting Orchestra, to get some works into performable shape, and he gave a number for the first time over the air and had written an enthusiastic article about Ives's work, mentioned in the above letter. The next letter followed immediately:

164 East 74th Street
New York City
Sat. Ma. 16 1946

Dear Elliott

Mr. Ives has decided he wants one sentence in the Herrmann notes left out—The last sentence in the first paragraph.

'Ives in the role of preacher speaks words of comfort, tenderness & hope.'

He feels that it is appropriate in a magazine article but not in a programme note,

With best wishes

Sincerely
Harmony T. Ives

P.S. It would be well, Mr. Ives thinks that the title of the score 'Central Park in the Dark' be changed to 'Central Park in the Dark Some Forty Years Ago.'

We are giving you lots of trouble.
[top of the next page] *Unanswered Question*

Enclosed is a page from the 'Boletín Latino-Americano de Música' which is marked to show that the passage in the square should be in the upper part of the score staves and not where it is written in the lower ones.

Mr. Ives doesn't know if Mr. Schenkman is using this score—he has no photostat score here but doesn't think it is put down this way in the latter.

Mr. Ives doesn't know if it will help to have the notes on the 2nd Str. Quartet used—and says to do whatever you think best.

As the Columbia University concert approached, plans for it began to change. For one thing Lou Harrison conducted a New York performance of the Third Symphony (which was to win Ives the Pulitzer Prize for that year), and it was decided to include some works of Ruggles on the concert. So a further telephone call elicited this letter:

164 East 74th Street
New York City 21
April 9th 1946

Dear Elliott,

Miss Dower telephoned me today asking me for programme notes & dates to be sent to you for the Columbia concert on May 21st.

On the last page of both scores 'The Unanswered Question (or Cosmic Landscape)' & the 'Central Park in the Dark Some 40 years ago' are typewritten photostat copies giving some description of the music from which programme notes could easily be made. These scores we think are at the Music Center. If not we will have photostat copies made & sent to you tho' if you are in a hurry for these it might save time if you call the Quality Photostat Studio—VA6-3058—& order them—the bill to be sent to Mr. Ives of course. Ask for Index nos. 229–230.

As to the 2nd Violin Sonata Mr. Ives says the titles to the 3 movements would almost do as programme notes. 1. Autumn. 2. Barn Dance. 3. A Revival.
The dates you ask for are 'The Unanswered Question'—sometime before June 1908 'Central Park in the Dark—' 1906 2nd Violin Sonata—1903–1910.

Mr. Ives hopes you do realize how very appreciative he is of all you have done & are doing for his music—You will of course send bills for any expense incurred to him. We are going to West Redding on the 15th of this month I think you have our telephone number if there is anything further you want to ask about.

I enjoyed the concert so much & was so glad Lou Harrison got such good criticism.
With our warmest best wishes

Sincerely yours
Harmony T. Ives

In the Yale Library there is, in Ives's hand, a "sketch for postscript to 9 apr. 46 (not sent)":

Though it is not an important matter, it would be well,—unless the programs for your May concert are already printed—not to put as a first public performance the 'Central Park—some 40 years ago'.

As it was cut down some in instrumentation for Theater orchestra (Mr. Ives doesn't remember the details) and (it) played between the acts in a downtown Theater in NY.

—He doesn't remember the exact date or the name of the Theater. There was no programme, but he thinks it was in 1906 or '07.

The players had a hard time with it—the piano player got mad, stopped in the middle and kicked in the Bass Drum. However don't put the above in the program—just not 'First Performance'—as he feels if not, it would be hardly fair to those old 'fellers' who stood up for a 'dangerous job.'

After the concert, since I was in touch with Mrs. Ives by phone, I called her up to have her tell Mr. Ives about the strong impression his works had made on many of us. We had done *The Unanswered Question* and *Central Park* at McMillan Theater with the "off-stage" string orchestra behind a curtain and the other orchestra in front of it, which gave a particularly magical effect.

After this, I was frequently away from New York, and there seems to have been no correspondence until I learned of Ives's death while I was a Fellow at the American Academy in Rome in 1954. My letter of condolence to Mrs. Ives, not yet found, was answered:

West Redding
Connecticut
October 3, 1954

Dear Elliott,
    From the length of time it has taken me to acknowledge your most kind and truly valued letter written to me at the time my husband died you might think I was not as moved by it as I was—I loved the things you said about him. I remember your visit here and Mr. Ives telling me, 'He says people think I'm crazy, *really crazy*'—and he used to recall that remark rather with wonderment.
    I am by no means adjusted to a life without him. He has for so many years been my care and my joy that my life seems emptied of its contents and I do not know how I shall fill it.
    Henry Cowell tells me you are still abroad—I know Rome and love it—better than Florence and hope you are gaining inspiration and laying up a store of rich memories and experiences.
Thank you so warmly

with kindest wishes
Harmony T. Ives

    John Kirkpatrick and Henry Cowell have been a great help to me in going over and rearranging Mr. Ives' MSS which are in a state of confusion.

IV

Some Other Composers

Gabriel Fauré
(1945)

There is no better example of the power of persuasion in the music of recent times than in the compositions of Gabriel Fauré. Unlike other musicians writing around the turn of the century, he was not interested in attracting the listener by large dramatic effects or sumptuous orchestration. Neither did he believe in the exploitation of any other of those extremes of musical language which overcome the listener by their violence or strangeness and all too quickly lose their effect. His music has a precision of outline, a marvelous clarity, and an intimacy of expression that differentiates it from that of his younger and more widely known contemporaries, Debussy and Ravel. It is the work of a man both simple and modest whose warmth of feeling and loving kindness reveal themselves in every detail. It is by these rare qualities that Fauré stands out as one of the great figures of French music.

During the seventy-nine years of his life, he saw the passing of Bizet, Saint-Saëns, and César Franck and the rise of Debussy, Ravel, and Stravinsky, and his penetrating criticisms for the newspaper *Le Figaro* show us how well he understood the changing scene. But in spite of the new developments, he followed the highly personal path which led him to the style of his late years. This later style had far more influence on the succeeding generation of Poulenc, Auric, and Milhaud than did the music of the impressionists.

Fauré's music is not widely known outside of France for two reasons. First, since a large part of it is vocal, the French or Latin texts must be clearly understood as the settings follow closely the fluctuations of the literal meaning. Second, because the musical language is reduced to the barest essentials, it is often not striking on first hearing. To appreciate it the listener has to pay strict attention; none of the seemingly secondary details must escape him. Using ordinary chords, scales, and arpeggios, Fauré works miracles in the underlying subtle harmonic progressions. Listeners accustomed to large rhetorical effects emphasizing every expressive detail will have difficulty orienting themselves in this restrained music, which has often been called perfect "though cold." But once the sobriety of Fauré is appreciated, it becomes obvious that such poignant and beautiful expression could not be achieved by the use of more colorful and dramatic means. Adherents of this music find in its understated romanticism a world of deep feeling that often puts to shame those who carry on with empty grandiloquence.

Fauré's music has its counterpart in the paintings of Edouard Manet, with their rather muted colors but definite outlines. This parallelism is also manifested in the relation of their works of the impressionists as well as to those of their antecedents. Goya, Courbet, and Delacroix demonstrate affinity with Manet; Mendelssohn and Schumann with Fauré. In both, flashbacks to earlier periods appear on close inspection. In Fauré there is a transparency and an economy that is rather Mozartean at times. In his ability to spin out one pattern and to catch all manner of different inflections in a continuous movement, he resembles Bach. A reminder of Couperin's explorations of the Watteauesque, or of the tender gaiety of the French madrigal school hangs over certain facets of this music. At one time in Fauré's life the modal scales attracted him for their kinship with Medieval music. Later, after Reinach and other musicologists deciphered ancient Greek notation and resurrected the *Hymn to Apollo* (published with a harmonization by Fauré), he was enchanted by the new discoveries because of their Attic flavor.

Like Manet, Fauré is particularly successful at characterization, and he is best known for his settings of religious texts or of those by Baudelaire, Verlaine, and other "Parnassians." The tender and resigned beauty of his Requiem portrays not the horrors of the grave but the sadness of bereavement, and a human, nostalgic picture of Paradise. Similarly, the charmingly fresh settings of Verlaine's *La Bonne Chanson*, and the Hellenic atmosphere of his two operas, *Prométhée* and *Pénélope*, depict with a sure touch each shade of feeling and capture the special character of the texts in a masterly way. Sometimes by a sudden modulation, by varying the accompaniment imperceptibly, or by a touching inflection of the voice, Fauré achieves more than do many others using complicated means. The love of the classic artistic principles—such as logic, order, and serenity—combined with a highly individual sensibility and a refinement of taste, suffuse his work, so that it if is not comparable to the art and literature of Fifth-Century (B.C.) Athens, as some have maintained, at least it is characteristic of one of the best sides of French music.

Like his vocal music, his instrumental works reveal a constant development. Of the same general type as the music of his teacher, Saint-Saëns (a composer who was "rediscovered" by Ravel in his later years), Fauré's First Violin Sonata in A and his First Piano Quartet in C Minor indicate those personal qualities which became more pronounced later. These are works of a graceful triviality; they possess an elegant lyricism or a humorous lightness that is characteristic.

By the time Fauré had reached his middle period, during which his Requiem was written, his music had deepened and had greatly widened in scope. At a time when he was moving on to his last and most unusual style, the incidental music for a London performance of Maeterlinck's *Pelléas et Mélisande* (1898) made its appearance, four years before Debussy's opera. The four movements—two rather light interludes in the middle, a nostalgic prologue, and the tragic final Adagio, which reaches a remarkable interior pathos—are entirely different from the Debussy score and have to be appreciated on the basis of quite another conception of the work.

As is evident from this work that uses such simple means, Fauré was not primarily interested in the orchestra. Sometimes he entrusted his orchestration to others, as in the case of *Pénélope*, but in *Pelléas* and the Requiem he uses the orchestra with full awareness of its capabilities. Simple harp arpeggios, a soft harmonic background, and a floating singing line suffice to paint the tender joy of Paradise at the conclusion of the latter work. It is the conception of a devout man full of sympathy and hope, forgiving his fellow men with Christian charity.

Gabriel-Urbain Fauré's own life exhibits the same order and modesty present in his music. It was spent in composing, teaching, reviewing concerts, and later in directing the Conservatoire. The one profoundly tragic event was the gradual impairment of his hearing, which began when he was about fifty-eight, as a result of arteriosclerosis. From his son's biography we learn that Fauré's ears distorted the extreme upper and lower registers of sounds, bringing them each a third nearer the middle. For a highly trained musician, listening to music under these conditions must naturally have been painful in the extreme. He gradually relinquished performing his own music, although until his death at seventy-nine he remained very prolific as a composer. In keeping with his character, this strange deafness was never mentioned and it was only known to his most intimate colleagues. For during this period, knowing only the profession of music and not living in a society which endowed composers liberally for their efforts, he had to continue in his positions as newspaper critic and director of the Conservatoire. That his opinion of the newer trends represented by Strauss, Ravel, and Dukas should have shown such understanding under this terrible handicap is remarkable. To read his criticisms now is to realize how seldom one may find an intelligent critic of new music and how many, blessed with two healthy ears, hear far less.

Born on 13 May 1845, in a town of southern France situated at the foot of the Pyrenees, the youngest of six children of a country school teacher, Fauré lived at home only five years. Until he was four he lived with a foster mother and at nine was packed off to Paris to study music. This early lack of home life must have played an important part in forming his outlook, though he never lost contact with his family and at his father's death was moved to write the Requiem. Boarding at the Ecole Niedermeyer in Paris until he was twenty-one, he learned a great deal about Gregorian chant, music of the Renaissance, and, of course, all the classics, largely through the efforts of Saint-Saëns, who was not only instrumental in raising the money to bring the boy there but in teaching him as well. After graduating, he became an organist in various churches and finally at the Madeleine, his career being interrupted by a short period of active military service in the war of 1870. Although neither a student at the Conservatoire nor a winner of the Prix de Rome, two requisites for important posts in that national institution, he became its director in 1905, and in 1920 retired after having completely renovated its policies. With César Franck, Edouard Lalo, and other leading musicians, he helped to form the Société Nationale and later the Société Musicale Indépendante, both devoted to the performance of new works. At these concerts almost all his songs and chamber music received their first performances. With constant concern for the music under consideration and little for drawing attention to himself, he worked as a reviewer on *Le Figaro*, one of the leading Parisian newspapers of the time.

In 1924, after a long life during which the number of his works mounted to op. 121, he put the finishing touches to his only string quartet and died a much venerated figure whose reputation has increased constantly since his death.

The Three Late Sonatas of Debussy
(1959/94)

The last works of Debussy, three sonatas for different combinations of instruments, represent both a summation of the principles of his earlier works and a new departure. Very little has been written about them—or, indeed, about the composer's musical output in general, perhaps in response to the fact that Debussy was very much concerned with what he considered the essential in music, the aspect of music irreducible to words. It is true that the works for the most part have titles, but in their inner workings he seems almost perversely to have avoided all the aspects of music which make good copy for the critics and musicologists. More "systematic" composers, such as Stravinsky, Schoenberg, and those of the various nationalist schools, have inspired the consumption of more typewriter ribbon than have more discreet composers, like Debussy, who turn an absence of systems into a system. Anyone writing about Debussy constantly senses this almost anti-intellectual side of his music: the fact that his forms are either so utterly simple or so obscure that they cannot be discussed in the usual terms of melodic development, counterpoint, or harmony, forcing one to fall back on such terms as color and atmosphere. Yet the music exercises a powerful influence on musicians, partly because of its thoroughly convincing expression and partly because it seems so completely to be following its own inexplicable methods, so remote from the common practices of music both before and since that time.

One of the most interesting features of the music is its extreme sense of freedom, its high degree of intuitive taste which keeps all the elements, from harmony to form, on the same level of divergence from conventional usages. It might, I think, be viewed as though in a private world of methods constantly changing from work to work. It is abundantly clear, both from his early works and from many of his statements about music, that Debussy's tastes and musical training were formed in the best French tradition—a circumstance which, perhaps, helped frame his private world and prevented him from falling into complete chaos.

In the later part of his life, with the appearance of Stravinsky, Schoenberg, Bartók, Satie, the Italian futurists, and other manifestations of what seemed to him a growing cultural anarchy, Debussy began to say, in his letters to friends, "Ne soyons pas modernes" ("Let's not be modern"). And he began a quest for the more rigorous yet suitable kind of unity in his works, noticeable in *Jeux*, the piano Etudes, and the three sonatas, a quest which was then interrupted by his suffering from the cancer that proved fatal in 1918. Other, more recent advanced composers, sensing this anarchy too, have in various ways attempted to give their music a stronger sense of form. But most of them have returned to older forms, older systems of building and linking ideas, and even of establishing the nature of musical ideas. Very often these older methods were unsuitable to the chosen harmonic and melodic material and produced an uncertain effect. What is most interesting, therefore, about Debussy is his effort to find a homogeneous method that would not rely on borrowed forms. And nowadays, since the novelty of the harmonic style of Debussy, which was the first thing that struck his contemporaries, has worn off—indeed, since the novelty of almost any aggregate of simultaneous sounds has ceased to be a matter for surprise—we are beginning to see in Debussy's music other, more significant aspects. Certainly the history of music reveals to us how revisions in thinking about form, about harmony, and about all the other features of music have gone hand in hand. Thus the case of Debussy could serve as an extremely valuable lesson, perhaps one of the most radical in contemporary music. But most composers of his time did not grasp any too clearly what Debussy was doing, and composers of a later time dismissed the quiet, rather misty world of his music as too dreamy and "escapist," rejecting many of his formal innovations along with his perfumed atmosphere. The world was more brutal, more violent. For instance, the sea, to most artists and writers, would have held some terrors, and yet Debussy's *La Mer* suggests little of this aspect. It moves in a shimmering buzz of elegant and mysterious sounds, for to him its symbolism was more one of motion, of ceaseless but ever-shifting play, of indistinct thoughts. His score seldom suggests the many kinds of drama which have often accompanied thoughts of the sea; there never seems to be any darkness in this or, indeed, in any of his music except *Pelléas*. This in itself was enough to estrange later generations from him.

During the 1920s, it must be remembered, there was a vigorous return to so-called classical forms, not only on the part of Stravinsky in such works as his Piano Sonata and Piano Concerto, but also in the works of Arnold Schoenberg, such as his Piano Suite (op. 25) and Third String Quartet. This set the pace for many years to come: the younger composers tended to follow this on the whole quite conventional approach to form, perhaps hoping to bridge the gap between the audience and their new music, which employed what were for the time such novel harmonies and melodies. In retrospect, it becomes clearer that this pastiche of classical form had certain very serious dangers, for it was not at all suited to the kind of tensions, conceptions, and expressions with which new music was concerned. As a result, we are now once again faced with the problem of finding both large-scale forms and detailed shapes that are consistent with our modern way of thinking. And it seems clear today that Debussy's music, perhaps more than any other composer's of the time, has settled the technical direction of contemporary music, if not its emotional tone. In many ways his works, particularly the later ones, presented such a new departure in musical thinking that all composers after him saw it as a kind of extreme, particularly in the matter of form, to which those even of schools where more definite outlines were considered important often reacted with more traditional and in many ways inert, misunderstood conventions of older music. The sonatas of Stravinsky, Hindemith, and many others represent a kind of parody of textbook methods of musical development and patterning, embedded in new ideas of sonority, new harmonic, contrapuntal, and rhythmic methods. But even in this music the avoidance of the various methods of conventional development is noticeable. So for its power, for its attempt to solve the problem of what is often called "musical logic" in terms of new musical situations and in terms that bear some analogy to contemporary views on the operation of human thought and feeling, Debussy's music is especially significant.

The three late sonatas of Debussy have much in common with the last works of a number of composers whose styles changed abruptly near the end of their lives, whether the life was long or short. This same sort of crystallization and clarification of intent, as well as a certain restraint or stylization of means, is noticeable in the last works of Bach, Mozart, and Beethoven, as well as in those of Fauré, Mahler, Bartók, Schoenberg, and Webern. And it is this special quality which has earned the late works of each of these composers pointed criticism on the one hand and cult status on the other, as in the case of *The Art of Fugue* or the last songs of Fauré.

In discussing Debussy's music, it has become customary to bring in the symbolist poets and the impressionist painters. It is easy to understand why: Debussy was linked to the poets by his friendship with Henri de Regnier, a minor figure, and by his habitual attendance at Stéphane Mallarmé's Thursday afternoon gatherings, from which resulted the mutual compliment of Debussy's musical "églogue" after Mallarmé's "Afternoon of a Faun" and Mallarmé's response in his charming quatrain about Debussy. Further, Debussy set many poems of the symbolists Verlaine, Mallarmé, and Maeterlinck, along with those of their precursor Baudelaire. As for the impressionists, some of Debussy's titles for his works suggest a commonality of subject matter: Monet's and Seurat's paintings of the sea, Manet's of Spain, and the influence of Japanese prints which is noticeable in some of Gauguin's work.

No doubt we are lucky, from the point of view of explication, to have had two such important movements as impressionism and symbolism going on at the same time in Paris. Yet society had undergone such a change that artistic movements occurring simultaneously no longer necessarily bore the kind of relationship to one another that they had done in the Renaissance and Baroque periods, any more than did the artists within the movements. From Manet to Monet there is a far greater shift than that of a single vowel; the differences between Rimbaud, Verlaine, and Mallarmé are vast. In any case, we are a good deal closer to this attempted analogy on the part of music historians than we are to many in the more remote past, and the deeper we delve into it the harder it becomes to clarify except in the most general terms. Impressionism and symbolism seem to have evolved rather independently of each other, with their traditions drawn from their own histories. Thus the influences of Constable, Delacroix, Goya, and to a lesser extent Corot and Courbet are noticeable in painting, while in poetry Edgar Allan Poe, Coleridge, and the French Pléiade as well as Baudelaire and the mad boy-poet Rimbaud are important. (In music, there is the influence of Berlioz as it filtered through the Russian Five and of Wagner as it was filtered through Franck.) The parallels are very hard to establish because each painter and poet is so different from the others. The main similarities inhere in the general point of view that they share with Debussy—the avoidance of big rhetorical and dramatic effects, the concern with the still, small, individual human voice in all its uniqueness, and the discovery of techniques and symbols, each personal to the poet or painter, in which to express this individualized world. It is important to point out in any discussion of this sort that "impressionism" in music really did not form a school because Debussy was its only important figure; there was no many-sided exemplification. For Dukas, Ravel, Roussel, Stravinsky, Schoenberg, Bartók, and De Falla, impressionism was only a passing phase.

Another very important aspect of the symbolist movement and to a lesser extent that of the impressionists is the idea of catching the spontaneous uniqueness of individual moments. Edmund Wilson, in his book *Axel's Castle*, expresses this very clearly:

> Each feeling or sensation we have, every moment of consciousness, is different from every other; and it is, in consequence, impossible to render our sensations as we actually experience them through the conventional and universal language of ordinary literature. Each poet has his unique personality; each of his moments has its special tone, its special combination of elements. And it is the poet's task to find, to invent, the special language which will alone be capable of expressing his personality and feelings.[1]

At first sight, this statement seems to suit the music of Debussy, but upon further consideration one realizes that the very nature of music is quite different from that of literature. Many poets of the time, in asserting that all art aspired to the nature of music, emphasized at once its abstract expressiveness and its absence of prose denotation. This left music, so to speak, no place to aim for—except the inner program of the workings of the sensibility, the stream of consciousness, to which French composers, who have a long tradition of program music, were particularly sympathetic. This exposure of the inner subjective life to consideration was, of course, becoming quite normal at the time. Bergson had stated that metaphysical truth could be arrived at only by the intuition, and that to follow the intuition one had consciously to suppress any attempts at reason. This fit in well with the views of the French psychologists, such as Charcot, who had become concerned with the workings of the subconscious.

1. Edmund Wilson, *Axel's Castle: A Study in the Imaginative Literature of 1870–1930* (New York: Charles Scribner's Sons, 1932), 21.

Now, the stream-of-consciousness school has had a remarkable impact on literature since the time of Rimbaud. One of its methods of operation is to find relationships of a personal or suggestive kind that follow emotional or other associative patterns rather than rational ones. In its earlier manifestations, such as in the work of Rimbaud and other symbolist poets, there was not much concern for formal integration: somehow form seemed taken for granted, and this was also true for Debussy. In its later manifestations, such as Joyce's *Ulysses* or *Finnegans Wake*, familiar and recognizable patterns of order are superimposed on the stream, very much as familiar musical patterns are imposed in works like Schoenberg's Third String Quartet or in Berg's *Wozzeck*. Thus what we now call the stream-of-consciousness technique was emerging in Debussy's day and this, I think, is an important key to any discussion of his music. It involves the discovery of musical relationships that do not follow the traditional patterns, relationships which may be called in some loose sense "logical" but which really proceed by more obscure routes, sometimes extramusical, sometimes stylistic, and sometimes by way of resemblances not often taken into account in musical dialectic.

An important crosscurrent to this trend in Debussy, which much more specifically affects his music, involves the ever more rapidly growing familiarity with the musical past. This, indeed, no less than the above served to disturb the familiar progress of musical tradition. It was in Debussy's lifetime that the forgotten past of the Western tradition began to be scrutinized; sometimes, in fact, it seems as though every experimental step, every daring extreme that contemporary composers have taken has been paralleled by the increasing oddness of the music that musicologists have uncovered. Thus, to the unsuspecting public, Perotin is on the same level of remoteness as Schoenberg. In this respect, composers and musicologists have collaborated in subverting what was considered the tradition of music at the beginning of Debussy's lifetime. This particular trend is scarcely noticeable in literature, while in painting the conscious resurrection of parallel earlier styles came more at the hands of Ingres, Courbet, and Corot—as well as Cézanne, who broke with the impressionists in his concern for form—than with the impressionists, who were more inclined to follow the lead of Goya and Velasquez.

The impact of these various kinds of newly discovered musics on Debussy is well known. Judging by the many titles he gave his works, there is an almost perfectly consistent love for remoteness or exoticism of subject, either ethnically or historically speaking. Relatively few of his pieces—such as *La Mer*, *Jeux* (a ballet about a tennis game), and the Nocturne "Nuages"—deal with more or less familiar subject matter. Of far greater interest to Debussy were: places geographically or historically far removed from his immediate surroundings, such as Spain (*Ibéria*, "Soirée dans Grenade," "La Puerta del Vino"), China ("Pagodes"), America ("Golliwog's Cakewalk," "Minstrels," "La Sérénade interrompue"), Greece ("Danseuses de Delphes," "Danses sacrée et profane"), or the Middle Ages (*Pelléas et Mélisande*, *Le Martyre de Saint Sébastien*, "La Cathédrale engloutie," "Et la lune descend sur le temple qui fut"); or mythological antiquity ("Sirènes," "Canope"); or special occasions, such as festivities ("Fêtes," "Feux d'artifice").

Of course, for a musician with as much musical projection as Debussy, the titles serve only as touchstones to suggest an experience that is directly and more forcibly translated into music. But still this remoteness is a pictorialization of the sense of remoteness from the commonplace of feeling, away from which his fastidious taste and sensitivity moved. It is not surprising that Debussy, like many writers and painters of the time, was also deeply attracted to childhood, which was then seen by adults as a period when impressions are fresher and more spontaneous, when the responsibilities of practical life have not directed the mind toward more prosaic things. And some of the melodic and harmonic material of his ballet *La Boîte à joujoux* and *The Children's Corner* is to be found in his Sonata for Flute, Viola, and Harp.

The titles of his works are in fact a list of the tasteful artistic/aesthetic preoccupations of the cultivated bourgeois society of his period much more than those of the symbolists and impressionists. They are in this respect like titles in Couperin, whom Debussy greatly admired. The abstruse, highly artificial world of symbols used to cloak Mallarmé's delicate philosophical reveries is very far from Debussy's more direct contact with the natural and familiar world of the cultivated classes of France. It was among these and the lesser painters and poets, neither members of the two important movements mentioned above, that the particular variety of exoticism and love of nature and the world of unruffled bourgeois calm and refined pleasure that is seen in Debussy is best exemplified. The warmth and charm of this world does suggest certain periods of Renoir, as well as the agreeable optimism of Paul Fort and of such writers as de Regnier and others whose names have never been known outside of France. Debussy did not really ever enter the strange hermitic world of the symbolist poets, nor did he ever become very interested in the everyday world as it was seen through the brilliant colored light effects of the impressionist painters. In a way, he belongs to yet a third movement, which musicologists should find a new name for.

It is perhaps significant that Debussy returned to abstract titles in his last three works, after so many programmatic ones had intervened since his String Quartet of 1893. This quartet shows Debussy in full command of the compositional methods current at that time, the unification of themes by the use of motivic cells, of sequences, of cyclical repetitions—a few motives incessantly expanded, modified, carried over from one movement to another—and of many of the usual characteristics of nineteenth-century French music, particularly that of the Franckian school: patterned rhythms, clear-cut phraseology, and simple crescendo techniques. From a technical standpoint, the work's most outstanding features are its harmonic freedom and powerful lyrical impulse, which immediately put it above almost any of the string quartets of the time. But the fact that Debussy, in the years between 1893 and 1915, wrote practically no works with abstract titles certainly does not reflect a lack of interest in form during that period. His piano and orchestral works, along with *Pelléas et Mélisande*, involved Debussy in many fascinating experiments that had the effect of liberating him from conventional concepts. This constant striving for freedom is stressed throughout his letters and critical articles. Debussy felt strongly that music had somehow to find its freedom in its poetic vision of the world, which led him to an appreciation of Beethoven's significance as an innovator in form as well as to a condemnation of the stereotyped formal methods of his day. It is interesting to note both the emphasis on freedom, on harmonious proportions and on freshness and spontaneity in his discussion of Beethoven's Ninth Symphony:

> It is the most triumphant example of the molding of an idea to the preconceived form: at each leap forward there is a new delight, without either effort or appearance of repetition; the magical blossoming, so to speak, of a tree whose leaves burst forth simultaneously. Nothing is superfluous in this stupendous work . . .
>
> It seems to me that the proof of the futility of the symphony has been established since Beethoven. Indeed, Schumann and Mendelssohn did no more than respectfully repeat the same forms with less power. The Ninth Symphony nonetheless was a demonstration of genius, a sublime desire to augment and to liberate the usual forms by giving them the harmonious proportions of a fresco.
>
> Beethoven's real teaching then was not to preserve the old forms, still less to follow in his early steps. We must throw wide the windows to the open sky; they seem to me to have only just escaped being closed forever. The fact that here and there a genius succeeds in this form is but a poor excuse for the laborious and stilted compositions which we are accustomed to call symphonies.

Later, he parodies the form in terms surprisingly like those Thomas Mann used in *Doktor Faustus* to excoriate contemporary music—and which in many respects could be transposed to our own present scene:

> A symphony is usually built up on a chant heard by the composer as a child. The first section is the customary presentation of a theme on which the composer proposes to work; then begins the necessary dismemberment; the second section seems to take place in an experimental laboratory; the third section cheers up a little in a quite childish way interspersed with deeply sentimental phrases during which the chant withdraws as more seemly; but it reappears and the dismemberment goes on; the professional gentlemen, obviously interested, mop their brows and the audience calls for the composer. But the composer does not appear. He is engaged in listening modestly to the voice of tradition which prevents him, it seems to me, from hearing the voice that speaks within him.[2]

Debussy's own formal methods developed rather slowly. For much of this time—as is to be expected—his songs are, on the whole, in advance of his instrumental works and his orchestral works are more advanced than his piano and chamber works. Thus the *Prélude à l'après-midi d'un faune*, written during the same years (1892–94) as his String Quartet, shows a much greater liberty with formal matters; and while "L'Isle joyeuse" is far less developed than *La Mer*, both were written around the same time (ca. 1904). His complete maturity of style comes in the piano works, in the *Préludes* of 1910. After this time there is a growing attempt to clarify his style and to eliminate elements that do not directly contribute to it. The three sonatas represent a clear effort

---

2. Claude Debussy, "Monsieur Croche the Dilettante Hater," transl. B. N. Langdon Davies, in *Three Classics in the Aesthetic of Music* (New York: Dover, 1962), 17–19.

to crystallize his method into melodic material against a very radically simplified background.

By the time of Debussy's maturity, it has become quite clear that his formal methods spring from two different sources, the Franckian cyclical method employed in the String Quartet and the method of continuous development used by the Baroque composers of which he was so fond. Unlike many composers of the nineteenth century, he did not treat the seventeenth and eighteenth centuries as a source of neoclassic stylization—as did, for instance, Tchaikovsky in his *Mozartiana*, or Wagner in *Die Meistersinger*—but more like Chopin and Schumann, both of whom were deeply influenced by Bach. His works abound in the concept of continuous development, though robbed almost completely of its contrapuntal aspect. At the same time, the cuts in continuity are contrasted and sometimes provide a diverting crosscurrent, which follows its own continuous development.

Thus "La Cathédrale engloutie" starts with a rising pentatonic motive quite statically harmonized, in C major; this is interrupted by a melodic section in B major and then the pentatonic motives resume in different versions and with different backgrounds in B and E♭, returning to C, in which finally a more melodic version of the motives appears. At the rather extended conclusion, again the opposing melody in B appears and after a transition the C-major melody is played in a new version. The short coda refers to the very beginning of the work. All of this material has very clear affinity with itself, and it could be said that the intentional cloudiness of the ringing bell-like pentatonic harmonies is directly paralleled by the cloudiness of the thematic formulations, which all run together even at points where the motives crystallize into a more continuous melody. There is no tendency to modulate within a phrase, although some of the degrees are altered to give a neomodal effect. Naturally this work also displays suggestions of organum and a very faint suggestion of Medieval melody, more of the troubadour type than plainsong—this to emphasize the literary aspect.

Each of the Preludes is of course stylized in some way to suggest its subject; the method is very varied but there are certain things always at work that were to be highly important in music after Debussy's time, always noticeable. One of them is that harmonies participate in this form-building development. That is, a certain chordal sound will be treated as an item or a motive in the form and be developed along with melodic motivic material sometimes quite unrelated to the motive. At times the motives are broken chords, as in "La Cathédrale": in fact, one chordal sound with variants often completely dominates a section or a whole piece. Sometimes this will be a chord of many appoggiature taken as a unit and not resolved until the conclusion of the piece, if ever. Often too there is a key harmonic progression which becomes a form-building factor. Another, quite prominent characteristic is that transitions from one idea to another in another key are accomplished by parallel chromatic progressions of triads or seventh or ninth chords, forming thus a disturbance in the tonal feeling but moving with the utmost simplicity.

The last three sonatas, the first for cello and piano written in 1915, the second for flute, viola, and harp in 1916, and the third for violin and piano completed in 1917, are obviously meant to be abstract works, for Debussy would not have hesitated to give them literary names if he had intended to convey programmatic content. In them we find all of his methods well exemplified, each work strikingly different from the others in character as well as formal plan, and each set out to present a different kind of idea sequence.[3] The three are not, of course, sonatas in the Classical sense; it is likely that Debussy was thinking of the late Baroque sonatas in his use of the term. For one thing, the three movements of the violin sonata, as well as the three of the trio, maintain a unity of key: all three movements of the violin sonata are in G and all three of the trio in F. Moreover, the cello sonata has a second movement mainly in the subdominant of D, which is the key of the first and last movements. Debussy apparently liked the blandness of unity of key and felt that the extreme digressions from the tonality within each movement provided enough variety. In this connection, the story of Debussy's short stay as a student in César Franck's organ class, as told by Louis Laloy, is both enlightening and amusing. Whenever Debussy would improvise, Franck would say: "Modulate, modulate," until one day Debussy became annoyed and said, "Why should I modulate when I feel perfectly satisfied with this key?" ("Je me trouve bien dans ce ton"). As for the sonatas, one notices that the modulations within sections are for the most part sudden and extreme and usually follow quite a long stay in one key. The modulations within phrases, on the other hand, are almost imperceptible and involve a kind of chromatic coloring to produce the expressive touches in his neomodal passages. Like other French composers of the time, Debussy employed various scale patterns which were thought to be like the Greek or Medieval modes and which have been called "neomodal." More to the point is that in Debussy there is a very strong sense of the expressiveness of small intervals—semitones, whole tones, and thirds—and many of his melodic phrases move within a very small range, a restrained quality that is consistent with his avoidance of modulation.

Indeed, throughout the three works, there is a kind of spasmodic quality which can be seen in the detailed working of his melodies, harmonies, and rhythms. It consists of establishing a pattern, dwelling on it by repetition of melodic motives, rhythmic patterns, and harmonic progressions, and then suddenly breaking loose from them to take up another pattern, in turn reinforced by the same sorts of devices. The breaking loose often involves extreme contrast: a remote modulation, a change of rhythm, a new unexpected melodic figure. This mechanism of climax both delayed and led up to by repetition is in direct contrast, of course, to the Classical pattern of music construction, which seeks its effects by mounting in gradual steps to the climax and then leading away from it. In these last sonatas, this expressive pattern is

---

3. Debussy intended to write six sonatas in all. The three completed are dedicated to his wife Emma-Claude Debussy with the letters p.m. after her name, abbreviating a term of endearment, "petite mienne" ("little mine"), by which he referred to her. In this unfinished gesture of homage to his second wife, Debussy gives a small hint of the tender, personal and human side of his nature, which still remains one of the most characteristic touches exhibited in his music.

skillfully managed so that the phrase patterns are often arranged to join into one continuous line one or more of these abrupt changes. This gives a richness of inflection and a sense of depth to meaning of an intimate sort that was rarely met with outside of Mozart, who was adept at rapid contrasts within the short space of a phrase or sentence. And this technique of repetition sharply distinguishes Debussy from the other (so-called) impressionists and suggests a very real relationship with Stravinsky.

Out of this accumulation of short, repeated melodic fragments, often standing in marked constrast with one another, a remarkable sense of dialectic emerges, of one musical idea suggesting the meaning of another, and the whole adding up to a kind of aesthetic satisfaction that is akin to that of works of the past. For if Debussy avoids the usual methods of development by repeating phrases almost identically, he emulates these methods in a play of hidden motives that appear in phrases of contrasting character. Thus, for instance, in the Trio sonata a whole series of contrasting melodic phrases is presented, one after the other, apparently unrelated—but in the same tonality as well as, more characteristically, sharing a single pentatonic motive. This gives a sense of unity of style. The movement begins with a rising arpeggio and a chromatic harmony that suggests the key of Ab, but this initial suggestion is immediately put aside until the middle section and a series of themes in or near F major appear.

The next thing to be noticed, aside from this melodic method, is the remarkable transparency of texture. Debussy in these last works has reduced his method to the most sober and most essential elements, and in this he is really more like some of the post-impressionists like Cézanne or the early Matisse. There is very little reliance on anything but melodic outline, accompanied by comparatively simple harmonies, and no counterpoint. Even the usual two-part layout of soprano and bass appears only here and there. The accompaniment also tends to emphasize the expressive accents of the melody and also its directional sense, or of thickening and thinning out for expressive effects.

This tendency towards simplification, of course, was in the air. It is noticeable in Mahler's later works, as in those of Fauré. And this simplification in Debussy also involved a stylization of an entire work, for each of these sonatas moves within its own sphere. The movements are not only in the same key or closely related keys, they do not present great contrasts between one and the others. What contrasts there are occur *within* movements: the Sonata for Flute, Viola, and Harp is predominantly gentle in tone, involving alternation between wistful ideas and rapid diatonic ones. It is perhaps the most unified of the three; its first movement contains one of the finest examples of his method of joining apparently unrelated ideas into large paragraphs. The rhetoric of question and answer so dear to the Classical composers is here extended to a kind of stream-of-consciousness method that was hinted at in the opening movement of Berlioz's *Symphonie fantastique*. Each idea is quite obviously linked to the previous by its opening motive, but besides this the tonality of F unifies this diversity of ideas, and certain recurrent pentatonic motives of three tones are built into each phrase and thus give a unity of style if not a sense of what is often called "musical logic." In fact, this kind of logic is clearly being avoided and for the most part the music never even suggests this. It is, therefore, quite a *tour de force* to have constructed these works of considerable length with so little reliance on the usual methods of musical continuation and yet at the same time giving such a complete sense of the many-sided experience, controlled and unified, that we have come to expect from an art work.

One could say further that the sort of unity experienced in these pieces has come about in part as a response to the violent problems of style in the nineteenth century. Debussy, and to a certain extent other French composers as well, began to think of the entire musical vocabulary as flexible, which led to greater freedom on the part of the composer in choosing the scale, type of harmony, type of motion, and type of unfolding of ideas for each piece. Ultimately, this extreme stylization became an element of formal coherence. In the Sonata for Flute, Viola, and Harp, there is a basic dependence on a few figures drawn from the pentatonic scale. These figures are ones already often heard in the music of Debussy, particularly in his "Doctor Gradus ad Parnassum" from *The Children's Corner*. A great deal is made of this established pentatonic material, with subtle departures from it in chromatic alterations. Thus all the harmonically relaxed melodic figures are drawn from this and the more intense or expressive material consists of departures from it. The very limited choice of material pervades the entire work and at once gives it a semblance of formal relationships, as if all the phrases in such often contrasting speeds and rhythms were related to each other. This tight stylistic coherence verging on formal order is likewise noticeable in the Sonata for Cello and Piano, which makes a great deal out of some melismatic figures suggesting Spanish flamenco music, though remaining always at enough of a distance from the original folklore so that the work can hardly be said to have more than a tinge of Spanish flavor. The Sonata for Violin and Piano is a much less tightly organized work from this point of view, although the cyclical elements are treated in more thoroughgoing fashion.

The boundary between narrowing down the character of a long work to exploit this material within a small frame of fairly definite procedures, and the notion of form in the usual sense of recurrent themes and motives, is hard to establish. Within this frame of limitation Debussy, in the Sonata for Flute, Viola, and Harp and in the Cello Sonata, builds continuities of great freedom. Each movement in the first work has many different speeds and different characters which nevertheless add up to a whole, not only because of the subtle sensibility which constrasts things that seem to have some relationship of spirit, but also owing to the rather clear relationships of motives and the general overall plan mentioned above, which would not be sufficient to maintain the interest during a work of larger size without more direct methods.

The actual details of shaping in all of these texturally simple works are very interesting. The first movement of the Sonata for Flute, Viola, and Harp, called Pastorale (there are no movements in "sonata form" in any of these works), consists of a series of phrases each quite contrasted with the other and each a little more intense than the previous until a much faster middle section appears, followed by a return to the series of themes of the first part, but in a different order. From this description, the movement might seem to be like a typical three-part form, yet there is one great difference: namely, that the interrelations of phrases are so subtle that the whole work has more the kind of unity associated with a sonata. This kind of unity is difficult to pin down. The musical mind, when confronted with music that seems so heterogeneous, tries to find relationships—but if such relationships do not eventually become recognizable, there is the distinct danger that the whole piece will begin to pall. Actually, these works are primarily melodic; there is no wealth of interesting texture, unlike many works of Debussy's middle period, or of intriguing harmony. It is the outline that is evidently meant to carry the work.

It should be clear that practically all I have mentioned in connection with these works flies in the face of the accepted musical practices of the time. The more one penetrates into these works, the more one realizes that everything in the theme is chosen according to a highly developed sense of musical taste and a very high critical standard of expression, with a keen sense of both coherence and uniqueness. Like all the best works of twentieth-century music, these have an inimitably special character in which all the various novel features are brought together into a harmonious whole.

Schoenberg and Stravinsky, among others, continued in this direction for a few years after Debussy before taking up neoclassicism, giving each of their works its special mark of unity as well as uniqueness. It often has seemed to people familiar with contemporary music that this was the true way for such music to exist—that the only valid function of art in our time was to produce these special works, each with an interior life of its own. This "useless quality" point of view can, of course, lead rapidly to anarchy, to the establishment of freakish principles often of a very unartistic kind. But as we look back through the first fifty years of our century, most of the music which impresses us was connected with this "Mandarin" aesthetic, as it was called by the literary critic Cyril Connolly. The other works which helped to preserve our sanity and music's respectability before a public at first scandalized, then bored by what it did not and might never understand continued both to furnish a background of modified tradition, insofar as they were competently done, and to further our understanding of the more remotely introspective works. It is obvious that the Mandarin kind of music may never have a large public, for its appreciation demands a very deep understanding of musical tradition, an appetite for adventure, and a high esteem for the individual. As our society becomes more transient, and as culture becomes more widely and thinly spread, it is very hard to see how such an attitude toward music can survive except among a very small group of specialists. One could well imagine that the tables might then be turned, as specialists mop their brows over remarkable oddities while the public applauds without understanding—and that this would become the established academic routine against which some new school would rebel. Some think that this has already happened. However, as long as the artist retains his special position in a democratic society, one is hard put to see how this tendency to express one's unique qualities could develop in any other way.

American Figure, with Landscape [Henry F. Gilbert]
(1943)

It has been characteristic of musical life in America to neglect the composers of its own past. Although almost all serious compositions presuppose a future audience whose tastes will be affected by them, in our country the death of a composer generally marks the end of his musical career. Quickly he is supplanted by new individuals anxious to promote their own works before they, too, shall be forgotten. And music that is easily forgotten by musicians is more easily forgotten by the public. Thus we develop the habit of evaluating each new work as having the same unimportance as its rapidly vanishing predecessor.

It may, of course, be true that many if not all of our previous composers have not produced music of great significance. On the other hand, they have occasionally written works which deserve attention because they mirror and communicate to us certain interesting, lovable aspects of the America of their day. Besides, many of the tendencies they set in motion still direct our musical thought.

At the time when Henry Franklin Belknap Gilbert was making his effort to write, as he put it, "some American music," nationalism was the subject of wide discussion by critics, musicians, and composers, including Gilbert himself. A general historical sequence of periods had been formulated to cover our national musical evolution: first, foreign domination, and imitation of non-native art music; second, collection of and familiarization with indigenous folk songs and dances; third, invention of a style consistent with folk material though without using actual quotations; and fourth, the musical millenium, emergence of the national masterworks written by native composers with a large native background and inheritance. This hypothesis, reflecting the historical doctrines of the late nineteenth century and especially the "millenarianism" so dear to America, had its obvious support in the facts of Russian musical history. True, also, to the thinking of the period in omitting the important influences of speculative thought and of religious music in the concert hall, this thesis gave folk songs a basic position as the root from which each national music culture is to grow. All the elements comprising the "manner"—rhythm, melody, harmony, and form—evolve from this germ and generate a style that is to be expressive of our native kind of "matter." To put it another way, in a search for a means of expressing the "matter" of our national consciousness, it was assumed that composers would inevitably follow this historical pattern.

The two interrelated doctrines of historical stages, and the antithesis of matter and manner, combined with our special brands of individualism and of progress, have deeply influenced the thinking of our contemporary composers, particularly those of nationalist intentions. The conflict of opinion over which of the four stages we are now in is the basis of many present arguments; while the manner-matter problem perpetuates itself in questions as to the "abstraction" in contemporary music and its "neoclassicism" or "neoromanticism."

When these doctrines were being considered at the turn of the century, there was a tendency to minimize America's longing for the refinement of feeling and taste of Europe, which found literary expression in Henry Adams and Henry James. But the founding of our conservatories and of our larger performing organizations had been largely motivated by this longing. They were more concerned with promoting an interest in the classical European repertory than in encouraging native compositions.

Obviously under the circumstances the cards were stacked against those composers who were following nationalist doctrines. At a slightly more advanced stage of musical development, their reception might have been very different. If we had been ready, their ideas might have penetrated our musical life. For at that very time, political and economic nationalism were being aggressively declared by such important Americans as Theodore Roosevelt and A. T. Mahan. It was in this same aggressive spirit that the school of American nationalist composers supported their doctrines. In literature the field had already been well explored by the generation of Whitman and Emerson. But in music, as in politics, these ideas still had the charm of novelty and adventure. Composers led lives and wrote music in conformity with them, and the four-fold historical scheme gave men of Gilbert's generation, who modestly placed themselves in the second and third periods, a bright future to anticipate for their music and, by that token, a deep-seated conviction which helped them carry on under conditions often adverse.

Throughout his fifty-nine years of life, from 1868 to 1928, Gilbert struggled against a physical handicap of an unusual sort, which had to be borne in an almost continuous state of extreme poverty. As he would ruefully explain, he was occasionally invited to medical conventions as "Exhibit A"—the only man to survive his thirties with the heart deformity known to doctors as the tetralogy of Fallot. He had been born with the right ventricle of his heart larger than normal, and therefore an unusual amount of blood flowed through the capillaries of his skin. This gave him the fiery red complexion which was his most striking physical characteristic, and also made him susceptible to many physical troubles of which he never spoke. To have persisted in a career of musical composition at a time when no money could be derived from it, and when he obviously had talents for several more remunerative occupations, illustrated the power of his faith. Bearing his difficulties in an outwardly carefree way, he courageously led the trying life of a pioneer American composer, and at its culmination ventured on a trip to Frankfurt, Germany, in 1927, as a representative from America to the International Society for Contemporary Music Festival where his "uramerikanische" tone poem *Dance in Place Congo* was being performed.

Gilbert was one of the very few residents of Cambridge, Massachusetts, who ever attained prominence unaided by some connection with Harvard. In its vicinity he was born, lived, died, and he was buried like a good Cantabrigian in Mt. Auburn Cemetery not far from William and Henry James. Both his parents were musicians and encouraged their son to continue in this path. As a result of their efforts Gilbert had an all-American musical education. At the New England Conservatory he learned to play the violin and studied harmony and counterpoint and finally took lessons in composition from Edward MacDowell, who had just returned from Europe. His violin opened up a source of income as a fiddler in resort hotels from Florida to the White Mountains. But even in his early twenties, Gilbert was interested in being a composer, and this conflicted with his hectic hotel-musician's life. By the age of twenty-four, Gilbert had had enough of this and set out to find a more grateful trade that might pay a little better. For the next ten years he gave up music almost completely and tried many different ways of earning his living. He worked in music publishing houses in Boston as an engraver and as an arranger. Wandering away from home, he even got a job as a pie-cutter in the Chicago World's Fair at the time of the hootchy-kootchy. During this period he learned about a great many sides of life in America, and gained the almost Whitmanesque knowledge and love of his country that so deeply affected his musical development.

At the Chicago Fair he met a Russian who thrilled him with stories of Rimsky-Korsakov, Mussorgsky, and the new kind of music they were writing. To familiarize himself and his friends with this music, Gilbert organized a few concerts of Slavic nationalist music at Harvard. His association with Arthur Farwell in Boston, the discussions they had about American nationalist music, which finally resulted in the Wa-Wan Press publications of American music, all tended to rouse him once more into musical activity.

Finally, Gilbert heard rumors of a new French opera about the common people and, shipping on a cattle boat, went to Paris in 1901 to hear Charpentier's *Louise*. This opera was the touchstone of his life, for he was so impressed by it that he decided to devote all his time to musical composition, come what may. At thirty-three, Gilbert came back to Cambridge, found a job minding a horse and cow in a barn at Somerville to pay his board, moved a piano in beside one of the buggies, and started to compose on a breadboard resting on a flour barrel. He was going down to rock bottom to create the true American native music.

From his barn, near Harvard, which was then educating such erudite composers as John Knowles Paine, Arthur Foote, Walter Spaulding, and Edward Burlingame Hill, Gilbert threw down the challenge. American serious music was too imitative "not only. of the methods of Europe but of its spirit—a spirit which, at the present day, is decadent—which covers its weakness in genuine inspiration with a wealth of invention; a glittering show-off of ingenious externalities; deceiving the unwary into attributing to it an undue worth and importance. The long arm of Europe still stretches its deadening hand of tradition and authority over our American musico-art developments, so that the true spirit of America is lost sight of, and that great potential spirit which is the birthright of the American composer, as of others in their lines of activity, has been thoughtlessly bartered away for a mess of clever European pottage."

In his struggle to cast off the erudite tradition and yet to surmount a crudeness and amateurishness that sometimes helped to stamp his music with personality and sometimes prevented him from realizing his intentions, Gilbert resembles Mussorgsky and Chabrier. Both these men seem to have impressed him with their vitality and unconventionality, and his music occasionally shows their direct influence. The prevailing tradition of the time was largely German, and the prestige and success of Dvořák's American works served to strengthen it. Like anyone reacting against an accepted custom, Gilbert was searching around for unconventional elements. These he found in American and Celtic folklore. From the Russians he took for his cue the vigorous, simple, and even crude style he needed to express the spirit of the America he loved. Like many composers of his time, he did not escape the influence of the saccharine chromaticism of Grieg, Dvořák, and MacDowell; but as time went on he gradually eliminated their overripe harmonies and helped to develop the harmonic style which has become the common currency of most popular music since.

Gilbert composed the greater number of his published works from about 1902 to 1913. During these years, he worked on an opera based on Joel Chandler Harris's *Uncle Remus* stories; but after having nearly completed the score he was finally refused permission to use the material. This was one of his greatest disappointments. The opera still lies in manuscript, unperformed, a somewhat remarkable fact considering the success which its *Comedy Overture on Negro Themes* has had in all the years since its first performance in 1911. Judging from this and from the delightful *American Dances* for piano, four hands, published by the Boston Music Company, which are also excerpts, and from the comment of those who heard Gilbert run through the opera, it is rich in the particular homey American humor that was one of Gilbert's most engaging characteristics as a musician and as a man.

Another good work dating from this period is the set of five rag-timey piano numbers, *Negro Dances*, written in a style that closely resembles the popular music of its day and yet raises it to the level of concert music without pretense or falsification of its spirit. At his best in gay, humorous, short pieces, Gilbert was often at a loss in the larger forms, where a lack of emphasis at important points, such as the climax or the end, makes his works seem too short. The *Symphonic Prologue: Riders to the Sea* suffers from this weakness, and perhaps all his other orchestral works of the period would be more effective if their proportions had been slightly amplified.

All kinds of Negro music aroused Gilbert's interest—minstrel, spirituals, Creole songs, and dances like the cake-walk—because that music seemed closely related to the spirit of all America. Its national popularity testified to that. He was not attracted to it because of its strangeness, and, though a Northerner, he never sought to play up the exotic element. He wanted to get at its forthright qualities of humor, sentiment, and vitality. This humor he attempted to express in the orchestral *Humoresque on Negro Minstrel Tunes*, with its gay setting of "Zip Coon" and comically sentimental second theme; its vigor and enthusiasm are reflected in the orchestral *Negro Rhapsody*,

"*Shout.*" His songs, not of great distinction, reveal the strong dramatic sense which pervades all his works. The *Lament of Deirdre*, the *Pirate Song*, and *Salammbo's Invocation to Tanith* are the best instances of this.

Gilbert's greatest popular success came with *Dance in Place Congo*, a twenty-minute tone poem on Creole tunes. Unlike his earlier works, its form is completely convincing, which is why it was more immediately effective. As in Mussorgsky's *Night on Bald Mountain*, there is the striking of a bell in a macabre night revelry which calls the New Orleans slaves back to their quarters. (In the Russian work the dead are called back to their graves.) Yet, although a very effective piece of its kind, it had somehow lost the simplicity and charm of his earlier music. The composer's preface in the printed score admits modestly that he was using the Creole melodies "much after the manner of Grieg or Tchaikovsky." This is not to say that the work lacks personality, for in spite of his admission (which may have been more to calm the public than to inform the critics) it has his characteristic rhythmic vitality and melodic interest. The score, with a ballet interpretation of its program, was performed at the Metropolitan Opera in 1918 and received many enthusiastic tributes. For Gilbert by this time was a composer whom audiences and critics were discussing. All our important orchestras played his music and he had even received acclaim in Russia. His reputation seemed made, most of his scores were published, and he seemed a fixture in American musical life.

But after the end of the war, "modern music" galvanized our audiences. Sides were taken, arguments raged, and the newer music with its tumultuous energy and the violent opinions it aroused made the cause of "American music" and Gilbert's in particular appear tame and faded. Jazz, too, was gaining over ragtime, and Gilbert's raggy pieces began to sound old-fashioned. Gilbert stuck to his guns and wrote the excellent *Symphonic Piece*, which had all the American qualities of his earlier work. It was performed in 1926 by Koussevitzky and deserves a rehearing today. But time was pressing on and the music of Gilbert had no publicity appeal. Younger composers were busy blowing their own horns. After the first fine frenzy of the modern music movement had died down and Gilbert was forgotten, a whole group of composers started rediscovering the virtues of simplicity, of ascetic Americanism, and of many other qualities which he had prefigured. They claimed these as their own invention, as if Gilbert and his fellow nationalists had never existed.

It would be unfortunate for our culture if the present generation were as easily swept aside as all previous ones have been, yet this is the lesson which our history seems to indicate.

Stravinsky in 1940
(1940)

The recent performances of Stravinsky's music, inspired by his presence in America, and particularly by the Town Hall benefit for Allied relief, which gave us a telescoped view of his development from *L'Histoire du soldat* to the *Dumbarton Oaks Concerto*, cannot, it seems to me, fail to raise important questions about his position in our musical life. Here is certainly one of the great figures of the period. He is now fifty-eight years old and his fame has been worldwide for more than thirty years. The important fact remains that, of all his rich and varied output, only two works, both of them early—*The Firebird* and *Petrouchka*—have won a definite place in the standard orchestral repertory. Is this situation the result of certain elements and a development peculiar to Stravinsky's musical nature, or does it reflect tendencies more general to the musical life of our time?

In the not so distant past, a work would find its way into the repertory if it displayed the civilized qualities of imagination, depth, and scope of feeling, a high degree of craftsmanship, and inspiration (and, of course, if it was scored for the normal symphonic or chamber combinations). Thus with the music of Brahms and Tchaikovsky. But although most musicians will agree that many twentieth-century works meet all these requirements, very few have been so recognized by the public. The reasons advanced for this increasing resistance—the standard repertory is large enough to fill several subscription seasons, nobody wants to gamble on doubtful items, the taste of conductors and performers is less revered than in the day when Brahms and Wagner could be put over "on faith" until frequent repetition should develop appreciation—are surface apologies. It is much more apparent that there has been a rather conscious "hardening" of attitude, shared and indeed to some extent now fostered by musicians, against "modernism," by which is meant the musical styles and the technical discoveries that are the special innovations of the past thirty years. How permanent this reaction will be is something that only time can tell. At the moments, however, the defection of the various European groups which chiefly nurtured these twentieth-century innovations and the accelerated pace at which American composers are now directing their attention to the native scene have temporarily fixed the attitude of both performers and audiences.

Reviewing his career, one might now question whether Stravinsky could have attained his prestige without the opportunity supplied by Diaghilev. Notwithstanding all his réclame and the tremendous interest of conductors and musical elite in each new work, his music since *Petrouchka* and *The Firebird* still seems, for the great public, too unusual in sonority and feeling, too disconcerting in its distortions of the familiar. This includes *Les Noces*, and to some extent even *Le Sacre*. His point of view has been rigidly set down as "cerebral" and mathematical, and it has earned the opprobrium of being "neoclassic." To give his all-Stravinsky programs he must include the two old works and add interest by his own appearance as conductor. Thus, assiduously, and by painfully slow steps, introducing newer and more typical compositions one at a time, he attempts to familiarize the public with his recent self. This year the *Jeu de cartes* and the *Capriccio* showed signs of thawing out the audience, although *Apollon*, like the *Symphonie de psaumes*, still remains remote and puzzling.

The Town Hall concert gave us an excellent view of the span of Stravinsky's most significant work. His stage music has always been dense and full enough of musical ideas to stand up in the concert hall. But in *L'Histoire du soldat* and the *Octuor*, we find the beginning of that remarkable series in which he concentrated and purified his musical personality. Both reveal his astonishing intensity, his succinctness, his ability to give a special unity and character to each work. All his music bristles with discoveries, yet in each piece, even in the dance parodies, there is a distinction, a sense of importance, a seriousness of purpose which few composers since the days of the early Romantics have so consistently maintained.

These two pieces also mark the direction he was to take in using familiar musical material, a habit which has proved so disturbing to many listeners. From *L'Histoire*, in which certain violin figures are derived from gypsy music, and the fanfare and other themes from ordinary military marches, down to his *Concerto for Two Solo Pianos* and *Dumbarton Oaks Concerto*, he has been building up a large vocabulary of so-called musical commonplaces. Sometimes they have been taken from periods, but so utilized that they spring to new life—as in *Pulcinella* and *Apollon* (Italian and French eighteenth century) or as in *Baiser de la fée* (nineteenth-century ballet). All these melodic, harmonic and rhythmic turns, whether of formal periods or from popular sources—derived from history and from the music of the ordinary man—have been completely transformed by Stravinsky and today are welded into one style, his own.

The *Octuor*, one of his first important non-theatrical pieces, is also one of the first successful attacks on the problem of creating music whose effect depends chiefly on integration, choice of theme, and development. To this example here with eighteenth-century forms can be traced the consequent use of dissonant counterpoint, canonic imitations, and motivic construction of melodies, which has characterized nearly all contemporary music since the appearance of the *Octuor*. From that date on, Stravinsky in his non-theatrical music has been bringing to a condensation point the various atmospheres of his stage works. With each new piece he comes more and more to grips with the problem of concert music.

The qualities which are the result of this process in the two-piano concerto were discussed here last year. In the *Dumbarton Oaks Concerto*, just introduced to New York, we see Stravinsky renewing his approach to the concerto grosso form. This is no easy task today. Since *Pulcinella* and the *Octuor*, many contemporaries have set themselves the same goal, and there are now hundreds of modern works of this genre. Unquestionably *Dumbarton Oaks* goes them all one better. In this piece for small orchestra, so gay and lively in the manner which seems to come most naturally to him, Stravinsky has carried out his ideas on a large scale and with rhythmic amplitude. The transparent second movement is tender and delicate, the remaining two vivacious and directly attention-compelling. With his newer austerity he avoids the more pointed effects of his earlier music and at the same time brings all the technical innovations of his past together with freedom and ease. Since the Violin Concerto, Stravinsky has been developing a single style, and in these new pieces we see it carried to its most refined point.

Igor Stravinsky, 1882–1971: Two Tributes
(1971)

I

In this period of sorrow, immediately following Stravinsky's death, it is hard to find words to express the many thoughts and impressions that must occupy the minds of many composers and musicians. For me the periods of overwhelming illumination and of profound gratitude for them, of irrepressible wonder, crowd into my mind as I recall the first time I heard *Le Sacre* (which I already knew in a four-hand piano arrangement) played live at Carnegie Hall in the mid-1920s, conducted by Pierre Monteux, and decided there and then to become a composer; or the subsequent fascination with which I was on the lookout for each new work, many of which, like the *Symphonie de psaumes, Perséphone, Jeu de cartes, Orpheus, Symphony in Three Movements*, the *Mass*, the *Cantata, Agon, Threni, Abraham and Isaac*, and *Requiem Canticles*, I had the good fortune to hear in their first performances. This experience, which I actually sought out, out of enthusiasm for the composer's work, was, of course, in this case, filled with amazement and surprise since his growth was a series of unexpected renewals of approach from *Fireworks* to *The Owl and the Pussycat*. Of course, it was easier during the late 1920s and early '30s to keep up because the Boston Symphony played each new Stravinsky work almost as soon as it was finished (unlike orchestras today) and kept some, like *Apollo* and *Capriccio*, in the repertory for years. It was because of this opportunity to know Stravinsky's works that the *Symphonie de psaumes* was so much appreciated by the audiences of the Boston Symphony—the orchestra that commissioned it in 1930. The same cannot be said of the *Symphony in Three Movements*, commissioned by the New York Philharmonic, whose audiences are still "protected" from the new. (It is to be hoped that Boulez will change this.)

Later, when Stravinsky's remarkable piano playing, filled with electricity, began to be heard here, as well as his conducting, many of us were grateful that this great composer had decided to come and live among us. I myself have a very vivid memory of him playing over the score of *Perséphone* (the humanistic rite of spring) with René Maison singing the part of Eumolpe, at the apartment of Nadia Boulanger in Paris a few days before its premiere. What impressed me most, aside from the music itself, was the very telling quality of attack he gave to piano notes, embodying often in just one sound the very quality so characteristic of his music—incisive but not brutal, rhythmically highly controlled yet filled with intensity so that each note was made to seem weighty and important. Every time I heard him play, in the Salle Pleyel, in Town Hall, or wherever, the strong impression of highly individualized, usually detached notes filled with extraordinary dynamism caught my attention immediately—and this was as true in soft passages as in loud.

Then, to my own surprise, I was privileged to meet him, to come to know and witness this remarkable man with his penetrating, brilliant, and original mind and dedicated spirit in action. A highly concentrated inner force, although by then considerably reduced in expression, seemed to govern him even during my last visit in December 1970, when we listened to recordings and followed scores together of *Le Chant du rossignol* and the last act of *Magic Flute*, which he particularly enjoyed, shaking his head and pointing out special beauties on the page.

Through these recent years, when I saw him now and then, certain things that I wanted to make clearer, at least to myself, have nagged at me, but I was never able to formulate them into questions that would bring the answer I wanted. The possibility of such questions came to me first during a time when Robert Craft was conducting my Double Concerto in Los Angeles, and Mr. and Mrs. Stravinsky invited me to their house on North Wetherly Drive. A little discouraged and shy in the midst of such august figures as Spender, Isherwood, and Huxley, who were also there, I went off into a corner, soon to be joined by Stravinsky himself, and we began musicians' talk until I got up the courage to ask him how he composed. At which he took me to his work room, and showed me a large book of blank pages onto which short fragments of musical sketches, roughly torn out of larger sketch-pages, had been pasted. Since the original sketch-pages had been papers of different qualities and colors and the musical fragments (sometimes only two or three notes) had been written on staves that were hand-drawn, often in quite fanciful curves, the scrapbook itself gave a very arresting visual impression. This was the work book for *The Flood*, which I don't think had yet been performed. He proceeded to explain how he chose fragments from his sketches, tore them out, shuffled them in different orders until he found one that satisfied him, and then pasted them down. I was genuinely surprised to learn of such an unexpected way of composing, of which, if I had not known whose music it was, I might have had doubts as to the results; indeed I was so surprised that I did not think of the questions which would continually recur to me from then on. Naturally, he explained that all the fragments were derived from one chosen piece of material (as was evident), but what was not evident to me was how these fragments could be made to fit together. Of course, the printed score of this "Musical Play," which I saw much later, contains passages of short bits of music interspersed between lines of speaking, and these do look very much like what I remember seeing, even in print.

Some time later, I began to realize that what I saw corresponded to glimpses I had had of this technique in his music elsewhere. The description and quotation of Stravinsky telling how he cut up the final "fugue" of *Orpheus* and inserted fragments of harp figurations characteristic of the work, given in Nicolas Nabokov's *Old Friends and New Music*, as well as in a brilliant lecture by Edward Cone on the *Symphonies of Wind Instruments*, recalled to me how pervasive crosscutting was in the music. I had not expected to see it so graphically demonstrated.

In his lecture, Cone shows how the *Symphonies* are made up of a series of different musical movements, each crosscut into the other. Sometimes the edges of the cuts are joined together by transitions or marked by cadences, but usually they are abrupt, coming at a point where the statement of a unified concept or impression is incomplete. In this, these cuts are unlike the articulations of literary works into chapters or stanzas, or of musical works into movements, or even of serialized movies or TV shows, all of which conclude with a completed action, although raising the question, "What happens next?" In Stravinsky, these are more often like random cuts, aimed, probably, as similar devices in the movies, particularly those of Eisenstein, at giving a sense of sampling different kinds of things from which the observer can form a concept of the whole.

Such abrupt articulation seems to have become a conscious device with Stravinsky from about 1916 (*Renard*) on. Naturally one of the questions this brings up as far as music is concerned (since visual things have a very different quality of concreteness) is how these abrupt fragments can be joined into continuities that give the listener a unified musical idea or impression.

In connection with this, one of the things I had always wanted to discuss, especially after I had publicly read the text of the soldier's part of *L'Histoire du soldat* (with Aaron Copland as narrator and John Cage as devil) for a performance given by Lukas Foss, was the lack of the usual continuity in the plot. For I was struck by the fact that there are at least three almost unconnected stories presented one after the other as if they were continuous. The second story starts back where the first one did with the soldier trudging down the road, as if it were the first time. I had also noticed that there was a similar plot structure in *Renard*, and a similar isolation of events so that previous actions seem not to affect succeeding ones—although the final result, the victory of the devil over the soldier or that of the barnyard animals over the fox (each finale presented almost as a separate story), fulfills expectations. In these two stories, the characters on stage and the audience are dealt with as if they had no memory, as if living always in the present and not learning from previous events—a dramatic situation that suggests the puppet world, like that of Punch and Judy, as the authors certainly intended, and also in a larger sense inescapable fate and universality of action such as that in the Everyman plays or that of the shades in the Hades of Gide's libretto for *Perséphone*, who ceaselessly repeat the gestures of living.

Whatever the intention, this kind of almost disjointed repetition immeasurably increases the pathos of both works. In fact, I came to believe, as I studied the soldier's part, that it was just because of this curious plot repetition, especially as it is coupled with music, that, although almost continually different in tiny details, is always drawing attention to its repetitive form, particularly harmonically and motivically. And it is through this that these two works gain their very urgent, compelling quality. For the soldier's violin seldom departs, from beginning to end of the work, from its basic musical material, drawn as it is out of the very fundamentals of violin playing, and from this is derived the tango, waltz, fox-trot, and devil's dance, as well as the striking end. Because of this underlying continuity of material, all the brief, almost discrete fragments, however roughly they connect with each other, end up by producing a work that holds together in a very new and telling way. Disjunction of motive exists in much of Stravinsky's music before this time—such as in the fisherman's song in *Le Rossignol,* in which (especially as it is presented at the end of the opera) each measure, although motivically related to its neighbor, is not connected to it by phrasing, harmonic leading, or rhythm.

Already in *Petrouchka,* of course, there is both a harmonic separation of crowd music from puppet music with a crosscutting of a rather conventional kind from one to the other. In *Le Sacre,* too, there is a use of different chord structures to characterize and unify each dance and to isolate it from its neighbors, a device that had already been used by Bartók in his piano Bagatelles, by Schoenberg in *Erwartung,* and in works by Scriabin and also by Ives. One question I did ask was whether all the chords in *Le Sacre* were related to one source chord (which may be partially or completely stated in the introduction). It was in January 1962, when I was teaching a course that dealt with *Le Sacre* and thought I had discovered such a chord. I showed him my conjecture and he politely turned away from it, saying that he had forgotten whether or not or how he had organized this work. (In connection with this I had meant to ask about the three or four different editions of the "Danse Sacrale," with different orchestrations and with the shift of the corona from the first to the third beat in the first measure, which, along with the change in harmony in the first and second chords and other similar places, not to speak of changes in barlines in the 1943 version, reveal either a change in the idea of the phrasing of the movement or a clarification of what was originally intended, all of which invalidates some French attempts at analysis.)

But to continue about the matter of "unified fragmentation," which really seems to have been carefully studied during the writing of works after *Le Sacre,* like *Pribaoutki* (1914). The idiosyncrasies of Russian folk song and liturgy, of jazz and military band playing, of the parlor parodies of Satie seemed to have played a role in this, which, once it was developed, furnished a pathway out of Russian folklore into an ever broadening musical world of technique and expression—always marked by what came to be recognized everywhere as the highly original and compelling voice of Stravinsky.

As a postscript, I quote my tribute written for the 16 June 1962 issue of the Hamburg newspaper *Die Zeit,* which, unlike American papers, contained a page of tributes to him written by composers from everywhere for his eightieth birthday:

> Stravinsky's music is filled with a remarkable sense of the power, strength, and movement of human life. As no one before him, he captured the immediate moment in all its freshness and vividness and welded it into sequences of music that enhanced its life. Formulae, schemata, and other routines which can fill out musical time and space have no place here. Everything is shaped by the musical concept, which he presents in the most telling and direct way. His entire work—a very personal, almost autobiographical mirror of the development of a composer in our time—when considered as a whole forms a typical composition by Stravinsky. It lives in and grows out of the present through which it passes, finding unexpected but highly evocative and convincing ways of progressing. It denies itself the tried patterns by which similar patterns were solved in the past. It is founded on a new approach to musical statement and expression often called "objective" but no less human for that.

The career of Stravinsky serves as an example of a highly civilized creator aware of the disasters and glories of our period, from which he has drawn very important musical conclusions. His art represents a profession of faith in the value and importance of music to which his work lends new glory.

2

If anyone can be said to have *lived* the artistic history of his time and embodied it in outstanding works, it is Igor Stravinsky. In mourning his death, musicians of succeeding generations suffer this loss as a loss of part of their world. The horizon has suddenly become narrower. For while each generation has tended to live out its particular version of the twentieth century, Stravinsky encompassed them all. The general public, however, for whom he was, as he was for musicians, one of the leaders of his time, mourns the Stravinsky of the early part of this century, when it was still possible for a composer to become world famous. It was a great privilege to have lived in his time, to have awaited year upon year the appearance of new works, each an unexpected departure, a new challenge, and yet always totally engrossing and convincing. He never gave up his status as an advanced composer, as he once said jokingly of himself.

Understandably, many have, and the temptation to continue in the same direction must have been very great for one who between 1910 and 1913, from his twenty-eighth to thirty-first years, caused an international furor with the three ballets, written in quick succession, that have remained in the repertory ever since. They revealed a composer who understood the style of ornamental, romanticizing Russian folklore inherited from Rimsky-Korsakov, and could present it more convincingly than anyone else. Yet the line of development which led him so quickly from *The Firebird* to *Petrouchka* and then to *Le Sacre du printemps* indicates that he was already on the way to a complete change of style. He had the courage to follow this direction, which found support from the new artistic trends in France at the time he finally settled there at the end of the First World War.

Here he soon became the leading figure of the post-war generation, the so-called neoclassicists, in sharp revolt against the former romanticism, impressionism, and fauvism. From then until the end of the Second World War, he explored many facets of this aesthetic with matchless power to convince, ranging more widely than other composers. So widely, in fact, that by 1945 there were indications that still another stylistic change was in progress. And, during the 1950s, he became the leader of this second post-war generation—sometimes called "serialists" because they followed the twelve-tone methods of Stravinsky's contemporary Arnold Schoenberg. From around 1954 to 1967, from his seventy-second to eighty-fifth years, he embraced the methods of this Viennese composer who had long been considered his opponent, outstripping in originality and power all the younger followers with some of his finest works. Naturally each of these about-faces violated public and critical expectations, dismaying and often angering admirers and discouraging many of his disciples.

Yet in no way could this development be considered an effort to be up to the minute, since the works at every stage carried such conviction and imposed themselves by so many remarkable qualities. All are decisively marked by the composer's highly individual way of thinking and expression, by a passion for his particular kind of order and symmetry, and by his quick and intense temperament. The approach to these conflicting styles was that of a poet or novelist toward different subject matters, the invariable being the artistic vision, expression, and handling. In Stravinsky the style was truly the man himself, his own voice, not the "styles" he used.

In fact, the voice became more itself through the adoption of these different aesthetics. In the nine large religious works, spread throughout his life, the sharpening of focus on personal religious experience, the gradual elimination of the extraneous with a consequent increase in seriousness fuses the great variety of methods into one coherent development. The non-religious works as well mark this progression toward the discovery of the essence of their respective genres.

Yet for all Stravinsky's deep artistic commitment, there is much lightness and wit. Impatient with romantic gestures, his was a quick, ironic yet compassionate nature, expressing itself in the brilliant flashes so evident in his secular works, in his television appearances, on the recent Columbia record of rehearsals, in the transcripts of his conversations, and in his actions. He could truthfully answer at eighty-five, with his broad smile, when I asked him what he was composing: "What can you write after a Requiem but a setting of *The Owl and the Pussycat?*"

On Edgard Varèse
(1975/79)

Despite the small amount of music Edgard Varèse left us—about two hours of playing time in all—written between 1920 and 1960 (exclusive of one early setting of Verlaine's "Un Grand Sommeil noir" for voice and piano, which goes back perhaps to 1906, and numerous unfinished works including *Nocturnal*), and despite the great similarities between all of these works, except for the Verlaine, which have led many to say that he wrote the same work over and over, his music has been the inspiration of two generations of American composers—those of the late 1920s and those of the 1950s and '60s, during which time his music began to be much prized in Europe.[1]

Varèse, of course, was one of a now somewhat unjustly forgotten group of experimental composers of the 1920s that flourished in many places: Russians, like the early Arthur Lourié, Wladimir Vogel, Ivan Vyshnegradsky, Nikolai Oboukhov, and Nikolai Roslavets—who settled in Paris, in Zurich, or tragically disappeared—or Americans, like Cowell, Ruggles, Ornstein, and

---

1. This paper is based on an article I wrote in French and read over the transatlantic telephone on 29 October 1975, for a broadcast over Radio-France (ORTF) of a program devoted to Varèse. They are the remarks of a composer and friend which make no pretense to musicological accuracy, since I have no time for research, and rely on memory and, I hope, as little fantasy as possible.

Ives, or those from many other countries, like Chávez, Roldán, Hába, and Petyrek. Of these, it now seems that Varèse was the most striking because he developed a new way of dealing with musical thought and structure. Carrying out a direction that perhaps came from Stravinsky, he made rhythm the primary material of his musical language and used it, rather than thematic linearity, as the thread which holds his compositions together. Usually sharply defined, his rhythmic process recalls the clicking and rattling of rather complex machinery that seems to produce broken, out-of-phase cycles of sound. These rhythms shape the order of presentation of the notes of vertical harmonies that are frequently static and lead them to burst or explode in unexpected ways. Whole sections of any of the characteristic pieces proceed by the varied repetition of short rhythmic cells, sometimes associated with pitched instruments, sometimes with non-pitched percussion.

There seem to be three main types of variations of such cells: first by the addition or subtraction of notes; second, by augmentation or diminution, usually between note values that have a two-to-three relationship instead of the more familiar augmentation and diminution by doubling or halving note values. Of course, as in much music of this period, such cells are frequently shifted from one part of a measure to another, since the barring frequently follows the downbeat accentuation of the leading line and the various inner beats are to follow their own stress patterns. A third way of varying rhythmic cells Varèse uses is that of distortion of their inner relationships: one part of a cell will remain constant on repetition while another is augmented or diminished, often giving the impression of a written-out rubato. The total effect is to produce a much more irregular scansion than that found in Stravinsky, whose irregular scansion is almost always measured by some constant, repeated unit, such as a continuous stream of eighth notes.[2]

In many ways, the mature Varèse scores contain constant irregularities similar to those found in early Schoenberg and Webern, where regularity of unit is often avoided, producing what has often been called "prose rhythm." In Varèse, for instance, there are seldom more than ten notes or micro-cells like flams, drags, ruffs, or paradiddles of equal duration in succession, particularly in the later works. It is true that in the very brilliant passages of *Arcana*, such as those just before and after rehearsal no. 5, there are much more extended passages of equal fast notes, perhaps to give the spaciousness characteristic of this work. In most, however, like *Intégrales*, *Octandre*, *Ionisation*, and *Déserts*, the maximum number of equal values seldom exceeds five, almost invariably preceded and followed by note values that prevent a larger-scale regular rhythmic pattern from being heard. In the Second Viennese school, which employs a somewhat similar practice, this irregularity was prompted, as has often been pointed out, by a desire to extend the notion of

---

2. In reading over this lecture in 1994, I realize that at the time I wrote it I was projecting onto Varèse's music a notion of irregularity of rhythm that is there only sporadically. Since then I have listened to *Arcana*, *Ionisation*, and other works in excellent live performances and have been surprised a bit by the large regular pulses I had not noticed previously, maybe because I had not heard very good performances or was not paying strict attention.

rubato. It was employed primarily to emphasize the expressive phrase structure, freed—apparently—from a regular beat, and to relate one such phrase or motive to another. Probably there was also an intention of avoiding repetition of similar note values, much as repetition of pitches was avoided.

Primarily oriented toward emphatically attacked rhythms, Varèse could be said to have made an amalgam of the Stravinskian and Viennese procedures, although he usually denied this when questioned about it. Certainly a development can be traced almost step by step in a chronological consideration of his scores. His early setting of Verlaine's "Un Grand Sommeil noir" reveals no sign of what was to be his rhythmic development. Like middle-period Fauré and early Debussy songs, it is an almost continuous stream of quarter notes. In this Aeolian E♭-minor piece there is little harmonic movement and a rather portentous tone, both of which one finds in his later, more characteristic work. With *Amériques* of 1920–21 and *Offrandes*, composed later in 1921, his future rhythmic preoccupations begin to take shape. They are much more developed in *Hyperprism* and come closer and closer to the method described above as he approaches *Déserts*, with the exception of *Arcana*, as mentioned above.

It is very important to realize that Varèse was not adopting this structuring as a means of furthering the almost hysterical expressivity sought by the Viennese composers, or as a means of blocking musical flow, but rather as a way of producing a new rhythmic structure with a high degree of forward drive not resulting from regular beat patterns. It was an original and fascinating conception which interested especially the generation after the Second World War: composers like Boulez and Stockhausen for a time tried completely to abolish any sense of rhythmic regularity both in the large and in the smallest details. Much of Boulez's *Structures* seems to be deeply concerned with this problem, and certainly the notion of serializing note values must have derived from a consideration of the rhythmic continuity of such works as *Intégrales*.

What has interested recent composers, also, is that Varèse's music does not depend on thematic motives for its continuity, but rather the relationship between vertical, harmonic structures, instrumental sonorities, spacings, and, of course, the play of rhythmic motives. This is what seems new and important, for his harmonic style with its almost constant chromatic saturation is not very far from that of the Viennese of the earliest part of the century. Even many of his ideas, as Stravinsky himself remarked, especially in the works before *Ionisation* recall quite clearly moments of *Petrouchka* and *Le Sacre*. Too, the use of percussion as the core of the orchestral sound had already been developed by Milhaud in *Les Choéphores* and by Berg in the first of his *Three Pieces for Orchestra*, which starts and ends with non-pitched percussion, modulating by degrees to the pitches of the orchestral instruments and then back to non-pitch, while the construction of a piece entirely for percussion had been effectively done in one of the movements of Alexander Tcherepnin's First Symphony. But even in his first American works Varèse carried these earlier devices much further.

The idea of treating percussion as an independent element in an orchestral fabric may go back further than Wagner's Nibelheim, but it is in this scene that the three types of usage in which rhythm becomes a primary element can be clearly distinguished: that of a purely orchestral treatment of rhythm, that of a purely non-pitched percussion, and a combination of both in which each is more or less independent of the other. Sharing in the general Romantic tendency to fade from one scene to another, Nibelheim is first suggested with triplet rhythms in the orchestra; gradually these are taken over by anvils of three different registral levels, all located in different parts of the stage, until eighteen are playing nine different lines of music, dovetailing their different contributions into a grotesquely entertaining vision of the horrors of factory work, which fades back into the orchestrated quarrel between boss Alberich and Mime, one of his downtrodden employees.

Varèse, coming at a later time with another aesthetic and another vocabulary, and with a desire to produce music that interested because of its internal patterning, carried these three phases—rhythmicized orchestra, percussion alone, and a combination of both with each contributing different elements to the total effect—to a much more extensive development. In general the pitched instruments, usually winds, tend to be treated as percussion instruments repeating short patterns of one or two fixed pitches and thus can be easily amalgamated into the total effect. The use of the orchestra without percussion occurs in short moments in each of the works, except, of course, in *Ionisation*, where the orchestra is omitted altogether, and in *Octandre*, where no percussion is used. In the latter, nevertheless, the treatment of instruments as if they were percussion—having isolated sound characteristics of timbre, pitch, and register—leads to irregularly repeated single notes, or two-note intervals, or to chords of various densities, or figures that oscillate between two (less frequently three) different but fixed elements. Very often two or three such repetitive continuities out of phase with each other are presented at once and in contrasting registers that make them clearly separable to the listener. Such a pattern is characteristic of almost all of *Octandre* and of the opening of *Intégrales*.

At the other extreme are the pure percussion passages that occur here and there throughout the works and find their epitome in *Ionisation*. It must be said here that Varèse's exploration of percussion instruments, his categorization of them—particularly illustrated in the way he used them—developed this whole field far beyond its previous state and has given rise over the past twenty years to a whole new generation of percussion players equipped to do things which would never have been thought of if his fascinating scores had not existed. The composing world in this respect, as in many others, owes him a great debt of gratitude. It was probably the teaching of Messiaen at the Conservatoire after the Second World War that brought Varèse, and particularly his use of percussion, to the attention of the young composers who were to form the Darmstadt school. And in return it was after their reputations were made that he began to use the vibraphone and magnetic tape, perhaps being influenced by them.

In Varèse's music, the combination of the usual orchestral instruments with the percussion is seldom of the familiar type—that which lends emphasis or color to orchestral rhythms and textures. It does occur in the big works like *Amériques*, *Arcana*, and *Déserts*, but in the last two rather rarely in comparison to the more usual stratification of orchestra and percussion so characteristic of his work, paralleling the stratification described in *Octandre* above. Such stratification occurs in textures in which pitched instruments and non-pitched percussion form two separate groups, each contributing different elements to the total effect, making a novel conglomerate of musical sound-material, part pitched and part non-pitched. Examples of this occur in *Offrandes*, where in the first song, "Chanson de là-haut," the percussion contributes articulative moments at the end of instrumental phrases, when it is not emphasizing instrumental motives, and in the second, "La croix du sud," where at the opening and ending the percussion is quite independent of the other instruments, having its own motives for the most part and only related to them in large phrase structure. Even here the various elements of the percussion itself begin to be stratified.

In the next work, *Hyperprism*, for the first thirty measures and again near the end, a much more elaborately stratified percussion adds its own motives to the repeated C♯s of the trombone and horns through the first eleven measures, relating to these to form a series of distinct phrases. Later the percussion fills in the end of a flute solo much in the same way as had been done in "Chanson de là-haut."

In the next work to use percussion, *Intégrales* of 1924–25, there is a much greater independence between the percussion strata and those of the orchestra. The opening section (first twenty-three measures) is broken into approximately eleven phrases, some consisting of the one note B♭ repeated and ornamented in various ways, while others start with this note and build up to a chord. What is interesting is how this phrase beginning on B♭ alone is accompanied in every case with a new and different timbre of percussion. At first B♭ appears all alone, next with softly ringing tam-tam and gong not struck on beats that coincide with the attacks of the B♭, the third time a castanet motive is heard, the fourth time a few notes on the switch, and so forth. Meanwhile another element of the percussion links the end of one phrase with the next so as to give the impression that the phrase structure of the percussion does not coincide with that of the pitched instruments. This becomes especially striking at the conclusion of the passage when the percussion drops out, allowing the orchestral instruments to make their crescendo on an eleven-note held chord all alone, and then come in, as if interrupted, continuing the material from the earlier section, so that the orchestral instruments seem to come to a cadence while the others continue as if this had not happened. The return of music similar to the opening near the end exhibits the same characteristics. *Arcana* of 1926–27 is much more restricted in this type of passage, as is *Ecuatorial* of 1933–34, while perhaps the most interesting ones of all come in *Déserts* after the first taped intervention, in mm. 87–114, and in the passage following m. 132.

In considering all of this, it should be borne in mind that we are talking of music closely related to that of the first two decades of our century, when the musical avant-garde felt it was on the crest of a wave signifying a brightening and progressive future and was aware of the responsibility that this might entail. In fact, Varèse, who composed most of the works we know between 1920 and 1927, remained during his whole mature life attached to this heroic period of the avant-garde. Coming late to this movement, he was able to profit by the music of his immediate predecessors. Living in America, he was somewhat protected from the rapid change of fashion in France after the First World War that led to the neoclassicism of *Les Six* and the *Ecole d'Arcueil*, which resulted in an almost complete neglect of his work there. In America, where trendiness, particularly in music, is neither as clear-cut nor as cultist as in France, fifteen years or so passed after the First World War during which Stokowski and many others encouraged Varèse and played his works. Even in the 1930s and '40s, after which interest in him revived, there was always a small group of Americans who continued to believe in the validity of the older avant-garde style, like Ruggles, Cowell, Riegger, and even Ives, who although he had stopped composing by that time still helped finance the publication of such music.

During the Second World War such activity was somewhat eclipsed. Stokowski like a number of others had lost interest in sponsoring avant-garde performances, and it became harder and harder to find ways of presenting Varèse's music here. Yet even during this period several of his friends made a great deal of effort to have his music played in order to help the composer maintain contact with live performance. I remember particularly a concert organized in 1947 at the New School to present extracts from his *Etude* for *Espace*, apparently never completed, for chorus singing and speaking in several languages at once and accompanied mainly by percussion. It proved a most stimulating score, suggesting a whole world of new possibilities not thought of at that time; it had certain affinities with Milhaud's *Mort d'un tyran* and the oratorios of Wladimir Vogel like *Wagadu* but was much more varied and flexible than either of these.

Varèse invariably had very striking ideas for his projected works. Long ago he used to have the reputation among his fellow students in Widor's composition class as one who appeared each week with one or two new measures of music and a new fascinating description of what he intended to write but never completed anything. If this story has any truth to it, it was not long before he did learn how to realize his unusual visions. One can remember here in New York passionate, fascinating conversations about future plans for works, and it is to be regretted that he did not have time to carry more of them to completion, since those that he did complete remain so enthralling.

Edward Steuermann
(1966)

The striking text of Kafka, "Auf der Galerie," used by Edward Steuermann for one of his last works, a Cantata for mixed chorus and orchestra (1964), furnishes such a significant comment on the type of performance to which he devoted an important part of his life, and his choice of this particular text such an insight into what must have been one of his attitudes about performance, that this discussion must begin by quoting it:

> If some frail, consumptive equestrienne in the circus were to be urged around and around on an undulating horse for months on end without respite by a ruthless, whip-flourishing ringmaster, before an insatiable public, whizzing along on her horse, throwing kisses, swaying from the waist, and if this performance were likely to continue in the infinite perspective of a drab future to the unceasing roar of the orchestra and hum of the ventilators, accompanied by ebbing and renewed swelling bursts of applause which are really steam hammers—then, perhaps, a young visitor to the gallery might race down the long stairs through all the circles, rush into the ring, and yell: Stop! against the fanfares of the orchestra still playing the appropriate music.
>
> But since that is not so; a lovely lady, pink and white, floats in between the curtains, which proud lackeys open before her; the ringmaster, deferentially catching her eye, comes towards her breathing animal devotion; tenderly lifts her up on the dapple-gray, as if she were his own most precious granddaughter about to start on a dangerous journey; cannot make up his mind to give the signal with his whip, finally masters himself enough to crack the whip loudly; runs along beside the horse, open-mouthed; follows with a sharp eye the leaps taken by its rider; finds her artistic skill almost beyond belief; calls to her with English shouts of warning; angrily exhorts the grooms who hold the hoops to be most closely attentive; before the great somersault lifts up his arms and implores the orchestra to be silent; finally lifts the little one down from her trembling horse, kisses her on both cheeks, and finds that all the ovation she gets from the audience is barely sufficient; while she herself, supported by him, right up to the tips of her toes, in a cloud of dust, with outstretched arms and small head thrown back, invites the whole circus to share her triumph—since that is so, the visitor to the gallery lays his face on the rail before him and, sinking into the closing march as into a heavy dream, weeps without knowing it.[1]

In spite of a typical Kafkaesque ambiguity, on one level at least, this can be read as a double view of the performing situation, contrasting the "behind the scenes," tired, routined "professional" aspect with its communicative, evocative intention. The deep ambiguity about which aspect is "real" and which "imagined" for the various participants, and also the comment one aspect makes on the other, is not lost on the "young visitor." Steuermann's setting casts a mask of highly sensitive, beautifully connected phrases over the whole text, avoiding any direct reference to the circus world (other than an occasional drum roll) or any other mimicry. In one continuously developed movement that minimizes the contrast between the two paragraphs and dramatic moments such as the young visitor's "Stop" or the rider's "great somersault," it passes over these quickly to emphasize a fleeting, alternately shadowy and excited nervous character. The score is one of delicate shadings, smooth transitions, with a mosaic of contrasting bits of material of much greater variety,

---

1. Franz Kafka, "Up in the Gallery," trans. Willa and Edwin Muir, in *The Complete Stories*, ed. Nahum N. Glatzer (New York: Schocken Books, 1971), 401–2.

character, and expressive scope than those of the late Webern cantatas, which it remotely resembles, although actually closer in character to the pre-twelve-tone Viennese works. In emphasizing musical over dramatic development, it bears out Steuermann's statement to Gunther Schuller: "His [Schreker's] approach was a little *theatralisch*, which was against the spirit of the Schoenberg school."[2]

This Cantata was given its first performance at the Juilliard School at a memorial concert devoted to Steuermann's works, one year after his death, and like the three other original works on the program—*Drei Chöre*, for mixed voices with instrumental accompaniment (1956); the Suite for Piano (1954); and the *Suite for Chamber Orchestra* in four movements (1964), together with a charming arrangement for three pianos of Schubert's *Wohin*—represents his personal development of the general style of the Schoenberg school, in an apparently original way. I say "apparently" because Steuermann's music and indeed a great deal written by those associated with or influenced by this school (other than Berg, Webern, and perhaps Krenek, Eisler, Pisk, and Weiss), like that of many who came to maturity before the Second World War, is hardly known in spite of the interesting but far too sketchy account of their work in Leibowitz's *Introduction à la musique de douze sons* (Paris, 1949) and a few articles by Adorno. This lack of recognition, performance, and publication prevents us from knowing the many interesting developments of this style and the musical influences as well as the individual originalities. That there was such a development can be clearly seen in works of Wellesz, Gerhard, Kahn, Apostel, Gielen (to name but a few at random), and Steuermann himself. The works of Steuermann heard at this concert represent what must have been a long development in a special direction. The style differs from the known one in its much greater freedom of pitch recurrence within each statement of the row, octave encounters, octave transpositions, and even tonal references. Partly because of similarities in technical features and in general character, this reviewer was reminded of some of the music of the very youngest generation of Polish composers—Krauze, Madey, and Meyer—heard at the Warsaw Autumn this year. This may represent a reaction against the "post-Webern" style—so different from the music of Steuermann, which emphasizes sensitivity, fanciful variety, and "heard" inner organization.

The special quality that informed his thinking, aside from the musicogrammatical traits mentioned above, is evident in all four compositions played, particularly the two composed in 1964. These reveal a wealth of imagination about musical syntax, as regards construction of motives and textures into phrases, phrases into sentences, paragraphs, total compositions, and the inner articulation of all of these. There is even a complexity of articulation that resembles the interplay of verbal syntactical structures and versification structures, which fall into lines and stanzas not necessarily coordinated with the

2. Gunther Schuller, "Conversation with Steuermann," *Perspectives of New Music* 3, no. 1 (Fall–Winter 1964):22–35.

Example 1. Edward Steuermann, Suite for Chamber Orchestra (1964), mm. 14–18.

former. Much imagination is expended on such things as the preparation for the beginning of a phrase, its type of actual "beginning" with varied degrees of new or referential assertiveness or with direct linking with previous ones, its "middle" comprising perhaps an expressive or accented point of emphasis, and its "end"—strong or weak, abrupt or prolonged. Similarly there is a great

Example 1. *(continued)*.

concern for interrelation of phrases, of cross-cutting one with another, of sharply delineated or ambiguous and concealed articulations. The *Suite for Chamber Orchestra* (1964) in particular maintains an interesting flow of constantly evolving dialectical statements made of short strands (often three-note motives) of contrasting intervallic, rhythmic, timbral, and dynamic content that in combination produce flexible phrases in a logical and expressive continuity (see Ex. 1).

Note the transition from m. 14 to m. 15 with the pivotal A passed from guitar doubled by viola to the cello, and the descending melodic interval A-C♯ in eighth notes, *piano*, suddenly expanded to A-C by the cello, in sixteenths, *forte*, also the linking fourth G♯-C♯ starting in m. 16 in the viola pizzicato, the picked up by the violin tremolo, *sul ponticello*, each softly, then suddenly attacked by the marimba tremolo *sforzando-piano*, which is held as a new phrase enters in m. 18, started by the viola, which refers, near its end, on the last quarter of the measure, to the pitches in question. This example, besides illustrating a frequently employed method of pivotal tones, also shows a linking by similar sonorities (the diminished triad in m. 14 is heard transposed in m. 15), and the interweaving of short motives of different character and intervallic content.

It is impossible to point out many such devices within the cumbersome limits of a printed discussion. But in thinking about them, the remarkable performance of Chopin's Preludes given by Steuermann a few years ago at the Juilliard School is brought to mind. For many this was one of the more memorable musical experiences of recent years. Discussing this performance after the concert, he explained, humorously referring to the fact that he was a Pole, too, that he had tried to find in each of these pieces that which interested him most as a composer and to bring these points to the attention of the listener, without, of course, violating Chopin's intentions. In performance, each prelude became a work of special character, different from the others not merely in general expression and sonority but even in thought process. Certain moments left a lasting impression—the way, for instance, the much-discussed E♭ came in at the end of the F-major Prelude as a structural event prepared throughout the piece, not as the commonplace effect of sonority it is usually thought of. And this moment was made to seem part of a whole series of similar events in other preludes, as part of the logic of the entire set. His performance made the listener sit up and listen so as not to miss the wealth of freshness seen in a work that is only too familiar.

Theodor W. Adorno, who studied piano with him in 1921, recalls:

> It is however true that the discipline and control that this kind of performance exacts from the performing musician is more than unusual and approaches the unbearable. Steuermann increased the ability to analyze concretely to a point of magnificent defeatism of Kafka proportions. When he despaired of all his pupils and wondered if they would ever learn to play the piano properly, he was animated by the fact that he asked the same question of himself—a question he expressed frequently and very seriously. . . . With talmudic strength, by interlinear vision, so to speak, he made the signs and markings of the score speak to him. But equally strong was his expressionist impulse: as a pianist, Steuermann freed musical expression in agitated eruptions from its taboos.[3]

3. Theodor W. Adorno, "Nachruf auf einen Pianisten: Zum Tode von Eduard Steuermann," *Süddeutsche Zeitung*, 28/29 November 1964.

Steuermann was born in Poland in 1892, went to Vienna to study with Busoni shortly before 1914, and joined the Schoenberg circle, to which he devoted his remarkable musical abilities not only as a pianist who championed Schoenberg's and other modern works from then until the end of his life, abroad and here, but as an arranger of them for piano, as their analyst, and as a coach imparting information about their performance that he had received from Schoenberg. His contact with this music gave a special, urgent quality to his playing of the classics. As Adorno says:

> Steuermann not only had an open, receptive mind for the modern radicals, but he was part and parcel of their very existence, and embodies the refutation of the fatal habit of separating actual composing from music making. The interpreter is doomed when he feels closer to music of a different age and relating to circumstances now remote, than to music that rises from his own historic moment.[4]

In his years in this country from 1936, he was at first in the difficult position of a refugee, and then during the 1940s and '50s of the typical advanced musician living in a society that did not favor his particular talents. Like many others of his time—Roberto Gerhard and Egon Wellesz in England; Wladimir Vogel in Switzerland; Stefan Wolpe, Erich Itor Kahn, and Ernst Toch here; and a host of others composing in a style unappreciated at the time—he suffered tragic neglect. By the time Schoenberg came to this country in 1933 the earlier period of interest in and even enthusiasm for the musical avant-garde both of America and Europe had passed. Enthusiastic support to these, as was given by Huneker and Rosenfeld in their critical writings of the early 1920s and by Stokowski at Philadelphia Orchestra concerts, had given way to the views of a new generation, which looked back on this music as "old-fashioned modernism." Conductors were following the lead of Koussevitzky in hailing neoclassicism and populism as the vital new trend. Nevertheless, the modernist groups never ceased entirely to be active and fought to give performances. One of the most energetic individuals in this was Steuermann himself, who, with Mark Brunswick and Roger Sessions, gave a series of Contemporary Concerts in 1939 and 1940 in which those interested heard, perhaps for the first time in America, excellent performances of the Viennese composers and others whose music had figured in the programs of Schoenberg's *Verein für musikalische Privataufführungen*. The very smallness of this effort, which continued, always aided by Steuermann as adviser, as organizer, and as performer, during the active years of the ISCM and then of its combination with the League of Composers well into the 1950s, had a very selective effect on the choice of music. Works of a composer such as Steuermann were by the very nature of things neglected, even by himself, in the effort to present performances of the as yet unfamiliar works of the well-known Viennese, those of the older American avant-garde, and those of the few young Americans who were developing along these lines and could find no place else to hear their works. The patient and self-denying

4. Ibid.

attitude of many in Steuermann's position at that time helped to lay the groundwork for the rediscovery of this avant-garde, which took place after the war, and helped to keep alive a way of thinking about music, of composing, that for a time seemed about to disappear. American musicians owe an immense debt of gratitude to this group and to Steuermann for, first, having kept alive our faith in this music, and, second, having made it as meaningful in performance as it had seemed in score.

His own attitude is best summed up in an article he wrote on the occasion of Schoenberg's seventy-fifth anniversary for the Australian journal *The Canon*:

> All this is Schoenberg's life: fight, incessantly from the very beginning; fight for the future, fight for the past—the past he overcame to show the future, the future he showed to preserve the past. These battles are history by now. . . . There is hardly a musician of our time not influenced by him, hardly any music conceivable which bypasses his work and thought.
>
> As the memory of the struggle becomes more distant it seems as though the fight had raged mostly around misunderstandings: matters of style, method, theory. These have been accepted, voluntarily or subconsciously, in faith or in protest, possibly laying the ground for new misunderstandings.[5]

Now that the music he fought for is being recognized, it is important for us to know the music of those who, like Steuermann, continued to carry its implications in unfamiliar directions.

Walter Piston
(1946)

For the past twenty years Walter Piston has devoted himself, with a consistency of purpose and conviction rare in our rapidly changing times, to one of the central problems of purely instrumental composition. From his earliest available work, *Three Pieces for Flute, Clarinet, and Bassoon*, in which he reveals himself already skilled and imaginative in the contemporary idiom, his major concern has been the creation of valid and imaginative concert music in the larger forms. It is hard to think of another composer of importance as prolific as he who has written so few theatrical and vocal works. Those who are remembered primarily for their instrumental music usually have a considerable list of less abstract and more literary work—operas, ballets, choral or vocal music, or incidental scores for the theatre or the films—to their credit also. But Piston, so far, seems satisfied with his single short choral piece and his one ballet and has focused his energies on a considerable series of pieces with such soberly appropriate titles as "Symphony," "Sonata for Violin and Piano," "Prelude and Fugue," and the like.

Through the years when the "avant-garde" moderns were busy exploring

5. Edward Steuermann, "A Great Mind and a Great Heart," *The Canon—The Australian Journal of Music* (September 1949), 111.

fantastic new sounds and sequences, often under the inspiration of literary and theatrical ideas, through the early 1930s when a new wave of nationalism and populism startled many into thinking that the concert hall with its museum atmosphere was finished as a place for living new music, down to the present, more conservative situation, Piston went his own way. He stood firmly on his own chosen ground, building up a style that is a synthesis of most of the important characteristics of contemporary music and assimilating into his own manner the various changes as they came along. As a result of this tireless concentration combined with rich native musical gifts, his works have a uniform excellence that seems destined to give them an important position in the musical repertory.

On surveying the course of his life, one is impressed by this quality of integration and direction. Once his particular field was decided on, the rest of his career was organized to suit. The rather speculative enterprise of uniting the different styles of contemporary music into one common style and using this in an ordered and beautiful way needs the peacefulness and sense of long-term continuity nowadays more frequently found in a university than elsewhere. Besides, as is well known, composing large works for the concert hall is one of the most unremunerative, if highly honored, fields of music in this country. It requires, therefore, a fairly steady source of outside income at least during its maturing stages if not afterwards, as well as a considerable amount of uninterrupted time. Few positions outside the academic world offer these advantages, and a university provides a place where long-range consideration of questions of broad scope are the rule rather than the exception. All these considerations must have determined Piston on an academic career. Before he decided, he tried out several alternatives, until he became more aware of his own capabilities as a musician. Once having decided, he took up a modest and quiet life as a composer on Belmont Hill overlooking Cambridge and Harvard, the scene of his teaching career.

His paternal grandfather, the one Italian member of his otherwise typically "down East" family, had already died by the time Piston was born in Rockland, Maine, in 1894. Life in a small community being what it is, the Italian heritage had already been considerably effaced. "Pistone" was changed to "Piston," and the composer's father, though half Italian, knew only how to count up to five in the foreign language. Like most Americans, the composer had little or no music at home, although several years after his family moved to Boston in 1905, the father bought young Walter a violin and his brother a piano. Up to this time, his innate musical abilities had had no chance to develop. But while he was teaching himself to play on both the piano and the violin, music began to assert its ascendancy. Engineering, which he was studying in a vocational high school, soon lost its interest. When Piston first played a march among the violins of the school orchestra, he immediately fell in love with music, but could not make up his mind to pursue it professionally until he had more training.

From this time until he was twenty-six, he tried different plans. First he made up his mind to be an artist, giving up the draftsman's position with the Boston Elevated Company he had taken on graduation from high school in 1912. Then he wavered several years between being a painter or a musician. During this time, he studied the violin with various teachers and earned his living playing in cafés, restaurants, and dance halls. In this way he acquired the intimate feeling for popular music that flavors many of his compositions. At twenty-two, still undecided, he went to the Massachusetts Normal Art School, where tuition was free. Here he came in contact with French art through his teachers and began to look towards Paris, where he later went to study.

This inclination towards French culture, which still slightly tinges his compositions, was reinforced by many impressions during Piston's student years. Rabaud and then Monteux succeeded Karl Muck as conductor of the Boston Symphony in 1918 and a great deal more new French music began to be heard. Boston had always been cosmopolitan in its relation to European cultures and France had frequently been favored. Puvis de Chavannes had crossed the Atlantic to paint his frescoes in the Boston Public Library. Edward Burlingame Hill had studied in Paris, and Henry F. Gilbert had made a pilgrimage to France on a cattle boat to hear Charpentier's opera *Louise*. There was, in fact, considerable precedent for a musician living in Boston to be attracted to the French tradition, and Piston's own personal qualities, his love of proportion and restraint as manifest in his compositions as in his elegantly penned manuscripts, predisposed him to regard this tradition with respect.

When the United States declared war, he volunteered for service in a Navy band; counting on his unusual ability to master an instrument, he claimed he could play the saxophone. Called up, he rushed off to buy an instrument and to borrow a manual from the public library; and in a short time he knew enough to be able to hold his own in a band stationed at the Massachusetts Institute of Technology throughout the war. He was already aware that the saxophone can be learned more quickly than any other of the band instruments. But this is only a trivial indication of a penetrating knowledge of musical instruments gained before and after this time. Indeed, his understanding of the different schools of playing, the different makes of instruments, and all the most practical matters of performance surprised and delighted his fellow students both at Harvard and later in Paris. His knowledge of the registers of the instruments and their qualities and the type of writing idiomatic for each is evident on every page of every score. He likes to give each orchestral player something interesting to do in the course of a work, no matter how subordinate the part. The pleasure he takes in such matters is always stimulating to his orchestration classes, and this care and understanding is a token of the thoroughness and realistic grasp with which he approaches every aspect of his art, from the type of pen to use in copying to the construction of a symphonic movement.

After the war, he resumed the study of the violin, hoping eventually to take a place in the string section of the Boston Symphony Orchestra. But the prospect of being a professional performer did not attract him as much as the possibility of entering upon an academic career—a possibility opened up by his studies in counterpoint with Archibald Davison of the Harvard Music

Department. Davison recognized his unusual abilities and was anxious to enroll him as a regular student.

Thus, in the fall of 1920, at the age of twenty-six, already married to the painter Kathryn Nason, Piston became a freshman at Harvard. To support the newly formed ménage, he continued fiddling for a living and also helped as an assistant in music classes at the college.

About this time, the placid routine of college music teaching began to be disturbed by the strangeness of the new music. Few had the vision of Edward Burlingame Hill, who kept his annual course in modern French music up to date with the latest scores from Paris. Almost no theory teacher had yet thought of renovating his courses to keep pace with contemporary music, which Piston was later to do. Students were beginning to bring in compositions that seemed to flout every idea that teachers believed in. No one had ever before doubted the pedagogical usefulness of the Beethoven sonatas. Yet one pupil raised a protest on being asked to analyze one, saying that he could not even bear to play it over. One of Piston's fellow students, Virgil Thomson, arranged a performance of Erik Satie's *Socrate* that is still talked about. But Piston was not among the dissidents. He applied himself to his studies so assiduously that he graduated *summa cum laude*.

It was not only through the ructions of classroom revolutionaries that Harvard was feeling the impact of the First World War. Several different trends expressed themselves in books by a few of the professors and give a deeper insight into the temper of the time. Internationalism was stressed as an antidote to the narrow isolationism keeping us out of the League of Nations. Ideas sprouted up here that opened the way for new developments in music in this country parallel to those taking place abroad. It was a short step to an international style in music, a common, exportable language interesting to musicians all over the Western world and subordinating the national and personal. And this language was to serve the purposes of serious art that does not rest on local color and that aims at universal validity. Such ideas were given particular consideration at this time, although they were not new. Edgar Allan Poe, for instance, had said that "the world at large" is "the only proper stage" for both reader and writer. It is because Piston's music moves on this stage with such mastery that it is so highly regarded by many Europeans.

Rejection of the Romantic gestures and emotional attitudes of the nineteenth century also marks the music of the time. This was absorbed by Piston along with other characteristics of modern music, but only in certain respects. He has not been affected by the various types of return to the primitive and childlike, or by the modern methods of pastiche which ape the mannerisms of other styles, past and present. Only occasionally does he follow rhythmic and melodic patterns derived from older music, such as that of Bach in the first movement of the Concerto for Orchestra, although this is purely modern in feeling and is not a comment on the older style but a direct expression of a character somewhat akin to that of a *Brandenburg Concerto*. Piston's use of classical forms closely related to those of Bach, Mozart, and Beethoven, as well as his sense of order and propriety, characterize his reaction to this trend.

It is important to realize the power of anti-Romanticism in the post-war period both here and abroad. It seemed to many the valid answer to a need to sweep away the grandiose illusions and the vaporous hopes fostered by the Romantics and a way of finding a stronger basis in reality for human conduct. Once more, as before the nineteenth century, artists wanted to be considered artisans, skilled craftsmen, the opposite of romantically inspired, erratic geniuses, and many of the newer composers took pains to foster this impression in their outward actions. In their music, they did not wish to exaggerate human feelings to titanic proportions but sought the well formed and the logically thought out.

Leaving the intellectually active atmosphere of Harvard, Piston, on graduating, went to Paris on a Paine Fellowship, intending to complete a thorough technical and professional training at the Conservatoire. When he was refused admission because he was thirty years old, he turned to Nadia Boulanger as one of the few outstanding teachers of the time who was sympathetic to contemporary music. By this time he was completely won over to new music, and, following all the performances of recent works, studying scores, he was able to master many of its techniques. His first works were played in Paris, and when in 1926 he returned to Harvard, where he has taught ever since, he brought with him the *Three Pieces for Flute, Clarinet, and Bassoon*, which Paul Dukas had called "Stravinskistes." These at once impressed many forward-looking musicians. Starting as an instructor, he rose to an associate professorship and the chairmanship of the music department. Afterwards, he relinquished the latter office because it interfered with his composing. He became a full professor in 1944. Working at his composition modestly and seriously, he has gradually gained prominence in the quiet way that characterizes all of his actions, so that Slonimsky in 1945 was justified in saying: "In the constellation of modern American composers, Walter Piston has now reached the stardom of the first magnitude. He has not exploded into stellar prominence like a surprising nova, but took his place inconspicuously, without passing through the inevitable stage of musical exhibitionism or futuristic eccentricity."[1]

So far, I have indicated the quality of Piston's native musical gifts, his love of *métier*, his openness to new developments, and his continuous devotion to the high principles of purely instrumental music. His early predilection for French culture, fortified by various trends in Boston and at Harvard, led him to study in France, and several ideas that were stressed in the post-war period, such as internationalism and anti-Romanticism, helped to crystallize his relationship to musical tradition. The nature of this relationship, so important a part of his musical personality, becomes apparent when we consider his point of view as a teacher.

The impact on music schools of the contemporary, and of the older periods brought to light by musicologists, demanded a complete revision of courses in

---

1. Nicolas Slonimsky, program notes for a concert of The Civic Symphony Orchestra of Boston (Paul Cherkassy, conductor), 18 April 1945.

music theory. Aims had to be redefined and new means of presentation devised. As a progressive new theory teacher, Piston tackled this problem and went to its core, attacking it in much the same analytic way that he applied to the study of contemporary scores. The standardized academic routine, which taught harmony and counterpoint according to outmoded and unimaginative textbooks, insensitive to the beauties of the great composers' use of these materials, seemed more sterile than ever as students came to know many different kinds of music. A thorough analysis of the use of harmony and counterpoint by the great composers particularly of the thorough-bass period seemed indicated as a point from which to branch out. In his books, *Harmony: Principles of Harmonic Analysis* (1941) and *Counterpoint* (in preparation[2]), Piston points out many important factors at work in older music, giving examples from actual scores and devising exercises to supplement these. He dwells on the problem of rhythm, especially of the rhythmic change of harmony, which so often enlivens contrapuntal rhythms without coinciding with them. He shows the relation of strong and weak progressions to strong and weak beats. In his own music a wide use of these principles greatly animates the motion. His plan is to continue this series of writings with a book on contemporary styles.[3]

His books, like his articles in magazines such as *Modern Music*, have a smooth and closely packed, thoughtful style that is in direct contrast to the dogmatic systematization of older textbooks. It has been said that the latter sought to organize their subject on the analogy of a book on classical mechanics, in which propositions are deduced from a series of fundamental axioms. However, few of the authors had the penetration of Archimedes, and the axioms as well as the deductions are not generally true. The result is the reduction of the subject to a routine of formulas divorced from living practice. Piston adopts a more inductive method, searching out fundamental principles, and is not interested in formulas that make easy examination questions and bad music.

His own compositions have been praised as exhibiting a new academicism; they have also been condemned for the same reason. But if the academic method consists in drawing up a system of rules that solve every problem of musical composition including that of expression, Piston's music as well as his teaching follows a very different direction. His opposition to facile, routine solutions is obvious even in the detail of his music. For in it, frequently repeated figures, static harmonies, and extended parallel motions

2. Walter Piston, *Counterpoint* (New York: W. W. Norton & Co., 1947). [S]

3. Piston did follow up with his *Orchestration* (New York: W. W. Norton & Co., 1955), but never published a book on contemporary styles. However, in a letter dated 21 September 1976, he wrote to us, "I am . . . very busy working on a Fourth Edition of my *Harmony* (W. W. Norton). It is supposed to deal more with the transition from XIX to XX centuries. Most fascinating and I am learning a lot." Less than two months later, on 12 November, he died. [S] The work was completed by his former pupil, Mark DeVoto, and brought out in 1978. [B]

are the exception rather than the rule. The broad application of general principles that give ample chance for freedom attracts him most. As Israel Citkowitz put it: "His insistence on the purity and definitiveness of musical pattern links Piston to that current of contemporary thought which has attempted to reabsorb classical principles into the music of today."[4]

This emphasis on principles rather than on codifications enables him to teach student composers without dictating their choice of style. In fact, he is against that contemporary academicism that substitutes a new routine for an older one, his opposition resting on the sensible ground that any style, even a contemporary one, gets out of date and may suddenly no longer suit the needs of the growing composer, who, without a basic training to fall back on, will have trouble starting afresh.

In class, Piston is affable, tolerant, and reserved. Though quiet he is far from the dry professor, because he casts over his subject a penetrating wit or a thoughtful seriousness that comes from a deep concern with the subject at hand. His sly humor is always good-natured and so aptly expressed that his words linger in the memory long after they are said. Having an uncommon respect for the art of music, he is fond of quoting the maxim, "Life is short and art long," and pointing out how it is the composer's business to keep learning. He is not ashamed of admitting how much he finds out from hearing his own works played. Usually willing to talk about his music to someone who is seriously interested, he is not inclined to talk about himself. When he does, it is with a dignified modesty that sometimes baffles those accustomed to the usual ways of musicians. These traits seldom fail to command the respect and liking of his students, especially those who share his concern for the art.

Because of the number and variety of Piston's compositions, it is hard to discuss them in the detail they deserve without taking a great deal of space. Certain broad points can be made which throw light on them as a whole. Because in his music the "form is the feeling and the feeling formal," some have felt that it is without emotion. It is, on the contrary, particularly rich in variety and scope of expression, and grows more so with the years. In certain of his more recent works—for example, the slow movement of the Second Symphony—a romantic expansiveness is noteworthy, paralleling the current trend. Contrast this with the last movements of the First String Quartet and the Sonatina for Violin and Harpsichord, whose wit and sparkle represent one of his most compelling traits. However, a flexibility of motion and of feeling is the distinguishing mark of Piston's music. Moods are contrasted so skillfully that they seem like a comment one upon the other, like the thoughts of a serious man with a sense of humor who can take up a subject and see it in different perspectives. Sometimes an ironic jazz theme comes to lighten the lyricism of a first section, as in the first movements of the Sonata for Flute and Piano and the Sonatina for Violin and Harpsichord. In fact, this use of a scherzando second theme in the first movement of a three-movement sonata is

4. Israel Citkowitz, "Walter Piston—Classicist," *Modern Music* 13, no. 1 (1936): 3–11.

fairly frequent and is an interesting way of preparing for a vivacious finale, usually accomplished by a separate scherzo movement in other composers' larger works.

He does not play up his contrasts to the hilt but usually stays on a certain level of sobriety, of modesty, and of elegance; he does not seek out dramatic effects, strange sonorities that contrast very high and low sounds often in unusually spaced chords, or use sudden silences. A standard of decorum is always maintained. The themes, for all their extensions and rhythmic gyrations, behave sensibly. Dissonances, though occasionally extreme, find their resolution in a relaxation of tension (Exx. 6–8 below). Phrases are clearly articulated with natural breaths and the extremes of range or dynamics are rarely touched. Nothing is insisted on at extravagant length. In fact all types of emphasis are used with a restraint that occasionally verges on the prim. Like any composer concerned with architectural clarity and order, he balances section with section using well-planned textures that allow each occurrence in the procession of events to claim its proper attention.

By his convincing and imaginative handling of all these problems of musical form, Piston has begun to occupy a place of great distinction among American composers. As Aaron Copland points out:

> Piston's music, if considered only from a technical viewpoint, constitutes a challenge to every other American composer. It sets a level of craftsmanship that is absolutely first-rate in itself and provides a standard of reference by which every other American's work may be judged . . . Without men like Piston, without his ease and ability in the handling of normal musical materials, we can never have a full-fledged school of composers in this country.[5]

The normal musical material of the time has been the goal of his search. He brings materials from many different scores and purifies it of freakishness. Most of the techniques of modern music are found thoroughly and rather impartially assimilated. There are chromatic and diatonic elements, linear counterpoint (Ex. 6), impressionist harmonies (Ex. 4), twelve-tone techniques (Ex. 14), and asymmetrical rhythms, sometimes combined within a single work. One of his main concerns, of course, as of many other contemporary composers, has been the use of the contrapuntal style within the sonata principle. But this is done with a clear sense of harmonic structure and motion that distinguishes his tendency from that of many others with similar aims.

In spite of the fact that most of his material comes from Europe, certain qualities mark the music as distinguishably American, particularly in more recent works. Since the Concerto for Violin and Orchestra (1939), it is no longer possible to say, as Copland did, that "there is nothing especially 'American' about his work."[6] But even in his Suite for Orchestra (1929), he

5. Aaron Copland, *Our New Music* (New York, 1941), 182.

6. Ibid., 183.

Example 1. Second Symphony, II, mm. 4–9, clarinet.

started including phrases and rhythms from our popular music and using rhythms that would have been impossible without a thorough knowledge of jazz. Later this native flavor becomes more pronounced, not so much by actual quotation of American material as by implication, as in the long-breathed clarinet melody in the slow movement of the Second Symphony (Ex. 1), or the lively second theme of the first movement of the same work (Ex. 2). Even within the frame of a major scale, Piston here shows his ability to be personal and spontaneous. But his American quality is also apparent, much more subtly and pervasively, in the sonority and texture of his music, which are quite distinct from those of any of the schools of Europe.

The works can be divided into two chronological groups, those written before 1938, the year of the *Carnival Song* and *The Incredible Flutist*, and those written after. If in the first period he is occupied with integrating and assimilating modern techniques, in the second there is an urge towards directness and simplicity. There was scarcely a sudden change of heart between one period and the other. Many tuneful and simple elements do appear in earlier works, as in the last movement of the Second String Quartet, while there are elements in his later works of the complexity and dissonance characteristic of his earlier ones, the difference being more a matter of what is stressed in each.

The first period culminates in the important First Symphony, where elements of the twelve-tone technique are integrated into Piston's style. It opens in a somber, poignant mood with one of the few examples of an ostinato in his music. The pizzicato bass contains nine of the twelve chromatic tones and

Example 2. Second Symphony, I, mm. 55–60, oboe.

the three others are supplied by the theme sung above it. But first, four measures are devoted to a statement of the ostinato figure with a soft timpani roll on the dominant of C, the tonality of the first and last movements; then a theme is stated above the ostinato (Ex. 3). A sonata-allegro movement soon follows whose main theme, drawn from the ostinato figure, is presented in one of Piston's most striking and boldly dissonant contrapuntal passages. Returning at the end of the first movement, the same ostinato figure helps to introduce the F♯ tonality of the second movement and provides material for its themes. The beginning of that movement illustrates Piston's unusual ability to combine different elements with spontaneous and convincing ease (Ex. 4). While one of the episodes of the final rondo comes from the introduction, the main theme with its driving power is built around the opening tones of the pizzicato bass inverted (Ex. 5). But quotations can only give an inadequate sample of a work that unfolds with dark and forceful eloquence in a close-knit and dynamic structure.

Its immediate predecessor, the Concertino for Piano and Chamber Orchestra, is in complete contrast, representing the witty and charming side of the composer as perfectly as the symphony does the serious side. It is a perfect summation of the lighter elements of Piston's music up to this time. One section contrasts with another with remarkable ease, and the orchestra is treated so as to throw the piano into the spotlight as the leader in an elegant conversation of instruments. In this work the frequent use of biting dissonances like the major seventh sounded in conjunction with the blandest consonances is characteristic of the harmonic sensibility of Piston at this period. Such harmonies began to make their appearance in the Suite for Oboe and Piano, where they were boldly marked in the Prelude (Ex. 6) and in the very Pistonian closing Gigue (Ex. 7). Note similar clashes in the string quartets (Ex. 8). They came to bold elaboration in certain passages of the Concerto for Orchestra, where the organization is polytonal. In this last, there is a brilliant and unusual second movement built on the plan of repeating in reverse in the

Example 3. First Symphony, I, mm. 4–10.

Example 4. First Symphony, II, mm. 1–11.

second half the jazzy material of the first half. Piston has frequently used devices like inversion and canonic imitation and other methods derived from the great contrapuntal periods of the past and still used by many composers today.

In the rondo of the Second String Quartet a whole section of the theme stated in four parts is recapitulated in inversion, the upper part becoming the bass and so forth (Ex. 9). His use of fugal writing in the course of a sonata movement is particularly effective because he knows how to imply a harmonic background of the same type as that heard in other parts of the movement (Ex. 10). Of the two excellently written and effective quartets, the second seems more integrated, perhaps because it uses the device of a unifying motive of minor and major thirds that appears in all the movements. It begins with one of Piston's finest and most expressive pieces of two-part writing—a melancholy, tender introduction that establishes not only the tonality of A minor but the mood of the whole work (Ex. 11).

Example 5. First Symphony, III, mm. 1–6.

Example 6. Suite for Oboe and Piano, Prelude, mm. 17–19.

These two parts are later repeated in double canon, a fragment of which is given in Example 8d.

The figure marked with a cross (in Ex. 11) is later used to form the harmonic background of a lyrical theme, after an allegro first section filled with a variety of different thematic fragments in the fashion of a similar place in the Beethoven E-Minor Quartet. The second movement suggests the mood of the beginning in a more intense and expressive way, while the last is quite diatonic and has a theme resembling ragtime (see Ex. 9). This work moves more freely and expansively than almost any other of Piston's first period.

As I have said, the ballet *The Incredible Flutist* marks a turning point. Being a very effective stage work and a charming concert suite, with its neat manipulation of the familiar dance forms, it is a work of a composer more accustomed to the concert hall than to the theatre, at least as we see the theatre today. Since Stravinsky and the French ballet composers, audiences have demanded of ballet scores the ability both to underline the action and dancing and to set the stage by giving a pronounced sense of environment. This type invariably results in pastiche music that sets the style, the period, and the

Example 7. Suite for Oboe and Piano, Gigue, mm. 1–9.

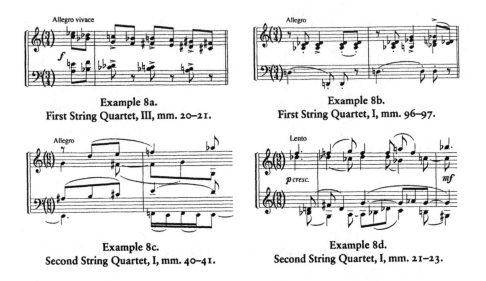

Example 8a.
First String Quartet, III, mm. 20–21.

Example 8b.
First String Quartet, I, mm. 96–97.

Example 8c.
Second String Quartet, I, mm. 40–41.

Example 8d.
Second String Quartet, I, mm. 21–23.

locale, either taking them seriously or poking fun. Piston's attitude, however, is more like that of composers of Italian operas who leave the Egyptian, Bostonian, Parisian, or Druid backgrounds to the costume and stage designers and concentrate on the foreground of human situations. It is about the circus coming to a village—any village. The only immediately noticeable concession to the circus environment is a short, comic band march. A more modish treatment might have emphasized or parodied the carnival tone and kept it up from beginning to end of the circus's sojourn. It may be that our tastes will change to a less realistic and stylized kind of treatment of theatrical subjects, and if they do, this elegantly written ballet will certainly attract the notice of ballet companies more than it has.

In the next year comes a transitional work of a surprisingly convincing unity, the Sonata for Violin and Piano. In this a Mozartean tendency begins to take shape, evidenced by a much more fluid synthesis and a more plastic joining of different materials. There is also a forecast of the melodic sweep that

Example 9. Second String Quartet, III:
a. mm. 2–4 b. mm. 93–95

Example 10. Sonata for Violin and Piano, III, mm. 132–36.

suddenly appears in the next work, the Concerto for Violin and Orchestra, written in the same year (1939), for it marks an abrupt change. It is as diatonic as the *Carnival Song* for men's voices and brass but far more tuneful. Its Mendelssohnian charm and facility and its amplitude of form leave one with a sense of completeness not always present in Piston's music. The earlier dissonant sharpness is avoided and the work moves in an atmosphere of warmth and brilliance that makes it an immediate success, although, for some strange reason, it is rarely heard. It ought to appeal to violinists because the orchestra never suffocates the solo part, as it does in most modern concertos. Most of the materials suggest in a very discreet way various kinds of popular music. The first theme has a simple freshness entirely new to Piston (Ex. 12). And the whole movement flows along in this engaging fashion from beginning to end.

A second movement of quiet, peaceful character contrasts a soft background of brass with the fragile voice of the solo instrument in a development that is unusually bland and reflective for this writer of poignant slow music. The finale jokes along gaily, stating its rondo theme against a comically broken-down bassoon figure (middle staff with stems down), changing, later, to more lyric moods (Ex. 13). Certainly this is a new adventure for Piston, and it anticipates, by his own critical awareness, the criticism of some at that time, which Aaron Copland expressed before knowing the work: "Piston is not adventurous enough. One would like to know less surely what his next piece

Example 11. Second String Quartet, I, mm. 1–12, violins I and II.

will be like. One should like to see him try his hand at types of music completely outside the realm of anything he has attempted thus far."[7]

A similar concern for directness and lucidity but on a more serious plane seems to motivate the Second Symphony, winner of the New York Music Critics' Circle Award last year. Its beautiful, songful beginning uses the same 6/4 measure and the same type of contrast between lyric and humorous material (Ex. 2 above) as the early Sonata for Flute and Piano, but there is a new, greatly intensified eloquence and expressivity. The frankly romantic second movement spins out its theme (Ex. 1 above) somewhat after the fashion of a large figured chorale prelude. Throughout there is a relaxation into grace typical of this second period. Some have complained that they felt the specter of the nineteenth-century French symphonists lurking here and there, referring perhaps to the heavily doubled theme of the last movement and its rather "heroic" atmosphere. But this feeling is soon dispelled after the statement of the theme by typically Pistonian interplay, with its new, airier character.

The most extreme step in the direction of relaxedness comes in the Quintet for Flute and String Quartet, music dominated by the gentle tone of the

7. Ibid., 186.

Example 12. Violin Concerto, I, mm. 16–31.

Example 13. Violin Concerto, III, mm. 15–24.

solo instrument. One feels in this piece, as in the two works with organ, *Prelude and Allegro for Organ and Strings* and *Partita for Violin, Viola, and Organ*, a desire to broaden the scope of his style, to incorporate new moods and methods. Mozartean grace as well as Mozartean combination of all the elements seem to inform the purely contemporary language. For instance, in the latter work, the third movement, "Variations," is built on a twelve-tone row (marked O in the example) and its inverted, retrograde, and retrograde-inverted (marked RI) variants. This material is treated tonally and is imbued with a tender and gentle individuality (Ex. 14).

Originality of detail, skill in construction, and imagination mark the series of short commissioned works, such as the *Fanfare for the Fighting French* and the *Variation on a Theme by Eugene Goossens*, and all are immediately distinguishable as Piston's. Being a most punctual and methodical worker who can always be counted on to produce music of high quality and imagination, he has received many commissions over the years. The League of Composers heads the long list of commissioning organizations, which include the Coolidge Foundation, the Columbia Broadcasting System, the Alice M. Ditson Fund of Columbia University, and the International Society for Contemporary Music.

Now the composer seems headed in a new direction, for the Sonatina for Violin and Harpsichord and the short *Divertimento for Nine Instruments* are written in a fresh vein that returns to the more pointed and terse style of his earlier works. The violin work, particularly, is attractive in its combination of newly found Mozartean fluency with the older, more acid harmonies and

Example 14. Partita for Violin, Viola, and Organ, III, mm. 85–90.

alert rhythms. Both works are organized into large paragraphs containing many contrasting phrases and rhythmic patterns, a most compelling means of avoiding the rather persistent and unrelieved moods by now only too common in recent music. There are a Third Symphony and a Third String Quartet in preparation that may apply this new-found flexibility to the serious style. But at this point one feels that it is much harder to predict Piston's future than it was in 1940.

One thing is certain: there will be no relaxation of quality or want of imagination, no matter in what line he continues.

In the whole field of contemporary music, Walter Piston occupies an important position. He has summed up the tendencies of the past twenty years both here and in Europe and given them broad and masterful expression. Although living in the time of the "lost generation," he found himself in his devotion to music. His unique contribution is to have done this particular work with outstanding excellence in a country where few have ever made a name for themselves as thoroughly craftsman-like artists. In literature several names come to mind but in music there is hardly one to be found before our time.

To have helped to establish a deep understanding of the value of craftsmanship and taste here and to have given such persuasive exemplification of these in his works is highly important for our future. For, not having as ingrained a respect and love for high artistic ideals as Europeans have had, we have often slipped into the trivial, chaotic, and transitory. Piston's work helps us to keep our mind on the durable and the most satisfying aspects of the art of music and by making them live gives us hope that the qualities of integrity and reason are still with us.

But this sounds like philosophy and Piston once said something about Stravinsky's *Symphonie de psaumes* that could well be applied to his own work:

Many were the philosophical speculations as to the intent and content of this music after its performance. But the musician must be satisfied that what one gets from any work depends on what one brings to it. In the *Symphonie de psaumes* he will sense unmistakably those elements he seeks in real music.[8]

Roger Sessions: Violin Concerto
(1959)

Roger Sessions's music has increasingly come to grips with the most serious and important issue that has faced contemporary music when considered in terms of its own internal development, that is, the important task of finding new forms for the new material. Many composers have been aware of the need to find a continuity that would allow them to translate into the most typical of musical dimensions, subjective time, the implications of the new twentieth-century world of rhythms, linear and textural shapes, harmonic fields, and all manner of new qualities of physical sound. We can see Debussy facing this problem in his late sonatas and *Douze Etudes*, Schoenberg in occasional early and late works like the *Five Pieces for Orchestra* and the Trio, Bartók in his Piano Sonata and Third String Quartet, Stravinsky in a number of works, particularly the *Symphony in Three Movements*. In this country, more than anywhere else, this matter seems to have engaged the attention not only of many younger composers, who have in their background a number of experimental works such as those of Varèse and Chávez, but also of the more traditionally oriented composers, of whom Sessions has been most devoted to this particular enterprise. It is a problem that has led the Darmstadt group to impatiently giving the whole musical vocabulary a thorough arithmetical shaking up, often without too much concern for producing audible and musically intelligible continuities of sound. For it is not an easy thing to develop a new and meaningful type of musical continuity. It must be undertaken by slow, rather intuitive steps, since the condition of "meaningfulness" presupposes a cooperative development in the composer and in some qualified listeners of a grasp of musical relationships not previously clearly recognized, coupled with an ability to test them against some standard of interest and meaningfulness.

Beginning with his music for *The Black Maskers* (1923) Sessions has gone through a musical evolution of unusual scope, since each of the three technical and aesthetic areas of his time became in turn a center of interest for him and contributed to his way of musical thinking. The devices of blurring, of crowding sonorities by figurational activity in "close position," the meaningful use of instrumental and registral tone color, the shimmering backgrounds that in him have become contrapuntal—these are some of the marks of an impressionism that was more prominent in his early works and that still can be glimpsed, although completely transformed, in such a recent work as his Third Symphony. Likewise, the sharply defined, vigorously incisive, rhythmic

---

8. Walter Piston, "Stravinsky as Psalmist—1931," *Modern Music* 8, no. 2 (1931): 42–45.

drive of primitivism and neoclassicism as well as the intense, highly concentrated and characterized gestures of expressionism furnished a springboard for the different techniques Sessions uses. To talk of his impressionist beginnings of around 1923, his neoclassic period from about 1926 to 1937, his expressionist period from then until now does great violence to the facts although it sheds some illumination. It is true that his "neoclassic" works are much more tonally centered than his more recent works. They also contain certain turns of phrase, figurations, rhythms that link them to other composers' works in this style. The recent compositions, however, while approaching the "atonal," employ materials and methods only very remotely related to any other composer's style. Even his use of twelve-tone patterns is freer and more personal than that of many others.

The significant continuity techniques, which are among the explicable things that give his music its interest and importance, seem to have become much more focused and intentional in the Violin Concerto (1931–35) than in the previous First Piano Sonata (1930) and the First Symphony (1927), a fact that of course does not detract from these latter as works of art. These techniques can be best illustrated by a comparison of Examples 1 and 2.

In Example 1, the very opening of the Concerto, the trombone plays directional motive "A," rising in five diatonic steps from tonic to dominant of B minor. This is immediately answered by the similar tone color of the trumpet playing directional motive "B" in the same dynamic and note values, a figure whose overall pattern is a rapid rise and descent over a diminished eleventh. However, within this arch the figure changes direction every two notes except for the three that descend at the end of the measure. Its character, aided by a crescendo and diminuendo mark, is much more intense, both because of the expressive jumps of augmented fourth, major seventh, and diminished octave and the total distance it covers and because of its chromatic nature. Likewise there are a number of perfect fourths which are very much a feature of this motive, as can be seen in the harmonies of "B" in the first measure of Example 6. To these two brass figures, two flutes add, in homophonic style, the suggestion of an interrupted cadence in E minor, against a pedal of F♯. As any musician realizes at once, these brief, striking, yet rather bare measures are filled with implications—they are in fact a tiny summary of a great deal that is to follow, even prefiguring the final cadence, which holds F♯ and D after everything else has been stopped by a short, accented tonic note in the bass. The two directional motives "A" and "B" are met with throughout the work.

Example 1. Roger Sessions, Violin Concerto, I, mm. 1–3.

Example 2. Violin Concerto, II, mm. 1–5.

Whether this is a consciously contrived feature or the result of a very integrated conception of another sort would be hard to tell from the score, particularly because the connection between one idea and another is not always as clear as that which exists between Example 1 and the opening of the Scherzo (second movement) shown in Example 2.

In Example 3, a later episode in the Scherzo, motive "A" does not appear until an introductory motive of minor thirds is dwelt on—perhaps derived from the first two eighths of Example 2. When it does appear, its intervals are different from those in Example 1 or Example 2, its joint to motive "B" is like that of Example 2, and the pattern of reversal of direction at each two notes is more strictly adhered to than in Example 2. That these three thematic ideas are related would be grasped quite quickly by the listener.

However, in the opening of the short third movement, a Romanza (Ex. 4), one cannot be so sure whether the rise of five notes over irregular intervals should be related to "A" and can be even less sure whether the descent is related to "B," although the last four notes suggest the possibility. Later in this movement the connection with "B" is made somewhat more definite. In the opening of the tarantella-like finale, a cadenza is played by the violin alone (Ex. 5). Many would doubt whether the composer intended to recall the opening, although certainly the similarity cannot be fortuitous.

This brief survey of some of the themes of a work whose main feature is a wealth of long, beautifully shaped singing or rhythmic lines and figurations that move in very broad sweeps is not intended to state whether such an overall unification of the themes was striven for by the composer or not, but simply to examine the score, and to point out a tissue of connections which must strike the listener at once since it seems to operate not only on a large scale but also in the joining even of details, and of one small phrase with another. For instance, this is evidently at work in the connection between two

Example 3. Violin Concerto, II, mm. 109–117 (rehearsal no. 44).

Example 4. Violin Concerto, III, mm. 1–3.

relatively dissimilar contrapuntal lines, the beautiful cantilena with which the violin makes its first appearance and the slow motion of regular eighths played by the violas in octaves (Ex. 6). There are obviously many degrees of similarity possible between phrases controlled by the same directional motive, and when directionality is used with other kinds of remote relationships such as imitation of outline, ornamentation, and simplification, directional inversions, and so forth, the play of these could be likened to the use of metaphor and simile in poetry that results in the fascinating effects described in Empson's *Seven Types of Ambiguity*.[1]

Example 6 also exhibits another important feature: the predominance of an overall process of continuity on which the harmonic, textural, dynamic, and expressive changes have only a slight deflective effect. Here the two separate registers, kept apart for many measures; the constant flow of eighths with approximately six in a group; the violin's gradual descent using a mixture of quarters, eighths, and long notes, with abrupt rises just before the beginning of each phrase; and the unity of dynamics represent a frame for uniform progress, just as Example 1 did. As in that earlier passage, there are many sudden shifts of intervallic tension, both melodically and harmonically. This way of combining certain techniques used in a uniform, rather neutral way with others used in an intense or highly irregular way is like the use of harmony in some works of Brahms and Fauré in which an overall melodic and figurational pattern of considerable regularity and restricted range persists while sudden, very intense harmonic changes are taking place. Stravinsky's works abound in examples of such dissociations of techniques, Alban Berg's in the coordination of techniques.

During the progress of the overall continuity pattern Sessions uses, there is usually an increase and decrease in definition and individualization of motive, of rhythm, or of some other feature or group of features. Sometimes only the increasing or decreasing portions of this pattern are used. For instance, the first movement of the Violin Concerto comprises three clearly separated sections, each introduced by what sounds very much like (but never is) a transposed repetition of Example 1, each time more extended and differently orchestrated. The first of these sections, fifty-six measures, of which Example 6 gives the first ten preceded by the last measure of the introduction,

---

1. William Empson, *Seven Types of Ambiguity*, 2nd ed. (London: Chatto and Windus, 1947).

Example 5. Violin Concerto, IV, mm. 1–5 (rehearsal no. 87), solo violin.

emphasizes the particular expressive quality found in Example 1 that comes from its bareness of texture, its regularity of rhythm, and its abrupt changes of harmonic tension. Over the fifty-six measures this quality is made more intense in the middle and finally more attenuated with no more literalness of repetition than can be heard in Example 6. The second section, on the other hand, draws an entirely different consequent from Example 1, a graceful, light motion of sixteenths built of a mixture of staccato and legato, repeated notes, and the interval of a sixth, the repetition of which over a held chord forms the delicate climax of the movement. The falling away of this is accomplished by repeating the climactic moment each time more softly. Thus the second section brings into greater focus the graceful quality implied in Example 1. The third and last section recalls the other two, gradually reducing them to neutrality and quiet.

More and more the notion of extended, continuously flowing sections during which ideas come to the surface, gain clarity and definition, and then sink back into the general flow has characterized Sessions's unique style, and he seems to have striven for this first here. When Sessions wrote this work, the twentieth-century concerto had reached a rather fixed stage of development through the combined efforts of Stravinsky, Prokofiev, and Hindemith. Shunning the Classical opposition of solo and orchestra, it had turned, of course, to the Baroque form for assistance in finding a way to organize concertos in which the solo was the prime mover and in which the orchestra is used mainly

Example 6. Violin Concerto, I, mm. 8–19.

to intensify and amplify the solo part. Sessions carries this method further than any of his predecessors. The violin dominates the orchestra in every sense, playing almost continuously a part of prime thematic or figurational importance; it is never dwarfed or overwhelmed in volume of sound, intensity of expression, or brilliance by the orchestra. Yet the orchestra has a typical life of its own. This remarkable feat not merely reveals high skill but must be the result of careful choosing of characters, themes, and all other devices with the final end in mind.

It was finished just before the Violin Concerto of Alban Berg, but under cultural conditions so vastly different that the achievement of such an outstanding work represents an even more remarkable artistic triumph—a triumph over the apathy, cultural confusion, and uncertainty that caused its subsequent neglect. For here there were then, and are even now, few incentives within or without the musical profession to recognize, encourage, cherish, or promote effectively such real excellence in our own music. If there were, this work would be as well known here (and elsewhere) as its outstanding European peers. Instead, like many important works it has been lent a specious importance by being tagged an "example" of some trend and thus given a ghostly existence in prose, when its special, powerful uniqueness that brings together so much into one imaginative whole is what gives it its importance. Even at the Thursday night performance, its premiere at the New York Philharmonic, played beautifully by Tossy Spivakovsky and conducted with care by Leonard Bernstein, the latter felt it necessary to introduce it with the brief description: "An interesting example of complicated music written here during the thirties."

In Memoriam: Roger Sessions, 1896–1985
(1985/95)

Everyone who came to know Roger Huntington Sessions and to admire his music was always deeply impressed by his integrity as man and musician. For us his high moral stand revealed itself in every aspect of his mature life: in his music, in his teaching, in his writings, in his moments of light-hearted humor in social gatherings. This quality has been evident to me ever since I heard his First Symphony performed by the Boston Symphony Orchestra in 1927. And what I wrote in 1940, on the occasion of an entire concert of his music (reprinted earlier in this book),[1] still substantially represents my opinion of his work, although my view has become much broader and more enthusiastic in light of the additional eight symphonies, much other music, and the many essays and books he wrote over the next forty-five years.

In one essay, Sessions states that his aim in composing was "to help build a really new and better inner world," because for him, as for many, modernism in the early part of this century was born of this optimistic, noble,

---

1. See "American Music in the New York Scene," 50–51.

and revolutionary intention.[2] I don't think Sessions ever lost his firm belief in this aim; through many years of neglect, years that brought changes of all sorts with vast effect on our musical life, his fundamental convictions remained unshaken—and now these convictions seem almost to have come from another time. Indeed, Sessions can be considered one of the very last composers to have formed his outlook in the era preceding the First World War and to have held to the standards of that period—as did Stravinsky, Bartók, and Schoenberg. Sessions was younger than they, and the terrifying issues that have confronted those of us younger than he were also very vital to him. As he wrote:

> Fascism . . . is only the logical conclusion, as it is certainly the result, of what one might all too easily regard as the dominating tendencies of our time. Its ultimate horror is not the fact that it is cruel beyond all conception but the fact that from beginning to end it is *phony*. It is an almost inevitable product of a culture which contains so much that is phony as does that of pre-War Europe and America . . . it is the final enthronement, by terror and blood, of all that is spurious in contemporary life, and the attempt to make of spuriousness the basic principle of the future . . . Our hour is at hand, and either we must begin to live seriously as heirs of a great civilization, or we must, in refusing that role, face destruction.

"What does this mean," Sessions continued,

> in terms applicable to musical life? American music is convention-ridden as has been that of no other modern nation. . . . The prevalent attitude towards music . . . is that of the late nineteenth century. Our standards are very largely external ones. We demand music that, whether "programmatic" or not, is evocative rather than inwardly expressive; or profess a "nationalism" which we conceive in terms of association or recurrent mannerisms rather than of traditions created by mature and significant works. . . . Our musical life is propaganda-ridden. This is, of course, partly an inevitable result of the situation which has made "American music," as such, a *cause* to be promoted. The result has been to a very large extent to place emphasis on "personalities," "tendencies," a "movement," rather than on music itself, which seems at times almost to be relegated to the status of a by-product.[3]

Elsewhere, he balanced these angry words with a recommendation:

> [Composers] must learn to write music . . . which has been a real, important, and primary experience to them. Music so produced will vary in quality, as individuals vary; it will vary in style and form, with the immense variety of America itself. But it will embody the authentic accents and gestures of American individuals. And what other Americanism do we want, or can we demand, in our music?[4]

2. Roger Sessions, "No More Business-as-Usual" (1942), in *Roger Sessions on Music: Collected Essays*, ed. Edward T. Cone (Princeton: Princeton University Press, 1979), 312.

3. Sessions, "No More Business-as-Usual," 306–12.

4. Sessions, "American Music and the Crisis" (1941), in *Collected Essays*, 303.

Sessions was an unusually gifted and widely read man: already at the age of fourteen, when he was admitted to Harvard, he had composed an opera. His staunch adherence to high principles probably was a result of his old New England background, which for a number of generations had been centered around Hadley, Massachusetts, although he himself was born in 1896 in Brooklyn, where his branch of the family had moved. At Harvard, he was already up-to-date and could play the score of *Elektra* on the piano practically by heart, so he told me. In fact, it seems that this early familiarity with such elaborate scores must have set a standard of orchestral composing for him— one that made great demands on players and conductors—which he maintained throughout his life. He retained this standard, even when such virtuosity became so expensive to rehearse that it was nearly impossible to find the time for it, except for already known works, whose success was assured. The young Sessions soon exhausted what he could get from the Harvard music department and began to study privately with Ernest Bloch, the Swiss composer who had just come to America. Bloch soon realized how gifted his pupil was and asked him to join him as an assistant at the Cleveland Institute, where he had been invited to teach. A little later, having received the Rome Prize in the early 1920s, Sessions started a long stay abroad, going from Rome to Florence to France—where he showed his First Symphony to Nadia Boulanger, who was sufficiently impressed with it to persuade Koussevitzky to conduct it in Boston—and then finally to Berlin, which he left when the threat of Nazism began to be taken seriously. Arriving in New York without a job, but with a reputation already established among the young progressives, he taught privately for a while in Miriam Gideon's apartment. Fairly soon thereafter he began his long university teaching career, mostly at Princeton, then for a few years at Berkeley. During the last two decades of his life he also taught at the Juilliard School, where we were colleagues. Certainly he was one of the leading teachers of his time, as the presence of so many of his former students in the National Institute of Arts and Letters testifies: Milton Babbitt, David Diamond, Vivian Fine, Ross Lee Finney, Miriam Gideon, Andrew Imbrie, Leon Kirchner, Donald Martino, Hugo Weisgall, and the many more who received Institute grants.[5]

For Roger, music was *gesture*,

the result of at least as many complex forces, impulses, and experiences, both individual and general, as every other gesture. Like every other gesture it is essentially indivisible, and while we can, obviously, note certain of its elements, we must nevertheless remain constantly aware of the fact that we are not thereby revealing its whole or even its essential meaning.[6]

5. As Sessions was a rather inactive member of the Institute, these choices were made entirely by his colleagues.

6. Roger Sessions, "The Composer and His Message" (1939), in *Collected Essays*, 12.

This attitude caused him to question the analytical theories proposed by Schenker, Hindemith, and Krenek and impelled him to rise to the defense of the practicing composer who followed his musical intentions without concern for their theoretical correctness. It was the natural result of his belief in the importance of intuition, which he always sought to develop in his students. Throughout his long stretch of university teaching, Sessions often expressed his dissatisfaction with academic life, both in his essays and in conversation with his friends. He was dismayed by the tendency to formularize so prevalent among his professorial colleagues, and he often complained of students whose approach was too intellectual, claiming to prefer teaching in a music school like Juilliard because students there had living contact with performed music. But as a committed teacher, he was always surrounded by a group of very loyal students, who did what they could to make his music known. For during most of his life he made little effort to promote himself or his music, out of the idealistic belief that our profession at best is devoted to high artistic achievement and that excellence will inevitably be recognized without the help of critics or public relations. If this belief seemed justified by his high reputation among musicians and by the fact that commissions kept coming his way—eight of his nine symphonies and many of his other orchestral and chamber works were written on commission—one must also acknowledge that, like many such works by others, his suffered the fate of receiving few if any performances after the first, even if well received at their premieres.

One result of his point of view, which puts such reliance on the musical understanding of performers, is very evident in his early scores, such as the First Piano Sonata, where performance indications remain very sparse. The expectation that the performer would enter into the spirit of the work and grasp the intention behind the notes is, of course, very much the way Classic and Romantic composers up to Brahms's time notated their music. The idea that phrase shapes, melodic inflections, subtle changes of dynamics should not or did not need to be written into scores was particularly prevalent in the early 1920s, when Stravinsky seemed to be following Bach in this respect. In Sessions's case, what with a tendency to build long expressive phrases using non-literal sequences and rhythmic structures that involve a hierarchy of stresses—weaker accents leading to and away from stronger ones—such sparse marking of inflection leaves a great deal up to the performer's comprehension (over-marking a passage can cause a performer to play very artificially). Any performer of Brahms, who marked his music quite simply, must be able to keep the music from sounding stodgy and pointlessly elaborated by many subtle gradations of dynamics, touch, and phrasing. This usually happens when Sessions's works are played by soloists or small ensembles. However, when we come to larger ensembles, and especially to the many orchestral works that Sessions wrote, the use of sparse dynamic marking presumes more time of careful preparation and more effort of imagination on the part of conductors and instrumentalists than they can usually give to new works, especially those by American composers.

Even performers who make real efforts in this direction have to confront the problem that the other recent trend in performing indications has inevitably led to. Mahler, then later Ravel, Debussy, and others needed to give ever more detailed instructions in their orchestral scores as they developed new ways of shaping phrases that could never be achieved without them, as well as new balances and new types of articulations. These were taken up by the Viennese and to an extent by the later Stravinsky and were finally carried to an extreme by those who serialized dynamics. Scores written in this way also included passages with no dynamic inflection, which to players familiar with this method meant they were to be played exactly as written, in a flat, even, uninflected way—just the opposite from the way Romantic composers had expected them to be played. Hence music such as that of Sessions requires a conductor who can persuade performers to understand the intention of his notation.

Sessions's example as a man of great artistic integrity who was also possessed of a forward-looking, adventurous vision underlay the remarkable works he produced and gave them a compelling aura. These works represent a large, opulent world of varied expression, highly imaginative and moving and often very timely, as was his oratorio on Whitman's *When Lilacs Last in the Dooryard Bloom'd*, dedicated to the memory of Martin Luther King and Robert F. Kennedy. Both his operas—*The Trial of Lucullus*, based on the play of Brecht, and *Montezuma*—deal with the hollowness of military success and its disastrous consequences. In 1964 I was fortunate enough to be a composer-in-residence in Berlin, at the same time that Sessions was, when *Montezuma* was given its first performances by the Deutsche Oper, and I was deeply impressed by it. It made an even greater impression on me a few years later in Boston, and later in a performance by students at the Juilliard School. On that last occasion, *Montezuma* was so severely criticized by the press that I doubt it will be revived in the near future. Sessions has had hostile reviews in the New York newspapers for many years, to such an extent that even his obituary was used as an opportunity to attack him on the grounds of the very academicism that he inveighed against in his essays.

Perhaps part of the reason for this hostility is that his works, being quite elaborate, need very carefully prepared and committed performances, which they have seldom received. Music that is really new often requires quite a number of performances before musicians can understand its meaning fully and are then able to express it to an audience. For Sessions, this need has been a formidable obstacle to public understanding. The long, beautifully shaped lyricism of his slow movements and the brilliance of his fast ones have too seldom come across at the many performances I have heard live or on records. His deeply romantic expressivity is certainly hard to bring out without a careful awareness of how to balance textures (half the time, I have noticed, the listener is hearing an inner part obscuring the main line, especially on records) and the sense of leading from one note, or one motive, or one phrase to the next—so important in Romantic music—is only too often neglected. This also explains, perhaps, why although no other American has written such a large body of excellent music, Sessions did not receive a Pulitzer Prize until he was eighty-five, for his Concerto for Orchestra—to the great embarrassment of many of us who won ours before he did.

By contrast to his symphonic and operatic music, Sessions's beautiful piano works have enjoyed the good fortune of being marvelously performed and recorded by many, including his pupil Robert Helps, and make it evident to anyone who listens what a master Sessions is. These recordings should have convinced critics and conductors long ago about the worth of his other works. When Sessions was a young man, the musical world was much more on the lookout for the remarkable qualities his works show, and these would have attracted serious musicians to devote whatever effort was necessary to bring them before the public in a compelling way. Nowadays, performers and conductors are so busy flying from one engagement to another that they have little time to study new scores. Public relations and publicizable gimmickry tend to control the tastes not only of the public but of musicians and critics. Fortunately, Sessions stuck to his principles to the very end of his life, and those of us who share his idealism believe, as he must have, that his works will shortly be given the chance they deserve, because of their exceptional power and beauty.

In Memoriam: Stefan Wolpe, 1902–1972
(1972)

Comet-like radiance, conviction, fervent intensity, penetrating thought on many levels of seriousness and humor, combined with breathtaking adventurousness and originality marked the inner and outer life of Stefan Wolpe, as they do his compositions. Inspiring to those who knew him, these inspiring qualities reach many more through his music. He was a man and musician for whom everyone who came close could not help but feel admiration and affection. Contact with him was such an important experience that he was understandably surrounded by many devoted friends and students who helped with his problems of publication and performances, helped in finding him teaching positions, helped to save his manuscripts during the fire of a few years ago, and helped to save his manuscripts when his physical condition was deteriorating. The force of his artistic personality, motivated as it was by deep conviction and by an innately original way of doing things, occasionally seemed to be utterly unconcerned with prudence and caution, yet frequently what he did turned out to be the only right way of acting.

I remember a very vivid day in England, when I was teaching at the music school at Dartington Hall, where Wolpe had come to visit. I asked him to teach my class of young English student composers—feeling that he, at least, would give the students one worthwhile class. He started talking about his Passacaglia, a piano work built of sections each based on a musical interval— minor second, major second, and so on. At once, sitting at the piano, he was caught up in a meditation on how wonderful these primary materials, intervals, were; playing each over and over again on the piano, singing, roaring, humming them, loudly, softly, quickly, slowly, short and detached or drawn out and expressive. All of us forgot time passing, forgot when the class was to finish. As he led us from the smallest one, a minor second, to the largest, a major seventh—which took all afternoon—music was reborn, new light dawned, we all knew we would never again listen to music as we had. Wolpe had made each of us experience very directly the living power of these primary elements. From then on indifference was impossible. Such a lesson most of us had never had before, nor have had since, I imagine.

Wolpe's work first came to my attention in the 1920s when he wrote workers' songs, somewhat of the type of Weill and Eisler, during the Weimar Republic. When he left his hometown, Berlin, as the Nazi menace grew, he went to Russia, Rumania, Austria, and what was then Palestine. During this period little of his was heard here, before he came to America to live in 1939. It was about that year that I reviewed his *March and Variations* for two pianos, written in 1931, as "the only work on the program with signs of real originality."[1] But it was with his *Songs from the Hebrew*, sung at the McMillan Theater at Columbia University, that Wolpe became one of the moderns I was and still am most enthusiastic about. Then we heard the piano Passacaglia, the amazing *Battle Piece*, the many wonderful chamber works, and finally the Symphony (1955–56), commissioned by Rodgers and Hammerstein in collaboration with the League of Composers–ISCM. It turned out to be one of the most remarkable but also one of the most difficult-to-perform pieces of our era.

When it was finally accepted for performance by the New York Philharmonic, six years after its completion, Wolpe, already ill, had the parts copied hastily so that later, at the last moment, the Philharmonic librarian had to do many of them over, for which many of the composer's friends contributed. The music itself proved beyond the level of difficulty that the Philharmonic could cope with, given its lack of experience with new music and its limited rehearsal schedule, despite the good will and valiant efforts of many of the performers and of Stefan Bauer-Mengelberg, who had been called in to conduct. As all his friends remember bitterly, only two of the three movements were performed and these not well.

Tragically, shortly before this performance-ordeal, while Wolpe was at the American Academy in Rome, he began to show signs of the illness, Parkinson's disease, which from then on fell like a heavy shadow on the body of this extraordinarily animated man. From about 1961 until his death in the spring of 1972, physically weakened often to the point of not being able to push a pencil across a piece of paper, he still continued, undiminished in spirit, to teach, think, and compose, producing more of his remarkable

1. See "Stravinsky and Other Moderns in 1940," *Modern Music* 17, no. 3 (March–April 1940): 164–70; repr. in *The Writings of Elliott Carter*, 74–81. [B]

works. In this phase of his life, the courage, determination, and will to live and act through his art were inspiring. Few have been put to the terrible test that he endured, and fewer have been able to carry on as he did under such circumstances.

Now, his physical life over, what emerges more clearly than ever is that the surpassing moral fortitude Wolpe exhibited in these last years is the very quality which gives the radiant power and originality to his work. His music, to me, unequivocally expresses his deeply felt conviction about the values of art and life—makes them immediately graspable—a most inspiring thing in these unencouraging times.

Two Essays on Goffredo Petrassi

1. The Recent Works of Goffredo Petrassi (1960)

The conception behind Goffredo Petrassi's recent music is much more difficult to grasp analytically than that of his earlier compositions. In the new works, all the elements of compositional technique have been subjected to reconsideration: it is as if they had been dissolved, shattered or dissociated, and then reassembled into new groupings. Every moment is conceived as a total texture rather than as a statement or development of a theme or motive; the total sound in all its different formations is the subject matter, the statement or expression of idea. The composer himself prefers to think in terms of "events" (*avvenimenti*) rather than of textures, reminding one of the meaning of "event" in the sense defined by Alfred North Whitehead: as a unit of action in a total sequence in which the event contains within itself not only its own history but as well its prefiguration of possible futures and its own individualized character.

Because of this novel approach, "traditional" analytic methods are not effective in coming to grips with a work such as the *Serenata* (1958) for flute, viola, contrabass, harpsichord, and percussion. At first hearing (and sight) it is clearly knit together by a kernel of three notes referred to frequently throughout. The general motion gives the impression of very varied improvisations in which each instrument in turn plays a cadenza touching upon the many different musical characters that arise from the instrument's special capabilities. These cadenzas are set off by tutti passages; the general character of the whole is not unlike that of the large Baroque organ fantasias. The charm and interest of this piece lies in a continuous series of explosions of the imaginative and unexpected. Constantly changing in rhythmic pulse, texture, dynamic shading, and timbre, the *Serenata* moves rapidly from one evocative quality to another, juxtaposing motives and complexes of sound from which emerge meanings that these motives and complexes could not have by themselves. Since the work proceeds more by contrast than by similitude, its connection of ideas is more often oblique than direct. The whole technique is very close to the symbolic or analogical expression found in much modern poetry.

Along with a great variety of timbre and techniques of sound production among instruments of definite pitch, Petrassi uses the percussion in the *Serenata*, as in the *Invenzione concertata*, not merely for color or emphasis, but more as a means of stating or completing musical ideas. In the *Serenata*, he bridges the gap between the percussion and the other instruments by the familiar yet effective device of ostinato, which together with frequent pedal points lends a unity to the imaginative variety of the work, bringing out the meaning of the various constrasting particles of musical thought by grouping them so tightly together that one hears each moment as a single complex but multifaceted unit.

This welding together of disparate and contrasting bits of musical discourse has gradually been developed by Petrassi in recent years. The *Invenzione concertata* (1956–57) for brass, percussion, and strings is an atonal work featuring many canonic sections in various tempi which follow each other without pause. Each new tempo, so to speak, both concludes and continues the one preceding it. In the String Quartet (1958), these contrasting tempi are even more interlocked, while in the *Serenata* (1958) the contrasting tempi are so fused that they frequently become part of the same "event."

Petrassi's recent development has followed the direction of a search for an expanded or emancipated discourse, a direction that most present-day composers have shown little interest in exploring. In fact, adherence to traditional conceptions of detail in musical structure, such as "chords," "counterpoint," "themes," "accompaniments," or of larger matters such as "phrases," "crescendi," and other techniques of emphasis, as well as "canon," "fugue," "sonata form," and "development of themes," has proved more durable than might have been expected earlier in this century. The need for such serviceable routines, which have worked so well for so many composers in the past, was challenged first by Debussy in his later period and, following his example, by the Second Viennese School before their conversion to the twelve-tone technique, as well as by Varèse and by Stravinsky in several works, particularly the *Symphonies of Wind Instruments* and the *Symphony in Three Movements*. In these, significant efforts were made to develop an emancipated discourse. However, when the apparent urge for order led to the dodecaphonic system and to neoclassicism, this progressive effort was temporarily put aside. One could say that it was resumed in the last works of Schoenberg and Webern, although Webern was far less experimental in these matters, since his intention was to reduce the musical matter to its essentials rather than discover a new discourse that could encompass many qualities.

As the importance of the Second Viennese School eventually began to be recognized, it became obvious that the continuing evolution of musical discourse towards greater emancipation was vitally important. The next, and quite natural, step in this evolution has been taken by Petrassi, whose development reveals not only a continual personal growth in expressive intention and philosophical outlook but also a steady effort at renewal of his musical vocabulary. His enthusiasm for valid new ideas, his never-ending curiosity about them, and his constant self-questioning have resulted in a series of changes of approach. But behind these changes, there is the strong sense of an individual living in and responding to our rapidly changing world. His works are the musical autobiography of a sympathetic and highly interesting individual, an impression that is intensified by the fact that themes are carried over from one work to a later one, not only revealing how much Petrassi values them, but also how such ideas can serve to generate new works that no longer have the same technical preoccupations.

Given the composer's *personalità percettiva*, it is not surprising that one contemporary influence after another has played across the surface of his style, even as that style has become more and more itself. From the point of view of the *Serenata* and the new String Trio one can see, in retrospect, certain characteristics of his music that have remained permanent. The most evident of these are the combination of reliance on short motives as a way of linking ideas together, and a tendency to irregularity of musical motion resulting from a desire for mobility of thought and character. There is much dramatic emphasis on change and contrast that results in short, lively, and vivid characterization of feeling. Because of his interest in musical mobility, Petrassi began some time ago to write works which eliminated pauses between the movements, as in his Second Concerto (1951), and now has arrived at a complete interlocking of characters and tempi. The progressive adoption of serial techniques from the *Récréation concertante* (1953) to the *Invenzione concertata* continues the interest in the motivic linking of ideas. Such serialism fulfills two basic functions: first, it furnishes a common source of interrelated motives or themes for an entire work; second—what was most important for the Viennese composers—it permits the setting of these motives or themes in a harmonic context. It is the former which interests Petrassi primarily and which explains his occasional use of the octave interval, avoided by the Viennese, and his preference for protracted emphasis on single harmonic areas instead of the typical fast harmonic motion characteristic of most serial music. In his music, there is much variety in rate of harmonic motion, and it is perhaps for this reason that he has never used the twelve-tone system strictly. Indeed, in his String Quartet, *Serenata*, and String Trio, he has abandoned it for the moment, although retaining much of its chromatic feeling and intervallic unity. The tone rows he has employed, as might be expected, are not of the highly structured kind, such as the symmetrical hexachords or interrelated groups of three or four notes characteristic of Schoenberg and Webern, but of a kind that features a motive, such as the eleven-tone series that opens the *Invenzione concertata*, of which the first four notes of the transposed retrograde inversion begin the next pitched phrase (Ex. 1).

Similar emphasis on a motive or interval can be found in the rows of the *Récréation concertante* and of the Fourth and Fifth Concerti. However, in the works written after the *Invenzione concertata*, a motive of a few notes without a tone row has sufficed as a principle of unification, returning to a

Example 1. *Invenzione concertata,* mm. 1–11.

method used in *Noche oscura* (1950). The String Quartet opens with four
notes later heard in important places, as at the opening of sections, in figurations, and as a generator of harmonies. Similarly, the *Serenata* opens with
a three-note motive, even more constantly referred to throughout the work,

Example 1. *(continued)*.

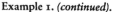

sometimes in its original form, sometimes in the various transformations associated with the twelve-tone method, and often only as a directional pattern of three rising (or descending) notes with the intervals changed (Ex. 2).

Each stage of progress from the *Récréation concertante* to the Trio has served to develop this discourse, which incorporates contrasting and varied characters and qualities within each "event" and in which their general activity and directionality acquire a more and more fantastic and inventive

Example 2. *Serenata,* mm. 1–20.

character. The interpenetration of movements becomes more complete, and the musical events, with their complexes of contrasting characters, take on a more personal and human character, resulting in a unique freshness of expression and feeling—one which could be achieved only by this free play of fantasy, without the rigidities of strict serialism. One might recall the free and inventive discourse of the eighteenth century, particularly the music of Haydn, which combines many qualities and techniques into a richly varied and dramatic unity. Of course, Petrassi's music is in no way a return to this style, but rather its remote descendant; just as the Mannheim school reacted against the unified and systematically patterned mode that characterized much of J. S. Bach's music, so today does Petrassi's music serve as an antidote to the systematic character of Hindemith, some of Stravinsky, some of the Schoenberg and Webern of the twelve-tone period, and much of the Darmstadt school.

Example 2. *(continued)*.

2. Some Reflections on "Tre per sette" (1986)

I have chosen *Tre per sette*[1] to analyze here, not because it is the work of Petrassi's that I cherish above all others—there are many that I like just as much: *Coro di morti, Noche oscura, Estri, Orationes Christi, Sestina d'autunno,*

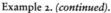

1. Petrassi's subtitle explains his title: "tre esecutori per sette strumenti a fiato." The seven instruments are: piccolo, flute, and alto flute; oboe and english horn; E♭ and B♭ clarinets. [B]

many of the Concerti, and others—but because since encountering it for the first time in 1983 I have had the good fortune to hear it many more times and thus know it best.

What impresses me in the large development of Petrassi's work, which I have known since hearing his *Partita* in Amsterdam in 1933, is the way it has constantly renewed itself, clarifying and focusing its language, reshaping the vocabulary for ever more personal needs. During the past forty years, Petrassi has written works of great variety of expression, each of its kind so convincing and moving—some noble and of mystical elevation like *Noche oscura* or *Orationes Christi*, others witty and charming, as the light-hearted *Tre per sette*—yet all recognizable as coming from the same fascinating musical vision. While he has always had a remarkable imagination for instrumental sonority and a vision that has covered a wide range of musical and human expression in his own personal way, Petrassi like many of his generation became more aware of new possibilities after the Second World War and gradually developed away from his earlier, somewhat neoclassical tendencies into his own special, chromatic style. In this new flowering he follows no preestablished approach, but depends on musical intuition, sometimes using dodecaphonic techniques, as in *Noche oscura*, at other times an apparently free association of tones, rhythms, and interrelationships. This fascinating freedom, which does not seem at all anarchic, is very characteristic of works preceding and following *Tre per sette* (1967). It was led up to by the *Serenata* of 1958 and finds elaborate expression in *Estri* and in the Seventh and Eighth Concerti. Petrassi's dependence upon intuitive insight means, of course, that his approach is difficult to reduce to a system of any kind.

On hearing *Tre per sette* for the first time, what struck me most was the imaginative interplay and contrasts of feeling and musical ideas and their interrelationships—dramatic, humorous, sensitive, and surprising. The listener is continuously left in a state of ambiguity about the tempi of any section, fast music being joined to slow music so that it is impossible to decide whether slow music is a pause in a fast section or fast music an ornamentation of a slow one. The opening soli by each of the three instruments present three different aspects of tempo in quick succession: the piccolo plays a rapidly accelerating rising figure, followed immediately by a descending arpeggio-like figure played as fast as possible by the clarinet; this in turn gives way to a fanfare by the english horn in moderate tempo, in regular note values of quintuplets (Ex. 3). These three phrases, joined together by the pedal note that concludes the piccolo's solo, are ambiguous not only in terms of tempo but also in their presentation of musical material. This opening passage is in a style that could be called "atonal," with no clearly dodecaphonic series: the piccolo begins with groups of notes derived from the whole-tone scale, and as its line rises the intervals become smaller, using more semitones. The clarinet figure, on the other hand, begins with minor thirds and ends with perfect fourths. The english horn fanfare features diminished and perfect fifths and finishes with a rising whole tone F♯-G♯, notes heard previously at the same octave by the piccolo. The first two soli are

Example 3. *Tre per sette,* beginning of m. 1.

pianissimo, while the english horn's fanfare begins mezzo-piano and ends fortissimo, its last note echoed pianississimo by the clarinet's long held flutter-tongue. These three elements are linked together in many different ways—the grace-note leaps in the piccolo and clarinet that start the work are picked up by the english horn and, as in many other sections of this work the recurrence of many pitches from passage to passage at the same octave level (although not in the same order) links passages of very different contours together. The english horn fanfare, however, is one element (and the only one) of the work which does return now and again at the same pitch, each time with a different sequel and often with a different articulation. This little phrase punctuates the work, sometimes as a concluding idea, at other times as an opening one for sections that are very free in character, often very unexpected, yet always linked in such a way as not to seem random or chaotic.

Unexpected, for instance, after all the solo and contrapuntal writing is the sudden G-major triad homophonically heard at the bottom of page 16 in the score (see Ex. 4), although its two outer notes have appeared frequently in the fanfare. This leads to several homophonic passages, employing eight of the possible twelve three-note chords. Of the four excluded here, the augmented and diminished triads have appeared frequently in arpeggiated figures, the chord of the diminished and perfect fifth has appeared in the fanfare, and the cluster of two semitones concludes the work in its closest possible position,

Example 4. *Tre per sette*, mm. 104–14.

after having been briefly referred to shortly before the G-major triad, and a few other places in different spacing (including the very wide spacing of the prominent cadence on page 5).

In describing such small details I have tried to show microscopically some of the pleasures the work contains for me. Beyond these, it is the extraordinary handling of textures and instrumental registers, as well as the brilliance of writing, that constitute Petrassi's absolutely fascinating musical world, that make it so rich, so human in its expressive variety, and hence so valuable.

To Think of Milton Babbitt
(1976)

There is no point in my discussing here the Rameau-like contribution of Milton Babbitt to the clarification and ordering of the twelve-tone method, or, indeed, his absorbing extensions of it. They will certainly be dealt with elsewhere in these pages.[1] His theoretical work, of course, has had inestimable influence on and importance to most American composers working in this domain and even to those, like myself, who are not centrally involved with it. Yet to be so brilliant and articulate an expounder and developer of music theory in print and in lectures has threatened to draw attention away from his most important work, his compositions, and unfortunately has left their artistic consideration to trivially-minded critics, content in their ability to go no further than to identify them as "dodecaphonic," thereby diluting the music's true interest before those not well versed in this field.

That Babbitt's music can be so classified is, in a way, obvious. That it is in a very real and special sense a great departure not only from the method as Schoenberg used it, but from all subsequent developments by Berg, Webern, Spinner, Gerhard, Skalkottas, Apostel, Steuermann, Kahn, and even Americans like Weiss and Perle or the post-War European serialists, does not seem to be generally appreciated. His music shares, of course, with these latter composers, the trend toward the "emancipation of discourse," but Babbitt's imaginings led him to this before the Second World War, preceding the Europeans by several years. His attitude toward this has been more responsive than most to the claims of rational order based on a realistic consideration of the process of listening with its accumulations in memory rather than on abstract number patterns, which he must have realized very early on was a rather primitive and random way of producing aurally chaotic, if sometimes surprising and novel, effects.

Very striking is the strong sense of integration in his work, its overpowering concentration on the particular premises of any given work. I can remember being so struck by this quality, among others, in his *Composition for Four Instruments* (first heard in 1951, I think) that I immediately persuaded *New Music Edition* to publish it. In all of his work, the originality of conception

---

1. Carter refers here to the double issue of *Perspectives of New Music* 14, no. 2 / 15, no. 1 (1976), conceived as a sixtieth-birthday tribute to Babbitt, in which this essay appeared. [B]

and the fastidiousness with which he avoids familiar musical devices have been most intriguing and attractive. Such novel ways of musical thinking can be, of course, perplexing at first, especially when performers lack an imaginative grasp of what they are playing, but it is a perplexity that disappears at later, better performances, although like many good modern works his do not lose their mysterious originality.

To one who enjoys artworks that take an imaginative effort to grasp in a serious way and who has often been rewarded for this effort by learning something unexpected, works like those of Babbitt are an absorbing listening adventure, particularly as they always reveal a quality of artistic imagination that encourages one to further familiarity. Works of this sort have, of course, been frequent in twentieth-century art, literature, and music. In the case of music, some, though by no means all, have proved to be accessible after repeated hearings and with performers that understood the music. Certainly the first American performances of the Viennese school like that of Schoenberg's Wind Quintet played by angry, loud, and somewhat uncontrolled performers at Town Hall in 1925 or of the Webern *Symphonie* a few years later left a very puzzling yet intriguing impression that has completely changed. What once seemed arbitrary, difficult, and complex now no longer presents problems, due to familiarity on the part of performers and listeners; indeed, if anything the Schoenberg sounds, today, a little too Regerish. Fully aware of the need to play good new works and repeat them over the years, Babbitt, as many of his colleagues know, generously devoted a great deal of effort during the 1950s and '60s to arranging concerts of modern music for the League of Composers and the ISCM in New York. During those years these concerts were the main hope of performance of many young composers. It was for the same series of concerts that Mitropoulos conducted *L'Histoire du soldat* and the Schoenberg *Serenade*, Jacques Monod gave the remarkable all-Webern concert in 1952 at the YMHA, and Steuermann played the complete piano works of Schoenberg.

The special demands of modern scores can only be solved by repeated efforts to play and listen to them, for their minute performing indications have to be understood in the context of the music itself and are often to be taken more as indications of the underlying qualities of the score than as literal demands. The problem of Boulez's *Marteau sans maître* with all its violent, sudden changes of dynamics, which to many performers seem to verge on the impossible and are seldom, if ever, carried out consistently, is to learn how literally unfaithful to the markings the performer has to be to give a true and effective performance of the work. Dynamic markings in Schoenberg's op. 23, for instance, seem, especially in the first piece, excessively extravagant and probably were not to be performed literally, but rather were meant to suggest the "expressionistic" character of the music.

The performance of Babbitt's scores, like those of many of his colleagues, poses many such questions. These are not confined only to scores written for live performers but extend also to music composed for those most erratic of performers, the tape deck and the loudspeaker. Matters of dynamic inflection, balance, and their rapidity of change, especially when they are treated as independent items of discourse as much of Babbitt's work does, pose serious acoustical problems in halls as well as many live-performance problems with instruments and the reactions of players. This has led some to raise the old, familiar cry that such scores are so written that a faithful performance is impossible. It is true that Babbitt, like many other composers, has had his share of uncertain, even incorrect performances. But, as is now so obvious, the generation of performers coming after the work was written finds a convincing way of playing music once dismissed as impossible. As this happens, Babbitt's special, highly imaginative and original work will become more widely appreciated.

For Pierre Boulez on His Sixtieth
(1985)

Unifying all the diversity of Pierre Boulez's extraordinary musical activities has been the intense desire to communicate musically the essence of our modern experience to musicians and audiences, to keep music at the forefront of modern activity. Unfortunately, in recent times the social position of music has been threatened because the profession and its public are caught, almost frozen in the rigid patterns of older musical thought as well as by the physical conditions of music making: antiquated instruments, inadequate concert halls, and standardized instrumental groupings. The determination to break this hard crust of institutional ice and to allow the new to take its artistic flight and reveal to us "Le vierge, le vivace et le bel aujourd'hui," as Mallarmé expresses it in the poem Boulez set to music so beautifully, has directed his continuously imaginative, enthusiastic, and energetic efforts for many years.

Apparently deeply conscious of this question as early as *Polyphonie X* and the first book of *Structures*, he declared his desire to make tabula rasa of accepted musical methods and call into question other parameters, such as rhythm and texture, and other traditional methods like causality, linearity, and form, which the earlier modernists had scarcely thought about—to bring himself, as he expressed it by quoting Paul Klee, "À la limite du pays fertile," much as Beckett and other writers, painters, and musicians of the time did, in order to learn the "language of abnegation." Yet today we can see that Boulez, unlike certain others at the time, called into question neither musical composition itself nor the fundamental concepts on which it is based. For his work has always remained within the frame of controlled, directed musical performance, centering primarily around the presentation of pitched and non-pitched sounds to listeners, expressing belief in the possibility of communicating his new visions under more or less familiar concert conditions—just as many contemporary writers do not call language into question, or the books which contain it.

As one of the most brilliant, artistic, and intelligent human beings of our time, he has supported his vision with astonishing energy and gusto by proceeding to renovate each aspect of our musical institutions. As a conductor and lecturer, he has given the works that form the background of present music such telling presentations that they have grasped listeners' imaginations all over the world and have made them receptive to further advances. It was in this spirit that he founded the Ensemble InterContemporain, which gives such convincing performances of new music. The following that Boulez's concerts have gained in Paris, London, Los Angeles, and other places where he has had the opportunity to prepare scores he considers significant has justified his belief in these scores and the remarkable enthusiasm that they evoke. His own compositions present the epitome of what he believes in with great panache as well as serious conviction. They are original and unique primarily because of their musical vision, which brings each of them into its own focus.

At IRCAM, following another line of attack, Boulez has expanded the horizons of musical sound materials and their manipulation and interorganization, studied the ways listeners perceive them in order vastly to enlarge the possibilities of musical communication. It is this enthusiastic belief in the benign potential of the future that gives his manifold activities, especially his own compositions, their rich visionary quality.

I remember very vividly Boulez in Baden-Baden at the ISCM Festival of 1955, when we were overwhelmed by the earlier version of *Le marteau sans maître*, conducted with such devotion by Hans Rosbaud. At that time, Goffredo Petrassi was the president, I was one of the vice-presidents, and the occasion was one of the better festivals sponsored by that organization—but at the final party Boulez jumped up on a table and with quite a flourish burned the festival program, pronouncing (with a good deal of reason) most of the music played at such festivals as "caduc."

From then until now I have often recalled Mallarmé's lines:

"... si contents
sur la soudaineté de notre amitié neuve ..."

His is a life whose birthdays give those seriously interested in the future of music an opportunity to celebrate with joy.

V

Life and Work

To Be a Composer in America
(1953/94)

I find that I am at something of a loss as to how to begin this talk, since it comes at a time when you might expect me to tell you something about my own music. As you know, a whole evening of it is being given here at your university tomorrow night.[1] I would like to thank those who are participating in the performance, for I know that my music is not easy to play. It makes unusual technical and musical demands on the performers, and it is hard on listeners who are unaccustomed to hearing new music. I know that part of my expression of gratitude to tomorrow night's performers should be to encourage you to go to the concert by giving a talk as challenging, as interesting, and as well worked out and rewarding as I like to think my music is. This I cannot do, for many reasons, the main one being that most of my effort has gone into the music itself and a very much smaller amount into verbalizing—especially about my own works. Indeed, the idea of talking about them makes me want to retreat behind William Butler Yeats's remark: "When I come to write poetry, I seem—I suppose because it is all instinct with me—completely ignorant."

Still, all composers have thoughts about what we do and why we do it, and have made efforts to explain it to ourselves and others. I have, it seems to me, carried on with my friends a fifteen-year-long conversation about all phases of contemporary music, so that a brief account of the gist of this conversation may help you to understand the outlook from which my music springs. At the outset I would like to stress that I do not feel myself to be a part of a school, or to be writing with a definite technical or philosophical program in mind. As I look at it, my music seems to be a series of crystallizations of states of mind and feeling at various times in my life, reflecting them in some way that I can no longer explain. Hearing it some time after it is written, I find that I can hardly understand how I thought of the musical ideas in them and feel that I can no more repeat what I did in them than I can turn back the clock and relive a day lived last year.

1. The program of 28 March 1953 consisted of: the Woodwind Quintet (1948), played by the Faculty Woodwind Quintet of the University of Illinois; Two Pieces for Kettledrums, "Recitative" and "Improvisation" (1949), played by Paul Price; the Piano Sonata (1945–46), played by Daniel Eller; and the (First) String Quartet (1951), played by the Walden Quartet of the University of Illinois. [B]

Yet we are all such products of the past that a description of what composers in my generation faced might help to explain what goes on now. For only fifteen or twenty years ago when we began to study music, the musical world looked entirely different to us from the way it does to students today. Two important changes had already occurred in contemporary music: the big revolution leading to the extended use of dissonant harmony had already subsided, and the second phase comprising "neoclassic" and more simply ordered styles had already been in existence for enough years to have completely won over the European composers of the generation after Stravinsky, Bartók, and Schoenberg. In the United States a first group of "modernist" composers had appeared who had started out in the extreme way that the earlier generation of Europeans had.

In the early 1930s none of this music was accepted by any but a handful of people, and its methods were neither established clearly enough nor considered important enough to have modified the traditional ways of teaching music. Indeed, the fact that there were many different kinds of contemporary music was not at all well understood. What few writers there were on the subject could only make the most obvious sort of distinctions. Even today, almost any generalizations about the first fifty years of the twentieth century are extremely hazardous, as I found out when I wrote the article on the subject for the new edition of the *Encyclopedia Britannica* three years ago. In fact, I must say that I see the whole development in quite a different light now than I did while I was writing it, and I expect that all of us will revise our ideas about our own period over and over.

Fifteen years ago, we could already see that the composers who came to maturity before the First World War were not only those who accomplished the violent break with traditional practices but were also the ones who led the return, around 1925, to a new kind of musical order. They had directed the modern movement in music and in a sense still do, although a number of them are dead. It is important, it seems to me, to realize that these individuals matured at a time when a very high standard of professionalism, of musical responsibility, was always maintained. The richness and broadness of scope of the musical scene before 1914 left its mark on the composers who grew up at that time. The fact that they reacted so violently against their period and introduced so many kinds of novelty at first appalled everyone. But as the dust and excitement has dissipated, it has now become apparent that the power of their revolt is at least partly owing to the cultivated background of that pre-War time. And the power of the music, such as Schoenberg's *Erwartung* and *Pierrot lunaire*, Stravinsky's *Le Sacre* and *L'Histoire du soldat*, and Bartók's early works with their remarkable completeness of realization, was in part due to the very high standard of artistic responsibility which these composers absorbed from the world in which they grew up. After the end of the First World War, the world became a very different place, and from then on there seemed to many to have been a gradual decline not only in technical command, in artistic vision, but also in liveliness of imagination.

I must say that when, as a boy, I was first attracted to the profession of music upon hearing of some of these extraordinary pre-War works, I completely sympathized with the iconoclastic attitudes they embodied, for I found older music rather boring. At that time, the full impact of the neoclassic movement as it was developed by Stravinsky, Hindemith, and the French Six, the twelve-tone systematization that took hold simultaneously in Vienna, and the special, newly formal approach that Bartók employed from about 1927 were scarcely known in this country. In fact, this more conservative trend did not reach here in its full force until 1937, which was when I began to compose. Before that, the extreme works of Aaron Copland—his *Piano Variations,* the *Statements*, the *Ode*, and the *Short Symphony*—and the works of Roger Sessions, Varèse, Ruggles, and Ives gave an American twist to the European modern movement which we found very exhilarating. For those of us growing up then, to compose modern music was to involve ourselves in a battle with the public which was exciting to wage and required a kind of courage and fortitude, even though we were sure that it would eventually be won. As music of this sort began to be accepted and played, a good deal of the liveliness and spirit began to evaporate, and a new, more career-minded kind of composer began to appear.

You can imagine what problem children we were in classes, when we kept insisting that old-fashioned technical studies would never help us write the kind of music we wanted to write. For myself, I remember working very hard with sevenths and ninths in my first harmony exercise, only to come to class with a paper which was an outrage not only to the teacher but to all the other students, who had written exercises in the familiar harmony-book style—a style I scarcely knew and could not stand. No one bothered to explain how harmony exercises were supposed to sound or why they should be written that way; it seemed that this was supposed to be self-evident. After a good deal of effort, I finally mastered this training, which seemed like nonsense to me then, if not to the teacher—for at that time hardly anyone in academe could conceive of a composer wanting to write in the modern style. I emphasize that this was only about twenty years ago.

As I look back on this today and see the widespread effects of fifteen years of teaching contemporary music and its methods to students, I am beginning to think that traditional training has a great deal to recommend it and now understand very well why Schoenberg always insisted on his students going through it. Musical training, it seems to me, should develop great control over the notes and a high degree of sensitivity to their many uses. This is not always accomplished in a training that is very free.

After the onset of the Great Depression in 1932 the older, more dissonant trend gradually spent itself in America, as it had already done in Europe. The public was not to be amused by *succès de scandale* and in this country definitely would not tolerate them. At this point, the modern music movement split in two. Many composers, such as Roy Harris, Aaron Copland, Henry Cowell, and Virgil Thomson, turned to a more easily accessible style that combined elements of neoclassicism with American folklore; and they were followed by others, such as Quincy Porter, Richard Donovan, Randall

Thompson, and Walter Piston, who shaped this style to their own ends. While this trend practically took over the American musical world, another retreated into the background: Wallingford Riegger, Roger Sessions, and a very few others persisted in a contrary direction. Sessions seems even to have gradually eliminated the more diatonic and accessible side of his music.

In spite of this change, which began to take place in the mid-1930s, the American public still would have none of any kind of modern music, so for the next ten years these styles were kept alive by groups like the League of Composers and later the International Society for Contemporary Music, in which composers made common cause and fought the battle for survival, development, and understanding against an apathetic public. Thanks to the League and its magazine, *Modern Music*, many new ideas were born, many composers were encouraged, and many teachers and many critics were afforded experience. When these musicians got out into the wide world and began to teach students and to write intelligent reviews of new music in the newspapers, public opinion began to change.

Though some have found it fashionable to scoff at organizations such as the League and the ISCM for being too special and sheltered, developing music written only for other composers, the importance of their role cannot be underestimated. Actually, their roots can be traced all the way back to the beginning of the Romantic era, when concerts became public events and people began paying for admission to them. From then on audiences, being of varied cultural backgrounds and of enormously different degrees of musicality, have invariably and understandably been conservative. It has been only through the efforts of small "pressure groups" of artists that young, original composers have been able to develop to maturity and finally make their mark with the larger public. It does not matter whether the music was of limited appeal, like that of Hugo Wolf or Gabriel Fauré, or of widely popular character like that of Schubert, Brahms, or Wagner: such music almost invariably arose and developed within the confines of a small circle, and in all probability this process will continue as long as there is a paying audience.

During the late 1930s and early '40s, when the great wave of refugees from Europe brought with it most of the eminent composers of our time to the United States, many of us watched in shock and disheartenment as their reputations dwindled almost overnight. Stravinsky, who was the most energetic and who had the largest and most varied repertory of outstanding works, soon began to emerge again. But there were others—Bartók, Schoenberg, Ernst Toch, and Ernst Krenek for instance—who had the greatest trouble in recovering from the transplantation. Their experience made us realize that a musical career in this country at that time was a far more hazardous pursuit even than we had thought. For it seemed that no matter how good one was, one could not count on performances or recognition. During the Second World War these composers faced the same difficulty in getting performances as did the rest of us, and many of their excellent works got no hearing or publication at all. When the war was over, their works, like our own, began to be performed in Europe more frequently than they ever were here and were often much better received, especially in their native lands.

By 1950, however, the popularizing and propagandistic efforts of the 1930s and '40s had begun to reap rewards. Contemporary music is now being fairly regularly performed at most important recitals and concerts, especially in big cities; and the rapidly growing public interest in it may soon parallel the sudden success of the new styles in architecture and design. Curiously, while this has been going on, almost everywhere in the Western world the youngest generation has been turning against the very popularizing movement that won over the general public and is becoming interested in a small group of composers who opposed it, such as the twelve-tone Viennese and our own Riegger and Sessions.

Things are changing for those of us who remained aloof from the prevailing tide and who were dubbed "old-fashioned modernists" ten years ago. I remember that when my first large work, the ballet *Pocahontas*, was given its premiere on the same bill as Aaron Copland's ballet *Billy the Kid* in 1939, mine was dismissed as cacophonous, as belonging to a dated, outworn style whose only purpose was to be unintelligible, while Copland's ballet was (quite rightly) hailed as ushering in a new, more transparent and understandable style. To my surprise, my score won the Juilliard award—and then was promptly forgotten. But to my even greater surprise, after I had persisted more or less on this path for a number of years, people began no longer to find my music so puzzling, and I began to feel that I had not been wrong to follow my own bent. In our hurried era, to go in and out of fashion more than once during one's lifetime is likely to happen to all of us.

For all a composer can do is to stick to his own vision, do what he thinks best, and let the future decide.

As we review these past years, there is, I think, a very real sense of decline in quality. Each succeeding generation seems less able to produce works of outstanding interest. Whether this is entirely a result of the terrible political and moral upheavals through which our civilization has passed, I leave to others to judge. But I do feel that this is no longer the time to be fooling with tricky fashions, with dubious artistic notions, with all kinds of triviality, that this is the time to work our hardest and our best if we want musical culture to survive.

The first generation of contemporary composers set a standard and maintained it throughout their lives. The high creativity of Igor Stravinsky is just as apparent in *The Rake's Progress* or the *Cantata* being performed here tonight as it was in *Le Sacre*. The same is as true of Schoenberg's String Trio as of *Pierrot lunaire*; it applies as much to Bartók's Second Quartet as to his Sixth. These composers, through all their changes of style and artistic milieu, have continued as wonderful examples of what can be accomplished in our time. They have been continuously creative, not satisfied with finding some trademark, some mannerism which would stereotype their music, but have kept to their larger vision as they have moved through many different phases and characters, spinning off new creative ideas as they went. It is almost as if a special logic, a special inner life had been invented for each important work. Their ability to achieve unity as well as uniqueness, original organization as well as strong projection of feeling, has enlivened concert and stage music and given it what it most needs to thrive.

It has taken us a long time to learn the lesson which should have been apparent from the very first. That is, that no amount of surprise or novelty can ever completely conceal the triviality of an imagination which employs these things for themselves without any real attempt to join them into a living, meaningful, and expressive flow. As Bartók and the others were keenly aware, it is not enough to find novel sounds and procedures; it is far more important to invent methods of joining musical moments together in a way that lends strength of character. The context of any musical event gives meaning to that event, a meaning that it can never achieve for itself.

In spite of this almost self-evident idea, most of the composers of recent times, while sometimes quite inventive in terms of melody, harmony, and rhythm, have all too frequently taken a conventional attitude toward form—as is obvious from the vast number of fugues and sonata-form pieces that have been written. Now, even to start with the idea of writing a fugue is to be forced to accept a whole range of predigested ideas that make the task of inventing an interesting flow far more difficult. It is very hard to chase out the specter of Bach and, if you like, Hindemith, and the same can be said of Beethoven and others in connection with sonata form.

Composers, it seems to me, have generally forgotten today how important musical flow and continuity are and have too often relegated them to conventional observances. This is a great mistake. For true novelty and progress in music now reside not in inventing new harmonies, new irregularities of rhythm, and all the rest, but in incorporating these into new patterns. It is high time that this field was explored more thoroughly, both in detail and in the large. And it is primarily from this point of view that composers of very recent vintage seem to be working. In part, their exploration has come about through the influence of the twelve-tone composers and their followers, whose work was not well understood until recently. As you know now, a great deal is being written about them and particularly about this technique, which has the great fault of being easily explicable in words. Consequently, the prestige of this technique has grown out of all proportion to its worth—and this development has led other composers to codify their methods in prose, which has provoked controversy upon controversy and drawn attention away from important questions.

It ought to be clear that the use of this technique is not the fundamental characteristic of the Viennese School. First of all, a twelve-tone system was propounded by Josef Matthias Hauer before Schoenberg and his pupils Berg and Webern took it up, and since that time composers of a great deal of music in quite different styles have applied this technique without sounding at all like any of the three Viennese. On the other hand, in comparing the works of these composers written before and after they started to use the method, one cannot fail to be struck by the fact that the character of the music hardly changed at all. Indeed, Schoenberg's *Five Pieces for Piano,* op. 23, dating from just before he began to compose twelve-tone music, verge so closely on the twelve-tone scheme at times that it is impossible to say whether he was consciously applying the method or not. The same is true of the Webern and

Berg works of this time. This leads to the realization that the really important features of this music are quite other. They involve a high degree of condensation, lending itself to rapid change and the quick, intense making of points. The use of equally intense melodic shapes, often broken up into short, dramatic fragments, joins with a very varied rubato rhythmic technique to produce a new kind of what might be called instrumental recitative. The rapid increases and decreases of harmonic tension, quick changes of register, and fragmented, non-imitative counterpoint are also worthy of note. This all adds up to a style of remarkable fluidity which seems to have been derived from the late works of Debussy but seen through the expressive extremes that characterize late German Romantic music, particularly Mahler and Richard Strauss. The fantastic delicacy and imagination of Anton Webern comes across as so new and so beautiful—now that we are just beginning to find performers who can present it effectively—that many younger composers are going to have a hard time recovering from it. The tendency to see the twelve-tone method as the genesis of these innovations is very unperceptive, for in many cases the row seems to be a kind of secret formula barely audible in the music.

This technique arose appropriately out of a concern for harmonic and melodic movement and does not regulate rhythm in any way. A number of attempts have been made to organize this field, and before I leave the discussion of techniques, I would like to point out some of the things I have done with rhythm. My Piano Sonata, the earliest work on tomorrow night's program, approaches this element in much the way many of my contemporaries have: equal units are joined together into irregular patterns. However, in the first movement these units are so quick that their rhythmic value is merged to form large irregular figurations that give the impression of a measured rubato. After this work, I began to explore the use of irregular units and their groupings. You will find in my [First] String Quartet sections in one speed followed by sections in another speed, say three-fourths as fast, sometimes sounding at the same time when they overlap. By bringing a much larger variety of rhythmic relationships together into one contrapuntal or rhythmic texture and relating them formally, I have tried to extend the scope of my musical flow. Using this large range of unequal musical units has been most stimulating and has sometimes suggested ideas that have meant a great deal to me.

But let me say at once that it is very easy to get the idea from any such description that the technique in question is the main point of the music, as if one were meant to listen for this and for very little else. Everybody knows, for example, that listening to Beethoven is not best done by cataloguing themes. What counts in listening to music is following the grand line, its forward motion, its reversals and dramatic and expressive moments.

For music is primarily flow in time, and its unity parallels the various kinds of flow of events about which we have feelings and thoughts. The dadaists' notion of the meeting of a sewing machine and an umbrella on an operating table was supposed to evoke the notion of utter incongruity, but if you put the sewing machine and the umbrella into the proper sequence with enough time between them, all sorts of meanings can be drawn, maybe even important ones. In any case, most older music followed a kind of cause-and-effect pattern, and it was possible to trace a straight line of causality from one end of a movement to the other. In late eighteenth-century music this basically linear presentation was broken up by musical asides which hinted that things were not to be taken at face value. Gay things were sometimes sad and vice versa, and this aside technique provided an added dimension to the music, although for the romantic it robbed the work of its intensity of expression. In any case, such patterns are what I consider to be the life of music. In a way, they are comparable to words and their grammatical interconnections. One word follows another, the second expanding or more often limiting the first, the third or fourth putting the previous ones in a new light. Then as whole groups of words, phrases, sentences, and paragraphs are heard these big groups react with each other, giving new meanings to what has gone before and suggesting what is to come. Meanwhile, in the listener's mind, other ideas not explicitly stated emerge until there is a vast wonderful web of meaning, of cross-references, of multiple planes of thought and feeling, of intentions, of realizations and of frustrations—all of which are brought together in the service of one vision to give the hearer a sense of a vital experience.

Just because the description of such processes is complex and cumbersome does not mean that such processes are complex and cumbersome in themselves. The music of Mozart deals in these complexities, particularly in his piano concerti and operas, with a transparency and a facility that is at once delightful and infinitely moving. (Whether these processes seemed so transparent and simple in his day is a question.) Today, unfortunately, such simplicity and facility in most cases seem associated with a primitiveness and naiveté that dilute any effort to recapture this marvelous quality. On the other hand, Stravinsky in *The Rake's Progress* has come closer to doing this than any other composer of our time, and his music is far from being either primitive or naive—or, for that matter, simple.

The Mozartean technique has much to recommend it, but from an entirely different point of view than that of its simplicity. For Mozart was a most remarkable inventor of plastic, many-faceted phrases, of ways of emphasis, of passing lightly over some things and emphasizing others, and a master of rapid changes of character all molded in flexible sentences and paragraphs. The fascination of a fluid and varied contour has always attracted Viennese composers. You can see this in Schubert and Wolf, occasionally in Brahms, in Richard Strauss, and more recently in Schoenberg and his group. Today, this flexibility is sought after by many grown weary of the stolid blocklike patterns of composers like Hindemith and Milhaud, or in some of our own composers, such as Roy Harris and William Schuman. In recent years, I have been anxious to work out a highly variable and flexible technique, and the change from a more blocklike structure in the Piano Sonata to the wide flexibility of my String Quartet can be traced through the Woodwind Quintet and the Pieces for Kettledrums, all of which you will hear tomorrow night.

As you may also notice tomorrow night, each of my works has sprung from a consideration of the instruments used in it. The special sound character of the instrumental combination has usually dictated to me all the ideas and their methods of development. In each case I have tried to find the type of music which would be the most idiomatic for the combination, for I am more concerned with sound than with abstract procedure. The totality of sound and its change from moment to moment has supplanted an interest in melody, harmony, and the other elements, and I use each of these elements for its sound character rather than for its constructive character. Debussy, in his later works, was really the first to compose in this way, and in various forms this interest in sound character has remained the preoccupation of many since his time. Expression and form-building, under this approach, are constantly shifting from one element to another. Sometimes a chord can become a deeply expressive feature, or a means of connecting one part with another; at other times, such connection can be accomplished by a rhythm, or by a stretch of counterpoint.

You will notice too tomorrow that there is a considerable change of character between each of my pieces and the others. This is partly due to the concern I have with instrumental media, but also to my concern with variety of expression and technique. Each work usually completely explores all the aspects of interest to me in the particular approach it uses—to the extent that when the work is finished, I have no further desire to write another piece anything like it. The other day one of my colleagues asked me why I did not write more piano music. He said that my Piano Sonata contained enough ideas to supply me with a whole repertory of pieces. All I could reply was that until I had some new and different ideas for piano music, I could not muster enough enthusiasm to write again for the piano. It is this attitude that has so far prevented me from writing any very simple works that might be more easily accessible and performable. I seldom come upon ideas at once interesting to me and also simple to play. Naturally, I try for them. But so far I have rarely been able to find any. It is far easier for me to find satisfying ideas for the rather complex music that I do write.

Ultimately, nobody interested in serious concert music really thinks that simplicity is a primary consideration in art. The primary consideration is rather the vision which leads a composer to do what he does best, most convincingly, and to follow his intuitions and imaginations and ideas to their most complete expression. A composer cannot completely control his natural bent. He can gradually educate and train himself in certain directions, but when it comes to the actual process of composition he is pretty much at the mercy of his intuition. At its best this intuition reflects the total man, his sense of responsibility, his self-discipline, his mind, and his heart. In our time, as André Malraux has suggested, one of the main sources of stimulus to the artist is the expression of his own special view of the world and of life, of those areas of feeling and technique which have the most important and most personal meaning to him. If he has not the urge to do this, his work does not seem to carry much weight.

Applying this point of view to music would help to explain the enormous variety of contemporary music, a variety which in my opinion is not great enough in imaginative concepts, for there are too many schools and too much imitation. Certainly from the public's point of view, modern music is too various to be easily understood. Yet in spite of the efforts of the mass public to keep composers in line over the past 150 years since the French and American revolutions, one by one the really vital composers have gradually brought the public around to their ideas, no matter how extreme these ideas had seemed at first. The appalling difficulty of the score of *Tristan und Isolde* and its obscurity to its first hearers is a case of such a development. There have been and will be many more, while the composers who flattered the tastes of their day are mostly unheard of now.

In this light, there is but one kind of advice to give any composer, and that is: Do what means most to you and it will, someday, if you are good enough and lucky enough, mean something to others. There is nothing sadder than a composer who tries to write for public consumption unsuccessfully, who turns out one piece after another intended to reach a mass audience but who like the rest of us gets few performances. There are never many really good composers at any one time, and it is a waste of effort in such a risky situation to court an easy success if it is not part of one's nature. As Edmund Wilson once said of the German painter George Grosz, who came to this country and hoped to give up his early style of brutal caricature and to try to find a way of painting that would be acceptable to American magazines: "He could only remain himself: an artist with a vision of the world which he could no more prevent his faculties from concentrating their forces to realize than a wild pig in labor with a litter of boars can give birth to china-pig savings-banks."[2]

The Composer's Choices
(c.1960)

The teacher to whom I owe the most, Mlle. Nadia Boulanger, frequently says to her students that a true artist can be recognized by the quality of his refusals, calling our attention sternly to the critical activity that lies behind all good artistic work. However, to say that the higher the quality of ideas the artist rejects, the higher the quality of his final accomplishment, implies a commitment to an order of values that may be possible only in a unified culture such as that of France. For unless there is some general agreement about grades of quality, it is obviously impossible for different individuals to judge, according to the same standards as the artist, the quality of refusals, or even to agree on the quality of the final accomplishment.

Mlle. Boulanger's remark, partly because of its emphasis on rejection, brings to mind the typical, highly cultivated French artists of the turn of the

2. Edmund Wilson, "George Grosz in the United States," in *Classics and Commercials: A Literary Chronicle of the Forties* (New York: Farrar, Straus and Giroux, 1950), 344.

century, such as Cézanne, Mallarmé, and Debussy, who not only rejected commonly held ideas about the subject matter of their arts but even within their own works were extremely fastidious about every detail regardless of all the obstacles that upholders of the conventions of ordinary life put in their way.

Something of the intensity of this devotion to art was made vivid to me while I was a student, on the day when the Stavisky affair resulted in bloody street rioting between rival political groups in Paris, closing all business offices and stopping public transportation. On this day our counterpoint class met. To reach it, some of us had to walk several miles across the frightening city. When we had assembled, Mlle. Boulanger criticized with melancholy exasperation the very few members of the class who had not appeared, saying that a riot might stop many ordinary affairs of life, but there was no reason why it should stop music.

I have thought of this day often when considering works created under difficult circumstances, and have wondered how many in our country would see any reason for a student to thread his way through a dangerous riot in which many were killed to learn the refinements of six-, seven-, and eight-part strict counterpoint—a discipline the nature of which few of them could understand, and the mastery of which still fewer would be able to recognize or value—and I have wondered whether this training or the precision of musical writing that results from it would seem to many Americans worth the risk which we took without question.

For few American composers can escape the impression that when serious music was brought over to this country, it was and still is but dimly realized by the public that the great compositions fundamental to the art were not things easily or cheaply produced, but were the results of human beliefs, of commonly shared moral and aesthetic values, of orderly, logical thought, and of the practical musical experiences of generations. And the standards set up by the music profession that had directed the fascinating musical development we all love are a direct reflection of these qualities. For instance, the typical traditional training of a composer, even today, centers around the learning of techniques that imply an attentive listener, experienced in following musical thought, who is also a cultivated person in matters of taste, quick to understand, and impatient with the obvious. This training consists, at the very least, in developing a respect for such an intelligent listener's expectations and abilities, and, at the very most, in using these as a means for eloquent communication. However, as often happens here today, when composers cannot always count on the listening ability of even a small part of their audience, or when this small part, if it exists, has no influence over the majority of listeners on whom most of the qualities and skills of even the accepted works of the standard repertory make little impression, what value can there be in learning to achieve the order and control which until now were thought to be so fundamental to the art?

It is against the background of this perplexing American situation that I would like to discuss some of the choices and refusals that I, as a composer, have made. Naturally I cannot judge their quality objectively, but in describing my musical development over the past twenty years, I hope to be able to dispel a little of the confusion and misunderstanding that surround the composer's work. If I dwell on the sound of the music—on what can be physically heard—it is because this can be talked about, while the musical content which must be grasped from direct attention to the sound cannot be put into words satisfactorily. It should be obvious that changes in musical vocabulary are the result of a human development in the course of which the musical content which I envisioned became more clearly defined and required a search for ever more adequate and precise means of expressing it; also as the character of the content changed and developed over the years, I was led to explore and invent other suitable new means.

My first large orchestral work, written in 1938—a ballet on the subject of Pocahontas—is full of suggestions of things that were to remain important to me, as well as of others which were later rejected or completely transformed because they no longer seemed cogent. Some of these features can be observed in the third movement of the ballet, a recording of which you are about to hear. First, the overall style made up of irregular rhythms, dissonant harmony, and a combination of diatonic and chromatic elements has remained fairly constant, although in the years immediately following this work I made a brief excursion into a more diatonic style, and then, after 1946, became increasingly more chromatic and dissonant. The rhythmic structure found in this work was delved into, expanded, and finally completely transformed. The construction of phrases here already shows a tendency to change character quickly, a feature that became much more important in my later works.

On the other hand, the way of forming musical material and texture, and the type of flow and continuity were abandoned. Observe, for instance, how the main gist of this work is almost always presented in the form of themes or melodic lines, either based on reiterative motives—a method I soon found unsatisfactory—or on long spun-out phrases, usually leading to a climax—a pattern I rarely use today. The background is filled in with rhythmic chords, figurations, and simple contrapuntal lines. Today the texture of my music is seldom that of a thematic foreground with an accompanying background. Notice, too, the constant rhythmic drive running through the fast part—a technique I have modified a great deal in the interests of plasticity. [Suite from *Pocahontas,* third movement, pp. 36–38 of printed score][1]

This work, now so easy to listen to, was considered difficult to play and to hear at its first performance in New York in 1939, and was received very coldly indeed by the public and the critics. And those colleagues who were my friends and whose opinions I respected were hardly more encouraging. However, the suite from the ballet was given the Juilliard Award for the Publication of American Music in 1941, and several hundred copies of the score and parts were printed only to gather dust on library and warehouse shelves,

---

1. The excerpts played during this radio lecture are identified from here on in bracketed insertions. [B]

unused, until 1959, when the recording, part of which you have just heard, was made in Switzerland by the Zurich Radio Orchestra conducted by Jacques-Louis Monod.

After the experience of *Pocahontas*, I felt that I had to write in a more controllable style, one that would be easier to perform and would appeal more directly to what I imagined to be the listening abilities of the average concertgoer, a point of view that a number of American composers adopted at the time. Of the few works I wrote in what seemed a more acceptable style, from 1940 to 1944, the *Holiday Overture* was the last and already shows a turning to more elaborate textures. This work again won a prize of publication, and again remained unperformed in this country for a number of years, although it received many performances in Germany during 1946 and 1947, none of which I heard. Recently it has been played by a number of orchestras here, among them the New York Philharmonic, directed by Dimitri Mitropoulos in 1958.

By the time I had completed the *Holiday Overture*, my interest was beginning to turn to other matters of a more specialized and personal nature. Since the music I had written with the aim of being accessible apparently interested few listeners and hence did not serve the purpose intended, I felt no compunctions about taking a direction that might be much more difficult to grasp.

By 1945, my preoccupation with modern dissonant harmony and what has since been called cross-accented counterpoint, of which the *Holiday Overture* is an elaborate example, was no longer central, and I became more concerned with the formation of musical ideas, of types and qualities of continuity, and with the fascinating possibility of musical flow and change. The opening of my Piano Sonata of 1946 will illustrate what I mean. It is the first passage in my works that is not primarily thematic. Its central idea comes from the total sound of the piano writing. Notice particularly the variety and flexibility of rhythm, the frequent changes of character, the oppositions of register, of manners of playing, and of slow and fast. All of these were to become increasingly important. [Piano Sonata, mm. 1–82]

In the opening of my Cello Sonata of 1948, I was interested in the musical meaning resulting from two simultaneous, but differently characterized, planes of music—a type of texture used to great effect in many operas, but seldom in concert music. Here the clocklike regularity of the piano is contrasted with the singing, expressive line of the cello, which, although accurately written out, sounds as free from the underlying beat as the jazz improviser from his rhythm section—the musical situation which suggested this passage. [Sonata for Violoncello and Piano, mm. 1–67]

As time went on, all kinds of new textural and rhythmic ideas began to appear. For instance, one of my etudes from *Eight Etudes and a Fantasy* of 1950 is a musical mosaic made up of a two-note motive constantly repeated in different transpositions. Out of this neutral material an overall pattern with a more articulate shape of its own emerges. [*Eight Etudes and a Fantasy* for woodwind quartet: Etude IV, pp. 7–11]

The last three examples briefly illustrate the numerous musical changes that occurred in my music from 1946 to the present. It is only in the realm of chamber music that such a a change could have taken place, could have been tried out in the America of these years, since it was, and still is, almost impossible to gain the necessary experience of actual live performances of works with any kind of unusual conception with the orchestras in this country. However, when the Louisville Orchestra commissioned a work from me, I decided to apply some of the ideas I had developed in my chamber music to the larger medium. I chose the form of a set series of variations, since the flow and change of musical character interested me a great deal at the time.

The work starts with activity on two different planes. On one there is a long singing line that flows calmly, resisting the change, and continuing through the introduction and the statement of the theme, gradually sinking below it. On the other plane, many brief dramatic ideas are presented during the introduction, followed by the statement of the lyrical theme which is the basis of the entire work, only part of which I shall point out now. [Variations for Orchestra, mm. 1–52]

Each variation has different features, and like different members of the same family, different relationships with the theme. For instance, in the fifth variation, all outlines are blurred and internal contrasts are reduced to accented attacks and held chords, which sound the notes of the theme together. [Variations for Orchestra, Variation 5, m. 259 (beginning of cymbal roll) to m. 288]

The work culminates in a rapid series of oppositions between many different characters, finally silenced by the trombones' loud statement of a new version of one half of the theme, while the strings play the other half softly. [The broadcast ended with a performance of the Variations in its entirety.]

Shop Talk by an American Composer
(1960)

When I agreed to discuss the rhythmic procedures I use in my music, I had forgotten, for the moment, the serious doubts I have about just such kinds of discussion when carried on by the composer himself. That a composer can write music that is thought to be of some interest is, of course, no guarantee that he can talk illuminatingly about it. It is especially hard for him to be articulate because inevitably his compositions are the result of innumerable choices—many unconscious, many conscious, some quickly made, others after long deliberation, all mostly forgotten when they have served their purpose. At some time or other, this sorting and combining of notes finally becomes a composition. By that time many of its conceptions and techniques have become almost a matter of habit for the composer and he is only dimly aware of the choices that first caused him to adopt them. Finally, in an effort to judge the work as an entity, as another might listen to it, he tries to forget his intentions and listen with fresh ears. What he is aiming at, after all, is a whole in which all the technical workings are interdependent and combine to produce the kind of artistic experience that gives a work its validity and in so doing makes all its procedures relevant. There is no shortcut to achieving this final artistic relevance. No technique is of much intrinsic value; its importance for the composer and his listeners lies only in the particular use made of it to further the artistic qualities and character of an actual work. If in discussing his works, therefore, he points out a procedure, he is bound to feel that he is drawing attention to something of secondary importance and by dwelling on it misleading others into thinking of it as primary. Schoenberg expressed such doubts in essays on his use of the twelve-tone method. And he was right, for certainly the twelve-tone aspect of his works accounts for only a part of their interest, perhaps not the most important part. For from op. 25 to his last works the number of different kinds of compositions he wrote illustrates the very broad range of expression and conception and the wide variety of musical techniques that can incorporate the system and yet be distinguished from it.

In any discussion of specifically contemporary procedures, there are a few serious risks involved that must be constantly borne in mind. The first is the danger of rapid and wide dissemination of oversimplified formulas that shortens their life. It is obvious that one technical fad after another has swept over twentieth-century music as the music of each of its leading composers has come to be intimately known. Each fad lasted a few years, only to be discarded by the succeeding generation of composers, then by the music profession, and finally by certain parts of the interested public, so that through overuse many of the striking features of the best works lost their freshness. It was hard, therefore, for those close to music to listen to these works for a time, and many of the better works disappeared from the repertory without a trace. Such a formula as the impressionists' parallel ninth chords, for instance, wore itself out in the tedious arrangements of popular music current until recently. Each of the trends of our recent past—primitivism, machinism, neoclassicism, *Gebrauchsmusik*, the styles of Bartók and Berg and now those of Schoenberg and Webern—has left and will leave in its trail numbers of really gifted composers whose music, skillful and effective as it is, is suffocated, at least for a time, by its similarity to other music of the same type. Of course, ultimately this faddishness is trivial, but its mercurial changes today have made the life of many a composer a great trial, more even than in the time of Rossini, who is now generally thought to have been one of the first outstanding composers to have given up composing because he could not change with the times.

The tendency to fad has been greatly encouraged by the promulgation of systems, particularly harmonic systems. Many recent composers following Schoenberg, Hindemith, and Messiaen have gained renown by circulating descriptions of their systems even in places where their music was not known. This kind of intellectual publicity can lead to a dead end even more quickly than the older fads derived from the actual sound of music in styles the composer did not even bother to explain.

The popularity of modern harmonic systems is, unfortunately, easy to understand. Textbooks led music students to think of harmony as a well-ordered routine, and when they found it to be less and less so in the years from Wagner to the present, they were much troubled—and still are—by the gap between what they learn and what they hear in modern music. For mature composers, lack of system is usually not much of a problem since they write, as they probably always have, what sounds right to them. This "rightness" has come, I suppose, from a developed sensitivity and experience that take time to acquire. When modern systems of harmony that were orderly and easy to explain appeared they filled an important pedagogical need for the inexperienced.

The very ease with which any of these systems can be used has its obvious dangers, as I have said. With the help of these and other shortcuts a vast amount of music is being written today, far more than can ever be played, than can ever be judged or widely known. At the same time there seems to be little corresponding development of discrimination, or even of ability or desire to listen to new music, and little expansion of opportunities for performance, at least in this country. The struggle to be performed and to be recognized makes it very hard for one not to become, even against one's will, some kind of system-monger, particularly if one uses certain procedures that are considered effective. For among students there is today a hunger for new formulas, and they constitute an interested public.

Obviously the only way to withstand the disturbing prospect of being swept away by a change in fad is to plunge into the even more disturbing situation of trying to be an individual and finding one's own way, as most of us have tried to do, not bothering too much about what is or will be sanctioned at any given moment by the profession and the public. We may then have to lead our lives producing works "too soon" for their time as Webern did, if they are not really "too late" since, if professional, they presuppose an attentive public which seems to getting rarer. We are caught in a development dictated by convictions impossible to change with the fads.

All this is to say that I do not consider my rhythmic procedures a trick or a formula. I do not even feel that they are an integral part of my musical personality, especially in the way I used them in my First String Quartet (1951), which delves elaborately into polyrhythms. As I have suggested, all aspects of a composition are closely bound together, and for this reason I cannot give an orderly exposition of any without bringing in a large perspective of ideas. So I do not know where to begin, and I need your help in directing this discussion to regions that will be interesting and useful to you. Almost anything I might say, I suppose, preferably on musical subjects, might be considered relevant to the subject you have so kindly invited me to discuss here.

Question: In the program notes of your Variations for Orchestra which you wrote for the Louisville performance, you described your method of variation as being a method of transformation, which you compared to the transformation from one life-stage to another of some marine animals. What did you mean by this?

Answer: As musicians you are all familiar with the problems of program notes. Technical discussions baffle the greater part of the audience and the few who do understand are apt to feel that the composer is a calculating monster, particularly since musical terms are ponderous, not always very definite in meaning, and too often give the impression of complexity when describing something very obvious to the ear. If I had described the augmentations, diminutions, retrograde inversions as they occur, this would have been positively bewildering to the public and would not have helped it to listen—certainly not the first time. So I tried to find a comparison that would help the listener to grasp my general approach. Serious music must appeal in different ways. Its main appeal, however, emerges from the quality of the musical material or ideas and perhaps even more from their use in significant continuities, but does not always depend on grasping the logic of the latter on first hearing. There has to be something left for the second time, if there ever is a second time.

As in all my works, I conceived this one as a large, unified musical action or gesture. In it, definition and contrast of character decrease during the first variations, arriving at a point of neutrality in the central variation, then increase again to the finale, which comprises many different speeds and characters. This work was thought of as a series of character studies in various states of interaction with each other both within each variation and between one and the next. Activity, development, type of emphasis, clearness or vagueness of definition, I hoped would also contribute to characterization. Formal, rhythmic, and developmental processes, as well as texture and thematic material, differ in each one for this reason.

The characteristic effort of the serious composer, as I see it, is not so much in the invention of musical ideas in themselves, as in the invention of interesting ideas that will also fill certain compositional requirements and allow for imaginative continuations. Serious music appeals to a longer span of attention and to a more highly developed auditory memory than do the more popular kinds of music. In making this appeal, it uses many contrasts, coherences, and contexts that give it a wide scope of expression, great emotional power and variety, direction, uniqueness, and a fascination of design with many shadings and qualities far beyond the range of popular or folk music. Every moment must count somehow, as must every detail. For a composer it is not always easy to find a passage that fits the particular situation and moment at which it appears in the composition, that carries to a further point some idea previously stated, that has the appropriate expressive quality motivated by what has been heard and yet is a passage that sounds fresh and alive.

As far as I am concerned, I am always interested in a composer's phrases and their shape and content, the way they are joined, the type of articulation used, as well as the general drift or continuity of a large section, and the construction of a whole work. The small details of harmony, rhythm, and texture fall naturally into place when one has interesting conceptions of these larger shapes.

Q: What do you mean by metric modulation?

A: If you listen to or look at any part of the first or last movement of my First String Quartet, you will find that there is a constant change of pulse.

This is caused by an overlapping of speeds. Say, one part in triplets will enter against another part in quintuplets and the quintuplets will fade into the background and the triplets will establish a new speed that will become the springboard for another such operation. The structure of such speeds is correlated throughout the work and gives the impression of varying rates of flux and change of material and character, qualities I seek in my recent works. The wish to accomplish this in the domain of heavily emphasized contrapuntal contrasts led me to work out the plan of metric modulation described by Richard Goldman.[1]

Q: Why are the contrapuntal lines in your quartet so much alike, using equal note values?

A: You cannot have listened to the work very carefully or looked at the score. Of the nine notes in the first four measures, there are seven different lengths, the longest eighteen times the shortest. There are, it is true, a few places near the beginning in which several contrapuntal parts, each of equal note values, are combined, but in complete polyrhythmic contrast emphasized by intervallic, bowing, and expressive contrasts. In these I was particularly anxious to present to the listener the idea of polyrhythmic textures in its most definite form, for even this quality of texture develops during the work, leading, in the second movement, to a four-part fragmented canon in continuous sixteenths and, in later movements, to lines of much notational irregularity. But even if the values were more frequently equal than they are, as for instance in the polyrhythmic, posthumous Etudes of Chopin, I cannot see that this would be a real objection, as you imply. Many a fine work has dealt in continuous streams of equal note values.

Q: Does your music have any harmonic plan?

A: A chord, a vertical group of pitches either simultaneously sounded or arpeggiated, like a motive, is a combination to be more or less clearly remembered and related to previous and future chords heard in the same work. Whether the composer is conscious of it or not, a field of operation with its principles of motion and of interaction is stated or suggested at the beginning of any work. The field may be tonal, employ traditional harmony, or it may be unrelated to traditional harmony, as my music seems to be nowadays, in which case I feel it imperative to establish clearly, near the beginning, the principles upon which the composition moves. Once this field of operation is established, its possibilities are explored, interesting new aspects of it are revealed, patterns of action of contrasting types emerge as the work goes along. A work whose world is not clearly defined loses a great deal of possible power and interest; one whose world is too narrow and restricted runs the risk of being thin, although if the world is unusual enough this narrowness can produce a kind of hallucinatory quality—one that I do not concern myself with in my works. This extension of the traditional methods of coherence can rarely be attained nowadays solely by intuition, I think, because of the vast number of musical means, new and old, that we know. Some

1. Richard Goldman, "The Music of Elliott Carter," *Musical Quarterly* 43 (1957): 151–70.

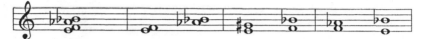

Example 1. First String Quartet: "key" four-note chord containing all intervals.

composers, it is true, insulate themselves from new musical experiences in an effort not to be distracted. Others, whose curiosity and interest prompt them to follow what is going on, feeling, perhaps, as Charles Ives did, that "eclecticism is part of his duty—sorting potatoes means a better crop next year,"[2] have to make a number of conscious choices and establish the frame in which to work before they can compose at all.

In my First String Quartet, I did use a "key" four-note chord, one of the two four-note groups that joins all the two-note intervals into pairs, thus allowing for the total range of interval qualities that still can be referred back to a basic chord-sound. This chord is not used at every moment in the work but occurs frequently enough, especially in important places, to function, I hope, as a formative factor. It is presented in various kinds of part-writing and interval combination, the number of notes is increased and diminished in it, in ways familiar to all of you. The chord, here in its closest position, showing its content of intervals of a diminished fifth and less, is also used both in many intervallic inversions and in total inversion (Ex. 1). An example of its use in counterpoint (Ex. 2) occurs in m. 477 of the last movement, where the quality of the chord is strongly dwelt on—each vertical combination except the last being made up of it.

Q: Did you try to shape the free writing found in your quartet into formal patterns?

A: Since I consider form an integral part of serious music, I certainly did. Strange as it may seem, the intention of composing a work that depended so much on change of movement and polyrhythmic texture involved me not only in special questions of clarity and audibility that one does not usually have to face, but in special problems of form also. One of the solutions I tried, to keep this rather free-sounding technique from seeming haphazard and thus lose its connection with the progress of the work and the attentive listener's ear, was to establish thematic patterns made up of components of different ideas that could be separated. This feature emerges in the last movement, many of whose motives are disintegrated to produce polyrhythms (Ex. 3). This is only one of the many ways I tried, hoping to give the impression of that combination of freedom and control that I greatly admire in many works of art.

Q: Do you use the twelve-tone system?

A: Some critics have said that I do, but since I have never analyzed my works from this point of view, I cannot say. I assume that if I am not conscious of it, I do not. Naturally, out of interest and out of professional responsibility,

2. Charles Ives, *Essays Before a Sonata, The Majority, and Other Writings*, ed. Howard Boatwright (New York: W. W. Norton & Co., 1962), 79.

Example 2. First String Quartet, III, m. 477.

I have studied the important works of this type and admire many of them a great deal. I have found that it is apparently inapplicable to what I am trying to do, and is more of a hindrance than a help. Its nature is often misunderstood, it is a building material and not the building, and it allows, I think, for certain greater freedoms than were possible using traditional harmony with its very strict rules of part writing, just as reinforced concrete allows for certain construction patterns impossible with stone. I must also say that having known many of these works all of my adult life, I hope the recent fad will not cause them to seem commonplace too soon. The results of total serialization are more recalcitrant to musical handling, I think.

Q: Do you mean to say that your rhythmic method is not a product of serialization?

A: It is not. It is true that like all music, mine goes from one thing to another—the pattern on which serialization is based—but my choices of where to start and where to go are controlled by a general plan of action that directs both the continuity and the expression. Single details, chords, rhythmic patterns, motives, textures, registers follow each other in a way that combines them into clearly perceivable larger patterns and then patterns of these patterns, and to me this cannot be easily accomplished with total serialization, at least the kind I study my way through in European articles these days. Perhaps another more useful and not so arbitrary kind of serialization could be devised. The present one resembles the turning of a kaleidoscope and usually produces not much more—or less—interesting results. Indeed it can be fascinating to listen to the total repertory of pitches, note values, timbres, registers, and dynamics being touched upon in rapid succession and from a point of view we are unaccustomed to. But the cumulative effect of this is self-defeating since neither the attention nor the memory is appealed to. For who can decipher, by ear, the complexities of total serialization in most works of

Example 3. First String Quartet, III, m. 244.

the sort? On the other hand, those in which this process can be followed are too obvious to be of any interest.

Q: What is your attitude about performance difficulty?

A: I realize with brutal clarity that orchestral music requiring a lot of rehearsal can, by the nature of American musical life, find very few, if any, performances. This is not true of difficult music for soloists or small standardized instrumental groups, for obvious reasons. Our orchestral musicians are trained to play in the demanding scores of Strauss, Mahler, Debussy, Ravel, and early Stravinsky. One might imagine that one of the obligations of a present-day composer would be to use the skills of these excellently trained musicians to their full, lest their abilities deteriorate for want of use; that the challenge of good, effective yet technically advanced scores would be helpful in maintaining high performance standards in an orchestra, if not in raising them, as it did in the past. But this does not seem to be a consideration here, and, as you and I know, new works that make an immediate effect with a minimum of effort and time are favored. The real effort goes into the standard repertory, where it is more widely appreciated. Therefore, composers who wish to write orchestral music and get it played here must tailor their work to these practical conditions, whether their ideas are suitable to such exploitation or not. Those who find that they can do nothing of interest under these conditions either give up writing orchestral music or, if they cannot, hope for European performances of their works. For these reasons, the scores of our composers often show a lack of practical experience that reveals itself in conventionality and timidity. How can anyone be adventurous, under the circumstances that obtain here? Any casual look at the European scores written since the war will show how far in advance of us even beginners are there in this respect. As in many other things, we may be willing to accept the final, accomplished results of European training and experimental efforts but we cannot afford and are impatient with the step-by-step experience needed to produce them.

Naturally, music that is both difficult and yet practical to play is not easy to write, and it may even be difficult to listen to. It does not make for a comfortable life to have this as one's mode of expression. There is an undoubted beauty in reducing things to their essentials or to their simplest form if something is gained thereby. A composer who cannot find an interesting and satisfying way of writing easy music is at least free, here, to use the level of difficulty he needs to set forth his ideas completely—even if this results in no performances. But I see no reason for being just difficult. Whenever difficult passages seem imperative in my works, I try to make them especially rewarding once they are played correctly.

For I regard my scores as scenarios, auditory scenarios, for performers to act out with their instruments, dramatizing the players as individuals and participants in the ensemble. To me the special teamwork of ensemble playing is very wonderful and moving, and this feeling is always an important expressive consideration in my chamber music.

Q: Have you ever thought of composing electronic music?

A: Naturally, I have often been intrigued with the idea of electronic music and have visited the Milan electronic studio several times to find out what is being done. I must say that almost all I have heard seems to me to be in a primary stage, and has not resolved some fundamental problems of matching and comparison of sounds that would raise it above the physical scariness that makes this music useful for television science fiction and horror programs. As far as composing it myself is concerned, you can imagine that since I am very enmeshed in the human aspect of musical performance, I would find it hard to think in terms of the impersonal sound patterns of electronic music. Certainly, impatience at not being able to hear my works in performance and impatience at the inaccuracies of some performances have occasionally made me wish that I could have a machine that would perform my music correctly and without all the trouble and possible disappointments associated with live performance.

Q: What do you think of Charles Ives now?

A: My opinions about Charles Ives as a composer have changed many times since I first came to know him during my high school years in 1924–25, but my admiration for him as a man never has. No one who knew him can ever forget his remarkable enthusiasm, his wit, his serious concern and love for music, and his many truly noble qualities, which one came to notice gradually because they appeared casually, without a trace of pompousness, pretension, or "showing off." Attracted to him by a youthful enthusiasm for contemporary music, I first admired, and still do, the few advanced scores privately available in those days, the *Concord Sonata*, the *Three Places in New England*, and some of the *114 Songs*. However, after I had completed strict musical studies here and abroad, I saw these works in a different light. Misgivings arose, which I expressed with considerable regret in several articles in *Modern Music* after the first performance of the *Concord Sonata* in New York in 1939. My doubts were of two kinds. First there seemed to be very large amounts of undifferentiated confusion, especially in the orchestral works, during which many conflicting things happen at once without apparent concern either for the total effect or for the distinguishability of various levels. Yet in each score such as the *Robert Browning Overture*, the *Fourth of July*, and the second and fourth movements of the Fourth Symphony, where this confusion is most frequent, it is the more puzzling because side by side with it are a number of passages of great beauty and originality. Even more disturbing to me then was his frequent reliance on musical quotations for their literary effect. In spite of these doubts, I continued for many years to help bring Ives's music before the public, since he would do nothing for himself, rescuing, among other things, *The Unanswered Question* and *Central Park in the Dark* from the photostat volumes of his work he had left with the American Music Center and arranging for their first performances in 1946.[3]

What interests me now is his vigorous presentation in music and essays of

3. See "Charles Ives Remembered" and "Documents of a Friendship with Ives," 98–107 and 107–118 respectively in the present collection. [B]

the conflict between the composer with vision and original ideas, the musical profession, and the American public. It is the living out of this conflict, made poignant by his strong convictions, the anger it produced, the various actions and attitudes it led him to, the retreat into a subjective world, and, unfortunately, the terrible toll of energy and health it took, that makes of Ives an artist really characteristic of America, not unlike Melville. Without the dimension of this struggle and the quality it gave his scores, his *Emersons* and *Hallowe'ens* would be of superficial and transitory interest.

His rage, which explodes between the waves of his transcendental visions in prose as it does in the scribbled comments in the margins of his musical manuscripts, reveals troubled concern over the problems of the American composer and his relations with the public. The music profession is castigated in one place as being more hidebound, more materialistic, petty, bigoted, and unprincipled than the business world. The latter, his refuge from the bleak, meager life of the conventional American musician of his time, he respected and identified himself with enough to adopt an American businessman's view of the artistic profession, one that was especially characteristic at that time of wealthy art collectors. Making of the artist an anti-businessman, Ives saw him as a prophet living in the pure, transcendent world of the spirit, above the mundane matters of money, practicality, and artistic experience. The nineteenth-century American dream of art and high culture, which Henry James liked to project against the sordid European background from which it came, was the source, as Aaron Copland and Wilfrid Mellers have pointed out, of Ives's greatest misfortune. In gradually retiring into this dream, he cut himself off from music's reality. Too many of his scores, consequently, were never brought to the precision of presentation and scoring necessary to be completely communicative to the listener—or so it seems now. One could say that Ives was unable completely to digest his experience as an American and make it into a unified and meaningful musical expression. The effort of remodeling the musical vocabulary to meet his own personal vision, almost without encouragement or help, was too great, and too often he had to let hymn tunes and patriotic songs stand for his experience without comment.

As I have said, Ives's life vividly presents the special conflicts inherent in the American composer's situation. Today, even more than in his time, the division between the musician's professional code of ethics, his traditional standards of skill and imagination established at another time in another place, and the present standards of behavior respected, sanctioned, and rewarded by the society that surrounds us, is very pronounced. The familiar training of a composer giving him knowledge and skill in the accumulation of musical techniques, past and present, and the development of skill in notating them, presupposes trained copyists and performers who can grasp what he means and respect his notations. It also presupposes critics and, if not a large public, at least an influential elite that will be able to perceive the sense of the composer's efforts and skill, value them, and enable him to develop them further, by giving them careful consideration. When one or more of the links in this chain is not sufficiently developed or is nonexistent, as is often the case here today, the composer has a bitter fight just to keep his skill, let alone develop it.

This misfortune can be laid to the general lack of unanimity about and concern for the profession of composing on the part of the mass musical public that plays such an influential financial role in America. By training, the composer learns to write for a musically educated public that is also an influential elite, which does not exist and may never exist here. He cannot help but feel that he will be heard by a large majority of listeners and even performers who disagree with him, if they have any opinions at all, on the most fundamental issues of his art. Questions of style, system, consonance, dissonance, themes, non-themes, being original or an imitator, which imply some agreement on fundamentals, are not the stumbling blocks. A professional composer has today, as Ives certainly had, the training to be "communicative," "melodious," "expressive," qualities considered to have a wide appeal, just as he is now trained to use advanced techniques that will be appreciated by only a few professionals. How shall he decide? He is free, here, to do what he likes, of course, but it does not take him long to realize that whatever he chooses to do, radical or conservative, his music will further divide into small sub-groups the handful of people who will listen to contemporary music at all. Not one of these small sub-groups has the power or the interest to convince the large public by publicity or other means of the validity of its opinions, as happens in the other arts here. While diversity of opinion is much to be welcomed, where so little support exists such splintering of interest, one must regretfully conclude, can lead to mutual cancellation of efforts and ultimately to their negation.

Even America's panacea, publicity, seems strangely useless in this field. Good reviews do not, often, lead to further performances, even if they do help to sell more recordings. One might have thought that Ives, now so much discussed and publicly admired, would be often heard. That a number of his recordings have been discontinued, that only a few of his easiest pieces are heard while some of his more remarkable works are still unplayed or scarcely known, is surely an indication of how confused and desperate is the relation between the composer, the profession, publicity, and the musical public.

The Time Dimension in Music
(1965)

It should be obvious that music must participate in the time dimension and all that this implies. A work that does not take into account the listener's ability to distinguish sounds, to grasp, remember, and compare in some way their combinations, both sequential and simultaneous, in small durations, intermediate lengths, as well as over the whole composition, is very unlikely to hold a permanent interest for the listener.

It is toward this time dimension that my own interest has been directed since about 1940, and whatever musical techniques I have used are contributory to the main concern of dealing with our experience of time, trying to communicate my own experience of it and my awareness of this experience in others. This, as I listen to most other contemporary music, is dealt with in a very routine way, in spite of the fact that sometimes most unusual and fascinating combinations of sound are being presented.

Before discussing my main topic—the time dimension and its various ramifications in contemporary composition—I would like to say a few words about the situation of many composers such as myself who grew up in the generation after the great musical revolutions brought about by Schoenberg and Stravinsky. It seemed to us at that time that the music of these important composers had completely reexamined the traditional postulates about music and the hearing of music. The "basic dimensions" of music—pitch, duration, volume, and timbre—had been "separated out" and examined anew. For example, we have Schoenberg's and Hauer's isolation of the pitch component— a process which eventually led to the twelve-tone system. We have works such as the third movement from the *Five Pieces for Orchestra* of Schoenberg and various *Klangfarbenmelodie* works of Webern, in which the element of timbre is more or less isolated and dealt with in a systematic fashion. Works such as *Le Sacre* and others of Stravinsky showed an analogous reexamination of various rhythmic and durational procedures. We were all aware almost intuitively at that time that these procedures were going on, but it was only later that the exact systematic significance of these developments became clear to us. It was this music, along with that of Americans such as Charles Ives, which was most interesting to me in my youth and which opened up enough possibilities in music to cause me to dedicate my life to it.

But this music was also part of a general cultural pattern. Many of these works which were so impressive to us as works of art contained in their hyperexpressivity a reflection of the retreat from reason and emphasis on "emotion," which was then current in all the arts, and, for that matter, in the very fabric of our social life. The appeal to the baser elements in human nature through mass propaganda, the rise of Hitler to power, the inability of many of the world's leaders to face the issues necessary for their survival—all these elements seemed to be a disastrous result of one aspect of a general point of view, another of whose aspects had furnished the artistic vision of the composers whose music we loved. For this reason, many of these earlier works lost their urgency—although, naturally, not their musical interest. However, it was through contact with the works of Schoenberg written during the Second World War, and especially with performances of his works I helped to arrange during the war and shortly thereafter, that this music began to have a more important meaning for some of us, who were then led to study it more carefully than we had. Contact with this and with the music of Ives and Ruggles led a few of us at that time to rethink our musical development and to strike out on a path still frowned on by the musical public and much of the profession in the United States, perhaps because of the poor, unenthusiastic performances that have given rise to much misunderstanding here.

To show one example—not directly related to rhythmic procedures—of how this idea of rethinking the basic materials of music had significance for me, let me quote the Fourth Etude from *Eight Etudes and a Fantasy* for woodwind quartet. Here the "simplest" possible interval—the ascending minor second—is made the sole basis for an entire movement. The second is, of course, transposed and moved to different metrical positions. But it is always a minor second up and it is always stated in contiguous eighth notes. This seemed to me to create a very interesting structure which I had never heard used before in music—a structure very similar to that of the parquet floor on which we are standing. You see, it is made of small blocks of wood—all of the same dimension.

In pieces such as my Piano Sonata and my Sonata for Cello and Piano I began to work with the rhythmic procedures which have proved to be so interesting for me in my later music. In the Cello Sonata, for example, the piano begins with a steady rhythm and plays that pattern for most of the first movement while the cello enters with a more free metrical pattern. This "stratification" of musical elements by metrical and other means became very important for me in such works as my First String Quartet. Here the first movement is a contrapuntal fantasy which is built on four main and several subsidiary themes each in a different speed and each having a different character. These themes of course have influence on each other and modify each other in the course of the piece. Yet a great deal of the interest in the First Quartet comes from passages in which four themes are stated simultaneously—interacting somewhat, yet also stratified by means of their being in different tempos. The fact of each theme being associated with a different tempo builds into the work the possibility and the necessity for metric modulation—a procedure in which the tempo of "beat" speeds up in an ordered manner between measures. Often, after many of these metrical modulations—which are in a sense analogous to the changes of key in a piece of tonal music—the piece will return to the original tempo. In my First Quartet, for example, the material played by the cello at the beginning of the first movement is marked quarter note equals 72. When this material returns in the first violin near the end of the entire piece, it returns at the speed of quarter note equals 72—though in this case the pitches are transposed up an octave and a fifth.

In this piece I was also very interested in examining the effects of the speeding up or slowing down of themes. The last movement, a set of variations, is made up of a number of ideas which become slightly faster with each repetition until they reach the "vanishing point"—until they can no longer be perceived as the same idea. The "minor-third" idea heard originally in the cello reappears frequently throughout the movement, gradually gaining speed until it is turned into a tremolo near the end of the movement. Another aspect of this idea (the same is true of the other ideas of the Variations, but is more obvious in this case) is that it is obviously not new to the movement marked Variations, but has been going on for some time in the previous movement. This brings us to the question of the plan of movements in the piece—a plan which is very much related to the general idea of metrical modulation.

Note that while there are really four movements in this piece, only three are marked in the score as separate movements, and these three do not correspond to the four "real" movements. The four "real" movements are Fantasia, Allegro scorrevole, Adagio, and Variations. But the movements are all played *attacca*, with the pauses coming in the middle of the Allegro scorrevole and near the beginning of the Variations. Thus there are only two pauses, dividing the piece into three sections. The reason for this unusual division of movements is that the tempo and character change, which occurs between what are usually called movements, is the goal, the climax of the techniques of metrical modulation which have been used. It would destroy the effect to break off the logical plan of movement just at its high point. Thus pauses can come only between sections using the same basic material. This is most obvious in the case of the pause before the movement marked Variations. In reality, at that point the Variations have already been going on for some time.

My interest in the speeding up and slowing down of themes is also reflected in various procedures in the Variations for Orchestra and the Double Concerto for Piano and Harpsichord with Two Chamber Orchestras. For instance in the Variations, of two secondary themes usually associated with the main theme throughout the work, one becomes successively slower and the other successively faster at each appearance. This kind of technique is demonstrated more obviously and on a smaller scale in variations four and six. Variation four has a measured ritard over a four-measure phrase from an original tempo to one half of that tempo (which is then doubled), and variation six has a measured accelerando over a six-measure phrase to three times the original tempo (which is then divided by three). The balance of each of these movements repeats the respective metric pattern of speeding up or slowing down. The combination of these two procedures is found in my Double Concerto. Beginning in m. 453 the harpsichord and all other instruments except the piano begin a measured ritard over a span of four measures to one-half the original tempo. This same ritard pattern is repeated three times after the original and then slows, in one large measure, to one-quarter the original speed. Meanwhile the piano has begun (in m. 453) a pattern of acceleration which continues throughout the ritards of all the other instruments. These means of metric stratification can be used in various ways to express different effects in the course of a work. In all these works I have tried to be as precise as possible about the effects desired and their manner of execution. Thus I do not write simply *accelerando* and *ritardando* at appropriate places, but I usually give specific metronome indications of the change desired. In a "measured accelerando" from MM 70 to MM 140 over a four-measure span, for example, one needs the MM indications 70, 83, 99, 118, and 140—adding 13, 16, 19, and 22, respectively.

As a final example, I would like to say a few words about my Second String Quartet. Here the four instruments are stratified according to their repertoire of intervals, their repertoire of rhythms, and their repertoire of musical gestures. The first violin, for example, specializes in the intervals of the minor third, perfect fifth, major ninth, and major tenth. Its fantastic and ornate character is borne out by its rhythmic repertoire, which is extremely contrasted. The second violin, on the other hand, shows very regular motion and moves steadily at its own metronome markings of 140, 70, and sometimes 280. The viola specializes in rhythmic relationships which are usually in the ratio 2:3 or 3:5, and the cello does not move at a steady tempo, but rather has accelerandos and ritards built in. This stratification of the instruments can be heard very clearly at the beginning of the piece. As the piece progresses, the diverse "characters" of the beginning come to influence each other and the repertoires of each "actor" begin to be shared. The work progresses through a climax involving each instrument's sharing the repertoires of each of the other instruments to an ending which serves a double function. There is a return to the intervallic stratification of the beginning, but there is also a sharing of functions—a fact made especially clear by the phrasing of the second violin, whose notes (usually individual pizzicato double stops), serve to end motives that had been played up to then by other instruments.

Two Sonatas, 1948 and 1952
(1969)

> . . . out of what one sees and hears and out
> Of what one feels, who could have thought to make
> So many selves, so many sensuous worlds,
> As if the air, the midday air, was swarming
> With the metaphysical changes that occur
> Merely in living as and where we live.

In prefacing a chapter about my music with this quotation from Wallace Stevens,[1] Wilfrid Mellers, author of *Music in a New Found Land*, draws attention to some of the main aims of my work. It is quite true that I have been concerned with constrasts of many kinds of musical characters—"many selves"; with forming these into poetically evocative combinations—"many sensuous worlds"; with filling musical time and space by a web of continually varying cross references—"the air . . . swarming with . . . changes." And to me, at least, my music grows "out of what one sees and hears and out/Of what one feels," out of what occurs "Merely in living as and where we live."

The two pieces on this record of are examples of this, since they treat of "metaphysical changes." For they were written during a time (1945–55) when I was preoccupied with the time-memory patterns of music, with rethinking the rhythmic means of what had begun to seem a very limited routine used in most contemporary and older Western music. I had taken up again an interest in Indian *talas,* the Arabic *durub,* the "tempi" of Balinese gamelans (especially the accelerating *Gangsar* and *Rangkep*), and studied the newer recordings of African music, that of the Watusi in particular. At the same time, the music of the early *quattrocentro,* of Scriabin, Ives, and the

---

1. From *Esthétique du mal* (New York, 1950). [S]

techniques described in Cowell's *New Musical Resources* also furnished me with many ideas. The result was a way of evolving rhythms and rhythmic continuities, sometimes called "metric modulation," worked out during the composition of the Cello Sonata (1948) and further developed in the other sonata on this record.

To sketch briefly another part of the background of these works (although they are to be considered primarily for themselves and not in relation to their time or their composer), I became interested in music as a boy through the exciting early works of Stravinsky, Bartók, Varèse, and others. Later, while I was a music student in the late 1920s and early '30s, the contemporary fashion changed and the latest thing—like, perhaps, live electronic music today—was the neoclassic revolt against the expressive and primitivist of the previous period. Music was to be anti-individualistic, to sound almost machine-made, and to use bits of "everyday music," pop, Baroque—anything that could be denatured into the cool, depersonalized character so much sought after. I found both directions increasingly unsatisfactory, and a return to older, "common-practice" music out of the question, so I took the steps described above.

Naturally any serious concern with rhythm, time, and memory must include the shaping of music, and I began to question the familiar methods of presentation and continuation, of so-called "musical logic," based on the statement of themes and their development. Certain older works, particularly those of Debussy, suggested a different direction. In considering change, process, evolution as music's prime factor, I found myself in direct opposition to the static repetitiveness of most early twentieth-century music, against the squared-off articulation of the neoclassicists and, indeed, against much of what is written today in which "first you do this for a while, then you do that." I wanted to mix up "this" and "that," make them interact in other ways than by linear succession. Too, I questioned the inner shape of "this" and "that"—of musical ideas—as well as their degrees of linking or non-linking. Musical discourse needed as thorough a rethinking as harmony had had at the beginning of the century.

These two pieces are, then, steps along the way from a prevalent neoclassicism toward a freer, more vital and sensitive musical language. Both relate to their time and also look forward. The Cello Sonata uses bits of pop, but manipulates these in a way that produces the special rhythmic handling characteristic of most of my subsequent music. The Sonata for Flute, Oboe, Cello, and Harpsichord (1952) ends with another kind of "everyday music"—a Venetian gondolier's dance, the *forlana*—but draws out of the characteristic rhythmic cell of that dance all sorts of rhythmic changes, a continuity which only later was to become widely used. Both works are also prophetic in that, encouraged, perhaps, by the example of Debussy's last sonatas, they avoid classical development, use sonority as an item of musical thought, and aim for a fluid, changeable continuity. The later sonata starts its slow movement with a one-note theme, continuing the idea of my one-note piece in the *Eight Etudes and a Fantasy* of 1949, a conceit that has become the stock in trade of the avant-garde during the past few years (the *Etudes* were played at the 1958 Warsaw Festival).

Finally, because these works are virtuoso pieces for all the performers, they were considered impossibly difficult to perform when they were written; but now, after frequent performances, these scores seem to have taught musicians to play them with comparative ease and fluency, so that the attention is not on the technique but on the music, as this record demonstrates.

When I was asked in 1947 to write a work for the American cellist Bernard Greenhouse, I immediately began to consider the relation of the cello and piano, and came to the conclusion that since there were such great differences in expression and sound between them, there was no point in concealing these as had usually been done in works of the sort. Rather it could be meaningful to make these very differences one of the points of the piece. So the opening Moderato presents the cello in its warm expressive character, playing a long melody in rather free style while the piano percussively marks a regular clock-like ticking. This is interrupted in various ways, probably (I think) to situate it in a musical context that indicates that the extreme dissociation between the two is neither a matter of random nor of indifference, but one to be heard as having an intense, almost fateful character.

The Vivace, a breezy treatment of a type of pop music, verges on a parody of some Americanizing colleagues of the time. Actually it makes explicit the undercurrent of jazz technique suggested in the previous movement by the freely performed melody against a strict rhythm. The following Adagio is a long, expanding, recitative-like melody for the cello, all its phrases interrelated by metric modulations. The finale, Allegro, like the second movement based on pop rhythms, is a free rondo with numerous changes of speed that ends up by returning to the beginning of the first movement with the roles of the cello and piano reversed.

As I have said, the idea of metrical modulation came to me while writing this piece, and its use becomes more elaborate from the second movement on. The first movement, written last, after the concept had been quite thoroughly explored, presents one of the piece's basic ideas: the contrast between psychological time (in the cello) and chronometric time (in the piano), their combination producing musical or "virtual" time. The whole is one large motion in which all the parts are interrelated in speed and often in idea; even the breaks between movements are slurred over. That is: at the end of the second movement, the piano predicts the notes and speed of the cello's opening of the third, while the cello's conclusion of the third predicts in a similar way the piano's opening of the fourth, and this movement concludes with a return to the beginning in a circular way like Joyce's *Finnegans Wake*.

The Sonata for Flute, Oboe, Cello, and Harpsichord was commissioned by the Harpsichord Quartet of New York and uses the instruments of which that ensemble was composed. My idea was to stress as much as possible the vast and wonderful array of tone colors available on the modern harpsichord (the large Pleyel, for which this was first written, produces thirty-six different colors, many of which can be played in pairs, one for each hand; the Dowd that Paul Jacobs uses for this recording even has "half-hitches," which permit the different colors to be played at half as well as full force). The three other instruments are treated for the most part as a frame for the harpsichord. This aim of using the wide variety of the harpsichord involved many tone colors which can only be produced very softly and therefore conditioned very drastically the type and range of musical expression, all the details of shape, phrasing, rhythm, texture, as well as the large form. At that time (in 1952, before the harpsichord had made its way into pop) it seemed very important to have the harpsichord speak in a new voice, expressing characters unfamiliar to its extensive Baroque repertory.

The music starts, Risoluto, with a splashing dramatic gesture whose subsiding ripples form the rest of the movement. The Lento is an expressive dialogue between the harpsichord and the others, with an undercurrent of fast music that bursts out briefly near the end. The Allegro, with its gondolier's dance fading into other dance movements, is cross-cut like a movie—at times it superimposes one dance on another.

The performances on this record[2] are remarkable, especially in view of some I have had to suffer through in the past. The outstanding technical and interpretative skill of each performer, each with his own individual way of playing and of joining the ensemble, comes through strikingly. The sonatas are reincarnated in a new, yet faithful way. Playing by such excellent performers brings to light new, unexpected aspects of these precisely notated pieces and is as lively, novel, and fresh as if the players were improvising.

String Quartets Nos. 1, 1951, and 2, 1959 (1970)

Hearing these two quartets now, I get the impression of their living in different time worlds, the first in an expanded one, the second in a condensed and concentrated one—although this was hardly a conscious opposition at the times of their composition. Each presents as different a version of humanly experienced time as the two imagined by Thomas Mann in "By the Ocean of Time," a chapter in *The Magic Mountain*, where he writes: "It would not be hard to imagine the existence of creatures, perhaps upon smaller planets than ours, practicing a miniature time-economy. . . . And, contrariwise, one can conceive of a world so spacious that its time system too has a majestic stride. . . ."[1]

---

2. Cello Sonata: Joel Krosnick, cello; Paul Jacobs, piano. Sonata for Flute, Oboe, Cello, and Harpsichord: Harvey Sollberger, flute; Charles Kuskin, oboe; Fred Sherry, cello; Paul Jacobs, harpsichord. [S]

1. Thomas Mann, *The Magic Mountain*, trans. H. T. Lowe-Porter (New York: Vintage, 1969), 546.

Although both quartets are concerned with motion, change, progression in which literal or mechanical repetition finds little place, the development of musical expression and thought during the eight years that separate them seems to me far-reaching. The difference, aside from that of their time-scales, might be compared to the types of continuities found in Mann's own writings, where in the earlier ones, characters maintain their characterized identities with some revelatory changes throughout a work, while in the Joseph novels, each character is an exemplification of an archetype whose various other incarnations are constantly referred to (as Joyce does in another way in *Finnegans Wake*). Recurrence of idea in the First Quartet is, then, more nearly literal than in the Second, where recall brings back only certain traits of expression—"behavior patterns," speeds, and interval-sounds—that form the basis of an ever-changing series of incarnations but link these together as a group. The musical language of the Second Quartet emerged almost unconsciously through working during the 1950s with the ideas the First gave rise to.

The First Quartet was "written largely for my own satisfaction and grew out of an effort to understand myself," as the late Joseph Wood Krutch (a neighbor during the 1950–51 year of this quartet) wrote of his book *The Modern Temper*. For there were so many emotional and expressive experiences that I kept having, and so many notions of processes and continuities, especially musical ones—fragments I could find no ways to use in my compositions—that I decided to leave my usual New York activities to seek the undisturbed quiet to work these out. The decision to stay in a place in the Lower Sonoran Desert near Tucson, Arizona, brought me by chance into contact with that superb naturalist Joe Krutch, who was then writing *The Desert Year*. Our almost daily meetings led to fascinating talks about the ecology of that region—how birds, animals, insects, and plants had adapted to the heat and the limited water supply, which consists of infrequent, spectacular but brief cloudbursts that for an hour seem about to wash everything away, and then very long droughts. There were trips to remote places such as Carr Canyon, the wild-bird paradise, but mainly it was right around the house that exotica (for an Easterner) could be seen—comic road runners, giant suguaros, flowering ocatillos, all sharing this special, dry world. It was indeed a kind of "magic mountain," and its specialness (for me) certainly encouraged the specialness (for me at that time) of the quartet as I worked on it during the fall and winter of 1950 and the spring of '51.

Among the lessons this piece taught me was one about my relationship with performers and audiences. For as I wrote, an increasing number of musical difficulties arose for prospective performers and listeners, which the musical conception seemed to demand. I often wondered whether the quartet would ever have any performers or listeners. Yet within a few years of its composition it won an important prize and was played (always with a great deal of rehearsal) more than any work I had written up to that time. It even received praise from admired colleagues. Up to this time, I had quite consciously been trying to write for a certain audience—not that which frequented concerts of traditional music, nor that which had supported the avant-garde of the 1920s (which in the '40s had come to seem elitist) but a new, more progressive and more popular audience. I had felt that it was my professional and social responsibility to write interesting, direct, easily understood music.

With this quartet, however, I decided to focus on what had always been one of my own musical interests, that of "advanced" music, and to follow out, with a minimal concern for their reception, my own musical thoughts along these lines. Now, in 1970, I think there is every reason to assume that if a composer has been well taught and has had experience (as was true of me in 1950), then his private judgment of comprehensibility and quality is what he must rely on if he is to communicate importantly.

Like the desert horizons I saw daily while it was being written, the First Quartet presents a continuous unfolding and changing of expressive characters—one woven into the other or emerging from it—on a large scale. The general plan was suggested by Jean Cocteau's film *Le Sang d'un poète*, in which the entire dreamlike action is framed by an interrupted slow-motion shot of a tall brick chimney in an empty lot being dynamited. Just as the chimney begins to fall apart, the shot is broken off and the entire movie follows, after which the shot of the chimney is resumed at the point it left off, showing its disintegration in mid-air, and closing the film with its collapse on the ground. A similar interrupted continuity is employed in this quartet's starting with a cadenza for cello alone that is continued by the first violin alone at the very end. On one level, I interpret Cocteau's idea (and my own) as establishing the difference between external time (measured by the falling chimney, or the cadenza) and internal dream time (the main body of the work)—the dream time lasting but a moment of external time but from the dreamer's point of view, a long stretch. In the First Quartet, the opening cadenza also acts as an introduction to the rest, and when it reappears at the end, it forms the last variation in a set of variations. Not only is this plan like that of many "circular" works of modern literature, but the interlocked presentation of ideas parallels many characteristic devices found in Joyce and others—the controlled "stream of consciousness," the "epiphany," the many uses of punctuation, of grammatical ambiguities, including the use of quotation. This quartet, for instance, quotes the opening theme of Ives's First Violin Sonata, first played by the cello in its lowest register after each of the other instruments has come in near the beginning. A rhythmic idea from Conlon Nancarrow's *Rhythm Study No. 1*, for player piano, is quoted at the beginning of the Variations movement. These two composers, through both their music and their conversation, had been a great help to me in imagining this work and were quoted in homage.

Since both these quartets are made up of many-layered contrasts of character—hence of theme or motive, rhythm, and styles of playing—they are hard to describe without adding to their apparent complications. Briefly, the First is in four large sections: Fantasia, Allegro scorrevole, Adagio, and Variations. This scheme is broken by two pauses, one in the middle of the Allegro scorrevole and the other just after the Variations have been started by the cello, while the other instruments were concluding the Adagio. The first section, Fantasia, contrasts many themes of different character frequently counterpointed against each other. It concludes with the four main ideas being heard together, fading in and out of prominence. This leads directly to a rapid Allegro scorrevole, a sound-mosaic of brief fragments, interrupted once by a dramatic outburst, then resumed, again interrupted by a pause, again resumed, and finally interrupted by another outburst that forms the beginning of the Adagio.

During this extended slow movement, the two muted violins play soft, contemplative music answered by an impassioned, rough recitative of the viola and cello. This Adagio forms the extreme point of divergence between simultaneous ideas in the quartet and has been led up to and is led away from by many lesser degrees of differentiation. The last section, Variations, consists of a series of different themes repeated faster at each successive recurrence, some reaching their speed vanishing point sooner than others. One that persists almost throughout is the slow motive heard in separated notes played by the cello just before and after the pause that precedes the Variations. This motive passes through many stages of acceleration until it reaches a rapid tremolo near the end.

Written in 1959, the Second Quartet represents quite a contrast to the First. In it, as mentioned previously, there is little dependence on thematic recurrence, which is replaced by an ever-changing series of motives and figures having certain internal relationships with each other. To a certain extent, the instruments are typecast, for each fairly consistently invents its material out of its own special expressive attitude and its own repertory of musical speeds and intervals. In a certain sense each instrument is like a character in an opera made up primarily of "quartets." The separation of the instrumental characters is kept quite distinct throughout the first half of the work but becomes increasingly homogenized up to the Conclusion, at which point the separation reemerges. The musical contrasts of behavior and material associated with each instrument can be brought to the listener's attention by a special stereophonic placement which helps to sort them out—as accomplished in this recording—although this is not absolutely necessary, since the total effect at any given moment is the primary consideration, the contribution of each instrument secondary.

The form of the quartet itself helps to make the elements of this four-way conversation clear. The individuals of this group are related to each other in what might be metaphorically termed three forms of responsiveness: discipleship, companionship, and confrontation. The Introduction and Conclusion present in aphoristic form and in "companionate" manner the repertory of each instrument. The Allegro fantastico is led by the first violin, whose whimsical, ornate part is "imitated" by the other three, each according to this own individuality; the same occurs in the Presto scherzando led by the second violin and the Andante espressivo led by the viola. The final Allegro, although partially led by the cello—which eventually draws the others into one of its characteristic accelerations—tends to stress the "companionship" rather than the "discipleship" pattern.

In between these movements are cadenzas of instrumental "confrontations" or opposition: after the Allegro fantastico, the viola plays its expressive, almost lamenting cadenza to be confronted with explosions of what may be anger or ridicule by the other three; after the Presto Scherzando, the cello, playing in its romantically free way, is confronted by the others' insistence on strict time; finally, after the Andante espressivo, the first violin carries on like a virtuoso, to be confronted by the silence of the others, who, before this cadenza is over, commence the final Allegro. Throughout the entire quartet, the second violin acts as a moderating influence, using its *pizzicato* and *arco* notes to mark regular time, its half, or double—always at the same speed.

On this record, Anahid Ajemian plays the second violin part with fascinating wit and humor where needed and with refined expressivity or robust vigor elsewhere. Indeed, all the members of The Composers Quartet—Matthew Raimondi, Jean Dupouy, and Michael Rudiakov as well as Miss Ajemian, accomplishing the difficult and unprecedented feat of maintaining both quartets in their repertory simultaneously—play their parts as if they meant what they were doing, as if it were very important, in order to reveal what both pieces are about, to play them accurately and musically. What more could a composer want of performers?

The Orchestral Composer's Point of View
(1970)

Merely to consider the possibility of writing orchestral music of any quality as a field of endeavor for a composer in the United States calls up a barrage of contradictory problems, each of which would seem to militate against any kind of new, vital, or original music being produced. It would even seem impossible to work out an intelligent program that would provide a situation in which this could be accomplished by anyone but a confirmed masochist seeking a heavy burden of self-punishment. The fact that such music has been written here, though not often, amid miserable circumstances, at great human cost to its creators, and in almost utter neglect—that Edgard Varèse, Charles Ives, Carl Ruggles, Stefan Wolpe, and others fought this desperate battle—means that these composers had such a strong inner vision that they were able to overlook the preposterous circumstances that surrounded them in our musical society, particularly in the orchestral field. Younger composers who write in an original way are often filled with illusions about the present situation (which, it is to be hoped, is changing), encouraged as they are by commissions, fellowships, and contests bent on stimulating what must seem like an appalling overproduction of an unwanted commodity. Such commissions, for instance, are very often given by those entirely concerned with publicity, a kind that feeds on the composer's reputation but is not interested in his actual work. This is clear from the fact that commissions are too often given by groups who have shown no previous interest in a composer's work by performing it or arranging for performances of it. Very often, a little research will reveal that the commissioners do not even know what kind of music the composer has written and hence is likely to write—with the curious result that the finished score comes as a disagreeable surprise to conductor and performers, who then churn through it desultorily or with hostility, misrepresenting the score to the public and ruining the possibility of future performances for a long time. The commissioning sums themselves are seldom attractive, and are usually far less than a professional copyist would be paid to copy the score. The rewards, if one cares about them—artistic results, kudos, and money—are so small that commissions rarely seem worth the trouble.

Composers with fewer illusions about the present orchestral situation in our country suffer through these nonsensical performances in the hope that they will get ones supported by educational funds, such as the Rockefeller Foundation-supported modern-music symphony concerts played in universities, or performances with some of our better conservatory orchestras (Oberlin, Iowa, Michigan, or the New England Conservatory), where student performers are eager to play new music and have plenty of time to rehearse and be taught the score by a conductor who really knows it thoroughly. A somewhat similar result can sometimes be obtained by performances with European radio orchestras, which do not play as well as American orchestras but can devote much more rehearsal time to new music. In fact, a number of American composers living abroad have been able to develop styles of orchestration by constant contact with orchestral performances that they could not have evolved in this country.

Because it is difficult to get multiple performances with American symphony orchestras, since they are interested mainly in premieres, composers do not write for this medium unless they are commissioned or have the stimulus of a prize contest. There is little satisfaction in a poorly rehearsed premiere. And, under the present rehearsal and performance situations, there are such absurdly small performance and royalty fees that the copying of the parts is seldom repaid except by potboilers. (No performance or royalty fees would be given at all if a number of us had not fought a bitter battle twenty-five years ago to establish what one would have thought was an obvious principle.) Prize contests do not solve the problem any better since the authority of juries is infrequently respected by musicians. Even when an honorific prize like the Pulitzer Prize has been given in music, sometimes resulting in a number of performances (as with my Second String Quartet), this can cause a great deal of dissatisfaction on the part of those who question the jury's choice.

Here is an example of what can happen at a prize contest: My *Holiday Overture* won a prize of $500, publication, and performance by one of the major symphonies, whose conductor was one of the jurors. The score and parts were taken from me, remained in the orchestra's library for four years without ever being performed, and were then returned. I had no copy of the parts, and I could not get other performances during this time, for when I tried to withdraw the parts, I was warned that I would lose the opportunity for a performance that might be scheduled very soon, if the parts were not in the library. Finally, I sneaked the parts out without the librarian's knowing it and had them photostatted. From these parts the work got its first performance in Frankfurt, Germany, and later in Berlin with Serge Celibidache conducting. The American orchestra never knew of this. Why it held up the *Holiday Overture* I never learned, but the experience did not add to my desire to deal with American conductors and orchestras.

Such mishaps are a constant part of the composer's routine. Conditions do not improve much even when such relationships are handled through a publisher, as has been my frequent experience since 1936, when my first orchestral work was written. The reasons for these vexations and others have been a constant source of concern for composers, yet no one has been able to find a way to solve them. Perhaps all these problems can be traced to the habit of applying traditional economic standards by a large segment of our population to all its efforts and products, which inevitably causes confusions and misapprehensions between composers and many performers, critics, publishers, and publics. Looked at in this way, a piece of music is assimilated to a typical item of consumption in the traditional frame of a consumers' market. However, such a piece cannot be physically owned as can a painting or sculpture, cannot generally be figuratively owned by being retained in the memory as can the contents of a book, movie, or play. This very fact means that its consumption value lies only in the immediate present during which it is heard and during which it must be experienced, if it is. Hence, it must cater to the listener's immediate abilities, interests, and experiences in much the same way a performer does on a far more accessible level. Although recordings have somewhat lessened the composition's mere present existence for the public, still it is the very evanescence, which is part of its attractiveness, that makes it an anomaly as an item of consumption and alters drastically the bases on which music can be compared to any of the other arts, both in terms of historical development and economic remuneration. This accounts for the underdeveloped nature of its economic aspect; particularly in America it was (and probably still is) assumed that musical repertory is a European importation and that Europe can take care of composers' payments and exploitation while we do not have to consider these seriously. From this it follows that the investment of money in publicity and salesmanship in compositions in the United States need be very little, since so little return can be expected.

However, with the explosion of the publicity industry, more and more emphasis has been put on the public image of the composer as the real item of consumption. His musical composition is only one of the contributing elements, others being his ability to perform, to talk, to write, to teach, and to be photographed—all of these being more salable, and hence more highly paid, than his music. The public, often, must wonder why composers persist in writing music that so few can understand. They must think—and perhaps rightly—that the musical work is intended to help his public image through reviews and reports in widely circulated periodicals, and thus lead the composer to more important positions in domains peripheral to composition, but more remunerative.

Except for American opera, symphony orchestra, and community-concert subscribers where the group must be very small, there usually exists a sizable minority of the musical public that understands what an important role new music could play. This special public realizes that the development of musical composition is affected by many more important factors than that of immediate popular consumption. This group has little power, even though its point of view—that contact with the new brings new attitudes toward the old, new insights into the art itself, and interesting, even important new experiences—is generally accepted in the other arts and in most of American life. Contemporary music, music that is to be listened to for itself rather than for its performance, is in another class from older music, and this distinction keeps it out of competition with the "performance industry," where the stakes are high, and whose efforts assume the solid foundation of accepted "masterworks."

A solid foundation? Commercial exploitation is destroying this as it did forests in the nineteenth century. So far, in America at least, no concerted effort of musical reforestation of the rapidly dying repertory of increasingly tired and worn-out classics is planned. (The mortality of the Francks, Regers, and Saint-Saënses is very high these years.) This improvident depletion of the repertory has gone on for years, while the twentieth-century composers were producing work after work that have been treated as seasonal novelties and dropped instead of being drawn in to replenish the failing repertory. The American public of symphony subscribers has not yet caught up with the Viennese music written fifty years ago, nor that of Varèse, which is thirty or forty years old. However, there is evidently another public for such music, as was proven by the success in New York of the all-modern music repertories of the BBC Orchestra and the Hamburg Opera in 1967. But the average subscriber has no part of this literature. For him the gap between contemporary music and his understanding has grown wider through the years, and it is ever harder for him to catch up. Unless this situation can be remedied, it will have a severe effect on the future of orchestral music. Often in recent years, composers have felt that the future of the symphony orchestra was doubtful. Needless to say, the artist who puts his faith in future recognition thinks a long time before he wastes a lot of time and effort on a medium which many think is dying. The contrast between this situation and that of chamber music, where contemporary music is welcomed, serves to emphasize that this plight is strictly a matter of the orchestral situation and not that of the composers, contrary to the assertion of Henry Pleasants's book *The Agony of Modern Music.* The orchestral brontosaur staggers with inertia and ossification; its very complexity resists change.

Now let us look at that institution, the conductor (seldom an American) of an American symphony orchestra. He is involved in a complex of economic and social problems in his community and orchestra that threaten to draw his attention away from musical ones; in tea-party strategies to keep and augment his audiences, in making himself a public personality, in helping to raise money, in getting better pay for his performers through recording contracts, in maintaining and raising performance standards without causing ill feelings. Keeping the orchestra alive and functioning must often seem to be the primary issue, while the actual giving of concerts and learning new repertoire becomes almost a secondary responsibility. Yet these latter duties—the backbone of his role as conductor—form a very taxing schedule. The extended seasons of the major orchestras devour an enormous number of standard works, few of which can be repeated more than once every two years, none of which can be performed without rehearsal and, on the conductor's part, without restudy and rethinking of interpretation. Understandably, the conductor has little time left to study the few new scores he may have scheduled, none to look through the piles of new music sent to him every year, and, certainly, very little time to keep up with the progress of contemporary music by following new trends through scores and recordings. His impossibly demanding tasks naturally force him to find time-saving solutions and not to do anything which will add to his problems. To satisfy the pressure of the progressive minority of his audience, he must inevitably find works that do not require much rehearsal, will not cause much dismay, or be too long or too unusual. He can hardly be blamed for not choosing more important scores under the circumstances. In fact, it is remarkable that as much important new music is played as there is.

The situation of orchestral musicians is not much better with regard to new music. The high cost of living in the United States naturally impels them to seek high pay for their very skilled efforts. They must participate in as many higher-paid services (concerts, broadcasts, and recordings) and as few lower-paid ones (rehearsals) as possible. This state of affairs limits the repertory of concerts drastically and, when combined with the extended seasons of many orchestras, results in overwork, fatigue, and tedium. When such musicians are faced with a new work which has been allotted a small amount of rehearsal time, insufficient to produce a good performance, many players, otherwise sympathetic to new music, become disgusted, while the unsympathetic performers are annoyed at being required to do many difficult and unfamiliar things that seem to lead to a pointless result. At a recent rehearsal of my Piano Concerto, an orchestral musician said to me: "Your music does not make sense unless the dynamic markings are followed." At most rehearsals and the majority of performances of new orchestral music, the players are so occupied with playing the right notes that they often forget to follow the instructions to play them softly or loudly. Music requiring careful observation of these distinctions needs extra rehearsals, therefore, in order to "make sense." A work like my *Holiday Overture*, in which the variety of dynamics is produced almost automatically by the addition of subtraction of instruments, can make sense without such care being taken, although it makes better sense when it is. One can easily imagine the frustration of an orchestral musician who works hard to master his part only to discover that he is being entirely covered by a neighbor who, instead of playing softly as his part indicates, is giving all he has.

Often the blame for the growing gap between audiences and new music is laid at the door of the orchestra's board of directors or of the audience itself. Most of the time, with both of these groups, there has been and still may be an interest in new music, in small amounts. However, if this curiosity is satisfied by poor contemporary music and not by the finest, a receptive attitude can readily turn to animosity, as has happened only too often. Many times when looking over the modern music played by orchestras for a certain period or season, one gets the impression of visiting an art museum where no examples of Picasso, Braque, Kandinsky, or Klee, but only the works of the latest recipients of the Guggenheim Fellowships had ever been shown. Everybody concerned with music—composers and musicians, as well as the public—has constantly to develop a background of understanding based on the best works of the recent past if they are to come to terms with new compositions. Recordings and scores can and have helped the public and composers, but the conductor and performer must have had direct performing contact with these works in order to be able to make quick sense out of the welter of new musical methods developed over the past sixty years. Most practitioners do not have the time or the encouragement from a good majority of those connected with music who are shortsightedly still milking the "masterpieces" dry.

As if all these practical problems were not enough to keep a composer from writing orchestral music, and they are not, the very instrumental makeup of the orchestra itself presents many serious difficulties in these years. Developed to play Romantic music based on a common practice of standardized harmony, rhythm, and counterpoint, of singing themes, of widening sonority by octave doubling, the orchestra seems to require this kind of music to justify its existence. Since most contemporary composers do not wish to compose this way, the orchestra has to be forced to do things which seem to violate its fundamental nature. For example, the dry incisiveness and powerful rhythmic articulation of Igor Stravinsky's music since 1920 does not fit the sonority expected from the orchestra. Also the whole growth of the orchestra, intensifying its Romantic character with Bruckner, Mahler, Strauss, and early Schoenberg, made the works of these composers and others unplayable outside large cities, especially in the United States, where they are a drain on the budgets of orchestras. Many European composers still feel the need, today, to write for large orchestra and can get their works played because of state subsidies—the Stalinist symphonies of Dmitri Shostakovitch and quite a few recent Polish and German works. American composers ruled out this possibility long ago. Aaron Copland recently revised his *Symphonic Ode*, written originally for a large Boston Symphony Orchestra, for a small group of instrumentalists.

Aside from the enlargement and increasing technical demands made by composers in the late nineteenth and early twentieth centuries, which limited their works to special situations that became rarer with each passing year, there came forth a realization which was expressed by many composers that the orchestra is no longer useful. In 1928, Schoenberg complained in an interview with Erwin Stein:

If it were not for America, we in Europe would be composing only for reduced orchestras, chamber orchestras. But in countries with younger cultures, less refined nerves require the monumental: when the sense of hearing is incapable of compelling the imagination, one must add the sense of sight. . . . But disarmament is as slow here as it is in other areas; so long as there continue to be nations which, in art, have not yet won their place in the sun, so long will America demand large orchestras and Europe maintain them; Europeans will remain incapable of acquiring that finesse of ear that artists long to see generally acquired as long as they continue to maintain large orchestras.[1]

It is significant that quite a number of the twentieth century's best composers—Schoenberg, Bartók, Webern—seldom wrote for the orchestra.

The orchestra's very instrumental makeup severely limits its possibilities of sound. All of the instruments of the usual orchestra playing a tutti can only be written for in a very few ways that will produce a balance of sound in which each element contributes significantly to the whole and is not partially or totally blotted out by more powerful instruments. A flute, for example, as sometimes happens in the Ives scores, playing a theme in its medium-low register against a full, loud orchestra playing above and below it, is unlikely to be heard at all, and scarcely contributes anything to the total effect. The fewer the instruments that play, the more possibilities of combinations there are. Recent Stravinsky works, like *Agon* and the Variations, treat the orchestra as a storehouse for many changing chamber music combinations, avoiding the full sound almost entirely throughout. This requires sensitive playing by the musicians and careful listening by the audience, which neither are prepared for, especially when many orchestral concerts take place in halls where acoustics prevent great delicacy of sound from being heard distinctly.

If there is still any point in composing for orchestra, it is to treat the medium with as much novelty of concept as one does harmony, rhythm, or any of the older musical methods, so rethought in our time. It is the compositions that are written for orchestra that will make it live. If these are dull and routine in the use of the medium itself, not consistent with the composer's thought, then the orchestra has to be left to the ever-diminishing repertory of the past.

To compose for the orchestra, as far as I am concerned, is to deal practically with the instruments, writing idiomatic passages for them, and, particularly, to compose music whose very structure and character are related to the instruments that play it. The entrance, register, sound of an oboe or a solo viola must be a matter of formal and expressive signification for the whole piece. The combinations of instruments are as much a compositional consideration as the material they play, even to determining the materials, and all must reflect the overall intention. The handling of the orchestra must have the same distinctiveness and character as the other components of the work. This

1. "Arnold Schoenberg on His Variations for Orchestra, Op. 31: A dialogue with his pupil Erwin Stein, originally published in *Pult und Taktstock*," 6 October 1928, trans. David Johnson, in booklet accompanying *The Music of Arnold Schoenberg, Vol. II*, Columbia Records M2S 694 (2 LPs, 1963).

concept of orchestral writing takes considerable imaginative effort, increased, as has been said, by the many built-in routines which the orchestra was developed to accomplish. The use of any one of these would be as much out of character in my music as a passage of conventional four-part harmony.

It took me many years of experience and thought to arrive at this technique of orchestral practice. My first works, the *Tarantella* (1936) for men's chorus and orchestra and the ballet *Pocahontas* (1939), were orchestrations and amplifications of prior piano four-hand scores, while the Symphony No. 1 (1942) and the *Holiday Overture* (1944) each began to move away from this procedure, the symphony dealing with orchestrally thought textures and the overture with orchestrally thought counterpoint. In fact the *Holiday Overture* began to use consciously the notion of simultaneous contrasting levels of musical activity, which characterizes most of my more recent work. *The Minotaur* (1947), a ballet, is another step toward direct orchestral thinking, which culminated in my Variations (1954–55), conceived as it is entirely in terms of the orchestra for which it is written. After this, each of my two concertos used a different approach to orchestral sound. The Double Concerto for Harpsichord and Piano with Two Chamber Orchestras (1961) makes the percussion the main body of the orchestra, the pitched, blown, and bowed instruments secondary, with the two soloists mediating between them. The Piano Concerto (1965) uses the orchestra mainly as an elaborate ambiance, a society of sounds or a sounded stage setting for the piano.

In every case, these works have taken into account the practical situation of the American orchestras that might be their performers at the times they were written. The complete change of aim and direction, amounting to a private revolution in musical thought, which went on through all these years in my chamber music, hardly found its way into my orchestral work until the two concertos. There was good reason for this decision since I was—and am still—made painfully aware with each orchestral rehearsal that the type of writing found in almost every measure of my chamber music could never come out under American orchestral conditions that I know or imagine. Orchestral passages of a far simpler structure have often proved serious stumbling blocks to musicians who always seem to face my scores with the belief that they will never make sense—although occasionally some performers find that they were mistaken. For these reasons, I have sought different goals in orchestral scores than in chamber music.

Up to now, although finding these were useless precautions, I have tried to fit the situations for which my music was written, carefully. The ballets used the size of the orchestra that would fit into the pit of Broadway theaters; the Martin Beck in the case of *Pocahontas*, and the former Ziegfeld with *The Minotaur*. The Variations, commissioned by the Louisville Orchestra, used the exact number of instruments that comprised that orchestra—a very small number of strings (nine players of first violins, and so forth) and the normal-sized brass section, which could cause serious problems of balance. My score allowed for possible enlargements of the string section in other performances. The Piano Concerto, partly to save rehearsal time, relegates much of the difficult playing to a concertino of soloists. Each of these self-imposed restrictions affected the form and plan of the work drastically, of course, and seem in no way to have helped the performance prospects of the work, as they have gone unnoticed. In the case of my Variations, when played by the Philadelphia Orchestra, the entire wind section was doubled through most of the work, as is sometimes done in Beethoven symphonies, without my knowing, until I arrived at the last rehearsal when the work was completely rehearsed. This resulted in a rather intense and coarse sound in fast passages, which I did not want. I realized, however, that this amplification of the orchestra was probably necessary because of the bad acoustics of the then recently opened Philharmonic Hall at Lincoln Center. When the work was performed there, one critic wrote that this work was seldom performed because it required such a large orchestra!

I made unusual orchestral demands in the score of my Double Concerto because the generous commissioner of the work, Paul Fromm and the Fromm Foundation, assured me of excellent musicians and sufficient rehearsals. Unlike my other compositions, this one presents many kinds of special performance problems, the main one being the harpsichord itself. The instrument is of always unpredictable volume, which varies from hall to hall as well as from instrument to instrument—a fact that I was so aware of that, during the work, all the other instruments usually stop altogether or play their softest in their dullest registers when the harpsichord is playing. These precautions do not prevent it from being lost and requiring amplification under many performing conditions but, as it is the soft member of a dialogue "pian e forte," it cannot be amplified very much. The balance and accuracy of the percussion, its damping, its sticking, have to be worked out with great care, otherwise the work will sink into a miasma of confusion, as it has on a number of occasions, especially when the hall is too resonant.

The work is built on a large plan, somewhat like that of Lucretius's *De rerum natura*, in which its cosmos is brought into existence by collisions of falling atoms, in the music by ten superimposed slowly beaten out regular speeds—five for the harpsichord and its orchestra on one side of the stage, and five for the piano and its orchestra on the other side of the stage. A musical interval is associated with the attacks of each of these and used in the introduction as if it were a percussive sound. The distribution of the speeds and intervals is given in Example 1a. As can be seen, the smallest ratio of speeds is 49:50, which is the one first presented. This fans out to the largest, 1:2, in intermediate steps, reading from right to left, during the introduction. The ratio 49:50 is represented by alternating rolls of the snare drum on the piano side of the stage at metronomic speed 25, and of the cymbal on the harpsichord side at speed 24.5, starting in an ornamented way in mm. 7 and 8 and resolving to the pure lengths combined with the associated intervals in mm. 10–12. Then harpsichord speed 28, perfect fourth, and piano speed $21\,7/8$, major seventh, appear in mm. 13 and 14—piano speed 21, major sixth, and harpsichord speed $29\,1/6$, augmented fourth, m. 17—harpsichord speed $19\,4/9$, minor third, m. 20; piano speed 31.5, perfect fifth, mm. 23 and 24—finally

RATIO	BETWEEN				SPEEDS		METRONOMIC SPEEDS	PIANO	HARPSICHORD
2					1/5	10	35		
	81					9	31½		
		25			1/6		29 1/6		
			32			8	28		
				50	1/7		25		
				49		7	24½		
			25		1/8		21 7/8		
		18				6	21		
	50				1/9		19 4/9		
1					1/10	5	17½		

Example 1a. Double Concerto: distribution and instrumental assignments of metronomic speeds.

harpsichord speed 17.5, minor seventh in m. 31, and piano speed 35, major third, m. 36. During these measures some of the layers of speed that have been introduced drop out, but they all begin to be sounded as the two climaxes, made by rhythmic unisons, approach. Four of the speeds that fill in the ratio of 35:17.5 are in a ratio of reciprocals, as the chart shows, and these reach a rhythmic unison in m. 45, while the other four speeds fill in 35:17.5 in a ratio of whole numbers and come to a rhythmic unison in m. 46. The two systems engender a pattern of regular beats in the case of the reciprocals and a pattern of acceleration and retardation in the case of the whole numbers as shown in the diagram, Example 1b.

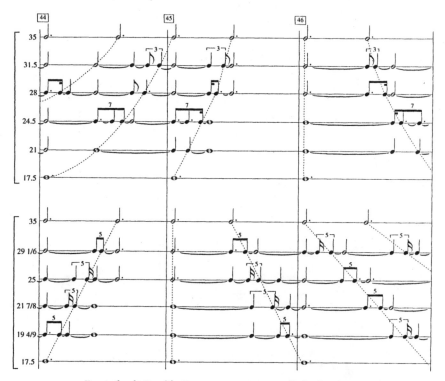

Example 1b. Double Concerto, mm. 44–46: rhythmic scheme.

After the introduction, the various speeds and their intervals are joined to-gether to produce polyrhythmic patterns of a lesser degree of density but a higher degree of mobility and articulation, different combinations producing different sections. How this is done can be seen in the harpsichord and piano cadenzas in which almost the entire repertory of both parts is presented in aphoristic form. The slow movement which emerges from the previous fast one at m. 312 and continues to m. 475, overlapping the beginning of the next section, uses alternations of accelerating and slowing up in a pattern that runs around the outside of the orchestra counterclockwise (percussion 4,3,2,1, harpsichord, contrabass, cello, piano) when accelerating and clockwise when slowing up. The central part of the orchestra, the winds, play a slow piece not related rhythmically to these motions, but maintaining their interval identity in each orchestra. Until the coda, the two orchestras adhere to a system of in-terval interrelationships that is different for each, as indicated in Example 1c. In general the piano and its group specialize in rhythmic ratios of 3:5 while the harpsichord group uses that of 4:7. The coda extends these ratios over many measures, producing long, slow waves of oscillating sounds, an orches-tration, so to speak, of the sound of a tam-tam heard in m. 619, dying away over many measures. The piano group at this point has important attacks every seventh measure with subsidiary ones every thirty-fifth quarter, while

Example 1c. Double Concerto: all-interval tetrachords and their combinations.

the harpsichord group emphasizes every fifth measure and secondarily every thirty-fifth dotted eighth—all with many subsidiary patterns and accents. The coda is the dissolution of this musical cosmos—Lucretius's "Destruction of Athens" or, perhaps, the triumph of Chaos at the end of Pope's *Dunciad*.

As in all my music, such intervallic schemes provide a somewhat ordered substructure (like the triadic harmony of the common-practice period, but more freely used because it is not adhered to so strictly) as a source of ideas of many degrees of interrelationship on several different levels at once.

With the many performances this work has had, I had a great deal of opportunity before the score was printed to try to get all its indications as foolproof as possible. There is a constant stream of unfamiliar ideas that can hardly be expected to come out "all by themselves" if the musicians have never before participated in a work that presents these particular problems. It is a great advantage not to conduct the music myself, so that I can find out just how explicit the score is to the conductor and players. When it is not, then I can make it clearer so it will come out well when I am not present. In it there are many problems of notation—such as the awkward dotted notations, used for quintuplets and septuplets in compound time, that have bothered performers in Warsaw and elsewhere. In defense of them, I do not think many passages which use dotted and undotted notes simultaneously could have been notated as clearly.

If I had not had the experience of my Variations behind me, I do not think I would have ventured to write orchestral works as unusual as the Double Concerto or the more recent Piano Concerto. It is strange to have a work like the Variations over the fourteen years of its existence not only become easier and easier for performers to play and for listeners to grasp but also gradually sound more and more the way I intended it to sound with each new performance. At its premiere in Louisville in 1956, the music sounded so confused, particularly in the very resonant gymnasium in which it was played, that I wondered if I had not gone off the deep end and written a score that would never sound as I imagined it. Although by far the hardest work the Louisville Orchestra had commissioned to that date, so I was repeatedly told, it was far simpler in performance demands than the chamber music I was writing at the time. The conductor, Robert Whitney, and the orchestra worked hard and well and made the fine Louisville recording of the Variations. After that, the work received, I think, no performances in the United States until 1964, although it was performed in the interim at Donaueschingen, Rome, Stockholm, Paris, and Liverpool. During its first years of existence, I was particularly eager to learn from live performances with different musicians in different halls, so that I could witness for myself just what was difficult, what was easy and why, what always came out well, and what was troublesome. I would have needed to hear lots of such performances by competent orchestras while the score was still fresh in my mind, in order to profit from its lessons in my next works. This did not happen, and by the time the score began to be played fairly frequently in places where I could be present, I had written my Double Concerto, which approached the orchestra in an entirely different way.

Under present conditions in America, it seems to be very nearly impossible to develop a personal orchestral style that also takes into account the practicalities of the performing situation. Either a composer must use the standardized, "tried and true" orchestral routines, or he must suffer for years through misrepresentative, tentative performances, which teach him very little. In situations where new music is taken more seriously, as in Germany, Italy, Sweden, Poland, and elsewhere, the composers' contacts with orchestral performances have often allowed them to develop highly distinctive yet practical techniques. In the United States, the prospect of troublesome situations is very discouraging—situations in which the performers assume that the composer does not know what he is doing, in which the score cannot come out as intended for lack of rehearsal time or because the conductor is unable to imagine how the score might sound if played correctly. These painful prospects, which a composer must face every time he plans an orchestral work, make it hard for him to follow his own ideas and to take the whole operation of composing orchestral music with the seriousness that he might devote to chamber music, where the musicians are eager to discover precisely the composer's intentions and to play the work to his satisfaction.

My most recent work for orchestra, the Piano Concerto (1965), presents a number of quite different concepts in orchestral use that involve difficulties of balance and, to a lesser extent, playing. For conductors unfamiliar with the late scores of Charles Ives and others, the orchestral score presents a forbidding appearance with its pages that sometimes divide the strings into many single parts. These pages are hard for performers to grasp and interpret, too, since they comprise as many as seventy-two different parts that need to be balanced and coordinated—especially in the fast passages near the end, in which the orchestra plays in 3/2 while the concertino plays in 12/8. The work consists in a different dimension of dialogue from the Double Concerto: the solo piano is in dialogue with the orchestral crowd, with seven mediators—a concertino of flute, english horn, bass clarinet, solo violin, viola, cello, and bass. These share with the piano its material and various characters. Like the Double Concerto, it employs no preestablished form but is a series of short, usually overlapping episodes, mosaics of fragments that derive from parts of the basic material combined in different ways. This basic material is formed of the twelve different groups of three notes, triads, six assigned to the soloists and six to the orchestra. Each of the twelve triads is related to one or more speeds and characters, as the chart shows in Example 2.

The triads, written in whole notes, show how each participates, and in what register, in the two twelve-note chords: A for soloists, B for the orchestra, which dominate the first movement and conclude it. The main triad for soloists is VII, for the orchestra, VIII, both sharing the augmented fourth. This relationship is stressed in mm. 19–22. After these, triads I and IX are frequently used. The black-headed notes in the example show the other spacings of the triads used, while the two-note intervals in boxes indicate the interval of the triad which is most frequently stressed. Each triad has its associated character or characters, and hence its own kind of continuity. Triad III, for instance, is constantly superimposed on itself in a way which leads to the large tone clusters in the strings, which become thicker and more frequent as the work proceeds. The first movement stresses the similarities between the triads of both groups. After the opening of the second movement—its first thirty measures, 349–78, being a transition from the first to the second large section—the music stresses the difference between the two groups. The orchestra has a constantly changing series of slow, soft chords that gradually become denser over many measures. At the same time, it keeps up a web of accented beats in many different speeds between 105 and 10 5/13 in as many as eight different layers going on at once. The piano and occasionally the concertino play a series of rhapsodic, cadenza-like sections based on the chords and intervals used in the first movement with the addition of the perfect fifth and the major seventh. Sometimes these soloists play accelerandi and ritardandi against the regular beating of the orchestra. The many-voiced chords of the orchestra become thicker and the eight polyrhythmic, regularly beaten out accents of the orchestra gradually approach a rhythmic unison as the piano dies

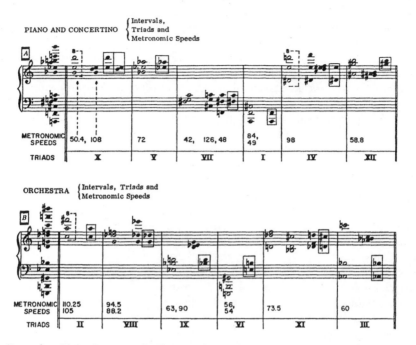

Example 2. Piano Concerto: distribution of intervals, triads, and metronomic speeds.

away repeating a single note. At this point the slow accents of the orchestra become very emphatic, the piano and concertino take up their parts, and the whole leads into a kind of battle between the soloists and the orchestra, with the orchestral strings playing fast passages of twelve-tone chords. The music subsides with a short piano solo in which all of its chords and characteristics are stated in a brief summary of its entire part, recalling each idea with quiet insistence.

Before the first rehearsal of the Piano Concerto, I was presented with the alternative of signing away my right of refusal to allow the work to appear on a recording (allowing the conductor alone to make this decision) or not having the recording made at all. Reluctant as I was to give this right up, since I could not be sure whether on hearing the piece for the first time "live" I would be satisfied with every part of it—or, even if I were, whether the performance would present the piece adequately—I decided to take the chance and was fortunate to have had two unusually good first performances from which to make the tape. Naturally, this surprising request was connected with the record's financing and other aspects of commercial recording ventures. Nevertheless, such a curious lack of consideration for the composer's artistic rights only adds to the general reluctance to write for orchestra that he gradually develops.

For all these reasons and others which come to mind every time I plan an orchestra work, I hesitate a long time. My first conclusion usually is that given the large amount of imaginative effort, skill, and experience demanded by the kind of work I am interested in writing, it will not be worth the effort (particularly in view of the disagreeable, absurd, and hypocritical situations that it will give rise to) since I always write music that cannot be expected to be a "hit" or a "scandal" with the audiences we know. The two or three thousand dollars (the Louisville was one thousand) I am paid for commissions recompenses my work at the rate of about twenty-five cents an hour. Artistically, there is not much to be said, either, for making the effort, given the inadequacies of most American performances, the apathy of most conductors and orchestral performers, and the consequent disaffection of audiences. As the satisfaction of a personal artistic need to write for masses of instruments, there is perhaps more point. Although if the composer feels this need without the concomitant one of writing for the public situation, there is no reason why he should use the usual orchestra setup if he considers it stereotyped—instead inventing his own combinations, which in the United States would, no doubt, rule out all possibility of performance. All in all, it is hard to understand why composers still commit the folly of writing for orchestra in our country. They do. Is it quixotic? Certainly the answer cannot be expected to come from our orchestras, who are too busy with their own organizational and financial problems to bother seriously about the work of composers foolish enough to see something in the orchestral medium.

On Saint-John Perse[1] and the Concerto for Orchestra
(1974)

During his tenure as conductor of the New York Philharmonic, Pierre Boulez gave two "Informal Evenings" outside the regular subscription series. One featured performances of works by Edgard Varèse and an interview with his widow, Louise; the other was devoted entirely to my Concerto for Orchestra, at which both Boulez and I spoke and the orchestra performed excerpts from the work before playing it all the way through. This took place at Philharmonic Hall, as it was then called, on 5 February 1974. The text given below is a kind of memorandum of what I had intended to say; Boulez assisted by reading the excerpts from Perse (in French) and of course by conducting the appropriate excerpts from the Concerto.

I would like to start this evening with a few words about the artist's vocation, as it is expressed in the poem I will later talk about. "The Wind with us as Master of song" is personified and speaks:

"I shall hasten the rising of sap in your acts. I shall lead your acts to maturation.
    And I shall sharpen for you the act itself like the splinter of quartz or obsidian. [. . .]

1. Saint-John Perse was the literary pseudonym of Alexis Saint-Léger Léger, a French diplomat who after the Nazi occupation of France in 1940 fled to exile in the United States rather than serve as ambassador to the U.S. for the Vichy government, and who was a staunch supporter of de Gaulle throughout the Second World War. He received the Nobel Prize for Literature in 1960.

And the Poet is with you. His thoughts amongst you like watchtowers. Until the evening, may he maintain, may he maintain his gaze on the fortune of man!

I shall people for you the abyss of his eyes. And you will turn into acts the dreams he has dared. And into the braid of his song you will weave the gesture he does not conclude. . . .

O freshness, O freshness rediscovered among the sources of language! . . . The new wine is no truer, the new flax no fresher. [. . .]" [IV,5][2]

Such convictions about the artist are the hopes that many share.

In particular, the rediscovery of freshness among the sources of language is something I have hoped for in developing the musical style of my works, which more and more find their sources in very elemental sound patterns, sonorities and motions, rather than in more traditional procedures such as thematic or motivic development. For at the time I agreed to write the Concerto for Orchestra for the New York Philharmonic's 125th anniversary, a number of special musical ideas were preoccupying me, and led me to see in the poem I have just quoted many patterns of thought, feeling, and poetic expression which gave direction to my piece.

An idea of how to write in a special way for the orchestra had been developing in my mind for quite a while. I had had a glimpse of it in my Variations, in which simultaneous layers of different musical characters were sometimes juxtaposed. In my Double Concerto, I had found an ending which involved an oscillating, wavelike fading in and out of different sonorities and characters, making polyrhythms out of whole systems of music—a technique which I wanted to carry out in a full-length piece. Around the same time, after many unsuccessful attempts to interest various conductors in performing Charles Ives's *Fourth of July*, the score of which I had known since around 1930 and had long been curious to hear, I finally persuaded the Italian Radio Orchestra to play it. And I found that Ives's use of strings divided into scales of tone-clusters, which form the background of much of the work, suggested a whole new way of treating the strings, which I worked with a little in my Piano Concerto.

Another intention was to extend to the orchestra the kind of individualization of instruments that I had tried for the four players of my Second Quartet. I thought that it would be moving to treat the orchestra as a crowd of individuals, each having his own personal expression and coordinated in a less stereotyped way than is usually done in orchestral writing. I began to imagine the players of the orchestra (and especially of the wonderful New

---

2. Saint-John Perse, *Winds*, trans. Hugh Chisholm, in *Saint-John Perse: Collected Poems— Complete Edition*, Bollingen Series Vol. 87 (Princeton: Princeton University Press, 1983), 225–357. Quotations from *Winds* follow Chisholm's translation for the most part; Carter has changed the rendering of a few words here and there. All ellipses (. . .) are part of Perse's actual text except for those set apart from the text, which represent Carter's abridgments. Designations such as "IV,5" refer to the location of quotations by canto of Perse's poem (arabic numeral) within its section (roman numeral). [B]

York Philharmonic) as members of a large group each with his own personality and his own kind of music to play, and each contributing to the general effect. I wanted to give each of the many marvelous players a chance to display his own ability, either alone or in small groups.

On a technical level, I was interested in investigating the possibilities of all the thirty-eight five-note and seven-note chords, and joining those of the most extreme dissonance with those of the blandest consonance. At the same time, I wanted to try combining accelerations and retardations in my rhythmic vocabulary, in order to produce a constantly hurrying and slowing down kind of tempo, rather than the polyrhythms of most of my previous music.

As I thought of all of this, I came across an article by Stephen Spender about Saint-John Perse's *Vents* (*Winds*), a book-length poem communicating a vision of the American continent being swept by the winds of change—winds that destroy and blow away the old, scattering seeds and bringing in the climate for the new in an ever-variable series of cycles.[3] After reading the poem, and as my interest in Perse's work grew with an acquaintance with some of his other poems—*Eloges, Anabase, Exil*—I came to realize that *Vents* would give a kind of shape and character to the multiple-layered music I wished to write, and that it corresponded to the form of the piece I had begun to imagine. The poem suggested a way of looking at all these intentions and using them for an expressive and, to me, meaningful purpose.

Vents was written by Perse during his wartime stay in the United States, in Maine, in 1945. It is, like his other poems, in the style of impassioned incantation, sometimes evoking primitive rituals even while describing the present. The general tone of the poem attracted me as a rebuttal to the rather passive, embittered view of life expressed in T. S. Eliot's *The Waste Land*, which seemed to explain what we saw around us especially during the Depression years when I was attending college. Also, it had a new meaning during the very years when this work was being written, in 1967 and '68, when there was, understandably, so much student unrest everywhere, even in Rome where I was working at the time. The extravagant rhetoric not only reminded me of much French poetry, such as Lautréamont's *Les Chants de Maldoror*, but also the prophetic books of William Blake and the Icelandic Sagas—*Burnt Njal*, for instance—and many long modern poems, like Kazantzakis's *Sequel to "The Odyssey,"* the *Cantos* of Ezra Pound, and *Paterson* of William Carlos Williams.

The general character of the poem and of the music is suggested in lines such as these:

These were very great winds over all the faces of this world [. . .] questing over all the trails of this world,
    Over all things perishable, over all things graspable, throughout the entire world of things. . . . [I,1]

---

3. Stephen Spender, "An Epic of America" [review of first bilingual edition of *Winds*, with English translation by Hugh Chisholm], *The Cincinnati Inquirer*, 19 April 1953. [B]

And following in the hurried footsteps of the night, amidst the spirit's worst dis-
orders, they instituted a new style of grandeur to which our future acts must rise;
    And when they had unraveled the living works from the dead, and from the best
the supreme, [. . .]
    One evening they restored to us the sharp face of the earth, [. . .] [I,3]

Perse's poem furnished not a story, but a kind of poetic vision of large-scale
change, and a series of characters, constantly in motion, frequently returning
like leaves on a whirlwind. Phrases such as "O you whom the storm refreshes" ("O vous que refraîchit l'orage") or "We had a rendezvous with the
end of an age" ("Nous avions rendez-vous avec la fin d'un âge") or "And you
had so little time to be born to this instant!" ("Et vous aviez si peu de temps
pour naître à cet instant!") recur like rhyming ideas throughout the work, as
do sonorities in the music, and as in the music at one point or another these
various phrases are expanded and their implications investigated. The third of
these phrases, for example, is developed in one place like this:

And still the Poet is with us . . . This hour perhaps the last, this minute even, this instant! . . . And we have so little time to be born to this instant! [. . .]
    This hour perhaps the last . . . this minute even! . . . this instant! . . . [III,6]

Of course, to a musician, who deals in instants, who depends on the alertness
of performers actually to be born to an instant of music, this idea has a very
intense meaning, and my work in one sense is a series of instants, more than
are many other pieces since it is constantly changing.
    Another feature that interested me as a composer was the jagged rhetoric,
which frequently interrupts lines of thought and feeling, leaving them suspended, while other feelings are interjected, something that is evident in every
part of the poem. For instance, the very opening, which like the musical introduction is short, quickly introduces the first important scene or situation of
the first part—but then immediately returns to the main idea:

These were very great winds over all the faces of this world,
    Very great winds rejoicing over the world, having neither eyrie nor resting-place,
    Having neither care nor caution, and leaving us, in their wake,
    Men of straw in the year of straw . . . Ah, yes, very great winds over all the faces
of the living! [. . .]
    These were very great winds questing over all the trails of this world,
    Over all things perishable, over all things graspable, throughout the entire world
of things . . . [I,1]

Actually the poem, like the music, seems to me to center around four main
ideas, which fade in and out sometimes being more stressed than at others—
although all four (and many more in the poem) are constantly being referred
to. The first of the four ideas to be stressed in the poem, as in the music, is
that of "men of straw in the year of straw":

And having exposed to air the attrition and drought in the heart of men in office,
  Behold, they produced this taste of straw and spices, in all the squares of our
cities [. . .]
  [. . .] And divinity ebbed from the great works of the spirit.
For a whole century was rustling in the dry sound of its straw, amid strange
desinences at the tips of husks of pods, at the tips of trembling things, [. . .] [I,1]

There is occasional nostalgia for the past that is being blown away (but this,
as well as a few other aspects of the poem, I rejected in the music):

Tonight we shall lay the dead seasons to bed in their ballgowns, in their laces of old
gold [. . .] [I,5]

And in this section two lines that particularly amused me as a musician:

Golden crocus, like a tuba's song in the mounting brass, we shall watch for you!
  And if the man of talent prefers the rose-garden and the playing of the harpsichord, he shall be devoured by dogs. [I,6]

The second section of the poem and the music deal with the freshness of
nature in the new continent as some of the early settlers saw it, as explorers
experienced it, and as painters, especially Audubon with his vivid portraits of
American birds, memorialized it:

New lands, out there, in their very lofty perfume of humus and foliage,
  New lands, out there, beneath the lengthening of this world's most expansive
shadows,
  All the land of trees, out there, on a background of black vines, like a Bible of
shadow and freshness in the unrolling of this world's most beautiful texts. [. . .]
  And there is a freshness of lands in infancy, like a perfume of things everlasting,
on this side of everlasting things, [. . .] [II,1]
                    . . . . . .
[. . .] Migrations of birds have departed across the breadth of the Century, drawing
to other cycles their great dislocated triangles.
  And there are millions of versts open to them, and the fleeing sky adrift like ice-
floes melting.
  To go! Where all unleashed animals go, in a very great torment of wing and
horn . . . [II,3]
                    . . . . . .
Swarms whistle by, freed of the hive—grapeshot of insects hard as horn! . . . . . .
  These flights of insects going off in clouds to lose themselves at sea, like fragments of sacred texts, like the tatters of errant prophecies and of recitations by ge-
nealogists, by psalmists . . . One has told them, one has told them—ah! what has
one not told them?—that they would lose themselves on the seas, and that they
should put about; one cried to them, one cried to them—ah! what did one not cry
to them?—that they should return, ah! should return among us . . . But no! they
went that way instead, where one is lost with the wind! (And what could we do
about it?) [II,4]

The third section of the poem and the music center on the phrase "O you whom the storm refreshes." In this section Perse reintroduces a figure first encountered in I,2—sometimes called a Narrator, sometimes a Poet:

> The Narrator mounts the ramparts. And the Wind with him. Like a Shaman in his bracelets of iron: [. . .] He has eaten of the rice of the dead [. . .] But his word is for the living, his hands for the fountains of the future.
> And his word is fresher to us than new water. [. . .] [I,2]
> . . . . . .
> For man is in question, and his reintegration.
> Will no one in the world raise his voice? Testimony for man. . . .
> Let the Poet speak, and let him guide the judgment! [III,4]
> . . . . . .
> "Litigation, I ignore you. And my opinion is that we should live!
> With the torch in the wind, with the flame in the wind,
> And that all men amongst us should be so mingled and consumed therein,
> That this growing torch may kindle within us a greater clarity. [. . .]" [III,5]

Finally, the last section of the poem and the music stress a vision of the future, followed by a conclusion which summarizes the whole:

> These were very great forces at work on the causeway of men—very great forces in labor
> Holding us outside of custom and holding us outside of season, among men of custom, among men of season, [. . .]
> And raised us, new men, to the very summit of the instant, they cast us one evening onto new shores and left us [. . .] [IV,6]
> . . . . . .
> ". . . We had a rendezvous with the end of an age. And here we are, close-lipped, among you. And the Wind with us—drunk with a principle bitter and strong as ivy wine.
> Not summoned in conciliation, but irritable and singing to you: I will irritate the marrow in your bones . . ." [IV,4]
> . . . . . .
> These were very great winds over the land of men—very great winds at work among us,
> Singing to us the horror of living, and singing to us the honor of living, ah! singing to us and singing to us from the very summit of peril,
> And, with the savage flutes of misfortune, leading us, new men, to our new ways. [IV,6]

The wind finally dies down and the music ends:

> Sing, sweetness, to the last palpitation of the evening and the breeze, like an appeasement of gratified beasts,
> And to its end, this evening, comes the very great wind. The night airs itself at other summits. And in the distance the earth is narrating its seas. [IV,6]

I never had any intention of writing a tone poem, of trying to translate Perse's poem into music; rather, I meant simply to use certain suggestions as to character and as to form that suited my purpose. The aspect of constant change, or the large motion of many small things set in motion by the wind, and the very notion of the wind as a kind of spirit, imposing its general patterns on things, all seemed to have a connection with the idea of a concerto in which many individuals could all be heard and helped me to imagine many parts of the Concerto for Orchestra. The large epic vision, the big rhetorical tone were less important to me than the sense of everyone having his chance to present himself.

Brass Quintet
(1974)

I am particularly happy that the world premiere of my Brass Quintet should be given as part of the BBC's celebration of Charles Ives's hundredth birthday, because it helps to repay the great debt that I owe him personally and musically. In 1924 and '25, when I was making youthful blunders in composition, Ives, whom I used to see at that time, encouraged me, and even over a number of years took an interest in my aspirations to become a composer. His remarkable personality has always been a great inspiration to me, but perhaps even more than that, the copies of the privately printed *Concord Sonata*, 114 *Songs*, and the photostat of the First Violin Sonata which he gave me formed a sometimes perplexing, but always exciting visionary bible during my formative years.

I can remember, vividly, the last time I saw him, when as a college student I had started to write the kind of Hindemith-like neoclassic music characteristic of the then young composer's revolt against the dissonances and confused Romantic textures of an earlier time. He looked at a little piano sonata and, I guess, rather disappointed, took me out for a walk in the woods overlooking the Connecticut valleys of Redding, where he spent his summers. Nature was at its most lush, and I remember clearly the mottled sunlight on the paths and rocks and his turning suddenly to me and saying something like: "How can anyone deny that there is a great being behind all this?" expressing typically pantheistic views, already well known to me then. In retrospect, this could have been taken as a kind of rebuke for the rather artificial music I was trying to write, but at the time, overcome by the beauty of the day and a profound respect for the man, I did not think so, although I did realize dimly that our directions were beginning to be different.

Yet now I see that many of our aims are similar, particularly in the primary concern for musical expressivity. For me this quality can be heightened, focused, and when necessary dramatized both in detail and in larger relationships, in a way that did not always interest Ives. Like him, I enjoy writing music of constant variety and change, but within a more highly focused and coherent sound-character and musical style than interested Ives. Coming at a later period, I have been much more concerned with flexibility and variety of texture and sound, while Ives, like many early modernists, relied at times on rather routine procedures to make dissonances, like the pedantic canon in *From the Steeples and the Mountains,* or the rigidly systematic use of harmonies built on intervals other than thirds found in *The Fourth of July* and the song *Soliloquy.* Unlike him, I have been concerned with finding idioms that would help express the special vision behind any particular work, that would give it its own identity and differentiate it from others. For this reason I have avoided conscious quotation of other music except for the one case in my First String Quartet of 1951, in which I quoted the opening theme of Ives's First Violin Sonata as a tribute to the composer whose works had suggested some of the general ideas of my music. Indeed Ives's music is one source of the notion of multilayered texture which has preoccupied me since 1948, the other sources being, of course, the operas of Mozart, Verdi, and Mussorgsky.

The Brass Quintet, which you will hear shortly, was written this past summer for its present players, the American Brass Quintet. It is representative of many things I have mentioned. Being almost constantly multilayered, like my Second String Quartet, it separates the players by individualizing their parts, but not as completely as did the string quartet, because each instrument shares parts of its repertory with one of the others. The first trumpet, for instance, near the beginning plays in a trio with the second trumpet and the tenor trombone, featuring the minor sixth in light, irregular chords, of which the character and interval become part of the repertory of the three participating instruments. A bit later the first trumpet plays another trio with the horn and the bass trombone, which features fanfares and quiet majestic music based on the perfect fifth, which then become part of the repertory of these three instruments. The horn, however, which has the largest repertory of all, also frequently uses the augmented fourth, which it does not share with any of the others.

All of these contrasting characters and their related musical intervals form a multilayered piece planned along the following pattern: Every third (that is the first, fourth, seventh, and so on) of its overlapping nineteen short sections is a brief five-part quodlibet in which the instruments oppose each other with contrasting parts of their individual repertories. Between these is a duo preceded or followed by a trio in which the two or three instruments join in music of similar character. Each duo and trio has a different instrumentation.

To make the general plan clear, let me describe the shape of just a few of the initial sections. The opening quodlibet starts as if it were a slow movement but is suddenly interrupted by the horn. This causes an outburst from all the five, each contributing a characteristic fragment. Immediately the first trio starts, with the two trumpets and the tenor trombone playing short, light chords in irregular rhythm, as mentioned, while the horn and the bass trombone continue the slow music of the beginning. These latter two stop for a bit and then start a somewhat rough, fast duo in which the bass trombone takes the lead. The trio still continues above this, pauses, and then starts up the slow music which leads to the second quodlibet. This general

pattern is followed throughout much of the piece, with variations of emphasis, timing, and, of course, contrasts of expression and character. At one
point, for instance, the two trumpets and the horn play soft, rapid, smoothly
flowing music that soon is combined with a duet for the two trombones playing glissandi.

The general plan is interrupted, midway through the work, by a relatively
extended unaccompanied horn solo, which is cut off by angry octaves from
the others. The slow music which began the piece and forms the background
of the first three quodlibets is abandoned after the last of these, only to return
in extended form near the end. The entire work, in fact, can be heard as one
long slow movement with interruptions.

Indeed another way of hearing the piece is to consider it as a meeting of
five brass players who have come together to play slow, solemn music. As
they start to do so, entering one after the other, the weak member of the
group, the horn, interjects irrelevant, disruptive ideas that momentarily upset
the plan. Given the atmosphere of discord that arises between the players,
each begins to assert himself, joining partners in small groups while the excluded ones try to bring back the slow music. The light, comic, flowing, excitable or lyric duos or trios, heard between passages during which all five al-
tercate, gradually stray from the project of playing slow music. Midway
through, the horn deplores its alienation in a long unaccompanied solo,
which arouses the others to a menacing duo for trumpets and an angry trio
for trombones and horn. All this leads to a violent altercation that finally is
settled by an agreement to continue the slow music of the beginning. After
quite a period of unanimity the players again begin to disagree: the tenor
trombone, never having had a proper solo like the others have had, stops
them for his, which is accompanied by a muted trumpet. There is an abrupt
and aggressive ending.

This quintet, rather than employing all the resources of color possible with
modern mutes for the brass, relies primarily on linear material, textures, and
the instrumental virtuosity for which the American Brass Quintet is notable.

Double Concerto, 1961, and Duo, 1974
(1975)

Both pieces on this record,[1] although written thirteen years apart, derive their
music directly from the performing situation. It was considered a matter of
great importance that the expression and thought arise from the unique
sound and performance techniques of the harpsichord, of the piano, and the
violin. There was a desire to get down to the physical origins of musical
sound and to take off from there. The Double Concerto, in fact, actually has
a shape that parallels this attitude, starting as it does by presenting gradually

---

1. Performers of these works on the recording in question are: for the Double Concerto, Paul
   Jacobs, harpsichord, Gilbert Kalish, piano, and the Contemporary Chamber Ensemble conducted by Arthur Weisberg; for the Duo, Paul Zukofsky, violin, and Gilbert Kalish, piano. [S]

changing percussion sounds that first "give birth" to a few musical pitches that in turn bring on the sound of the piano and then the harpsichord, which in their turn become more and more articulated and differentiated, only to sink back eventually to a more chaotic, undifferentiated state near the end.

Both of these works were written in response to specific requests; both had to wait until ideas arose whose expression seemed to require those pairs of instruments for which I had been asked to write. This was particularly true of the Duo, where the right idea presented itself only after about ten busy years of writing other things. In the case of the Double Concerto, the response to a request from Ralph Kirkpatrick for a piece for harpsichord and piano ended up in music that surrounds each of the soloists with a small orchestra and two percussion players, serving sometimes to intensify the special qualities of the solo instruments and at other times to blur their differences.

Each of the works heard here has two sound sources treated as opposing members of a pair, with differences of sound quality and types of expression reinforced by giving each member of the pair individualized musical materials, harmonies, and rhythms. In the Duo, the contrast between the violin and the piano, both stringed instruments, is fundamentally a gestural one—between stroking and striking. Using a great variety of bow strokes, the violin can be made to produce many different types of attack: it can also prolong its sounds and give them a variety of tone colors and inflections, such as swelling and fading or becoming more, or less, intense. On the other hand, the finger of the pianist strikes a key that catapults a felt-covered hammer up to the string more or less suddenly and forcefully, depending on how the key is struck. Once the hammer has started the string vibrating, the player has no further control over the sound—which immediately begins to die away—except that he can cut short this decay by raising the finger from the key, activating a damper.

The piano's loss of control over its sound is shared with the harpsichord, which, moreover, has only a remote control of dynamics—these are scarcely affected by the pressure of the finger on the key, being produced mainly by stops (operated, in this case, by pedals) that add or subtract the number of strings set into vibration by the plectra when the key is struck. These stops, however, give the two keyboards of the harpsichord a vast array of tone colors, since they control jacks that vary in their plucking materials—quills or leather—and pluck the strings at different places along their length.

The piano has eighty-eight notes (usually) and can play very loudly and very softly; the violin covers only the upper fifty-four notes of the piano's range and can be overwhelmed by the piano even when playing its loudest. The harpsichord called for in the Double Concerto lacks the piano's uppermost seven notes, but has four rather soft notes below the lowest piano note (these are heard in the harpsichord's last chord, just before the end); even at its loudest, it is very much softer than the piano playing moderately (in the fast duet in the middle of the Concerto, the piano has to play very softly for the harpsichord to be heard). This contrast between the two solo instruments dictated the antiphonal character of the Double Concerto, so that the harpsichord would not be overwhelmed by the piano. The changes of stops that give great variety to the harpsichord's sound were worked out as carefully as possible (harpsichords are not standardized), with certain harpsichord timbres being associated with particular effects in the orchestra, as at the end of the introduction, when the harpsichord's mute (lute) stop is answered by wood percussion and pizzicato strings. The harpsichord's solo cadenza has a great number of sudden changes of registration, which reveal almost the full color range of the instrument.

Given the point of view from which these pieces were written, there is little question of one instrument's imitating another in sound (as often happens in the Classical style), and for this reason there is almost no imitation of musical material between the members of each pair. The harpsichord and piano in the Concerto, and the violin and piano in the Duo, are each given music idiomatic to their instruments, meant to appeal to the imaginations of their performers and cast them into clearly identifiable, independent roles. The intention is to stimulate performers into giving vital, personal performances and through these to transmit the message of a new, important, and special experience to the listener. Since the instruments and the highly developed ways of playing them already possess a quality of special experience in and of themselves, frequent exploitation of unusual sound effects or of chance playing was avoided, for in these works it would have reduced the special quality to the ordinariness and obviousness of chaotic confusion.

The music gives the impression of being continuous, of evolving constantly from beginning to end. Although the Double Concerto falls more clearly into sections than does the Duo, it is constantly prefiguring what will happen and recalling what has happened, bridging the pauses and changes of character by numerous internal connections. The seven sections of the Concerto are symmetrically arranged. The brilliant Allegro scherzando and the Presto (sections 3 and 5) each feature one of the two solo instruments, the piano in the former, the harpsichord in the latter; in each movement, the featured instrument and its orchestra are frequently interrupted by the other instrument and its orchestra playing at a dynamic level opposite to that of the main group. In the central Adagio, the "choreography" changes: the entire wind section, in center stage (although still divided into groups), plays slow music, while in the background the two soloists, strings, and four percussionists surround the winds with accelerating and decelerating patterns that alternately move clockwise and counterclockwise.

The Introduction and Coda also form a fundamentally symmetrical pair. The Introduction "breaks the silence" and gradually piles up two-by-two, polyrhythmically, the ten speeds and associated tone colors and musical intervals used in the entire work. The Coda begins with a crash and then, like a large gong, dies away over many measures in wavelike patterns, with many diverse tone colors fading out and returning—each time slightly different, and each time with less energy—until the work subsides to a quiet close.

Thought about this work suggested a literary analogue to the concerto's expected form—Lucretius's *De rerum natura*, which describes the formation of the physical universe by the random swervings of atoms, its flourishing, and its destruction. Bit by bit, however, a humorous parody of Lucretius in Alexander Pope's *Dunciad* took over in my thoughts, in lines like:

> All sudden, Gorgons hiss, and Dragons glare,
> And ten-horn'd Fiends and Giants rush to war;
> Hell rises, Heav'n descends, and dance on earth;
> Gods, imps, and monsters, music, rage, and mirth,
> A fire, a jig, a battle, and a ball,
> Till one wide conflagration swallows all.

The beautiful end of Pope's poem seemed to articulate in words the end of the work I had already composed:

> —the all composing hour
> Resistless falls; the Muse obeys the power.
> She comes! She comes! the sable throne behold
> Of Night primeval, and of Chaos old!
> Before her Fancy's gilded clouds decay,
> And all its varying rainbows die away.
> Wit shoots in vain its momentary fires,
> The meteor drops and in a flash expires.
>
> Nor public flame, nor private, dares to shine;
> Nor human spark is left, nor glimpse divine!
> Lo! thy dread empire, Chaos! is restor'd;
> Light dies before thy uncreating word:
> Thy hand, great Anarch! lets the curtain fall;
> And universal Darkness buries all.

The Duo, as has been said, derives its character and expression from the contrast between its two very dissimilar instruments—the bow-stroked violin and the key-struck piano. The mercurial violin music, at times intense and dramatic, at others light and fanciful, constantly changes its pace and tone of expression; the piano plays long stretches of music of consistent character and is much more regular both in rhythm and in style. The piano makes extensive use of the pedal to mask one sonority with another and then gradually to uncover the second—as in the very first measures. In fact, the long opening section for the piano forms a quiet, almost icy background to the varied and dramatic violin, which seems to fight passionately against the piano. After this beginning, the music is joined seamlessly until the end.

In the course of the work, the violin focuses on one aspect of its part after another—and often on two or more aspects at a time—playing in a rubato, rhythmically irregular style, while the piano constantly plays regular beats, sometimes fast, sometimes slow. Toward the end, while the violin is involved in a very fast and impassioned music, the piano becomes more and more detached, playing a series of regular rhythmic patterns, each successively slower than the previous one. As the piano reaches a point of extreme slowness, the violin is heard increasingly alone, isolating for a few measures at a time the various elements of its part, with the quiet and more lyrical aspects given more prominence than previously.

The general form of both works on this record is quite different from that of the music I wrote up to 1950. While this earlier music was based on themes and their development, here the musical ideas are not themes or melodies but rather groupings of sound materials out of which textures, linear patterns, and figurations are invented. Each type of music has its own identifying sound and expression, usually combining instrumental color with some "behavioral" pattern that relies on speed, rhythm, and musical intervals. There is no repetition, but a constant invention of new things—some closely related to each other, others remotely. In both the Double Concerto and the Duo there is a stratification of sound, so that much of the time the listener can hear two different kinds of music, not always of equal prominence, occurring simultaneously. This kind of form and texture could be said to reflect the experience we often have of seeing something in different frames of reference at the same time.

The Double Concerto was commissioned by the Fromm Foundation and is dedicated to Paul Fromm. It was written during 1969–61 and was given its premiere in New York, 6 September 1961, at a concert for the Eighth Congress of the International Musicological Society, with harpsichordist Ralph Kirkpatrick and pianist Charles Rosen, conducted by Gustav Meier. The Duo for Violin and Piano was written in 1973–74 to fulfill a commission by the McKim Fund in the Library of Congress and is dedicated to my wife, Helen. It was first performed by Paul Zukofsky and Gilbert Kalish at a New York Philharmonic Prospective Encounter, 5 March 1975.

Music and the Time Screen
(1976)

The sense of the above title was suggested to me by Professor Edward Lowinsky, the well-known musicologist, once when I was lecturing at the University of Chicago. He said something to the effect that "time is the canvas on which you consider music to be presented, just as the spatial canvas of a painting furnishes the surface on which a painting is presented." Such a provocative comparison reaches in so many directions that it is difficult to discuss it in some clear and intelligible way. Analogies between the structure and character of time and those of space tend to be superficial, if not pointless, because we experience these dimensions in such different although interconnected ways. Yet, if the "time screen" on which music in this statement is said to be projected is considered to be a stretch of the measurable time of practical life, while the music itself may be incorporating another kind of time but needs measurable time for its presentation, then it can, no doubt, be compared to the space screen of a flat, rectangular canvas on which the imaginings of the artist about space are projected, and there is some point to the comparison.

However, it becomes much more tenuous if we try to compare the connections a composer can make in a composition between "sooner and later," which, although existing in "clock time," can also gain many special meaningful relationships because they involve patterns related to the experience of time of both composer and listener, and the "up and down" or "right and left" of a picture, elements that, although also physically in the picture, also participate in the artist's and observer's common experience of weight, shape, color, and visual texture, which can only be applied to time metaphorically.

It is not my intention here to indulge in such comparisons but to describe how, out of a consideration for the special temporality of music, I have attempted to derive a way of composing that deals with its very nature. To start with, I must briefly deal with the formidable subject of time, a most confusing one because no common vocabulary exists to help us—the "real time" of the Bergson school is very far from that of electronic composers, and the various conceptions of "ontological time" do not relate to each other, while the relationship of "public time" (of Martin Heidegger) to "clock time" (for some, synonymous with "mathematical time") and the latter to such a notion as Pierre Suvchinsky's "chronometric time" is hard to establish. In an effort to isolate the particular field under discussion, I would like to start by quoting Charles Koechlin, who proposed four aspects of time:

1. Pure duration, a fundamental of our deepest consciousness, and apparently independent of the external world: life flows by. . . .

2. Psychological time. This is the impression we have of [the above] duration according to the events of our existence: minutes that seem centuries, hours that go by too quickly. . . .That is, duration relative to the circumstances of life.

3. Time measured by mathematical means; all of which depend on visual methods—sand clocks, clocks, chronometers. . . .

4. Finally, I would like to talk of *musical time*. To us musicians this fact does not present itself as it does to scientists . . . *Auditory* time is without a doubt the kind that comes closest to *pure duration*. However, it appears to have some connection with space in that it seems to us measurable (by ear) and divisible. The divisions embodied in musical note-values (whole-notes, half-notes, etc.) lead to a *spatialization* of time very different from that (based on vision) which Bergson talks about. Besides, as concerns the measure of this [musical] duration, the role of musical memory possesses an importance that seems to escape many.[1]

To expand these aspects further: the first, "pure duration," is evidently the same as Bergson's "real" or "subjective time," *la durée réelle*, which can be known only by intuition, or, as Susanne Langer, whose *Feeling and Form* has been illuminating on these matters, comments: ". . . every conceptual form which is supposed to portray time oversimplifies it to the point of leaving out the most interesting aspects of it, namely the characteristic appearances of passage."[2]

1. Charles Koechlin, "Le Temps et la musique," *Revue Musicale* 7, no. 3 (January 1926): 45–62 (my translation).

2. Susanne K. Langer, *Feeling and Form* (New York: Charles Scribner's Sons, 1953), 114.

Koechlin's second aspect, "psychological time," would be more or less clear from his definition if Heidegger had not expounded a whole philosophy in *On Time and Being*, which, as I understand it, combines the first and second of the above aspects in an impressive demonstration that every human (*Dasein*)[3] is experiencing duration according to his own life pattern, tinged as it inevitably is with expectation, dread, and with the certainty of an end in death, as well as with the sense that the experience of living in time is a common human condition.

Of Koechlin's third aspect, "mathematically measured time," Langer says it is "a special abstraction from temporal experience, namely *time as pure sequence*, symbolized by a class of ideal events indifferent in themselves, but ranged in an infinite 'dense' series by the sole relation of succession. Conceived under this scheme, time is a one-dimensional continuum."[4] Finally, of "musical time" with its relation to "pure duration," Langer remarks: "The direct experience of passage, as it occurs in each individual life is, of course, something actual, just as actual as the progress of the clock or speedometer; and like all actuality it is only in part perceived, and its fragmentary data are supplemented by practical knowledge and ideas from other realms of thought altogether. Yet it is the model for the virtual time created in music."[5]

The ambiguity of the term *time screen* becomes evident with the isolation of such aspects, for while it can be said to be a mathematically measured stretch of time (painfully evident at broadcasting or recording sessions), still, the fact that music is intended for listeners creates the impression that "musical" or "virtual" time is being projected on a time screen of the listener's "pure (or 'subjective') duration," with all its added capabilities of interpretation, memory, and shifts of focus of attention. The relationship between two of these aspects is made clear in Langer's discussion of the experience of time, which is based on contrasting it with "clock time":

> The underlying principle of clock-time is *change*, which is measured by contrasting two states of an instrument, whether that instrument be the sun in various positions, or the hand on a dial at successive locations, or a parade of monotonous, similar events like ticks or flashes, "counted," i.e. differentiated, by being correlated with a series of distinct numbers. . . . "Change" is not itself something represented; it is implicitly given through the contrast of different "states," themselves unchanging.
> The time-concept which emerges from such mensuration is something far removed from time as we know it in direct experience, which is essentially *passage*, or the sense of transience. . . . But the experience of time is anything but simple. It involves more properties than "length," or interval between selected moments; for

3. I use the expression "human (*Dasein*)" exactly as it is used in Martin Heidegger, *On Time and Being*, trans. Joan Stambaugh (New York: Harper & Row, 1972), 1–24. It refers not only to existence or presence but also to the cognitive activities associated with this.

4. Langer, *Feeling and Form*, 111.

5. Ibid., 113.

its passages have also what I can only call, metaphorically, *volume*. Subjectively, a unit of time may be great or small as well as long or short. . . . It is this voluminousness of the direct experience of passage that makes it . . . indivisible. But even its volume is not simple; for it is filled with its own characteristic forms, as space is filled with material forms, otherwise it could not be observed and appreciated. . . . The primary illusion of music is the sonorous image of passage, abstracted from actuality to become free and plastic and entirely perceptible.[6]

Such ideas as these did not become important to me until around 1944; up to that year I had been concerned with other matters and thought of "time" much as many others did. I was familiar with (but somewhat suspicious of) the various proposals made to organize time according to mechanical, constructivist patterns frequently discussed in the 1920s and '30s. Like many other approaches to music of the period, this was primarily concerned with purely physical possibilities and their juggling. Some applied numerical patterns to note values derived from the tuning of the musical scales (as Henry Cowell proposed in *New Musical Resources*[7]); others followed the schematic methods presented in *The Schillinger System of Musical Composition*[8]—two points of view taken up later and subjected to serial permutation by Olivier Messiaen, Pierre Boulez, Karlheinz Stockhausen, and others. As the first phase of modernism began to die away with the rise of populist ideas during the late 1930s and the 1940s, composers, for the most part, returned to the more or less familiar ways of musical thought, and this matter, which began to interest me then, found little corroboration among most of my colleagues.

As one whose interest in music was aroused by hearing the "advanced" music played in the 1920s in the United States and whose musical education took place during the years of change to the populist style, and who then, out of political sympathy, wrote for a while in this style, I still view with considerable perplexity the renewal of many of the so-called experiments of the earlier avant-garde style, few of which led to interesting results then and seem, even today, to be rather unproductive. In any case, around 1945, as the populist period was nearing its end (as we now see in retrospect), I felt I had exhausted my interest in that style and started a thoroughgoing reassessment of musical materials in the hope of finding a way of expressing what seemed to be more important matters—or at least more personal ones.

In retrospect, I can see that it took several years to clarify intentions. During this time I wrote my 1946 Piano Sonata, my 1947 *Emblems*, and my 1948 Woodwind Quintet and Cello Sonata, all of which foreshadow future preoccupations. By 1948 and 1949 I had become very concerned with the nature of musical ideas and started writing music that sought to find out what the minimal needs were for the kind of musical communication I felt worthwhile.

6. Ibid., 112–13.

7. Henry Cowell, *New Musical Resources* (New York: Knopf, 1930), 45–108.

8. Joseph Schillinger, *The Schillinger System of Musical Composition* (New York: Carl Fischer, 1946), 1–95.

There were the *Eight Etudes and a Fantasy*, for woodwind quartet, and six of the *Eight Pieces for Timpani*. The seventh of the wind etudes, based on the pitch G4 (which can be played on all four instruments), draws, out of the four possible tone colors and their eleven combinations and many variants due to dynamic and attack differences, a musical discourse entirely dependent on contrasting various types of "entrances": sharp, incisive attacks as opposed to soft entrances. In the third etude, the three notes of a soft D-major chord are given different emphases by changes of tone color and doublings. In the fourth etude, a unit of two eighth notes, rising a rapid semitone and resting, serves as the generator of an entire piece constructed after the fashion of mm. 16–35 (Ex. 1), a mosaiclike technique I have used in many different ways.

At the same time, a whole complex of notions about rhythm, meter, and timing became a central preoccupation. In a sense, this was explored according to the principles of "clock," or in this case "metronomic," time, but its relationship to the jazz of the 1930s and '40s that combined free improvisation with strict time, and with early and non-Western music, as well as that of Alexander Scriabin, Ives, and Conlon Nancarrow, made me always look toward ways that could incorporate into "musical time" the methods that interested me. The desire to remain within the realm of the performable and auditorily distinguishable divisions of time kept me from exploring the field of polyrhythms, for instance—as someone else might have done who was primarily concerned with mathematically measured time.

A few years previous to 1948, I had come across the ideas of Pierre Suvchinsky in his article in the May–June 1939 issue of *La Revue musicale*[9] and in Igor Stravinsky's long discussion of them in *Poétique musicale*.[10] Here again, it was a question of the experience of time with an opposition between what Suvchinsky calls "Khronos," which appears to be a version of "pure duration" ("real" time), and the many different "psychological" times—expectation, anxiety, sorrow, suffering, fear, contemplation, pleasure, none of which could be grasped if there were not a primary sensation of "real," or "ontological," time. Different composers stress different combinations of "real" and "psychological" time—in Haydn, Mozart, and Stravinsky, the music is what Suvchinsky calls "chronometric," since the sense of time is equivalent to the musical process of the work. Musical time is equivalent to ontological time, while the music of the Romantic composers, particularly that of Wagner, is "chrono-ametric," since it has an unstable relationship between the time of the music and the psychological time it evokes. Such thinking (which I am not sure I agree with) led me to the idea of the opening of the Cello Sonata of 1948, in which the piano, so to speak, presents "chronometric" time, while the cello simultaneously plays in "chrono-ametric" time.

With my Cello Sonata, a whole collection of rhythmic practices began to be developed. Ultimately these were to expand the basic divisions and

9. Pierre Suvchinsky [Souvtchinsky], "La Notion du temps et la musique," *Revue Musicale* 20 (May–June 1939): 310–20.

10. Igor Stravinsky, *La Poétique musicale* (Cambridge: Harvard University Press, 1942), 19–24.

Example 1. *Eight Etudes and a Fantasy* (1950), Etude 4, mm. 16–35.

groupings of regular pulses to include polyrhythmic patterns and rubato, shaped into several methods of continuous change. One, which first found its way into the Cello Sonata, has been called "metric modulation." The technique is illustrated in a passage from "Canaries" (Ex. 2), one of the pieces for timpani. To the listener, this passage should sound as if the left hand keeps up a steady beat throughout the passage, not participating in the modulations and playing the lower notes B and E at the slow speed of MM 64, while the right-hand part, made up of F♮ and C♯, goes through a series of modulations, increasing its speed a little at each change. Starting with the same speed as the left hand—64 to the dotted quarter—the right hand substitutes regular quarters (MM 96) for them in the next measure, and in the third measure these quarters are accented in pairs, and then triplets (MM 144) are substituted for the two previous quarters. The notation is then changed at the double bar so that the previous triplet quarter equals the new quarter, which then in its turn is accented in pairs for which, once again, triplets are substituted (these are now at MM 216). The whole process is then repeated on this new level, bringing the value of the quarters in the twelfth measure to MM 324—with the left hand still continuing its beat of MM 64, now notated in durations of eighty-one sixty-fourth notes. The maintaining of two layers of rhythm, in this case one retaining a steady beat while the other changes its speed step by step, is characteristic of many passages written since that time. Obviously, too, in music built, as this is, on four pitches, the matter of the formation of ideas with such minimal material was a constant preoccupation, as were the various ways of opposing as well as linking these ideas into phrases and larger shapes.

The preoccupation with reduction of musical ideas to their simplest terms became a general formal trend in some works. For instance, the Adagio of my First String Quartet, with its strong opposition between the soft, muted music of the two high violins and the loud, vigorous recitative of the viola and cello,

Example 2. *Eight Pieces for Four Timpani* (1949/66), "Canaries," mm. 61–76.

is the presentation in their simplest terms of the oppositions of rhythm, theme, and character that are characteristic of the entire work, while the Allegro scorrevole is a reduction of the typically diversified texture to a stream of sixteenth notes with a seven-note theme, fragmented into diversified bits that form a constantly changing mosaic (Ex. 3). This section itself has as one of its characteristics a tendency to be interrupted and then to return. One of the

Example 3. First String Quartet (1951), I, mm. 356–67.

interruptions is formed by the relaxing break usually placed between two movements.

What preoccupied me through the 1950s was a desire to find a new flow of musical thought and expression—a tendency to which the previous efforts seemed to be leading. This tendency was not a very pronounced one during the earlier part of the twentieth century, although Debussy expressed dissatisfaction with the conventional methods of "thematic development" of his time. This led him to explore static as opposed to sequential repetition and to reduce thematic material, especially in his last works, to elemental forms containing motives that formed the basis for a spinning out of coherent, ever-changing continuities, a procedure probably derived from the study of plainsong as taught at the Parisian Schola Cantorum in the 1890s. Stravinsky was to adopt this nonsequential development after 1913, as were many outside central Europe, such as, for instance, Edgard Varèse. However, by the mid-1940s the excessive use of ostinati and the rather limited uses of plainsong continuity began to seem outworn, especially since the serial technique seemed to provide other possibilities. There was, as is well known, at the end of the Second World War a sudden interest in Europe in all the forms of modernism previously banned, which once more brought back in music the earlier concern with special sounds, irregular divisions of time, and groupings of these according to the serialization of their physical parameters, with only a very elementary concern for their possible interpretation by the listener. This return to old-fashioned avant-gardism was, of course, stimulating, because it put so many things into question—but only peripherally, since it sidestepped the fundamental issues of music from the point of view I am describing here. In effect, none of this was really "experimental" or advanced, as intended, since its approach to "musical" or even "virtual" time was as routined as the regimes of the patients in Thomas Mann's *The Magic Mountain*.[11] It was, on the contrary, an effort to find a more significant temporal thought, such as Hans Castorp (who never had his broken watch repaired) sought in Mann's novel, that directed my own development in the 1950s and '60s.[12]

It was with such an aim that the Second String Quartet and the Double Concerto for Piano and Harpsichord with Two Chamber Orchestras (written at the same time in 1959–1961) were planned. The primary questions were: How are events presented, carried on, and accompanied? What kind of changes can previously presented events undergo while maintaining some element of identity? and How can all this be used to express compelling aspects of experience to the listener? In both works, the purely instrumental sound material—the four string instruments in the Quartet and the harpsichord and

---

11. Thomas Mann, *The Magic Mountain*, trans. H. T. Lowe-Porter (New York: Vintage, 1969). This novel contains many passages dealing with various aspects of time, especially the chapter "By the Ocean of Time," 541–48.

12. Marcel Proust deals with the subject exhaustively in his *A la recherche du temps perdu*, 15 vols. (Paris: Gallimard, 1927). See especially the last pages of the last book, "Le Temps retrouvé," 15:249–61.

piano and their associated chamber orchestras in the Double Concerto, each with their unique expressive and sound capacities—was sufficient, and I saw no reason to extend beyond the usual methods of playing. In the Quartet, each of the four instruments has a repertory of musical characters of its own, while contributing to the total effect in many different capacities, sometimes following, sometimes opposing the leader, usually according to its own capabilities—that is, according to the repertory of expression, continuity, interval, and rhythmic patterns assigned to it. Each is treated as an "individual," usually making an effort to cooperate, especially when this seems helpful in carrying on the musical enterprise. The work begins and concludes (Ex. 4) with each instrument contributing—sometimes the briefest fragments, each characterized in its own fashion—to a mosaic that joins these into one large, audible pattern, a concentrated version of the pattern of the entire work.

While the Second String Quartet deals with the separation of four instruments of more or less similar tone color, expressive qualities, dynamic capabilities, and performing techniques, the Double Concerto uses soloists of such different capacities that an entirely different approach seemed necessary. The problem in the Quartet, given the kind of concept behind it, was to differentiate instruments of similar character, while the problem in the Double Concerto, as I saw it, was to join together instruments of very different basic characteristics. The harpsichord, as is obvious, is dynamically much softer than the piano when both are playing their loudest; its attack is much more incisive, however, while its response to the fingers is more mechanical. Dynamic shadings, which are the basis of a pianist's technique, are almost unobtainable by touch on the harpsichord, which has, to compensate, at least on some models, a vast number of possible mechanical-registrational color changes. The idea, therefore, of contrasting two worlds of musical expression and sound had to be carried out quite differently. It should be obvious that the idea of allowing four (as in the case of the Quartet) or two (as in the Double Concerto) different streams of music to be heard together in any one of the possible uncoordinated ways that have been used by Ives and others in recent years will, from the point of view I am describing here, produce a form of entropy, a degrading of the possibilities of communication, which to me have ever to be revitalized and sharpened. Furthermore, while such works as mine do not always receive performances that present clearly all the materials, their relationships and expressive intentions, still, these are there in the score, and performers and listeners can gradually come to recognize them after successive performances. If they were to be played quite differently every time, as is the intention of most aleatory scores, there would be little possibility of learning to hear and interpret more and more of what is in the scores.

So, to join the piano and harpsichord into one world of music that could have many inner contrasts, I chose two small orchestras, each with two percussion players, and, since this was to be an antiphonal piece, the two orchestras contained instruments that would underline the qualities of the soloist they were associated with and, in the case of the harpsichord, add dynamic volume to supplement its lack of dynamic range. It might be objected that the

Example 4. Second String Quartet (1959), mm. 599–607.

harpsichord could be amplified to make up for this, but I have always pre-
ferred to hear instruments, as well as people, present themselves in their own
individual way without mechanical amplification, which gets in the way of direct contact, the whole point of a live concert. Under good acoustical and
well-rehearsed conditions the harpsichord is perfectly audible and balanced in

the way I consider effective for this piece. Because this work, as I got into it, took on the character of a percussion piece, with the soloists acting as mediators between unpitched percussion and pitched instruments, composing for percussion suggested certain ideas that do, indeed, have a rather "clock time" oriented attitude. This is especially true in the coda, which starts with a crash on the largest tam-tam and then is organized as a dying away of this crash over many measures, using the possible patterns of fading in and out of various partials in different phases of the sound-shape of the music, with each different phase filled with various character patterns recalling ideas from the whole work. Indeed, this piece, even more than the Second String Quartet, depends for its material on the sound of intervals, combined with various tone colors. Any figurative material that exists is directly derived from the intervallic sounds associated with each group and each section of the piece.

These works, as well as those previously mentioned, depend on a special dimension of time, that of "multiple perspective," in which various contrasting characters are presented simultaneously—as was occasionally done in opera, for example, in the ballroom scene from *Don Giovanni*, or in the finale of *Aida*. Double and sometimes manifold character simultaneities, of course, present, as our human experience often does, certain emotionally charged events as seen in the context of others, producing often a kind of irony, which I am particularly interested in. In doing this so frequently, and by leading into and away from such moments in what seemed to me telling ways, I have, I think, been trying to make moments of music as rich in reference as I could and to do something that can be done only in music and yet that has rarely been achieved except in opera.

The concept of the Second String Quartet and the Double Concerto had this dimension built into them, as does my Piano Concerto, which pits the "crowd" of the orchestra against the piano's "individual," mediated by a concertino of seven soloists. Here, the conflict was conceived as one of orchestral music that becomes more and more insistent and brutal as the work continues, while the piano makes more and more of a case for variety, sensitivity, and imagination. Over a very long stretch of time in the second of the two movements, the orchestral strings build up more and more dense, softly held chords, which form a kind of suffocating blanket of sound, while at the same time the rest of the orchestra plays patterns of strict, regular beats that increase in forcefulness and are layered into more and more different speeds. Against all this, the piano and instrumental soloists play much expressive, varied music, which near the end of the passage finally becomes more insistent, with the piano crowded into repeating one note, the one note missing in the middle of an aggregate of eighty-one other notes (Ex. 5).

Of course, in these works, all kinds of uses were made of metric modulation, both as a mode of proceeding smoothly or abruptly from one speed to another and as a formal device to isolate one section from another. Generally, these work together, for very often a new section with a different speed and character starts while another layer continues at the same speed. In the course of exploring metric modulation, the idea of dealing with accelerandi and

Example 5. Piano Concerto (1965), II, mm. 599–609 (two-piano reduction by the composer).

ritardandi intrigued me. The first notational solution of an accelerando, which speeds up regularly from beginning to end of a piece, occurred in the sixth variation of my Variations for Orchestra (1955), in which a scheme of six measures in 3/4 time speeds up during its course to three times its original pace, at which point there is a switch of notation, and a part previously playing quarter notes is written in triplets of eighths, while in other parts dotted quarters become eighths, dotted halves become quarters, and eighths become sextuplets of sixteenths. Yet, while each of these notational systems sounds as

Example 5. *(continued)*.

if it were continuing a regular acceleration, the beat has returned to the speed of that of the first beat of the six-measure scheme (Ex. 6). The entire variation is projected onto this scheme, which repeats itself over and over. Its usefulness here proved to be that the canonic theme could be brought in at different places in the scheme, so that successive entrances, if brought in sooner (for example, as a dotted half-note in m. 298), would sound slower, or, if brought in later, would sound faster. A whole pattern of total acceleration was thus achieved, for one of the final entrances occurs with the first note of the theme lasting the full six measures, the second note lasting the first three measures, the third note lasting the last three measures, the fourth to eighth

Variation 6

NOTE (for the conductor):
The *accelerando* extending over each group of six measures should be a
very regular speeding up from ♩ = 80 to three times that speed each time.
Figures such as that of the clarinet at measures 294–295, which extend
over the double-bar and change from quarters to triplets of eighths, should
sound as if they were continuing to accelerate in quarters.

Example 6. Variations for Orchestra, mm. 289–99.

notes lasting dotted halves, the next eighteen notes lasting quarters, and so
forth. Similarly, the place at which the triplets of the theme are stopped comes
later and later in the six-measure scheme, so that faster and faster notes are
heard, until triplets finally invade the very last measure, sounding the fastest
note values heard thus far. The matter of projecting regular beats against such

a pattern interested me, too. In this variation, the harp gives the impression of playing in slow, regular time the notes of one of the ritornelli against the music just described. Sometimes, systems of accelerations, retardations, and regular beating have been combined, as in the slow section of the Double Concerto (mm. 314–466) and in many short stretches of the Piano Concerto.

The Concerto for Orchestra of 1969 carries out the idea of waves of sound, used briefly in the coda of the Double Concerto, over a duration of more than twenty minutes. With this intention in mind, I started work, developing an overall dramatic and expressive plan and choosing the musical materials and form. After these had been clearly formulated, I came across the long poem *Vents* by the French poet who calls himself Saint-John Perse.[13] His Whitmanesque description of the United States swept by the winds of change seemed to revolve, as did the music I was writing, around four main ideas in the poem: (1) the drying up of autumn, suggesting the dryness and death of a previous time—men of straw in a year of straw; (2) the swiftness and freshness of the winds that blow away the old and bring the new; (3) the exhortation of a shaman-poet calling for a rebirth and a destruction of worn-out things; and, finally, (4) the return of spring and life. These ideas are brought together in many different contexts, blended and mixed as the poet constantly stresses the motions of the wind. The music, too, has four main characters, and, while hints of all four are being referred to constantly, the concerto picks out one facet after another to dwell on at some length, subordinating the others. Thus, while there can be said to be four movements, these are almost constantly heard in combination. The orchestra itself can be seated, when there is enough space, in such a way that the four strands of music are separated stereophonically as well as in timbre, material, and expression. The wind itself was thought of as being a composite of many elements, and the concerto treats the orchestra as groups of soloists, dividing each of the bodies of strings into five or more soloists that form the basis of each of the four sections: the celli, combined with harp, piano, wood percussion, and middle-register winds, are related to the autumnal rattling of pods and straw; the violins with flutes and metallic percussion, to the freshness of the wind; the basses, combined with tuba, timpani, and sometimes trombones, to the poet's invocations; and the violas, trumpets, upper-middle winds, and snare drums, to the reawakening.

Technically, the piece is constructed on a use of all the thirty-eight possible five-note chords (ten of which are symmetrical and twenty-eight invertible) that are distributed among the four movements, as shown in spacings typical of their movements in Example 7. Also shown is how the eleven two-note intervals, the twelve three-note chords, and the twenty-nine four-note chords, considered as components of the five-note chords, are distributed. (The inversions of the five-note chords and the seven-note chords, sometimes used, are

13. St.-John Perse, *Vents* (*Winds*), trans. Hugh Chisolm (New York: Pantheon, 1953); repr. in *St.-John Perse: Collected Poems—Complete Edition*, Bollingen Series Vol. 87 (Princeton: Princeton University Press, 1983), 225–357.

omitted in the example.) Rhythmically, each movement has its general tendency: movement I is formed of groups of retarding phrases, each starting a little faster than the previous (see Ex. 7); movement II starts very fast and gets slower throughout the entire work with each successive appearance; movement III is made up of accelerating phrases, each starting at a slower point (as in Ex. 7); while movement IV gets faster from beginning to end.

The work starts with an introduction, "These were very great winds over all the faces of this world,"[14] in which a twelve-tone chord is presented in four groups (or chords) of three notes (Ex. 8). Each of these groups forms the basis of one of the movements (as numbered), and "places" that movement in character in orchestration, tessitura, and general rhythmic behavior. Then, after a clamorous outburst, based still on a combination of the four basic materials, the other three movements subside and allow the dry rattling of the first movement to predominate (mm. 24–140). During this section, music from movement II makes several brief appearances, the most extended of which is at mm. 42–47. The same is true of fragments of movement III, as at mm. 117–20, and of IV, as at mm. 79–80. After a brief tutti, movement II proper starts (mm. 141–285), which suggests the freshness of the wind. Here, too, are occasional incursions of bits of other movements. This leads to a four-layered tutti that subsides into the recitative of the third movement (mm. 286–419). Finally, the fourth movement occupies most of mm. 420–532. This movement made its vestigial appearance in m. 30 at a slow speed that increased at each reappearance until its real emergence following m. 420, after which its speed continues to increase. The coda, from m. 532 to the end, is multilayered, alternating rapidly between the four sets of materials, which, at times, change their characteristic tessituras. The work finally dies away, sounding fewer and fewer notes of the characteristic chords of each movement.

The musical material of this Concerto is entirely built of similar and contrasting items of sound. Intervals and chords are the characterized immediacies, or "nows," out of which motions of constantly changing shapes flow. It is a work fundamentally organized to produce the "virtual image" of "passage" discussed above. As such, it has to do, at least to me, with an image of internal time-consciousness of which Edmund Husserl says:

> The sensible nucleus . . . is "now" and has just been and has been still earlier, and so on. In this now there is also retention of the past now of all levels of duration of which we are now conscious. . . . The stream of lived experience with its phases and intervals is itself a unity which is identifiable through reminiscence with a line of sight on what is flowing: impressions and retentions, sudden appearance and regular transformation, and disappearance and obscuration. This unity is originally constituted through the fact of flux itself; that is, its true essence is not to be, in general, but to be a unity of lived experience.[15]

---

14. Ibid., 226–27.

15. Edmund Husserl, *The Phenomenology of Internal Time-Consciousness*, ed. Martin Heidegger, trans. James S. Churchill (Bloomington: Indiana University Press, 1966), 149–57.

Movement I

(e) Rhythmic basis: groups of retarding phrases, each starting a little faster than the previous.

Movement II

(e) Rhythmic basis: starts very fast and gets slower throughout the entire work with each successive appearance.

Movement III

(e) Rhythmic basis: accelerating phrases, each starting at a slower point.

Movement IV

(e) Rhythmic basis: gets faster from beginning to end.

Example 7. Concerto for Orchestra (1969), technical aspects of each of the four movements:
a. five-note chords; b. four-note chords; c. three-note chords; d. two-note intervals;
e. general retarding or accelerating tendencies.

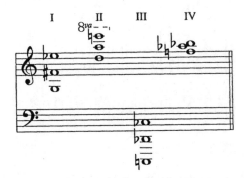

Example 8. Concerto for Orchestra. Compositional basis of each movement:
three-note chords that together constitute the twelve-note chord.

It should be obvious that the general approach to music rather fragmentarily presented here could be susceptible of exploration in many directions—that what I have done seems, even to me, like just a beginning both technically and artistically, although the works are meant to be considered primarily in themselves. It has cost considerable imaginative effort, since the artistic horizon of the American composer is not expanded by life in a society that is unable to furnish him with artistic and intellectual ideas and critiques of sufficient depth, clarity, and quality to be of much use. In fact, to have indulged in the foregoing explanations and to be faced with the prospect of their being used as a substitute for listening to the music itself and fed into the general hopper of American educational, artistic statements—later to be ground up and to come out as undifferentiated fodder to be forcibly fed to the young and permanently regurgitated at exams—is apparently the terrible fate of such efforts as these and the disheartening result of America's ambivalence toward the arts. Yet a composer cannot but be grateful for an opportunity to express verbally ideas important to him (for otherwise who would?) in the hope that they may be really helpful to a few others.

Perhaps the only consolation is that any such descriptive discussion as this has really consistently, although not intentionally, evaded the issues and visions most important and significant during the act of composing. For what is discussed here (as should be obvious, but never seems to be) is the outer shell, the wrapping of the music. The reason for writing it—for developing it in the way described, for weighing every note, chord, rhythm in the light of their expressive intention and their living, spontaneous interrelationships, and the judging of it all, almost unconsciously, against a private standard of what gives me genuine sensuous pleasure, of what seems fascinating, interesting, imaginative, moving, and of urgent importance—cannot be put into words. It is, I suppose, what is easily brushed off with words like *involvement* or *commitment* to music, as well as to what Perse somewhat portentously calls "the horror . . . and honor of living."[16]

16. Perse, *Vents*, 352–53.

"Elle est la musique en personne": A Reminiscence of Nadia Boulanger[1] (c.1985/95)

The first time I met Nadia Boulanger was at the end of a bus trip from Paris in early spring of 1932, when I asked the driver to stop where she had indicated in her letter, at the end of a long alley of linden trees which led to her house in Gargenville, near Juziers in the Seine valley west of Paris. It was in the late morning; we talked a good deal about many things in French, and she said, "Vous êtes comme nous, vous parlez si bien le français." And she invited me to lunch—kasha and a little salad—with her mother, Raïssa Ivanovna. As we talked I became absolutely fascinated by this extraordinarily lively woman who was so interested in contemporary music and so knowledgeable about it.[2]

When we first agreed that I would study with her, she asked me how much money I had, and I told her that I would be receiving a rather small allowance from my father annually, a thousand dollars a year. She asked me to pay her one half of that, but later revised her request when she discovered that it caused me a good deal of hardship (it was difficult to live in Paris, even in those days when everything was so cheap, on five hundred dollars a year): having learned, apparently from another student, that I was having to earn money by singing in the choir of the American church, copying music, and giving lessons in English, she generously offered to let me postpone my payments for lessons until I could afford them.

I remember that shortly after my first visit with her, we agreed that I would rent a room in a local farmhouse near her house and study with her during the summer, in the countryside of Gargenville. It was an absolutely fascinating time. Although she drove to Fontainebleau to teach a few days each week, there were those other days when she would call us up suddenly (there were other students boarding in farmhouses in the general area) and we would meet together and talk. Sometimes she would call us up after dinner and we would go for walks in the fields, often until very late at night, discussing music, art, and all sorts of matters. What I remember best from these conversations was a story she told about Maeterlinck and Georgette de Blanc, one of

1. The French embedded in Carter's title—"She is music personified"—was, according to Saint-John Perse, an aphorism of Paul Valéry's about Nadia Boulanger. Perse incorporated these words into his homage to Boulanger on the occasion of her eightieth birthday (1967). Carter, in turn, quotes this homage in his uncollected essay "France Amérique Ltd." (see Appendix 2). [B]

2. To illustrate her remarks she played little bits of Stravinsky, as well as music that I still remember, music that she returned to throughout my entire student period, the waltzes of Schubert. Much later, toward the end of my stay as a student, she used various of his waltzes in final exams in the history of music, invariably mystifying her students while at the same time illustrating the extraordinary range of types within one style of these beautiful pieces—for her students would identify one as by Chopin and another by Johann Strauss, still others by Richard Strauss and even Ravel.

his later wives, who was very determined to make her husband work hard in his old age and write as much as he could. She arranged a nice studio for him to work in every day, for most of the day, coming out only for lunch. However, he would never allow anyone to go into the room and locked it as soon as he went out so that no one could go in and clean. After many weeks of this regime, she finally broke into the room and discovered that Maeterlinck, instead of writing literature as he was supposed to have been doing, had been industriously making paper birds, filling the whole room with them. To be told this story by one's teacher was extraordinary; it seemed to indicate that you can lead a horse to water but you can't make him drink. This revealed the human side of Nadia, which perhaps more than anything else made her particularly endearing.

There were many different approaches which Mlle. Boulanger adopted toward her students. I remember occasionally bringing in incomplete compositional sketches, and she would always say "Ça c'est l'espoir"—that's hope. And she even told a story about Varèse, who had been in her class at the Conservatoire. Varèse, she said, used to bring in every week a little sketch of a few measures and the teacher, I've forgotten who it was (maybe Widor), would say, "Well, now, Mr. Varèse, this is very interesting, go on and finish it." And the next week there would be another little sketch, and the following week another different one; there was never anything finished, and finally the teacher got very angry and sent Varèse away from the class. Like so many of her stories, this one fascinated us—in this case because a few of us even then realized that Varèse was a very interesting composer, that he obviously had extraordinary ideas, but that he seemed to have great problems in carrying these ideas out for the length of a piece. He did not develop them in the way that was taught in the Conservatoire, so as a student he probably had a good deal of trouble in consequence.

Nadia would occasionally reverse her insistence on the strenuous discipline that she demanded of her students. She wanted me, for instance, to study piano with Annette Dieudonné, a lady who made me practice only exercises, arpeggios, and scales, because I didn't play the piano very well. I finally said to her that I couldn't stand the rigor of this particularly French approach, that it upset me a great deal to practice such exercises four, five, or six hours a day and never learn a piece. She understood that, and relented. Similarly, I remember the last time I saw her as a student, I was getting ready to leave for America from the little hotel that I lived in at 41 rue M. le Prince, Hotel Stella, that is still there, still has music students in it. She called off her classes, came over in her car, and helped me pack. I was a very disorderly and always rather confused young man, and so she made a list of the people she thought I ought to take presents home for; we agreed I must bring a present home for my mother, and another for my father, and we decided what kind of presents would be suitable. Then she went out and bought them. She also gave me a present, the *Pensées* of Pascal—very typical of her and a deeply touching reminder of her religious devotion. I still have those volumes.

All through the time I studied with her, there were similarly striking changes from very strict, rigorous demands to very human understanding. For instance, she always insisted that her students copy their counterpoint exercises very well. I made an effort to do so, and when I got to the stage where she found my copying praiseworthy, she then suggested that I might come to her house and copy parts for the Bach cantatas, which at that time she was having us perform at her apartment at the rue Ballu and for which parts were not then available in France. So I remember going at ten o'clock at night, after her lessons were over, and working in her dining room, being given an occasional small glass of whiskey to keep me awake, until two or three o'clock in the morning copying parts—and then having to struggle to get home. Mademoiselle lived, after all, near the Place Clichy, and I in the Latin Quarter on the other side of the city; late at night a bus ran once every hour to the Châtelet, where one had to change—all in all a very long and tedious route, especially when one was a little bit worried about walking around so late at night in my district and in the one where she lived. When I had spent quite a number of nights at this, she said, "You know, Carter, if you didn't copy so neatly and if there were spots of ink on your copying, I wouldn't ask you any more"; so I put a few spots of ink on my copying.

There were three kinds of private lessons that Mlle. Boulanger gave, at least to me. One of them was when I had done nothing, another when I had done harmony or fugal exercises, and a third when I brought in compositions. Sometimes the latter two were combined. When I brought in nothing she would give me a lecture about some subject that she felt I should know something about. Sometimes it was a lecture about care in workmanship, pointing out that a good workman took care of all the details, even those that were not immediately visible. She would turn over a chair, for instance, in the living room and show how the workmanship in that chair was not good, and that the fact that it hadn't been carefully worked on even in an invisible place somehow vitiated the effect of the chair, which if it had all been carefully worked at everywhere would have made a very much better, more beautiful and more striking impression. Or she would point out that even the more relaxed moments of Mozart or Stravinsky were not filled in with *pacotille* (cheap material) but with musically imaginative, valuable touches. At another time, she would discuss some piece of music she had been thinking about, perhaps one of the Bach cantatas we had been singing, or a mass by Josquin des Près, and she would call to my attention modulations, developments of themes, or linear beauties. Once I remember discussing the first movement of the first Beethoven string quartet, in which she observed that the motive at the beginning first jumps down to a lower note (C) and then immediately at its next appearance to a note one step higher (D), and that at the end of the movement this leads to a long scale which goes upwards step by step. In fact, this whole notion of step motive was very important at the time because Stravinsky's neoclassic works abounded in motives that moved step by step over long stretches of time, and gave the impression of growth and tension just by their upward or downward motion. I remember very vividly the lecture that she gave to me on Strauss's *Salome* when I asked her what to notice when I went to hear it that night at the Opéra. She played over the opening of *Salome* (a work that she really deplored) and brought to my attention that extraordinary slowly mounting chromatic scale in the strings, against which many different motives later to appear in the opera are projected, giving that strange, unearthly, and ominous sense of terror that pervades the work, established quietly yet intensely at the very beginning of it.

The second kind of lesson was usually given over to harmony exercises— or later to fugues, which I must say I wrote rather unsatisfactorily at that time, because the great problem with writing such academic exercises was making the enormous leap from the kind of counterpoint that we learned with her in her Ecole Normale classes, from the Dubois counterpoint book, to the Gedalge fugue book, which suddenly required us to write fugues that used stronger and more frequent harmonic progressions and required the kind of development of thematic structures that we had no experience in and had to learn by studying the works of Bach. I used to bring in fugues which were distressing to me because with the great familiarity I gained with the *Well-Tempered Clavier* (in fact, I played over a good deal of it almost every day of my entire student life), the despair one felt at the impossibility of writing something that had some similarity to Bach, some of the quality of Bach, was very crushing. However, I did write fugues, and she pointed out how one could get a great many different ideas out of one small motive, and how one could develop these, and she would play over examples from the *Well-Tempered Clavier* (which she knew by heart), showing how Bach could draw something even out of motives consisting of two notes a semitone apart. This was invaluable. She would take the prescribed fugue subject from Gedalge and improvise various kinds of fugal expositions, show how motives could be drawn to make transitional sections and different episodes. She made the most pedantic subjects reveal fascinating possibilities.

The third kind of lesson was devoted to looking over compositions. Two occasions I remember very well. One was when I had written a composition that used a great many parallel major sevenths. She pointed out to me that, while these were very intense intervals, when they are used in such an indifferent way, running around in parallel motion, they cease to have this intensity, and in fact soon become more tiresome to hear than thirds or sixths. Playing from memory the passage that uses this method in *Le Sacre du printemps* (rehearsal no. 94), she showed that it was effective because in between the parallel sevenths were trills that gave them an entirely different and much heightened harmonic meaning.[3] The other occasion came when she made a point about redundancy in a composition: that if one started a new section with a new idea and then, once that was under way, returned to the idea of the

3. Around 1968, my wife visited southern Tunisia with Darina Silone and brought back a rather primitively made type of musette which had two pipes and two mouthpieces closely bound together, so that both pipes were stopped together as the holes were adjacent to each other. On it one played scales and tunes in parallel (approximate) minor seconds—which called to mind this passage from Stravinsky.

previous section, one would spoil all the freshness of that new idea. And she played, as I remember, an example of this from a work by Igor Markevitch, saying that she had tried to dissuade him from doing this, but that he had insisted that that was the way it had to be done. Very much later, as I wrote my Double Concerto, I reached that point where, at the end of the long introduction, the piano starts playing its second movement (an Allegro scherzando), only to be immediately stopped by a long cadenza from the harpsichord—and I recalled that lesson and amused myself by doing quite the opposite of the redundant practice that Nadia had criticized, by introducing the next movement before the previous movement was over and having it sidetracked but finally having it taken up again more decisively.

Various kinds of drills emerged from these lessons. To help us learn how to write fugues effectively, Nadia encouraged us to play at the piano two parts of a three-part fugue, or three parts of a four-part fugue, while singing the omitted part. I went through a good many fugues of the *Well-Tempered Clavier* in this fashion, trying as I did so to memorize the parts linearly. There was a constant pushing of one's technique. Of course, the sense of what it was to be a professional, to be highly trained, was always self-evident to us from our contact with Nadia Boulanger, who had extraordinary skills of every kind: a very good ear, an ability to sight-read the most difficult complicated orchestral scores at the piano and to sing operas at sight with convincing dramatization—also an ability to grasp the character of the music that she was involved with, when she conducted madrigals or any other music. Her wonderful recording of Monteverdi, for instance, shows very clearly that she was well aware of how to make the character of the different madrigals come out vividly—an ability that extended to any repertoire, from Bach cantatas to contemporary music. She also held to what was considered important in the 1930s and '40s, the notion of maintaining a very strict, almost rigid tempo in the course of a piece. She used to imitate the way in which Paderewski played Chopin, keeping the left hand, the waltz or mazurka rhythm, very strict and with the right hand playing a kind of rubato. She pointed out how this rhythmic drive, so characteristic of Stravinsky, gave music a type of dramatic character and power that it would never have if it were played with the kind of rubato favored by many performers, which she was always deploring; even in illustrating to us the most Romantic music, she would give it a strong rhythmic propulsion. Although there might be slight variations and slight rubati within the small phrase, the big sense of rhythmic progress was something she treasured very deeply and encouraged us all to appreciate. I remember distinctly also that we were much concerned with the upbeat in music, with the upbeat for instance in Bach—which it seemed to me she always sought to find as soon after the previous downbeat as possible. If the first beat of the piece was on the downbeat, that was the end of an unheard phrase and almost immediately after that, the upbeat to the next measure started. This, I think, came from the views of Mathis Lussy and also perhaps from Riemann; Mademoiselle made us very aware of this dramatic and important quality. It was really not anti-Romanticism so much as a way of projecting even Romantic music, giving it a dramatic forward motion that perhaps was not characteristic of performances, let us say, in the time of Liszt or even of Chopin.

Mlle. Boulanger was very loyal in her tastes and her allegiance to certain composers, especially the French composers—Debussy and Ravel, of course, and also Gabriel Fauré, whom she had known. We used to argue quite often about Fauré because it seemed to me that the instrumental works, especially the later ones, were disturbing, being so repetitious. The works seemed to be built on a series of beautiful harmonic changes, but also on routinely literal transpositions of whole sections. Of course to me the songs were very beautiful, but what bothered me also was that the late songs had such very thin accompaniments that it was difficult for them to be projected under normal concert hall conditions. This was something that we discussed occasionally and had some disagreement about. However, the very refined and subtle quality of Fauré's harmonic changes, combined with the extreme simplicity of his figurative language, such as conventional arpeggios, and also his melodic lines which often just moved up and down scales, was something that Nadia considered a very beautiful restraint and an elegance that I must say to a certain extent her students were called upon to admire. And certainly the works of Stravinsky that were written during the period of my study, like *Perséphone*, showed a certain similarity to Fauré, although I imagine Stravinsky would have been the first to deny it: that is, a classical restraint, which at the same time had a touching loveliness to it, especially characteristic of the more lugubrious works of Fauré, such as the late song cycles: *L'Horizon chimérique, Mirages, Le Jardin clos*, all of which had a languorous, melancholy nostalgia and revealed a quality so *fin de siècle* French.

The atmosphere of crisis that arose in Paris around the same time I arrived there persisted throughout the whole period of my studies—in fact, it became steadily worse, with the Reichstag fire, the trial of Dimitrov and van der Lubbe, Hitler's sudden dominance of Germany, and the onset of the dramatic series of events that would lead, finally, to the outbreak of the Second World War. In Paris it was a time of massive unemployment, because the French were having a hard time economically; the franc was very low against the dollar and it was quite cheap for Americans to live there. Although the time was very troubled, many distinguished people continued to live in Paris, such as James Joyce and Gertrude Stein, who were championed by Sylvia Beach. I knew Sylvia Beach very well, from her Shakespeare and Company bookstore where I went frequently to borrow books and to buy them when I could afford it. There was a constant stream of refugees from Germany as Hitler gained more and more power. Many of these refugees came to Paris and began to participate in the musical life there, all the while having a hard time getting along. People like Kurt Weill lived in Paris for a while, as well as quite a few lesser-known composers, some of whom became friends of mine. Despite the difficult conditions of that era, Mlle. Boulanger was not terribly sympathetic; she was preoccupied with her work, with teaching music, with France, and she kept all this aspect of the times at a distance. No one, however, could have ignored the explosion of the Stavisky affair, with shooting and killing on one violent night in the Place de la Concorde and elsewhere. We had a counterpoint lesson at the Ecole Normale the next day, and in order to attend class I had to walk across several miles of a terrified Paris, since the Métro was no longer working. Mademoiselle was there, of course, but when most of her students failed to appear, she said, with melancholy bitterness: No matter what happens, music must go on. This very devotedly professional attitude, I must say, greatly impressed me at the time, amidst all the very complicated political and artistic matters that occupied our attention then. Certainly this particular point of view could not have failed to exert a powerful appeal, this sense that music was much greater than any of us; and that it had to live and persist was something that carried me and many of her students, as well as many other musicians, through difficult periods in our lives.

The great project that went on throughout my entire student period was the exploration of the Bach cantatas. We students met every Wednesday afternoon and read through one, two, or three cantatas, singing the choruses, while there were usually vocal soloists like Doda Conrad and Hugues Cuenod and performers who came to play the obbligato solo and orchestral string parts. And since there was an organ in her apartment, we were able to give rather creditable readings of one cantata after another with Mlle. Boulanger pointing out the wonders, the details, the word-painting, the modulations, the imitations, the counterpoint, the wonderful structure of line, that have remained indelibly fixed in the minds of my contemporaries. She herself, of course, was one of the pioneers in this intense concern with the Bach cantatas, which are only now becoming available on recordings. We even performed the best cantatas, those that were particularly well liked, publicly in the Salle Cortot de l'Ecole Normale or at private gatherings, such as those of the Princesse de Polignac. It soon became apparent to us that Stravinsky himself was interested in the Bach cantatas as well as in Renaissance and pre-Renaissance music, and very often we would discuss his use of material from these various sources in the music he was writing at the time, such as the *Duo concertant* and *Perséphone*. As I look back on our readings of the cantatas, sung always in German with Mademoiselle correcting our pronunciation, I cannot help but think how remarkable this enterprise was in view of the anti-German feeling prevalent in France at the time.

When she conducted the cantatas, even when she played accompaniments for Romantic songs such as those of Schumann or Fauré, or of the early Baroque such as Monteverdi, Mlle. Boulanger taught us to feel an inexorable, constant beat, a push forward regularly like the march of time throughout the work. This gave the piece of music its forward motion and a great sense of continuity. There was no dwelling, so to speak, on beautiful moments, but these passed one after the other without being lingered upon, put into sharp focus by her beautiful sense of phrasing. This was one of the ways we were encouraged to play, hear, imagine, and appreciate music, and of course another element was *la grande ligne*, the long line of the music that flowed from beginning to end in one grand melodic sweep. Mlle. Boulanger was very fond of showing how Beethoven achieved this, and also Bach and Mozart. We were constantly encouraged to think about this particular aspect of large-scale continuity in its linear and rhythmic sense—certainly an invaluable lesson. We were shown how these formed the backbone of one work after another, especially the Bach cantatas.

These Wednesday afternoons were remarkable for another reason, for after we had played and sung through the Bach cantatas, there would be a large tea party, served in great style with all kinds of cakes, and with many guests. We occasionally met Paul Valéry, Igor Markevitch, Raymond Duncan in bare dirty feet. Many of the important intellectual people of that time in Paris came, and the students were always very grateful to be able to talk to them during these Wednesday afternoons. Mme. Boulanger, Raïssa Ivanovna Michetsky, was always a very charming and amusing hostess on those occasions. She had been brought up with a different point of view about music: she used to complain that those Bach cantatas were a little severe for her taste and wished we would occasionally sing an operetta to lighten the atmosphere. The deceased father Boulanger had been an operetta composer, but Raïssa Ivanovna, so it was said, was the one who accompanied her daughters Lili and Nadia to their classes at the Conservatoire and made sure they did their homework.

Although even here, in such large courses, there seems to have been a re-solve to maintain a strict and very ordered discipline, in fact Nadia Boulanger was very fond of varying this discipline, even breaking away with a sense of freedom and exploration, always willing to try a new approach. She never seems to have given these Wednesday afternoons in the same way from one period to another. In previous years, for instance, she had focused on the Beethoven string quartets, and in the 1920s, I learned from Aaron Copland, they were devoted to Berg's *Wozzeck*. Many years later, coming to visit her at a Wednesday after the Second World War, I heard her going through De-bussy's *Le Martyre de Saint Sébastien* with the students singing the choruses. She was always pushing forward, never repeating herself and always finding a fresh new point of departure. Over the years, this was in itself an extraordi-nary lesson in self-renewal. She was not a woman who did anything by rote; although it is true that on one level she expected the student to have all the technical skills resulting from rote, like playing the piano, solfège, figured bass, transposition, everything very highly developed, nevertheless from that point on there was always a sense of adventure. While doing lessons, for in-stance, she would suddenly remember a passage from Mozart's *Idomeneo*. I remember that famous "Placido il mar" from *Idomeneo* which she brought out to me at one lesson, showing how beautifully the chorus was written, how fine and sensitive were the part writing and voice leading, and how the murmuring accompaniment never obscured the part writing of the chorus.

The curiosity of Nadia Boulanger was insatiable, not only about music, but about a wide variety of other things, including languages and literature. When I was a student, she was memorizing the sonnets of Shakespeare, in English, one after the other, practically one per night, it seemed, for she was appar-ently a chronic insomniac. I was very often called upon to listen to her recite them and to correct her pronunciation. This curiosity of course extended to other music at a time (1932–35) when the vast corpus of Renaissance and pre-Renaissance music was beginning to be brought to light, published, performed, and intensively discussed. She was right in the forefront of all this musicological exploration. We would come upon her one week full of ideas about Guillaume de Machaut, and the next week she would be carried away by Monteverdi, or Janequin, or Claude Gervaise. At the same time she would be looking over new works by contemporary composers like Hindemith, so that we found her full of insights and appreciations that were quite new and very refreshing. At the same time in Paris there were, of course, the activities of Henri Expert, Guillaume de Van, and others who presented the French madrigal and earlier music. I remember hearing an entire concert of Perotin in the lower level of the Ste. Chapelle sung and played on "old" instruments, which many of us found absolutely fascinating. When we discussed such things with Mlle. Boulanger, she shared in our enthusiasm. Her curiosity extended into painting too. I remember that extraordinary day in Venice when she, having memorized the guide book to Venice—a city which she was visiting for the first time—led me around to see paintings by painters that I would never have expected to see in remote churches that she had learned about. This kind of curiosity is something that we don't expect to see much anymore, yet it is one of the things that (quixotically perhaps) I find myself imagining to exist in the audiences for which I write my music: the same kind of curiosity that I have and that all people have whom I have known and admired, the curiosity to find out what is new, to assess it, and to try to come to terms with it.

The way in which Nadia Boulanger's interest extended into all sorts of fields—music foremost among them of course—was something that I encountered with renewed appreciation long after my student years, at frequent intervals throughout the rest of her life. I remember once in the late 1950s when the Domaine Musical brought the Südwestfunk Orchester, with Hans Rosbaud conducting, to the Salle Pleyel to play Schoenberg's *Five Pieces for Orchestra* (op. 16), Berg's *Three Pieces* (op. 6), and Webern's *Six Pieces* (op. 6). These works at the time were seldom played, and I had never heard them played well. I knew that Rosbaud was an excellent conductor—he had conducted my Variations in 1956 or '57—and I was very eager to hear this concert, as well as a rehearsal. This was possible, as I was passing through Paris at the time. I managed to get into the Salle Pleyel for a rehearsal, and the only other person in this huge hall, sitting in the audience, was Nadia Boulanger with the three scores of the three works to be played. She asked me to sit with her, and we followed the scores closely, listening, she making comments all the while—particularly about Berg, whose music she said sounded like the seasick music (*musique de mal de mer*) that her students used to write in the 1920s. She was very impressed however with the Webern score, and especially by the performance that Rosbaud gave. Then much later, very near the end of her life, six months before she died, I happened to be in London and came to Paris, not only to see her, but also to hear the last performance Boulez gave of *Lulu* at the Paris Opera. I visited her at 36 rue Ballu. Her illness made her unable to move, but in spite of that she was amazingly lively. The first thing she said to me was about *Lulu*—that it may be a *chef d'oeuvre* but was certainly hard on the nerves (*ça tape sur les nerfs*). Although I had never mentioned to her that I was going that evening to *Lulu*, this was the first thing she greeted me with. Then we discussed at great length the merits of Dallapiccola's music, which she admired a great deal, and among many other musical things the works of Boulez. She was very interested in his musicianship and his remarkable imagination.

Many young Americans going to college, both in my time and since, were more educated in artistic appreciation than in artistic skill; I knew contemporary music very well, and was fascinated by the many new works that were being played in Boston and New York during the 1920s and early '30s. When I came to compose music during my late twenties and early thirties, however, my efforts seemed to me primitive and, very naturally, infuriatingly inferior to the kind of music that I admired. For, being untrained, I was totally unable to approximate in any way on my own what I thought was excellent. This distress led me, finally, to look beyond America for my further education. I had first studied as a graduate student at Harvard, where Walter Piston had just returned from studying with Nadia Boulanger, and when I graduated with an M.A. in 1932 I decided in turn to go to her, the only teacher I knew except for Schoenberg who took contemporary music seriously and was willing to teach it. As I think back over these fifty years, it seems to me that I must have been very much like some of the students who apply to Juilliard and are turned down because they appear so inept. My own ineptitude worried me deeply, and I was willing to do anything to learn how to overcome it, and to gain the kind of command I would need to write the kind of music I aspired to write.

To help, Mlle. Boulanger had me return to elementary harmony exercises and work through all five species of strict academic counterpoint up to eight parts. She watched over my progress in these with enormous care. I would bring in a group of harmony exercises and realizations of figured basses of Dubois that were very standardized and dreary. And I must say that my results were often that way too. Mademoiselle would show that, if the voice leading were slightly different, the result would be more expressive and much more musical. She would change an exercise around a little bit and, in explaining why, completely convince one that it was much better that way. I was very much more at home in the counterpoint class: it wasn't long before I was able to write those long strings of half-note suspensions or strings of quarter notes that moved up and down in graceful curves while still fitting into the very rigid rules of the old Cherubini-derived Dubois counterpoint book which we used. In fact, Mlle. was insistent on stricter rules than those adhered to in the Cherubini style, which of course in its turn had come down from Padre Martini. She was very fussy about this—no hidden octaves, no hidden fifths, passing notes could not be left unresolved, many details of this sort—and we gradually learned, within a very rigid framework, how to write musically interesting lines. Since I had also been very much absorbed in Renaissance music before I came to Paris, and since while I lived there I sang in Henri Expert's chorus, the use of counterpoint especially in the Renaissance was something that I loved very much and used as a model. Over the three years I studied with Nadia Boulanger, I developed a considerable skill in writing in an elegant style two-, three-, four-, five-, six-, seven-, and eight-part counterpoint, double choruses, canons, and invertible counterpoint. In these exercises I experimented with all sorts of patterns I found in Renaissance music, which pleased Mlle. Boulanger a great deal. This was my most fruitful work as a student. I continued to compose discouraging pieces that seemed never to approach the quality that I wanted, though I struggled very hard to attain it. I don't think these impressed Mlle. Boulanger very much either. I was a great admirer, for instance, of Bartók, and in those years she was not much interested in his work. She had been at one time but now felt that this was an older, excessively dissonant style, and she was more attracted to a newer, neoclassic, more formalized language like that of Stravinsky from the period of the *Symphonie de psaumes* up to that of *Perséphone*. I tried very hard to write my kind of music, and I received a good deal of criticism because she felt that what I was doing—and I agreed—didn't embody what I wanted from myself, was not comparable to the quality of the counterpoint exercises that I was able to produce rather easily. So after my several years' study, at the end of 1935, I came back to America feeling that I hadn't yet learned how to compose as I wanted to. And really it was not until about 1936 or 1937 that I began to be able to write the kind of music that really interested and satisfied me, like the *Tarantella*, rather a derivative work I guess, but with what might be considered a good deal of liveliness and freshness, and some other music for a Latin play given by the Harvard Classical Club in 1936, Plautus's *Mostellaria*. (It is actually hard to say exactly at what stage of development I began to feel the balance of dissatisfaction and satisfaction with my own work tilt slightly toward the latter, since the balance between the two has always been nearly even at the time of completion of any work, and it is only after a considerable time that I can get any real satisfaction from it.)

Thinking back to more than fifty years ago when I first began my studies with Boulanger, what I remember most was what was for me a violent return to the pedagogical methods that my French governess inculcated during my early childhood: rote learning, the imposition of what seemed like almost impossible and apparently pointless exercises to "strengthen the intellectual muscles." In the case of Boulanger, to play the piano with reversed hands, so that left played what was written for right and vice versa, was like conjugating all those irregular (but never used) French verbs in the past subjunctive and so forth that I learned as a child. Between that time and my study with Boulanger, I had gone to more or less progressive schools in New York where there was little emphasis on memorization and much on puzzle solving and that sort of thing. So the return to this earlier way of learning was very difficult for me. Now, I still remember vast quantities of useless French verbs and much less of what is in more common use.

As I look back at it, while the teaching of Mlle. Boulanger was in many ways immediately effective, it produced no real result until a number of years after I had left. What I actually learned from her is still somewhat undefinable: a deep devotion to music, a sense of responsibility, an ability to pay careful attention to each note. She was always drawing attention to the detail, even in the simplest harmony exercises. Even in one that was correct, so to speak, with no fifths or octaves, still she would show that within this small frame it was possible to do things that made a very real musical sense, and that if done slightly differently made no sense at all. And there was a constant developing of the standard of what it was to have, say, an elegant line, or a strongly characterized one—all sorts of very different characters that could be incorporated into even the simplest kind of music, like a harmony or counterpoint exercise.

I still have a feeling that I learned much less about actual composition from her at the time, although I am sure that all the criticisms of all my compositions were very helpful. They didn't really bear fruit until much later. She herself, indeed, was surprised a good many years later, in 1943, during the Second World War, when she lived in Boston, and I brought my song *Voyage* to her. She said that it was a very striking piece (*très frappant*)—though not much more than that, which upset me somewhat. Then later, in 1952, when my First String Quartet was played in Paris, she came to the concert, and afterwards she said, looking me very strongly in the eye, "Carter, I never thought you would write anything like that!" Again, I didn't know whether it was a compliment or not, but in any case it somehow suggested her recognition that I had begun to achieve what as a student I had been unable to do.

The extraordinary example of personal quality that Nadia Boulanger set was really what was important, and this remained a kind of fundamental pattern that influenced her students throughout their lives. It was an impressive view of life and art, impelling one to make important demands on oneself, to pay strict attention to the material of the music and to make the very best choices one could, choices that were, one hoped, beautiful and also particularly eloquent. I have a feeling that I never would have composed the kind of music I began to produce around 1940 if I hadn't been taught this human lesson. It was not only a special kind of personal contact; it was a vision of music, and of how wonderful, how impressive, sensitive, moving, and eloquent music could be. The ideals of workmanship, of care, of detail, and of large conception she instilled very deeply, and they have remained ever living in a way that I do not think any other teacher could ever have made them for me.

Reminiscence of Italy
(1988)

My first memory of Italy comes from a trip to Venice, Florence, and Rome with my mother, in the early 1920s. The smell of the canals in Venice from the windows of the old Danieli Hotel and the pigeons of the piazza San Marco are all I remember of Venice; I cannot remember anything of Florence, but I do recall very clearly the old Hotel de Russie in Rome on the corner of the via del Babuino and the piazza del Popolo in the building where the present RAI offices are. We ate out of doors at the foot of the Pincian gardens in the evening and during the day took a Cook's tour which included an audience with the Pope. At this, my mother, whose parents had come from the North of Ireland and who was violently anti-Catholic, told me not to kiss the Pope's ring as it would certainly have germs on it. Disobediently, I did, and my mouth was wiped (secretly) by my mother's handkerchief. I had been greatly impressed with the seriousness of the occasion and the solemnity with which everything was accomplished and felt it was an important act to kiss the ring, in spite of the germs.

As I grew up and became more politically conscious, and began to read books such as Silone's *Fontamara*, I repressed whatever desire to visit Italy that I had. This desire was developing nevertheless during my college years at Harvard, where I read Dante, Pirandello, and Croce, and began to study music and art. Even in the late 1920s and the '30s, new things from Italy aroused my interest: paintings by Campigli, Severini, de Chirico, and others, and performances of works by Gian Francesco Malipiero, such as his *Sette canzoni* played in New York, as well as Ottorino Respighi's *La campana sommersa* and Alfredo Casella's *La giara* at the Metropolitan Opera. And for several years, when Casella conducted the Boston Pops (popular concerts played by the Boston Symphony after the regular season), we were privileged to hear many works of Ravel, Debussy, Stravinsky, and others including those of Casella. I followed all of his efforts to present new works in Boston during that time with great enthusiasm.

During the period of my studies with Nadia Boulanger in Paris, from 1932 to 1935, my interest in things Italian overcame my dislike of Fascism and I made, as I recall, two trips to Italy. One I remember vividly was on a special round-trip fare during an Anno Santo (perhaps 1933) when, in order to get the free trip back to Paris, I had to go through a Fascist exhibition in the Exhibition Palace on the Via Nazionale, showing all the rather bloody triumphs of the Duce. Already some of the wonders of Rome were beginning to come alive for me; at that time, like many young intellectuals of my age, I was only interested in Romanesque, Medieval, and modern art, and I searched around Rome avoiding (fashionably) the Renaissance and Baroque. Shortly after that, I visited Florence and Venice during Easter with Ruskin's books in hand looking at mosaics, painting, and sculpture made before Giotto. I had meanwhile visited many Romanesque churches in France—for to me, with the political ideas I had then, this was the real art of the people, as opposed to the decadence that set in with the upper-class art of the Renaissance and later.

It was on this trip that I saw Nadia Boulanger in Venice; although she was visiting the city for the first time herself, she led me around (having memorized the Guide Bleu), giving the gondoliers instructions in quite good Italian, walking into churches she had never seen and pointing to unusual paintings in dark corners more professionally (and intelligently) than if she had been a guide. Later she called me "conventional" for not ordering iced coffee with panna at the Caffe Florian where she took me at the end of the morning before lunch.

In 1953–54, I was awarded a Prix de Rome and came to the American

Academy with my wife and small son. Although we could have stayed for two or three years, I decided to stay only one year because we had to rent an apartment outside the Academy, on the via Trebbia, and I did not enjoy traveling from the piazza Fiume to the Janiculum (where my studio was) every day—and because the Fellowship money I received from the Academy did not even cover the rent, not to mention the cost of the American school for my son, where he was not too happy. During that year, however, Nicolas Nabokov, a good friend and, at that time, director of the Congrès pour la liberté de la culture, was composer-in-residence at the American Academy and organized a large contemporary music festival in Rome in the spring of 1954 at which was presented my First String Quartet. This work made, apparently, some impression on three Italian composers whom I esteem highly, Goffredo Petrassi, Roman Vlad, and Luigi Dallapiccola, each of whom congratulated me and became a lifelong friend.

The following year Petrassi was elected president of the ISCM, and Vlad and I vice-presidents, and we met at the ISCM festival, held in Baden-Baden in 1955. During my 1953 stay in Rome I composed most of my Variations for Orchestra and have returned there to the American Academy each time I planned to write a large work. In 1963 I wrote much of my Piano Concerto there, in 1968 my Concerto for Orchestra, in 1979–80 my piano piece *Night Fantasies*—for there I have been able to concentrate for long periods and have had the great pleasure of seeing my Italian friends and visiting the art in Rome that I love, which now includes not only that of the Renaissance but that of the Mannerists and the Baroque sculptors, painters, and architects.

Italy has shown me great kindness: the three concerts of my music in a single day at the Venice Biennale of 1981; the performances at the Pontino Festival, at the Accademia Filharmonica, and at the RAI in Torino and Rome; the invitation to talk on musical expressionism at the Maggio Fiorentino of 1964; the Premio delle Muse, "Polimnia," given at the Palazzo Vecchio in Florence in 1969 by the Associazione Artistico Letteraria Internazionale; and the booklet of my writings translated into Italian and published by the Scuola Civica di Musica di Milano in 1986,[1] as well as the present publication of the translation of David Schiff's book[2]—all of these, among many others, are evidence of Italian interest in my work, for which I am profoundly grateful.

1. See special issue of *I Quaderni della Civica Scuola di Musica* (Milan), no. 12 (April 1986), dedicated to Elliott Carter and ed. Alessandro Melchiorre.

2. David Schiff, *Elliott Carter*, Italian trans. Francesca Pontani Wagner and Raffaele Pozzi, I edizione italiana aggiornata dall'Autore [includes complete text of *The Music of Elliott Carter* as published in 1983 by Eulenberg Press along with additional material by Schiff, some of it previously published in English as separate articles, together with seven articles headed "Scritti di Elliott Carter"] (Naples and Rome: Edizione scientifiche italiane, 1990). "Ricordo dell'Italia" appears on pp. 567–70.

VI

Philosophy, Criticism, and the Other Arts

More about Balanchine
(1937)

In these last months we have had the good fortune to see three excellent examples of George Balanchine's choreography well rehearsed and well presented by the American Ballet troupe.

Most modern American and German dancers return directly to the gestures of primitive ritual or the miming of basic physiological activities. Balanchine treats these matters within the Petipa ballet tradition, a frame that theatricalizes by making everything more objective, and which he revitalizes by bringing it close to our present feelings. This tradition gives coherence and intelligibility to raw material that in itself has little more than ethnological interest. With these elements he has developed a type of choreography singularly poignant and poetic as well as new and original. Though at times resembling it in outward method, it is in direct contrast to Modern Dance technique.

A great difference between these two types of dancing is in the interrelations of the people on the stage. Modern Dance generally shows us individuals in the throes of self-induced emotions, who by their apparent disregard of the looker-on seem to move within a ritual like that of the church. Groups of individuals also take part in these ritual dances without contact, apparently swayed by a simultaneously experienced emotion. The relationships are not human and emotional; they might exist between schools of small fish. Sometimes we see satirical situations such as the genius-hero being tortured at the hands of a fantastic society conjured up for the occasion without any social validity.

In Balanchine's world, relationships are expressed in lyrical terms. Being of our times they often have some trouble, but this makes them the more appealing and immediate.

For Stravinsky's *Baiser de la fée*, which pays homage to Petipa in its choreography as the music does to Tchaikovsky, Balanchine invented some of the finest soli and *pas de deux* since the days of the Imperial Ballet. In the third scene the formal numbers between Gisella Caccialanza and William Dollar, remarkable for their tenderness, brilliance, compactness, and variety, are strictly within the classic tradition. This type of invention is as rare as it is important. For instance, in the Paris performance done by Bronislava Nijinska, the solo variations were boring, dull, and badly planned, so that the whole work was spoiled. Balanchine's worked-out steps were frequently more interesting than the music though he always followed it closely and sensitively.

The *Card Party* [*Jeu de cartes*] (in which William Dollar as the joker danced with brilliance and imagination) has a rather untheatrical libretto, for a pack of cards is a pack of cards and gives little chance for contrast. Balanchine invented a choreography that had to be followed carefully to be appreciated, as all its effects were microscopic. He interpreted the cards as a comic, perverse society and avoided any of the serious implications of the gaming house with its atmosphere of tension and of suicidal anxiety, a suggestion of which might have added body to the work. In the dancing itself there was many a reference to jazz, which is certainly a good way of revivifying ballet technique and skillfully added to the general grotesquerie and cuteness of the ballet.

Apollon musagète, seen by a few early comers, was Balanchine's masterpiece. Though in part a reprise of his former choreography for Diaghilev, it was less static and had greatly gained in feeling since its Parisian performance. The jerks from one statuesque pose to another were no longer in evidence and in their place was a very beautiful plasticity having both nobility and repose.

No one has ever worked out flow in dancing as well as Balanchine. In *Apollon*, as in his *Serenade*, there was a constant line of movement which bound all the steps together and never ceased until the curtain fell. There was something magical and stirring about this drawing of invisible lines in the air. The solo variations were very fine creations, especially those of the three muses, showing a highly creative imagination at work in every small detail. Balanchine's greatest successes have been in this lyric and poetic vein, as in *Errante* and *Orpheus*.

With the Dancers
(1938)

When I consider how often large, official artistic ventures miscarry, I must admit that the Dance International (which was held all through the month of December) did a real service in bringing American ballet and the modern dance to a larger public than they usually reach. There were, of course, more than a few "society" events of mediocre quality at the Rainbow Room and bad exhibits of costumes and scenery. But the two performances at the Centre Theatre were justly successful in showing where America stood in the two fields. There was a minimum of attempt to play down to the public and a maximum to attain a high artistic standard. The films of exotic dancing were also an excellent feature of this mammoth project.

The ballet, by its very nature and background, is easily led into vulgarization; its evening went farther in that direction than in that of Modern Dance, especially as three Broadway entertainers, Patricia Bowman, Paul Haakon, and Paul Draper, were on the program. Nevertheless the two men at least showed how remarkable a technical development ballet and tap have reached in the commercial theatre. The ballet groups were more serious.

Catherine Littlefield's troupe, always astonishing for its great number of performers, gave a better performance than usual, probably because the choreography had only the most elementary quadrille steps and contained a great deal of the obvious pantomime in which her troupe is most at home. *Barn Dance* was an amusing piece based on fiddler tunes in conventional arrangements. It caught in a showy way the atmosphere of these social dances and proved a pleasant piece of Americana. José Limon and Felicia Sorel carried the Dance Centre's otherwise uninteresting performance of *El Amor Brujo* with some intense Spanish tantrums of the expected kind.

The Ballet Caravan's *Showpiece*, to a specially commissioned score from Robert McBride, was the only group work with any notable dancing during the evening. It showed in a fresh new way how well each of the members of the small company danced, how able they were despite a certain immaturity. The work has a great deal in its favor. There is little fuss and pretension about it. Straightforward, with no attempt to build up an elaborate atmosphere, it shows young people doing ballet dances in bright costumes before a black curtain. Throughout, the choreography was ingenious and, within the limitations of the classic steps, had imagination. Probably because of a certain formlessness and lack of emphasis in the music, the ballet did not achieve a natural and theatrical articulation. This somewhat clouded the brilliance of the dancing.

The Modern Dance evening of the festival was a summary of what the courageous people in this city have achieved in the last ten years of hard work. It began at the beginning of the movement, Ruth St. Denis coming out of her retirement to perform some of those Oriental numbers that still, as in *White Jade*, retain the beauty and delicacy of gesture for which she is renowned. Like Swinburne's Greece or Rossetti's Middle Ages, Ruth St. Denis's Orient is superficial and false, but it is theatrical.

The remainder of the program was devoted to Martha Graham, Doris Humphrey, Charles Weidman, Tamiris, Hanya Holm, and their groups, dancers who have gained a large and enthusiastic audience and who are supported on every hand. Personally I cannot share this enthusiasm. In making the following attack I believe that I am also voicing the opinions of many who, like myself, are concerned with the future of dancing in this country.

Once Miss St. Denis's pupils, though now in violent reaction against her prettiness, Graham, Humphrey, and Weidman have continued her tendency to falsify. Instead of misrepresenting the Orient, which is pardonable and perhaps necessary to a culture so basically different, they misrepresent our contemporary American life to us. For they show it in the light of a special state of mind, that of the Germans right after the war, suicidal, hysterical, and not typical of the rest of life, then or now. In America, famine, inflation, and complete disillusionment have not existed on a large enough scale to be part of our common background; they remain a matter of speculation to most of those who attend the dance recitals. If these tragic things are to be shown strongly they must reveal a more cogent point of view.

Each performance at the Centre Theatre, after Miss St. Denis's, presented a group of discontented, unhappy, tortured, self-destructive people on the stage. This naturally arouses a feeling of pity and sympathy in the audience and leaves it with little respect or interest in the performers as artists. Instead of giving the audience a dance work to enjoy or be instructed by, the adherents of this school present themselves as people acting under an intense emotional strain. And, as if this were not embarrassing enough, they appear to be quarreling with and loathing the audience. Every gesture that might take on a meaning if fitted into context is quickly frustrated by the succeeding one; the atmosphere is of confusion and uncertainty and hardly conducive to the presentation of an idea. The music is no less frustrated, without line, point of emphasis, natural sequence, or development. Doubtless the dancers believe (and with some justice) that modern life is disintegrated and frustrated. But there have been works—and there are going to be more—that show this strongly and clearly without being so technically submerged by their message that they are weak and ineffective: Berg's *Wozzeck*, Weill and Balanchine's *Seven Deadly Sins*, and Blitzstein's *The Cradle Will Rock*.

What the dancers want to say about society may be significant and valuable. It should be said as strongly and with as much conviction as possible in order for the idea itself not to succumb to the very forces they criticize. Moreover, their message is not delivered on the stage, but via their program notes. Shan-Kar has a much less important announcement to make to Western society, and yet out of his performances comes something, remote as the sources may be, that is more true than anything the modern dancers have yet been able to achieve. He deals with certain basic facts about human feeling and gets his results through a very highly developed technique and a thorough muscular control. His discipline is so great that the moment he comes on stage and makes a gesture, no matter how slight, he arouses a feeling of respect toward him, as an artist, and this is maintained throughout the performance. What he does, not what he is, alone must be considered. And what he does has to do with the body and its parts from eye to toe. The modern dancer's body is always used monotonously as a whole, and the lack of disciplined gesture, hence concentration of meaning, dissipates the message.

The theme of revolt against bourgeois society (and I suspect against any form of society) is a recurrent one with artists. But surely the direction should be not toward that of emotional, chaotic conflicts as these dancers seem to maintain but toward greater physical, intellectual, and emotional discipline; that is the only road to liberation from the society they loathe. The single tendency in this direction to be noted at the Centre Theatre was in Hanya Holm's group, which presented a portion of their large work *Trend*, given previously in complete form at Mecca Temple. There was real beauty and significance of movement though, as so often in these large works, the level of stylization was uncertain. Obvious realistic parody stood side by side with the most abstract and obscure movements. The insect-like machine gestures at the beginning of *Trend* and the remarkable spasmodic convulsions of isolated individuals during the "cataclysm" were quite extraordinary; they showed what this type of dance could be if it were freed from the personal hysteria that now surrounds it and made more straightforward.

As this issue goes to press, I should like to include a note on the all-American evening the Ballet Caravan has just given at the Avery Memorial in Hartford. Virgil Thomson's *Filling Station*, which had its premiere on this occasion, and Paul Bowles's *Yankee Clipper* seem to me to be outstanding American ballets.

Filling Station is a pointed satire on the way Americans think about the different classes of their society. As if in a movie, the characters are all brought together at a gas station, where a holdup is staged by gangsters. Paul Cadmus has dressed all this with remarkable cleverness and style; in fact his scenery and costumes almost walk away with the work. Lew Christensen's choreography, however, is both expert and witty, and Thomson's score, like old-time, pre-sound film piano-playing, does not underline the action, move by move, but forms a running background that catches the simplicity of character and situation amusingly. His jazz number is one of the best satires of this style that I know.

Bowles's work has the much more usual relation between ballet music and action, for each situation is made into an appropriate dance. It is straightforward and episodic, like all conventional ballets. Nevertheless it is the Caravan's most deeply felt work. Having to do with the old story of the clipper-ship sailor who is gotten by the sea, the dancing and music are at times boisterous and at times tender. Bowles has written some of his best music in the tuneful sailor dances. He manages to retain his own personality while making pastiches of exotica. Loring's choreography is most convincing in its wistful moods, and the whole is worth seeing because of its touching and evocative charm.

Remembering Balanchine
(1991/95)

I saw all the Balanchine ballets that were done at the Théâtre des Champs-Elysées in 1933, when I was a student in Paris. It was a most remarkable occasion: in my opinion, Balanchine never did anything quite as interesting as that again. It has always seemed to me that this was one of his finest moments. At the performances of these ballets, I met my old college acquaintance Lincoln Kirstein, who later became an off-and-on friend and commissioned my two ballets. He, of course, felt even more passionately than I about what we were seeing and took action to bring Balanchine to the United States. Quickly realizing the level of skill that Balanchine's choreography would demand, Kirstein soon established the School of American Ballet and, after that, a succession of performing companies so that his dancers could gain stage experience: first the Ballet Caravan, for which Aaron Copland's *Billy the Kid* and my *Pocahontas* were written; then the Ballet Society, for which I composed

The Minotaur; and finally the New York City Ballet, with Balanchine as choreographer mostly using dancers trained at the school who had had experience in the previous companies.[1]

Balanchine said to me once that one of the problems he faced, when he first arrived in the United States, was that he felt obliged to do ballets that were guaranteed to be successful, felt that he owed it to Kirstein to insure the success of the new company. As a result, with the passage of time it seemed to me that he began to lose some of that novel character that was so striking at the beginning of his career. It occasionally reappeared, as in the Webern ballet, *Episodes* (1959), and in some of the Stravinsky ballets, but in general his whole attitude underwent a gradual change. It was unfortunate that he ended up having to run the company, that there was no institution at the time that could hire him to do solely what he did best. For in 1933, with Edward James's money, in Paris and London he had been able, for the first time in his life, to do exactly what he wanted to.

Occasionally he had that kind of opportunity again. Gluck's *Orpheus* (1936) at the Metropolitan Opera, with Tchelitchew's sets, was a very unusual and moving spectacle. I don't know how they got the money together for *Orpheus*, but unfortunately it was not a success and was never done again. I went to the rehearsals with Tchelitchew, whom I knew fairly well at that time. In that production I remember one scene with what looked like actual trees with roots hanging down. The underworld was a whole forest of roots and trees, with the trunks of the trees visible halfway up the stage. It was extraordinary. At one rehearsal, I overheard Lucrezia Bori, one of the directors of the Opera at that time and a very important person, declaring her disbelief, in absolutely scandalized tones, that anything like that had been allowed at the Met.

Also done at the Metropolitan, the Stravinsky-Balanchine *Jeu de cartes* (1937), or *Card Game* as it was called later, wasn't such a good idea as a ballet in itself, though the music was wonderful. Balanchine seemed unable to get beyond the mere idea of a pack of cards, and it would have been better too if he'd made the Joker more devilish. The music is full of parody, suggesting *The Barber of Seville*; Figaro there, like the Joker, is a character who breaks everything and causes problems. *Le Baiser de la fée*, which Balanchine also staged first at the Met, was another matter, a very good production, but it disappeared all too quickly. It must have been too elaborate and costly to stage repeatedly. The ending of the ballet was like the ending of *Errante*, with the main character climbing up a rope ladder to the top of the stage. Another Balanchine ballet I remember was Stravinsky's *Danses concertantes* (1944). This was a beautiful ballet, with wonderful scenery and costumes by Eugene

1. [1994 note] It's hard to believe that for many years the New York City Ballet had only very modest support from the general public and critics while it performed at the City Center, and that it was only in Balanchine's last years, when the company performed at Lincoln Center, that it attained its great success. Lincoln Kirstein had persisted in his visionary enthusiasm and devoted support against what must often have seemed frustrating odds to produce, finally, America's most outstanding ballet company.

Berman that were lost—a great shame. In the Ballets 1933, there was also *Mozartiana*, with an extraordinary set by Bérard. The front drop was an enormous red curtain painted in a very rough style with the little child Mozart playing a grand piano.

My first exposure to Balanchine's work was on the Riviera in 1932, when I saw *Cotillon*. The ballet was mysterious: things happened that seemed inexplicable. The Hand of Fate, I remember, was the important figure in the entire work. Toumanova was the heroine; she was ravishing at that time. *Concurrence*, also in the 1932 season, was different, much more straightforward. The plot was clear, although I don't remember the details. It had much less atmosphere, a humorous piece in the common world of people but as seen through the eyes of modern painters.

I came to know Balanchine through the composer Nicolas Nabokov, a great friend of mine for many years, and through Tchelitchew. I wrote the music for the ballet *The Minotaur* with the idea that Balanchine would do it, but then in 1947 he went to Paris and John Taras choreographed it instead. I don't think Balanchine ever liked the music very much—which puzzles me even now because it still sounds (especially in a recent recording) so much like his kind of music![2]

Balanchine and I had talked about the libretto, and he had made many suggestions; it was a collaborative effort. The basic idea was mine, however: to create a kind of balletic picture of the concentration camps. This idea already had a certain currency, because everyone had just become aware, in that period right after the Second World War, of the horrible things that had taken place in the camps. The Minotaur devouring its victims in the labyrinth was of course symbolic of it all. I think Kirstein wanted Balanchine to do this ballet, and that Balanchine was doing what he thought Kirstein wanted him to do. He did seem to be interested. There was one important moment in the ballet which he invented: when Pasiphaë is raped by the bull, she falls over panting, and her heartbeats become the hammering and building of the labyrinth. That transition from one scene to the other I put into the score. This analogy between the heartbeats of the woman who became the mother of the Minotaur and the labyrinthine imprisonment of the Minotaur seemed really quite moving to me.

I often used to go to Balanchine's rehearsals in the old studios of the School of American Ballet at 59th and Madison. I remember meeting the novelist Céline there one time. Watching Balanchine indicating the movements of the dance, showing the choreography to his dancers, one could easily get the impression that he was just improvising, inventing things moment by moment with no larger plan. But any such impression would vanish in the actual performance: the big picture that Balanchine had had in mind all along would become completely clear.

2. Elliott Carter, *The Minotaur* (first recording of the complete ballet). New York Chamber Symphony of the 92nd Street Y, conducted by Gerard Schwarz. Elektra Nonesuch CD 9 79248–2 (1990).

Some years ago, in a conversation with Allen Edwards, I spoke about my interest in and thinking about musical time. They were very much stimulated, I said,

by the kinds of "cutting" and continuity you find in the movies of Eisenstein, particularly *Ten Days that Shook the World* and *Potemkin*, and such as are described in his books, *Film Sense* and *Film Form*. I was similarly interested by the onward-moving continuity in the ballets of George Balanchine—every individual momentary tableau in the best of his ballets is something that the viewer has seen interestingly evolved, yet it is also only a stage of a process that is going on to another point; and while every moment is a fascinating and beautiful thing in itself, still what's much more fascinating is the continuity, the way each moment is being led up to and away from—something you are not aware of in the ballets of most other choreographers as being anything of interest or which has even been thought about much. Indeed, the Balanchine ballets have been very stimulating to me in this way ever since 1933 . . . They have been important as an example, in another art, of what one might do with music: one wanted to have very vivid moments, but what was more interesting was the process by which these moments came into being and by which they disappeared and turned into other moments.[3]

It is important to notice that Balanchine doesn't follow the music exactly. His choreography derives much of its interest from being a commentary on the music and not a specific Mickey-Mousing from one measure to another. Take *Serenade*, for instance: there are different movements in the score, but in the ballet when one movement ends the people who are to dance the next one are already onstage; he has linked up the movements, and the choreography is in some ways made more continuous than and different from the music. This remains fascinating for a musician to see, how he is constantly developing a choreography that is connected to the music but somehow tangential to it. Balanchine's ballet on Bizet's Symphony in C is also quite extraordinary. All sorts of patterns are created with the dancers rushing across and around the stage, producing a series of visual impressions that lead from one to the other.

One of the things you never knew about Balanchine's ballets was whether there was an element of fun in it all. The humor of that period was very concealed: people did things very seriously when they were meant to be funny, as in some of Cocteau's work. You couldn't always tell whether you were meant to laugh at it or not. This is one of the things that is interesting about Balanchine's work, its occasional ambiguity of character. In *Serenade* a whole regimented group of dancers stands statuesquely, each with one arm raised, while the soloist comes in, tries to find her place, takes up the common pose—then suddenly all the others leave and she remains standing abandoned, alone. In the context of the previous balletic action, in which the many dancers move in unison, solemnly, as if in a ritual, the appearance of this single misfit can give rise to many feelings. Is she simply absent-minded, or is she pathetically trying to fit in, or just foolishly late or willfully against

3. Allen Edwards, *Flawed Words and Stubborn Sounds: A Conversation with Elliott Carter* (New York: W. W. Norton & Co., 1971), 99.

the crowd? This is left in ambiguity. Of course, along with whatever such feelings they may evoke, such striking concepts as this one have a kind of profound affective originality which is far more impressive than the invention of detail in itself. In fact the detail, whatever it is, gains from being related organically to the larger patterns of the dance and its expressive concepts.

I don't ever remember Balanchine laughing, even with Nabokov or Tchelitchew. But I remember him smiling a great deal. Like Stravinsky, he was fond of puns—not surprising, of course, in a person who, being foreign, is constantly thinking about language. And he was given to little comic turns as well. Stravinsky, on the other hand, was broadly comic, even to the point of being extravagantly too funny, clownlike. Balanchine was never like that. He was muted in some curious way, as a person—controlled, somehow.

I don't much like to go to the ballet any more, for all I see is work that either very pedestrianly follows the music or else is so divorced from the music that two or more different things can be going on at the same time, as in the work of Merce Cunningham and others. This I find disturbing in its random and rather arbitrary character. One gets little sense, as one does with Balanchine, that music is being thought about and commented upon in dance. Balanchine always makes one wonder just what it is that he is seeing in the music. This is constantly provocative; it keeps one awake.

Some of the Massine ballets on big symphonies were very striking: the *Symphonie fantastique* of Berlioz, one of the Tchaikovsky symphonies, and the Fourth Symphony of Brahms. Massine was much more literal than Balanchine; he had a good sense of the spectacle and made everything a big production. But his ballets had none of the intensity and fascination that Balanchine was able to achieve without any scenery and without much show.

I recently attended a festival of music in Turin, where the leading architect was Iuvara, who with other Italian architects designed so much of St. Petersburg. St. Petersburg, Balanchine's home, is really more Italian than anything else. And it's that fancy, that element of elaborate, extravagant Baroque, that you find in Balanchine and in Tchelitchew. There is in their work a Russianized version of late Italian Baroque architecture which Iuvara and the other artists in Turin excelled in. You see a great deal of that in Turin, in the churches, in the Stupinigi hunting lodge. Perhaps Balanchine's whole sense of sumptuous extravagant design came from St. Petersburg.

Balanchine and Stravinsky remained very close throughout their lives in America and had similar attitudes about many things. Stravinsky turned away from the overt Russianizing that had characterized his early work and became more interested in Tchaikovsky, less in Mussorgsky, Borodin and the rest, eventually changing entirely into a neoclassic composer. In this sense he was a good deal like Balanchine, using classical material in his own personal way. Both of them were refugees, so to speak.

One of Balanchine's last ballets, *Robert Schumann's "Davidsbündlertänze"* (1980), is most compelling. It is obvious that its central feature, one that conditions every part of the ballet in some way or other, is a portrayal of what the entire suite of Schumann's piano pieces is about—and, by extension, what

Schumann's vision of music was in general. Even the life of Schumann is somehow expressed in the choreography. Balanchine was genuinely interested in who Schumann was, in the whole world of which he was a part, and in the madness that grew until it finally overtook him. The way in which Balanchine manages to express this is very moving.

A certain fascination with the affliction of madness was of course an important aspect of the German Romantic movement in general. And one finds an affinity with German Romanticism, in this work of Balanchine, in the always present idea of constant flow, expressed by the wind blowing, and by the dancers being carried with it as they enter. The dance doesn't accomplish this note by note or beat by beat, but rather conceives the whole in terms of a meaning larger than the small details of the music. Already in the Ballets 1933, *Errante*—which used Schubert's *"Wanderer" Fantasy*, with very striking, all-white sets by Tchelitchew—showed a clear connection to this German Romantic aesthetic, as did *La Valse* (1951), both in their sense of fleeting moments. Balanchine found this idea very affecting, and in a way all of his work is marked by it—from *Cotillon* right to the end.

Theatre and Films
(1943)

Kurt Weill's new score for *One Touch of Venus*, coming after last year's *Lady in the Dark*, reveals his mastery of Broadway technique. Apparently he can turn out one success after another with a sure hand. Weill, who orchestrates and arranges his own work, whose flair for discovering and using the stylistic earmarks of popular music is remarkable, has finally made himself at home in America. Where in pre-Hitler days his music underlined the bold and disillusioned bitterness of economic injustice, now, reflecting his new environment and the New York audiences to which he appeals, his social scene has shrunk to the bedroom and he has become the composer of "sophisticated" scores.

The present one represents quite a piece of research into the phases of American love-life expressed in popular music—the barber-shop ballad, the barroom song dripping with bloody murder, the serious and comic parodies of Cole Porter, an uproarious mock-patriotic *Way Out West in Jersey* in the best college spirit style. Even the orchestration with its numerous piano solos in boogie-woogie and other jazz styles constantly recalls nightclub atmosphere. Traces of the mordant composer of *Die Dreigroschenoper* and *Mahagonny* occur rarely and only in places where Weill is not trying to make an impression. Compared to his other American shows, the music is neither as ingenious and as striking as *Johnny Johnson* nor as forced as his made-to-order jobs for *The Eternal Road* and the railroad show at the World's Fair. But in the atmosphere of Broadway, where so much music is unconvincing and dead, Weill's workmanlike care and his refined sense of style make up for whatever spontaneity and freshness his music lacks.

Aaron Copland and Alexandre Tansman have been chosen by Hollywood to write scores for two new films. The results ought to convince our producers that good symphonic composers have something to offer which the usual Hollywood musician does not. Copland's score for the Samuel Goldwyn production of *North Star* is excellent in a technical way that, for instance, Victor Young's music in *For Whom the Bell Tolls* is not. Young serves up a rich variety of different kinds of Spanish music in the styles of Albéniz, Granados, and others, which seem to have no direct relevance to the characteristics of the plot except to emphasize the locale. Copland, on the other hand, comes to grips with actual particulars of plot, character, and mood of the specific picture and emphasizes the points which author and director make. He does this by using fragments of Russian folk song submitted to a process of development and arrangement and, besides, also makes them sound very much his own.

North Star is about a Russian agricultural community before and after the Nazi invasion. The picture falls into these two parts, but they do not play off against each other with sufficient dramatic meaning. The peaceful first part stresses picturesqueness rather than efficient modern collectivization (as a Soviet film probably would have). The comrades seem to be living in the familiar old Russia of peasant song and dance days in a neat, charming operetta atmosphere. No reference to preparation for war is made and no suspense is built up to prepare the spectator for the catastrophe. In these early sequences Copland has written three delightful songs to words by Ira Gershwin and a big dance scene which catches the Russian warmth and lustiness. This music with its childlike gaiety is often reminiscent of his *Second Hurricane*. The "going to school" and the two quiet sleep scenes are the best of this side of Copland.

Interrupting a song, *No Village Like Mine*, sung by the young people who are the heroes of this picture, Nazi bombs begin to fall, dive-bombers spit fire and death on the town, Nazi troops march, Russian guerilla bands are formed, and the music has the perennially difficult job of being both background for action and for war noise. One of the most successful musical war sequences so far written, because of its plastic use and intensity of style, it employs music sometimes to join one explosion with another and sometimes to modulate from one mood to another, as in the sequence in which Marina and Damian kiss in great quiet before the latter goes on his perilous mission. The most beautiful and dramatic piece is in the background for the scenes of the women burning their own homes before the Nazis come. At every point the intelligence and the personal elevation of Copland's music is recognizable, even in his arrangement and orchestration of the *Internationale*.

Alexandre Tansman's score for Duvivier's *Flesh and Fantasy* starts out with a bit of title music surprising for Hollywood. In the vigorous, dissonant, and contrapuntal style of his *Triptyque*, and indeed of many another modern score, the music takes off in a very arresting way. Also excellent and interesting is the long dance-music sequence providing the background for the Mardi Gras episode. After this, the score becomes more and more routine, except for those eerie moments when by many a strange effect it points up rather ordinary-looking scenes with a Freudian significance, notably those on shipboard. But by and large, screwiness has its limits in Hollywood and love scenes impose certain hallowed musical patterns which even Tansman could not break through.

The Genial Sage
(1948)

I first came across Paul Rosenfeld's name in 1925, I think, when I acquired his book of critical essays on modern composers, "Musical Portraits" (I wrote the date in my now tattered copy of the volume). These essays helped shape my thinking about and gave me a greater appreciation for the music of Schoenberg, Scriabin, Debussy, Ravel, Ernest Bloch, Charles Loeffler, and Leo Ornstein. Rosenfeld's criticism reached me at a crucial time in my life, when I was exposed to many of the "modernist" influences that in retrospect have turned out to be very important to my formation. Still pasted into my copy of "Musical Portraits," for example, is the program of the 1925–26 season at the Met, at which were performed "Petrouchka," "Rossignol," "Skyscrapers" (John Alden Carpenter) and "La Vida Breve" (De Falla). I find the 1925 date in my volumes of Gertrude Stein, Ezra Pound, and e.e. cummings, and 1926 in all the volumes of Proust's "A la recherche du temps perdu" published to that point, as well as my scores of Schoenberg's piano works opp. 11, 19, and 25, "Pierrot lunaire," and Stravinsky's "Le Sacre." These were the years when I subscribed to "The Dial" and to the German modernist periodical "Simplicissimus." During this time, and throughout the 1930s and '40s, Rosenfeld in a constant stream of writings served as a kind of advocate for modernism in all its various phases. The memorial volume in which the following remembrance appeared contained many other, eloquent tributes by Edmund Wilson, Marianne Moore, Charles Ives, Aaron Copland, William Schuman, and many others.[1]

The first time I met Paul Rosenfeld he was writing an article about young composers. This was in the fall of 1937. To hear my music he asked me down to his apartment in Greenwich Village.

It was a sunlit morning when I went there and he opened the door to rooms crammed with books and phonograph records. There was a sense of profusion and loving curiosity that always impressed me in the quarters of college professors. There they seemed accumulations of the old. But here they were the working objects of the present. The paintings of Marin and the photographs by Stieglitz that covered his walls framed a modern life with the new and vigorous tones that Paul wrote about so brilliantly. The whole gave the impression of energetic serenity that we feel in ancient portraits of Chinese sages.

He sat me down to his Steinway piano and listened and talked, and somehow seemed to catch something out of what was to me my hopelessly inadequate presentation of my music. He asked questions—surprising and challenging questions—that I wondered about for days afterwards. I liked him.

That was the beginning of an acquaintance that fed on occasional meetings, where we had the opportunity for snatches of critical conversation. I remember particularly one night at the Museum of Modern Art as we recalled

---

1. See Notes on Sources (Appendix 1).

the exciting days when the music of Varèse stirred up storms of anger and enthusiasm. Now all that seemed to have given way to mildly expressive pieces by men more concerned with getting ahead in popularity than with reflecting new and convincing sound worlds.

At almost every one of such meetings we somehow got to talk about Charles Ives. For Paul and I at that time were publishing articles about this American composer. Generally we talked with the attitude of people who would not let their disagreements be final. He argued that the spirit of Ives's music was remarkable, and I that his music did not convincingly express any such spirit. Paul was right. Ives's vision in music was too significant for us to neglect it simply because he lacked a technical equipment in music.

To phrase Ives's significance I suggested a biography of him as a businessman and a composer, against the American background out of which he developed. Paul, I pointed out, was the only writer who had the wide grasp of the situation and who could see into the motivations, into the time itself that had caused the interesting conflicts in Ives's life. Paul felt that he was too busy on his book about literary genres. Then he tried to excuse himself because he did not want to write anything more about music until he had gotten more precise technical knowledge himself. I persisted until, in the end, he consented to do the book if I collaborated to take care of the technical aspect.

So during Paul's last winter, after a decade of acquaintance and merging consonance—over innumerable cups of coffee and tea, during late dark afternoons—we talked and planned. It seemed to us vitally important to think through the age-old problems of the artist's relation to tradition, and the question of distinguishing a living tradition from sterile conventionality. Also, there was America's relation to European tradition, and the relation of experiment to creative imagination and expression. All this seemed to stand in vital need of redefinition in the light of our contemporary world.

The work of Ives represents a coming to terms with our present-day environment. We—Paul and I—saw Ives as a touchstone to bring all the problems of the artist and his times into pattern. How to describe most clearly the lines of such force made us talk and plan. We talked and planned too much and too long, and now we—sadly—no longer can.

Introduction to a Poetry Reading by W. H. Auden
(1969)

As a composer of music, I would like to use this opportunity to thank Mr. Auden publicly for his wonderful writing for and about my art. What composer can resist the lines about himself:

> Only your notes are pure contraption,
> Only your song is an absolute gift.

Or about his work:

You alone, alone, imaginary song,
Are unable to say an existence is wrong,
And pour out your forgiveness like a wine.[1]

From this and other things he has said, we can see he's an ideal listener, having a great fondness for the art, which led him to wide experience of its literature, and this in turn has resulted in wise thoughts and judgments, essays, libretti, and, finally, poems.

Because of his direct experience of music's immediacy, he never falls into that only too common kind of cultural alienation which substitutes abstractions about music for the imaginative involvement with what Karl Marx called "the living flower." This cultural alienation results in the non-listening to works of music and joins large parts of the establishment to whole sections of the avant-garde. Mr. Auden's breadth of comprehension and interpretation, based as it is on listening, keeps him above such trivialities and makes him someone to pay attention to even if you don't agree with him.

Much of his writing on music is occupied with fundamental matters—the attempt to define the identity of Western art music, describe its characteristics, and relate them to those of the other arts, and, finally, to life. Thorny questions all of them.

He often says things forgotten by musicians themselves, such as: "A verbal art like poetry is reflective; it stops to think. Music is immediate, it goes on to become."[2]

In extolling the particular quality of Western art music, he points out that it is unlike all other kinds because it, as he says, deals with "our experience of Time in its twofold aspect, natural or organic repetition, and historical novelty created by choice. And the full development of music as an art depends upon a recognition that these two aspects are different and that choice, being an experience confined to man, is more significant than repetition."[3]

To a composer his most fascinating encounter with music is the way in which he and Chester Kallman tackled the matter of opera libretti and produced three excellent ones: *The Rake's Progress* for Stravinsky's masterpiece, as well as *Elegy for Young Lovers* and *The Bassarids* for Hans Werner Henze. In seeing and hearing these works, a composer, especially, appreciates the fact that Mr. Auden never forgets that the music is the main thing in an opera and that the libretto should give ample opportunity for it.

Messrs. Auden and Kallman realize, as few librettists have, that the basic problem is to justify art music as the central element in the stage production. This justification has to be intrinsic to the plot or to the subject matter itself, has to inform every dramatic situation and verbal text to make the enterprise convincing—as it so seldom is nowadays, so seldom, indeed, that many have

1. W. H. Auden, "The Composer" (1938), in *Collected Poems*, ed. Edward Mendelson (New York: Random House, 1976), 148.

2. Auden, "Notes on Music and Opera," in *The Dyer's Hand and Other Essays* (New York: Random House, 1962), 466.

3. Ibid., 465.

wondered whether opera could ever become a living art form again. Mr. Auden has made a significant effort to revalidate it.

Of opera he remarks: "A credible situation in an opera means a situation in which it is credible that someone should sing. A good libretto plot is a melodrama in both the strict and the conventional sense of the word; it offers as many opportunities as possible for the characters to be swept off their feet by placing them in situations which are too tragic or too fantastic for 'words.'"[4]

Finally in this connection, let me read something I have always enjoyed very much although I don't agree with it since, being a musician, I don't have a very clear idea of what the word *sensible* means. He writes: "The theory of 'music-drama' presupposes a libretto in which there is not one sensible moment or one sensible remark: this is not only very difficult to manage, though Wagner managed it, but also extremely exhausting on both singers and the audience, neither of whom may relax for an instant."[5]

And so now let's hear something sensible from Mr. Auden.

Music as a Liberal Art
(1944)

Music, considered less as a practice than as an art with whose nature, history, and present state every educated person should be familiar, has suffered a decline.

On the university campus today the Victorian Gothic library, the Greek revival laboratories, the academic halls present an imposing bulk behind which, in some out-of-the-way corner, the reticent little music building seeks shelter. Music departments are too often staffed by professionals with little capacity to see their subject in a broader light than the teaching of special techniques demands, who tend to be less articulate than their academic colleagues. The thoughtful student who is no virtuoso finds little to his taste in a department that teaches skill without an appeal to reason, that attempts to demonstrate many styles but fails to take up the basic question of style itself, of philosophic and historic meaning. The purely practical approach is largely responsible for the low estate to which music, as a vital part of our intellectual equipment, has fallen.

In less exalted settings, music as a subject develops growing importance. Wartime propaganda devotes much effort to exploitation of the art. A nation's use of music is offered to prove its advance from barbarism, its degree of culture, refinement, civilization. By way of radio, discussions about music now reach the masses and make a claim on their consideration before the higher academies have done much to raise the subject from its present depressed level.

Historically, of course, music is no poor relation of the arts and sciences. In the golden age of Greece it occupied a post of honor. The Platonic dialogues

4. Ibid., 471–72.

5. Ibid., 472.

show music to be never very far from the thoughts of Socrates and his fellow Athenians. Besides offering witty, elegant, and often profound comment on the subject, the dialogues give music an important philosophical role. In the *Timaeus*, Plato tells a "likely story" of a creator who imposed on originally irreconcilable elements the mathematical pattern of the ratios of a musical scale, in order to fashion the soul of the universe. Elsewhere, as in *The Republic* (Book III), Plato finds that music imposes order on the motions of the body and the soul, teaching gracious and harmonious conduct and giving the young student a knowledge of good and evil. Three years, says Plato in the *Laws*, should be devoted to learning how to play the lyre and to kindred musical subjects. Philosophical discussions must be included so that the student will never be deceived by "appearances" and forget the true music of which this earthly music is only a shadow. For a music lover only interested in sounds, the kind that conservatories then as now produced, Plato had contempt. They are "the last persons who would come to anything like a philosophical discussion, if they could help, while they run about at the Dionysiac festivals as if they had let out their ears to hear every chorus; whether the performance is in town or country—that makes no difference—they are there."[1]

The moral benefits to be derived from the study of music as Plato saw it gave music great importance in the Academy of Athens, where its relation to geometry and astronomy was endlessly discussed. This early association of subjects later played an important part in the plan of the Medieval university. Here music, one of the "seven liberal arts," now systematized as a discipline, became a branch of mathematics. As the art of measurement, it was an object of major study for several centuries. Under this alliance with what we today call mathematical physics, our aural art, though occupying a lesser position, was widely cultivated. And in the Renaissance, so long as Medieval thinking continued to dominate education, no education, according to Thomas Morley, was complete without some actual musical training in playing or singing.[2]

That the practice of musicians was deeply influenced by the liberal arts discipline is written on the pages of every treatise of the period. In turn, the practice of music itself influenced thinking in many different fields, as witness the treatises on architecture by Palladio and on astronomy by Kepler. Kepler in the early seventeenth century drew extended analogies between Copernican heliocentric theory and the art of polyphony of his day, contrasting it to Ptolemy's analogy between Greek music and the geocentric theory. His method enabled him to describe the orbit of the planet Mars, a mathematical mystery before his time.

Aristotle in his *Politics* has another approach to music. He lists it under three headings: education, amusement, and intellectual enjoyment. "Amusement is for the sake of relaxation, and relaxation is of necessity sweet, for it is

1. Plato, *The Republic*, Book V, trans. Benjamin Jowett, in *The Works of Plato*, ed. Irwin Edman (New York: Modern Library, 1956), 434. [B]

2. See Thomas Morley, *A Plaine and Easie Introduction to Practicall Musicke* (1597); modern ed., *A Plain and Easy Introduction to Practical Music*, ed. Alec Harman (New York: W. W. Norton & Co., 1973). [B]

the remedy of pain caused by toil. . . . In addition to this common pleasure, felt and shared by all . . . may it [music] not have also some influence over the character and the soul? . . . Rhythm and melody supply imitations of anger and gentleness, and also of courage and temperance, and of all the qualities contrary to these, and of the other qualities of character, which hardly fall short of the actual affections, as we know from our own experience." After describing in detail the effects of various kinds of music and pointing out which are desirable, Aristotle concludes, "Music has a power of forming the character, and should therefore be introduced into the education of the young."[3] Together with the discussion of imitation in the *Poetics*, this and similar passages exerted a powerful influence on the philosophy of music and education even as late as the eighteenth century.

However, music in order to assume its classical position in the hierarchy of studies and bear an intelligible relation to them does not require a particular system of philosophy. From the fourth century B.C. through the seventeenth of our era, there were many changes in philosophy, while music's traditional place remained fairly constant. Most of the great music of the past that we admire, and much of the literature, have some relation to this tradition of the liberal arts. Its terminology still is used in our discussions of aesthetics, even though meanings have become vague, and its example is a challenge for us all to think more deeply.

In America today, the objectives of education are being redefined, the plan of studies reworked in an attempt to give people a broader and more understanding view of the world. To expand their knowledge of music, a few suggestions might be taken from those periods when the art was an integral part of education and of life.

Several methods have already been tried. One of the most familiar is the historical approach, in which music joins hands with other arts and is studied century by century. Its chronology is synchronized with important historical events, the development of court life, the effect of wars, the influence of one school on another. This is unquestionably useful and in the right direction, but as a method it places too little emphasis on the very ideas which have most deeply shaped the artistic works under consideration.

In at least two centers, the University of Chicago and St. John's College in Annapolis, where drastic reforms of the whole educational system have been put into effect, the relation of music to various philosophies is now stressed. At St. John's, music has actually been taken out of the music building. It is no longer the special study of the specialist, of the budding professional. Instead it is examined in the classrooms, seminars, and laboratories, in an effort to give it a working relationship with all other knowledge. Since the St. John's plan is the most familiar to me, I would like to present it as an illustration of how music can be brought back into the general life of a university.

At St. John's all students read a certain number of works, from Homer to

3. Aristotle, *Politics*, Book VIII, Chapter 5, trans. Benjamin Jowett (New York: Modern Library, 1943), 328–31. [B]

Freud, that have been influential in forming our total Western civilization. Some are read in translation, others form the basis of laboratory experiments, still others provide texts for mathematics and language courses; all are discussed in seminars. Included in this study during my stay at St. John's were several works of music—a Gregorian mass, a mass of Palestrina, a work by Bach such as the *Goldberg Variations*; and scheduled for the future were an opera by Mozart, a symphony of Beethoven, and music by Stravinsky and Debussy. These were coordinated chronologically with the rest of the reading. However, the college is not concerned primarily in giving a serial picture of various stages of Western civilization, but in having the student know the problems that have confronted us and learn to evaluate the efforts at solution. So musical works were chosen that not only represent their periods but are still being heard today.

The fundamentals of music were demonstrated in such a way as to clarify the intellectual traditions of the subject. The frequent mention of music in the works of Plato, Aristotle, and St. Augustine was thus made vivid and understandable. Music was examined first in the physics laboratory, so that students learned to distinguish intervals, to recognize, for instance, the fifth, whose effect Galileo says "is to produce a tickling of the eardrum such that its softness is modified with sprightliness, giving at the same moment the impression of a gentle kiss and of a bite."[4] Here also simple notation was taught, as well as the formation of modes and scales, key relationships, and chord structure. The students tuned sonometers according to all kinds of systems. In a class on the measurement of time, they found out about rhythm and meter, in another they studied the construction of musical instruments and acoustics. One class, held each month, was a concert, another a lecture dealing with music in its formal aspects.

The main emphasis was on preparation for the hearing and understanding of actual works. Scores and recordings were made available, and, whenever possible, the music studied was performed at concerts. Each work was then discussed on two successive evenings for about two hours, often more because the talk became so lively. One of the most recurrent topics was, naturally, the meaning of music. Did it, like language, refer to something other than itself, and if so, what? Or was a work of music an ordered pattern of sounds that awakened feelings and thoughts in us as a by-product of our enjoyment of its beauties? Is listening to music simply a pleasant pastime or is it more? What does music bring to the meaning of the words in Gregorian chant? What relation has notation to what the composer imagines and to what the performer does? And so on through all those profound questions that naturally arise in students' minds but are so lightly, so carelessly, brushed by in most music courses. Here arguments developed, sides were taken, controversy was important. Music became a matter of interest, whether it was approached by the scientific, the literary, or the artistic, and it gave one type of student an understanding of the other.

4. Galileo Galilei, *Dialogues Concerning Two New Sciences*, trans. Henry Crew and Alfonso de Salvio (1914; repr. ed., Evanston, Ill.: Northwestern University Press, 1968), 107. [B]

The introduction of music into such a plan of study, indeed into any general plan, has far-reaching results. It stimulates a consideration of the aesthetic problems bound to come up in a course on literature or the other fine arts; it can endow laboratory experiments with a quality of imagination often lacking in the more elementary subjects. When students see the interconnection of all these things, their understanding grows in richness. And since today no widely accepted aesthetic doctrine unifies our thought on the various aspects of music, such a plan at least conjures up the past to assist us; it helps to raise the various philosophical questions involved. In one way or another these questions must be considered, for it is not enough to devote all our efforts to acquiring the technical skills essential to instrumentalists, composers, or even listeners. There must be good thinking and good talking about music to preserve its noble rank as a fine art for all of us, and the college is one of the logical places for this more considered attitude to be cultivated.

Time Lecture
(1965/94)

The subject of time, specifically as it relates to music, lends itself to many different interpretations. Here I will limit myself to discussion of just a few of them. For Westerners, it is natural to begin with the Pythagorean philosophy, so beautifully expressed in Plato's *Timaeus*, where the "father and creator" found that it was impossible to bestow eternity in all its fullness on a created being—the heavens—in the same way as existed in ideal beings, and so "resolved to have a moving image of eternity, and when he set in order the heaven, he made this image eternal but moving according to number, while eternity rests in unity, and this image we call time. For there were no days and nights and months and years before the heaven was created, but when he constructed the heaven he created them also."[1] From this point on in the dialogue, Plato himself quickly becomes involved in the thorny problems of the subject—the past and the future, he says, are forms of time, which itself imitates eternity and revolves according to number. Alluding to the familiar Platonic attitudes toward being, he continues: "Moreover, when we say that what has become *is* become and what becomes *is* becoming and that what will become *is* about to become and that the nonexistent *is* nonexistent—all these are inaccurate modes of expression."[2] And the discussion ends with an allusion to the *Parmenides*, in which the remarkable statement occurs that "Whatever is becoming older than itself, if it is to have something *than* which it is becoming older, must also be at the same time becoming younger than itself."[3]

1. Plato, *Timaeus*, transl. Benjamin Jowett, in *The Collected Dialogues of Plato*, ed. Edith Hamilton and Huntington Cairns, Bollingen Series 71 (Princeton: Princeton University Press, 1961), 1167.

2. Ibid.

3. Plato, *Parmenides*, transl. F. M. Cornford, in *The Collected Dialogues of Plato*, 935.

This Pythagorean concept of time and of its numerical orders and divisions is of course very similar to Pythagorean thinking about musical intervals. Throughout the history of music, such thinking has given rise to many speculative efforts to divide musical time in all sorts of ways, stimulating the development of various systems of notation to express such divisions: not merely the simple ones of 1:2, 1:3, 2:3, and 3:4, but more complex or "irrational" ones, such as 5:17. At some point, composers noticed that many of these more remote relationships suggested the rather impulsive playing of many a performer and could be used, in explicit notation, to lend a similar impression. The music of various centuries before and during the Renaissance—as well as certain rather obscure music of later periods—and, in modern times, the works of Scriabin, among a number of other Russians, and of Charles Ives carried out hints found in Chopin that suggest a similar kind of speculation, in that rhythmic complexities suggest the imitation of improvisation.

This abstract Pythagoreanism is not the only point of view about time to be found in Greek thought; as in the matter of musical intervals, there was a pragmatic version as well. Classical Greek had three different words for time: *aion*, meaning a long period of time; *kairos*, the critical moment for action; and, of course, *khronos*, a certain definite stretch of time, such as a season. In an attempt to deal directly with time, especially musical time, the contemporary Russian music critic Pierre Suvchinsky, in a number of articles,[4] elaborated ideas that were developed much further by Gisèle Brelet in her book *Le Temps Musical* of 1949. Brelet's point of view, derived also in part from Bergson's philosophy, holds that time is the principal constituent of music, and that various kinds of time—objective or chronometric time, subjective time, experienced time—go toward making musical time the incarnation of the essence of time. Musical time, that is, is immanent in and transcends its outward form. According to Suvchinsky, "The personal musical experience of the composer is based above all on an experience of time that is specifically musical—of *khronos*—in relation to which the actual music only plays the role of a practical concretion."[5] Musical time, says Gisèle Brelet, taking a similar stand, is at once the product of thought and experience. Founding an entire philosophy and musical approach on this special notion of musical time, Mlle. Brelet asserts that all other aspects of music—harmony, counterpoint, form, and rhythm—must find very different descriptions and explanations from their traditional ones. She ends the introduction to her book with the statement that "If music is wisdom [as the Chinese say], it is not because it reflects the order of the cosmos, but because rather it reflects the *temporal order of the soul*, because at the very heart of sounding forms is the source of all wisdom, the *knowledge of time*, which is what excites our highest pleasure

4. See, in particular: Pierre Suvchinsky [Souvtchinsky], "La Notion du temps et la musique," *Revue Musicale* 20 (May–June 1939): 310–20; idem., "Igor Stravinsky," *Contrepoints* 2 (February 1946): 19–31.

5. Suvchinsky, "La Notion du temps et la musique," 312.

and interest in music and is its true significance."[6] Here may be recalled Stravinsky's many statements related to this kind of thinking, among them: "The phenomenon of music is given to us with the sole purpose of establishing an order in things, including, and particularly, the coordination between *man* and *time*."[7]

This view stresses the difference between "subjective" or passive time—*temps pathologique*—and objective, active, or empirical time—*temps empirique*—both of which have to do with human experiences of time. Musical time can become stiff and lifeless and lose its distinctive character when schematic or abstract patterns are imposed on it with no relationship to experienced time, *temps vécu*. Such schematism hinders musical time from attaining the living continuity of our experience of change. It substitutes intelligible systems or intellectually ordered time for our human time experience.

On the other hand, subjective time, with all its unpredictability and irrationality, can destroy musical time in another way, by being taken too literally and causing the composer to attempt to present such subjectivity in all its confusion and uncertainty and unclarity of motive. In fact, even to try to express this at all in musical terms is already to accept certain kinds of musical forms. Mlle. Brelet points out that psychological duration cannot produce a form in the full sense of the term: the nineteenth century did not create forms representative of itself and capable of surviving it by integrating themselves into our musical thought, like the fugue or the sonata. The forms of the nineteenth century (she continues), too influenced by psychological time, are essentially derived from the process of dissolution of Classical forms which have lost their meaning and from this process of dissolution no positive and original system was born. Romantic form, therefore, has a negative and negating character—it negates harmony, melody, tonality, rhythm, and finally even thematicity—that is to say all the determining characteristics which introduced intelligibility into the process of musical flow in previous times.[8] Unfortunately, ideas of this sort become a springboard for an attack on Wagner, who according to Brelet lost all sense of musical order in his attempt to present subjective time, and for affirmation of Tchaikovsky, who was able to devise a form of musical time that incorporated the power of subjective time but gave it an appropriate musical-temporal order. The upshot of both of these philosophies is, as might be expected, praise for the neoclassic Stravinsky for having found a truly formal art, an ordered time that has its sources in empirical time (that of action or gesture) and is thus the most living of musical times.[9]

6. Gisèle Brelet, *Le Temps musical: Essai d'une esthétique nouvelle de la musique* (Paris: Presses Universitaires de France, 1949), 61; my translation.

7. Igor Stravinsky, *An Autobiography* (New York: Norton, 1962), 54.

8. Brelet, *Le Temps musical*, 421–46 passim.

9. See, for example, Brelet's chapter "Musiques du temps rationnel et de l'éternel présent," 661–90.

To raise objections to these interesting but rather too generalized notions is easy; to attempt to construct another kind of pattern that is more valid is difficult, especially on such an abstract level. Certainly, the idea of presenting actually lived time in terms of its chronometric duration must have arisen with operas that were based on more or less realistic plays. The most varied, most absorbing and exciting and most compressed six minutes of opera, for instance—the first scene of *Don Giovanni*—could never have been written before Mozart's time, for up until then there were no musical techniques flexible, aphoristic, and varied enough to give form to such a heterogeneous collection of musical ideas and characters—presented here in a rapidity of succession, and with a force of direction, that even today is breathtaking. Each dramatic point, often in complete contrast to the previous, is made clearly, forcefully, and so quickly that the opera starts in a rush and with an impetuousness that seems directly related to its subject, and gives us in one complete picture all the facets of the situation, the comedy, the horror, the pathos, the scandalous swagger of the hero, at once attractive and repulsive.

To consider this unified but vastly varied sweep of music is to realize how music had changed from the time of Bach and Handel. The piece by Handel (familiar, at least at one time, from Harvard Glee Club programs), "The foolish lover squanders his moments brief of joy—never they come again, never, never, never they come again," which follows its leisurely course, going through all the various gestures we expect in Baroque music, repeating each idea over and over, is a simple example of what I mean. One could imagine a Mozart comic character like Despina, playing games with moments brief of joy as she poked fun for instance at a foolish lover, tantalizing in terms of timing—just as we could imagine a Romantically extended complaint on the same text with much emphasis on "never"—or a twentieth-century aphoristic comment, with some exceedingly brief moments, never coming again. It could be a description of many whole works of Webern and some of Schoenberg, provided that the notion of squandering were left out. The leap from a routined and orderly comment on such an experience (as in Handel) to its direct embodiment in music is enormous, and to accomplish it without sacrificing musical sense or intrinsic interest was a challenge not easily or quickly met. What ultimately made this leap possible was a complete overhaul of musical vocabulary and syntax, specifically in terms of its functioning in time.

Thus it seems that by Mozart's era composers were beginning to deal with musical pacing, with the combination of contrasting ideas and characters and with the resultant effects that such new techniques could produce. With Mozart and Beethoven, statement of idea became a multifaceted matter. Ideas, especially in Mozart, were often the amalgam of many separate contrasting musical techniques and characters—for instance in *Don Giovanni*, where different characters in different dramatic situations unite in one large musical ensemble that plays off each against the other and yet makes an overall unity, which in turn impels a new musical meaning to emerge from the whole. Mozart was particularly unusual in his statements of ideas, while Haydn and Beethoven were adept at finding unexpected characters related to the whole. Beethoven was constantly inventing new and surprising methods of continuity and of unification and even of statement—which depend very intimately on the emphasis given by their timing, by their succession (as in the late Bagatelles), and sometimes by their simultaneous presentation, a method more characteristic of Mozart. Harmonic progression and rhythmic pattern as well as standardized textural and even registral norms form the background against which these events—made up of contrasting themes, motives, and keys coordinated with octave doublings to amplify the sonority and dynamic changes—take place.

With the Romantic period, one could say, quite in contrast to the post-Bergsonians, that very new possibilities of form were discovered. First, a new look was taken at the Baroque method of continuing in a more or less uniform character. For there was first of all a desire to extend and intensify musical characters or moods, to have the listener come under their spell. Already in Chopin and Schumann the sound of a chord—often an inverted dominant-seventh chord—became the unifying factor of a section, as did a certain type of texture or figuration, while the thematic interest was reduced to very little. The Chopin Preludes are a series of highly condensed, short statements that depend for their unity on their sound, and for their motion on their figuration, rather than on motives and themes. This is like the first prelude in the first book of Bach's *Well-Tempered Clavier*—but the difference is that Chopin makes a great deal out of tiny inflections, unexpected contrapuntal encounters between parts, and modulations, so that the moments of these short works are very lively and unexpected.

Wagner's *Tristan*, of course, lives primarily by its harmonic world and by the special sound of the dominant seventh chord and its preceding and succeeding harmonies, which are in large measure to be classified as irregular progressions and resolutions. The work often seems like a compendium of the uses of the dominant seventh, both unaltered and altered, and its homonym the augmented sixth. It is obvious from listening to Wagner, especially *Tristan*, that the very reverse of what is often held against him is true. At best he was a master of interesting extension and prolongation of material with a great sense of timing—the opposite of Mozart, who cherished the aphoristic—which drove him to find ways of prolonging in one large sweep long stretches of material and moods of similar types. This is an intellectual feat of another kind; it allowed him to control rhythmic pulses, counterpoint, dynamics, and orchestration in new patterns pregnant with possibilities for the future. To build a special sound world, with all of its elements permuted from their usual routines into something with their special character appropriate for the concept to be presented, is to deal with the listener in an entirely different way from any that had ever been attempted before—at least on such an elaborate scale. The listener has to perceive new time relationships, new motivation to dissonances, new continuities—and, once familiar with the new way, begins to see its motions.

Now Wagner had but one typical, slow speed of presentation, and a reaction against this sluggish method that became a little too obvious, once familiar, soon set in. Yet in showing that all the aspects of musical sound are subject to extension, transformation, and development in the course of a work and can contribute to its projection in time and add depth to the flow of sound by multiple types of comparison and recall, Wagner achieved what was impossible in the period of common-practice harmony, texture, rhythm, and format. The melody-and-accompaniment format and the contrapuntal format began to seem only two of a large number of possible total sound formats—just as in late Beethoven and Brahms one finds the expansion of possibilities beyond linear motion that consists simply of a progression to a climax and then to a cadence, with various types of conventionalized extensions and interruptions. In fact, with Wagner we can see all the beginning of a tendency to reconsider the materials of music in the interest of vastly extended continuities.

Debussy, Scriabin, Stravinsky, Schoenberg, Berg, and Webern, as is well known, took up this reconsideration of elements and their coordination; but except for a few examples in each of their works, the question of timing and consequently of memory was secondary to the exploration of new compositional possibilities. Stravinsky, Webern in his early works, and Schoenberg in *Pierrot*, the *Vier Orchesterlieder* (op. 22), and the String Trio have all shown an interest in this time aspect, as has Berg, both of whose operas have distinct affinities with Mozart in respect to timing and joining of disparate ideas.

Unfortunately, with the post-War school, a new kind of Pythagoreanism has arisen, leading to the application of simple mathematical ratios and permutations to time divisions which, with the help of more "irrational" divisions of values, gives the impression of persistent irregularity from an entirely different point of view, an experimental point of view, or a "dissociation of the senses" (Rimbaud), and the manner of dealing with time and memory has beome very obvious, almost primitive. Things continue for a while in a more or less uniform way and then switch to another, contrasting stretch of similar concept. This is actually a denial of memory and time, which corresponds to the treatment of these we receive as readers of newspapers and advertisements, as targets of almost any kind of public communication which reduces everything to superficiality and ultimately to loss of identity. To quote Rilke (from "Der Dichter"):

> Du entfernst dich von mir, du Stunde.
> Wunde schlägt mir dein Flügelschlag.

In my own music, I am keenly aware of the ways in which some of these concepts of time can affect even small details and make them able to participate in larger constructions. For it is the large continuity and conception of progress which determines the choice of all the materials in my recent work—any given moment, for the most part, is a bridge from a previous one to a succeeding one and contains both the elements of unexpectedness as well as intelligible relation to the past and anticipation of the future, not always fulfilled in the way anticipated.

The *Gesamtkunstwerk*
(1966/94)

To prepare for discussing the combination of arts into one art form, it would perhaps be best to consider the differences that exist in the first place between the various arts. One must distinguish at the outset between painting, architecture, sculpture, literature, and film on the one hand, which deal in fixed objects, and the performance arts on the other, such as music, dance, and theatre. This distinction is not absolutely rigid—sculpture can move, film involves performance in some sense, music can be recorded—but it is nonetheless a meaningful one. The combined and integrated artwork, the *Gesamtkunstwerk*, became a conscious conception with Richard Wagner and deals primarily with two of the performance arts, music and theatre.

The main repertory of music consists of scores that indicate with considerable precision what the performers must do to produce the work. This precision is largely outward; it is left to the performer to interpret or understand the music—that is, to modify or amplify in a host of different ways the general indications—and project it to the audience. It is a mistake to think—as has so often been done with modern works—that the typical musical score is prescriptive to performers to the extent of always producing identical performances. In fact, the more different kinds of imaginative inner coordinations there are in a work, the more facets of interpretation there are. It is part of the composer's job to provide works with many possible interpretations by the performer as well as many possible interpretations by the listener, while at the same time maintaining an overall identity for the work. Similarly, a play may have characters, situations, plot, and a philosophical point that gives it its identity, yet with these in view it is susceptible to an infinite number of different interpretations in performance, all clearly related to the basic idea and throwing light on it.

Obviously, the theatre is much more concerned with actual human beings in action or passion and their relationships with themselves and things as these are seen and heard. Most of the operations of the theatre, from "happenings" to plays of high formalism, such as Noh dramas or the plays of Corneille, involve actors and their audience. The degree of difference between actor and spectator can be made to seem very little or very great: the audience's role can range from near identity with the actors to passive observation.

The actor-audience relationship exists in other arts too, although in every other art the particular medium—sound, paint, dance motions—has developed its own inner structure, meaning, and life, and in consequence requires a certain familiarity with the medium or works in the medium before it can engage the attention. The very fact, however, that the musical score, like the play, needs a *performance* to bring it into existence means that the work is being constantly modernized. Scores and plays that performers can no longer see any point in fall into neglect. And those that seem to have a point at any given period are performed so as to stress that point in terms of the style of the period. The modifications of text in performances of Shakespeare in the eighteenth century are well known; the modifications of Bach, Handel, and Scarlatti in the nineteenth century are before us in old editions. These give some idea of how different past performances were.

What is interesting is that with an art like film that depends entirely on reproduction and is preset and rigid as a book or a piece of sculpture, the acting and production very rapidly become dated—even a passage of four or five years is very noticeable. This is also true—but at a much slower rate—of musical performances stamped on piano rolls, and recordings, in which the extravagant performances of a previous period are hard to listen to seriously. Roland Barthes, in *Mythologies*, describes this vividly, in the article "L'Art vocal bourgeois":

> It would seem impertinent to lecture an excellent baritone, Gérard Souzay, but a disc on which this singer has recorded several songs of Fauré seems to me to illustrate very well an entire musical mythology in which the main signs of bourgeois art are found. This art is essentially one of signals (*Signalétique*): it continuously presents, not emotion, but the signs of emotions. This is exactly what M. Souzay does: having, for instance, to sing the words "une tristesse affreuse," he is not happy with the simple semantic contents of these words, nor with the musical line which supports them; he has to dramatize the phonetics of the frightful (*affreux*), wait, and then cause the double fricative to explode, to unleash misfortune in the very thickness of the letters; no one can ignore the fact that it is a question of particularly terrible pangs. Unfortunately this redundancy of intention stifles both the words and the music, and particularly their connection, which is the very object of vocal music. It is in music as it is in the other arts, including literature: the highest form of artistic expression lies nearest to literalness (*littéralité*), that is to say of a certain kind of algebra: all forms must tend toward abstraction, which as everyone knows is not contrary to the sensual element.
>
> And this is exactly what bourgeois art refuses to accept: it always wants to take its consumers for simpletons, for whom all the work has to be done and the intentions overstressed, for fear they will not be sufficiently grasped (but art is always ambiguous, in a way, it is always contradicting its message, and particularly music, which is never literally either sad or gay).[1]

Looked at from this point of view, the *Gesamtkunstwerk* so elaborately written about by Wagner seems to be a purely bourgeois conception, which as Debussy pointed out took its consumers for simpletons, since in his prose texts Wagner is always stressing the intention to express emotion, on the stage by words and actions as well as in the singing and in the orchestral music, and accompanying entrances of characters or mentions of important ideas with leitmotifs in the most obvious way. Its main problem, however, is that the various arts cannot remain on an equal footing. In Wagner, the music finally takes over in all the best works, reducing the words to very simple, almost primitive emotional expressions, and the stage action to such slow motion that in recent years directors have made of it a kind of ritualistic, almost hieratic gesturing that does not pretend even to suggest reality.

1. Roland Barthes, "L'Art vocal bourgeois," in *Mythologies* (Paris; Editions du Seuil, 1957), 189–90; my translation.

In Mozart's and Verdi's operas, the stage action, largely of a characteristically theatrical type, alternates with music which takes over and either destroys the stage action or becomes a portrayal of some background effect—like the dance music, the thunderstorm music, and the convivial singing of the banquet scene in *Don Giovanni*. When the theatre takes over, musical pattern becomes less important than its character, and the main interest resides in the theatre, just as in ballet the actual dancing and its choreographic pattern invariably take precedence over the music. However, just as in opera, there are infinite fascinating combinations. The choreography of many works of George Balanchine, for instance, carries out such constantly interesting patterns and counterpatterns to the music on which it is based as to be a kind of explication or commentary on the musical text, which puts the music in a novel light. But in most cases, where there is any degree of visible activity during music, most people, being more visual, begin to think in theatrical rather than musical terms.

In the following quotation, it should be obvious that instead of putting the claims of music and drama on an equal basis Wagner is actually simplifying drama, simplifying both the poetic language and the action to such a point that music will inevitably play the most important, formative role in his work, reducing the dramatic action and the characterization to what Barthes would call "signals" of the musical events with very little convincing quality.

Let us take a hasty glance at the form of our supposed drama, so as to assure ourselves that—for all its necessary and fundamental, its ever newly-shaping change—it is a form essentially, nay, uniquely *one*. But let us consider also what it is, that makes this unity possible.

Just as the joinery of my individual scenes excluded every alien and unnecessary detail, and led all interest to the dominant Chief-mood (*verwaltende Hauptstimmung*), so did the whole building of my drama join itself into one organic unity, whose easily surveyed members were made out by those fewer scenes and situations which set the passing mood: no mood could be permitted to be struck in any one of these scenes that did not stand in a weighty relation to the moods of all the other scenes, so that the development of the moods from out each other and the constant obviousness of this development, should establish the unity of the drama in its very mode of expression. . . . Just as, in the progress of the drama, the intended climax of a decisory Chief-mood was to be reached only through a development, continuously present to the feeling, of the individual moods already roused: so must the musical expression, which directly influences the physical feeling, necessarily take a decisive share in this development to a climax.

Let us not forget, however, that the orchestra's equalizing moments of expression [which take place while the characters sing the language of daily life] are never to be determined by the *caprice of the musician*, as a random tricking out of sound, but *only by the poet's aim*. Should these "moments" utter anything not connected with the situation of the dramatis personae . . . then the unity of expression is itself disturbed by this departure from the content. A mere absolute-musical embellishment of drooping or inchoate situations—a favorite operatic device for the self-glorification of music . . .—such a trick upheaves at once the unity of expression, and casts the interest of the ear on music no longer as an expression, but, in a manner, as herself the thing expressed.[2]

Wagner here, of course, touches on the fundamental point—the problem of relating both text and theater to music—that was being fought out around him at the time in the battle between the critics who sided with him and those who sided with Brahms and "absolute" music. Yet this battle had been fought for centuries, usually in the name of Greek tragedy, which has always had a great influence on Western theatre. Wagner himself was a great reader of the Greeks, and it was after the powerful dramatic pattern of these works with their choruses, chorus-leaders, dancers, and solo speakers that opera developed. The contrast between the more hieratic plays of Aeschylus and Sophocles and the more overtly dramatic ones of Euripides may explain why opera, very soon after its inception, divided into two opposing branches. One branch is represented by the Florentine Camerata and Monteverdi, and later by Gluck and Wagner, who wanted the music to emphasize the dramatic verbal and physical action; while, in opposition, Alessandro Scarlatti, Lully, and even Rameau favored the more hieratic pattern of the formalized, static arie da capo. This dichotomy was resolved to an extent in the later works of Verdi, who even in his earlier work had found remarkable ways of reconciling the two attitudes. Of course, Richard Strauss's *Capriccio* poses the problem of which is more important—words or music?—in opera, and works it out humorously on stage, sugared up with Viennese charm. Later, Schoenberg engages the same issue in expressionist terms, presenting it in a powerfully religious context and showing the opposition between reason, in the almost naturalistic *Sprechstimme* of the difficultly articulate Moses, and magic in the fluent aria-singing of Aron.

The naturalistic setting of words—that is, setting them in a way that will follow the normal rhythm and inflection of the voice—presents a problem, since we do not speak rhythmically. A number of years ago, when Virgil Thomson was an active critic, many American composers used to fear his technical criticisms of word settings. It has been a general matter of concern for some time that English has seldom been set effectively, or in a way that renders it intelligible when sung, since the time of Purcell. Our language, for instance, has many words with groups of final consonants that need to be clearly heard if the words are to make sense to the listener, yet that inevitably make a break in a vocal line.

Besides actual word and sentence setting, of course, there is the matter of giving these the kind of individual inflection with which they might be said by the stage character in his stage situation. When the words are declaimed in

2. Richard Wagner, *Opera and Drama* (1851), trans. William Ashton Ellis, in *Richard Wagner's Prose Works*, Vol. 2 (London: Routledge and Kegan Paul Ltd., 1893; reprint, New York: Broude Brothers, 1966), 343–46. The second paragraph has been inserted from Wagner, "A Communication to My Friends" (1851), trans. William Ashton Ellis, in *Richard Wagner's Prose Works*, Vol. 1 (London: Routledge and Kegan Paul Ltd., 1892; reprint, New York: Broude Brothers, 1966), 369. [B]

some more emotional or rhetorical way, with strong stresses on musically important words, the imitation of these inflections—increasing or limiting them by greater or lesser melodic leaps and by holding certain syllables—becomes a matter of theatre. The composer must determine all this beforehand, obviously, in a way that the playwright does not need to.

But besides all these detailed matters of word setting (what might be called "realistic" word setting), there is the larger matter of their composite meaning over a series of lines and paragraphs or stanzas—and, in opera, the actor's gestures and actions as they coordinate with the meaning of the words which somehow, too, have to be reflected in the music. On the other hand, if the music is to have an interest and a coherence of its own—which is the point of opera—then it must establish its own pacing and its own pattern, which must inevitably affect the naturalistic presentation of words and actions.

There is, of course, the non-naturalistic solution involving the establishment of a convention—the interjection of song or aria in which both the action and the plot are frozen in a period of time and the actor presents a musical monologue expressing the feelings or attitudes evoked by the immediate state of affairs. This, being individual comment (or duet, and so forth), can have a special poetic language, with repeated words and phrases, since this is a more or less static presentation of an elongated moment. The development of this convention of musical numbers in opera and their interrelationship with the onward flow of the stage action was developed with great subtlety by Mozart and Verdi, among many others. In a way this change of emphasis from action to passion, while like the monologues of Greek and Roman as well as Elizabethan and many other plays built on the classical model, is like the changes of angle and location of the moving-picture camera, which alter the viewer's comprehension of a situation by focusing on a special aspect of it.

This attitude, which characterized the number opera, is evident in this letter of Verdi:

> Today I have sent off to Ricordi the last act of *Macbeth* finished and complete . . . You will laugh when you hear that I have written a fugue for the battle!!! A fugue? I, who detest everything that smacks of the schools and who have not done such a thing for thirty years!!! But I will tell you that, in this instance, that musical form is to the point. The repetition of subject and countersubject, the jar of dissonances, the clashing sounds express a battle well enough . . .[3]

With the rise of public concerts in the early part of the nineteenth century, the whole question of theatricality—of extramusical effects—began to be discussed and considered seriously. We know of the great lengths to which Paganini went to publicize himself, spreading rumors about nonexistent love affairs before he appeared at a concert, dressing to suggest a diabolic character

---

3. Letter to Léon Escudier, dated 3 February 1865. This translation is adapted from two others: in *Letters of Giuseppe Verdi*, trans. and ed. Charles Osborne (New York: Holt, Rinehart, and Winston, 1971), 137–38; and in Mary Jane Phillips-Matz, *Verdi: A Biography* (Oxford: Oxford University Press, 1993), 481–82. [B]

on the stage, producing new sounds that no one could imitate on the violin—all in all putting on a very theatrical show of wild improvisation. Evidently he was such a remarkable violinist that those who came to hear the music were not put off. We know too of Liszt's showmanship, and of the constant efforts at publicity and public relations with which Wagner drew attention to himself (as is evident in his autobiography)—to such a degree, indeed, that Nietzsche lost all faith in his integrity, and sneered at him for using a religious theme in *Parsifal* (when he had been an atheist all his life) that was bound to be successful, purely to get his opera-theater in Bayreuth out of debt.

Concerts in the nineteenth century, in their own special way, became newsworthy events, and this quality of newsworthiness remains one of their social dimensions. The matter of improvisation, concerned as it is with the uniqueness of an event, as well as with acting out a performance and stressing its theatricality, is very much bound up with this quality. In listening to the old recordings of many performers of the last century, and in reading about them, we realize that one aspect of many performances was the impression of the extreme, almost improvisatorial liberties that were taken—an impresson that lasts until we have heard many such examples and have come to realize that a whole repertoire of techniques was in conscious use, like the catch in Caruso's voice at "Ridi, Pagliacci": techniques as mandatory for certain types of performers as the routines of improvisation taught to students of jazz. How much actual, spontaneous improvisation, a technique that naturally draws attention to the performer away from the music, is really occurring is hard to know—for the first thing that all performers of popular music tend to do is to learn routines, often modeled on those of other successful performers, which can carry them through a dull day while still producing a good audience impression. In music of every period such routines were highly stereotyped—the figured-bass player could rarely come up with a realization that seemed any better than hack-work, certainly almost never with the spontaneity of, let us say, the written work of Bach. The same is true of the cadenzas for concerti, and the improvisation on themes that organists used to do—and it is also largely true of popular musical practice from the era of the Viennese waltz to the present day. In whatever type of serious music which permits a degree of improvisation, composers make efforts to avoid too formulaic a performance. So it is generally true that carefully written scores produce the most unroutinized performances because, in preventing performers from playing in their usual way, they suggest another kind of spontaneous reaction—to the musical concepts underlying the music—which has greater potential for liveliness than is usually the case with improvisation.

Improvisation, of course, is possible only in a musical style that has become so fixed, like that of Baroque music or jazz, that it permits almost effortless musical invention—which is usually a signal that the style is about to lose its vividness. But there are also some new kinds of improvisational methods in which a private or special style is devised, which the performer or a group, by dint of much practice, learns very thoroughly, in order to be able to cover a multitude of unexpected performance situations through ready routine.

In the end, improvisation is undertaken mainly in appeal to the theatrical side of musical performance and rarely reaches the highest artistic level of musical thought and expression developed in Western music. In improvisation, the matter of the musical "work" is brought into question. Each performance in an art like theatre, opera, dance, or music has its special relations to the fixed "work" or score. It is a very different kind of affair from painting or literature, in which each element of an inanimate object is subject to the choice of the creator. But music of the most familiar type does display certain aspects of object-art, in that it is highly prearranged by the artist and deals with a non-natural medium that is the result of careful but special cultivation—the medium of instrumental or vocal sound. It is like painting in that it tends to use these special, once called "musical" sounds against a background of silence, as painting uses special pigments on a background of canvas. It does not ordinarily use objects with which we are in daily familiar contact, such as words or people, or views of objects and people as do literature, theatre, and film. Even when the whole world of sounds once excluded as noise began to invade music, this noise was usually processed, distorted, controlled—as much as are the bits of burlap or newspaper and so forth found in the work of Kurt Schwitters and other makers of collages.

Besides the Wagnerian manifestation of the *Gesamtkunstwerk* as a combination of different arts appealing to different senses, there was a parallel development in Germany and later in France which stressed the notion of correspondence of the senses. Ideas about the relationship between individual musical pitches and colors had been discussed by Diderot and by Schlegel, and in the Romantic period the whole question of synaesthesia began to be examined—by Coleridge, De Quincey, and Edgar Allan Poe, who wrote passages like: "Suddenly lights were brought into the room . . . and issuing from the flame of each lamp, there flowed unbrokenly into my ears a strain of melodious monotone."[4] Through this time and later, many attempted to establish direct relationships, as did Baudelaire and René Ghil, and of course Rimbaud in his sonnet on vowels. Color scales were invented for color organs, one of which was used by Scriabin in his tone poem *Prométhée*.

As Edmund Wilson says in *Axel's Castle*:

To approximate the indefiniteness of music was to become one of the principal aims of Symbolism.

This effect of indefiniteness was produced not merely by the confusion I have mentioned between the imaginary world and the real; but also by means of a further confusion between the perceptions of the different senses [quoting the famous lines of Baudelaire]: "Comme de longs échos qui de loin se confondent . . . / Les parfums, les couleurs et les sons se répondent."

Later, Wilson sums up:

4. Quoted in Edmund Wilson, *Axel's Castle: A Study in the Imaginative Literature of 1870–1930* (New York: Charles Scribner's Sons, 1932), 13.

The assumptions which underlay Symbolism lead us to formulate some such doctrine as the following: Every feeling or sensation we have, every moment of consciousness, is different from every other; and it is, in consequence, impossible to render our sensations as we actually experience them through the conventional and universal language of ordinary literature. . . . The Symbolists themselves, full of the idea of producing with poetry effects like those of music, tended to think of these images as possessing an abstract value like musical notes and chords.[5]

One can find examples of similar thinking among the expressionist writers and painters in Germany at the turn of the century. In the expressionist manifesto *Der blaue Reiter* of 1912, there is a play by Kandinsky, *Der gelbe Klang* (*The Yellow Sound*, a storyless stage presentation of colors, music, and pantomime). Part of Scene 2 reads, for instance:

The blue mist recedes gradually before the light, which is a perfect, brilliant white. At the back of the stage, a bright green hill, completely round and as large as possible.
The background violet, fairly bright.
The music is shrill and tempestuous, with oft-repeated A and B and B and A♭. These individual notes are finally swallowed up by the raging storm. Suddenly, there is complete stillness. A pause. Again is heard the plangent complaint, albeit precise and sharp, of A and B. This lasts for some time. Then, a further pause.
At this point the background suddenly turns a dirty brown . . .[6]

A far more convincing and remarkable example of this type is Schoenberg's *Die glückliche Hand*, a one-act symbolic opera that combines a very elaborate orchestral score with precise indications of changes of colored lights, synchronization of the actor's gestures with singing, and orchestral music. In this work, written in 1910–13, one aspect of *Gesamtkunstwerk* finds its most complete expression, even as to authorship—for Schoenberg not only wrote the text but designed the scenery and prescribed the various performance coordinations. The notion that each moment must have its individuality and character had already led him to write a one-act opera, *Erwartung*, that caught fleeting, dream-like, irrational changes of mood in a long, never-repeating score of music. *Die glückliche Hand* synchronized in great detail the stage action as well as the lighting with the music, so that they would play an almost formal role in the musical development, just as the music played an important role in the theatrical development by suggesting motions as well as moods.

This detailed coordination of music and physical stage action was developed further by Alban Berg in both *Wozzeck* and *Lulu*. In *Wozzeck*, Berg even goes to the length of composing into the score the moment when the

5. Wilson, *Axel's Castle*, 13, 21.

6. Wassily Kandinsky, *Der gelbe Klang*, in Jelena Hahl-Koch, *Arnold Schoenberg–Wassily Kandinsky: Letters, Pictures and Documents*, trans. John C. Crawford (London: Faber & Faber, 1984), 119.

stage curtain rises or falls on an act. Each time it is done differently—once, two measures before the music begins, once as it begins, once six measures after. The ends of acts are similarly planned: the speed of the curtain is indicated each time. These two works of Berg are perhaps the only really completely successful examples of *Gesamtkunstwerke*, particularly *Wozzeck*, not only because in both the play and the music are each so remarkable by itself, but because the main elements of the theatrical production have been very carefully composed into the timing of the score. Even in these works, however, the audience's attention will constantly fluctuate between the words, action, and music. In *Wozzeck*, for instance, the orchestra asserts itself in a long symphonic interlude just before the last scene, while in *Lulu* there are separate musical numbers, recitatives, and even spoken sections that harken back to the Verdian tradition almost as much as to the Wagnerian *Gesamtkunstwerk*.

Around the time of *Lulu*, which as a *Gesamtkunstwerk* includes the then new art of cinematography—a silent film accompanied by orchestral music—the problem of a new kind of unified art work, that of the sound film, began to be taken more seriously than it had been during the silent film period. Sergei Eisenstein and Alexander Pudovkin first wrote on the sound film in 1928; Eisenstein developed an elaborate theory about the synchronization of music with films which he carried out in *Alexander Nevsky* in 1938. His book *The Film Sense* gives very precise information not only about his ideas but about the details of his actual practice. First, concerning the general attitude:

Any definitions [of musical content] that even touch this approach of a *narrowly representational comprehension of music* inevitably lead to visualizations of a most platitudinous character—if for any reason visualizations should be required:

["Barcarolle" from Offenbach's *Tales of Hoffmann*]: Love: a couple embracing.

If we add to the pictures evoked by the "Barcarolle" a series of Venetian scenes . . . the "illustration" of the lovers . . . [is] blotted out. But take from these Venetian "scenes" only the *approaching and receding* movements of the water combined with there reflected *scampering and retreating play of light* over the surface of the canals, and you immediately remove yourself, by at least one degree, from the series of "illustration" fragments, and you are closer to finding a response to the *sensed inner movement* of a barcarolle . . . Music and visual imagery are actually not commensurable through narrowly "representational" elements. If one speaks of genuine and profound relations and proportions between the music and the picture, it can only be in reference to the relations between the *fundamental movements* of the music and the picture, i.e. compositional and structural elements.[7]

In an interesting chapter on the synchronization of the senses, Eisenstein discusses the combining of sound with film, audio-visual montage. With the coming of the sound film, he developed the idea of what he called vertical

7. Sergei M. Eisenstein, *The Film Sense*, trans. and ed. Jay Leyda (New York: Harcourt, Brace, and World, Inc., 1942), 161–63.

montage, which was basically the development of various kinds of visual and aural simultaneity—the latter not merely of actual sounds but of music. He discusses the type of what he called polyphonic visual montage,

> where shot is linked to shot not merely through one indication—movement, or light values, or stage in the exposition of the plot or the like—but through a *simultaneous advance* of a multiple series of lines, each maintaining an independent compositional course and each contributing to the total compositional course of the sequence . . . The several interdependent lines virtually resemble a ball of vari-colored yarn, with the lines running through and binding together the entire sequence of shots . . . The general course of the montage was an uninterrupted interweaving of these diverse themes into one unified movement. Each montage-piece had a double responsibility—to build the *total line* as well as to continue the movement within *each of the contributory themes* . . . Montage is actually a *large, developing thematic movement*, progressing through a continuing diagram of individual splices.[8]

The problem of adding a sound track to this kind of visual montage that had an organic relation to what he called "a complex composed of film strips containing photographic images" required much experiment to find

> *an inner synchronization between the tangible picture and the differently perceived sounds* . . . To relate these two elements we find a natural language common to both—movement . . . In the more rudimentary forms of expression both elements (the picture and its sound) will be controlled by an identity of *rhythm*, according to the content of the scene.[9]

From here, Eisenstein goes on to point out that the synchronization can be metric, rhythmic, melodic, and tonal. The film and its sound track can match element for element, or can be a combination of unlike elements that result in a dissonance between the aural and visual—each existing for itself and not uniting in an organic whole. Synchronization does not presume consonance, of course, but the play of correspondence has to be compositionally controlled. One element or type of synchronization can lead the other, music can predominate over the visual, rhythm can be the determining factor in some scenes, tone in others.

In his book, Eisenstein gives a detailed description of how the "Battle on the Ice" sequence in *Alexander Nevsky* was constructed in terms of his concept of audio-visual montage, which incorporates almost every conceivable type of combination of music and visual action in the service of this particular narrative, presentational intention. Similarly, there occurred almost every type of collaboration between the composer, Prokofiev, and the film director, from filming scenes based on precomposed music to composing music to fit already filmed sequences—so that perhaps one of the most elaborately worked out audio-visual sequences resulted. The work today still fascinates

8. Ibid., 75–76, 81.

9. Ibid., 77, 81–83.

with its complex construction, although as a battle scene it seems curiously lacking in vividness, perhaps partly because of the weakness of the music.

Much more recently, experimentation in the combination of music and films has been pursued by a small group working under the auspices of French Radio-Television, a Service de la Recherche that is able to combine experimental visual sequences with musical scores of every conceivable type, specifically commissioned or developed for the purpose. This group has been very active since 1960 and has produced some seventy short films; some, like those by the Polish painter Piotr Kamler, are remarkable kinetic colored abstractions. Many of the leading advanced composers have contributed scores to these films, collaborating in various ways with the director. These works, very uneven and varied, attack the problem of combining music, speech, or other so-called natural sounds with visual material from many very experimental angles, proceeding in far less systematized fashion than in most recent "commercial" films. In most of the examples I have seen, the visual motion and character forms the basis on which the music is built or with which the music is contrasted, and the musical form and continuity relies on the interconnections of images—although there are a few, like *Fer chaud* (hot iron), a film by Brissot about the work of futurist sculptor Schoffer, with a preexisting score by Xenakis, in which the entire action is controlled or, at least, planned around a musical order.

That the fascination of this unified artwork remains constant in our time is shown by Antonin Artaud's discussion of it in connection with his notion of the theater of cruelty:

> The theater of cruelty intends to return to all the old tested and magical means to win over the senses.
>
> These means, which consist of the intensity of colors, of lights, of sounds, which use vibration, trepidation, repetition whether of a musical rhythm or of a spoken phrase, which bring in tonality or the communicative enveloping of a lighting effect, can obtain their entire effect only by using *dissonances*.
>
> But instead of limiting these dissonances to a single sense, we intend to make them jump from one sense to the other, from a color to a sound, from a word to a lighting effect, from a nervous activity of gestures to a flat tonal character, etc. etc.[10]

This in many ways parallels Eisenstein's conceptions.

Just as in Wagner's time a movement against his concept of music drama arose in the name of absolute music, so in the time of Schoenberg and Berg was a polemic launched against the approach that their work exemplified—this one by Bertolt Brecht, in the name of the theatre of ideas:

> Our existing opera is a culinary opera. It was a means of pleasure long before it turned into merchandise. It furthers pleasure even where it requires, or promotes, a certain degree of education, for the education in question is an education in taste. To every object it adopts a hedonistic approach. It "experiences," and it ranks as an "experience.". . .

---

10. Antonin Artaud, "Le Théâtre de la cruauté (second manifeste)," in *Le Théâtre et son double* (Paris: Gallimard, 1964), 190; my translation.

The opera *Mahagonny* pays conscious tribute to the senselessness of the operatic form. The irrationality of opera lies in the fact that rational elements are employed, solid reality is aimed at, but at the same time it is all washed out by the music. A dying man is real. If at the same time he sings we are translated to the sphere of the irrational. (If the audience sang at the sight of him the case would be different.) . . .

The great struggle for supremacy between words, music, and production—which always brings up the question "which is the pretext for what?": is the music the pretext for the events on the stage, or are these the pretext for the music? etc.—can simply be bypassed by radically separating the elements. So long as the expression *Gesamtkunstwerk* (or "integrated work of art") means that the integration is a muddle, so long as the arts are supposed to be "fused" together, the various elements will all be equally degraded, and each will act as a mere "feed" to the rest. The process of fusion extends to the spectator, who gets thrown into the melting pot too and becomes a passive (suffering) part of the total work of art. Witchcraft of this sort must of course be fought against. Whatever is intended to produce hypnosis, is likely to induce sordid intoxication, or creates fog, has got to be given up. *Words, music, and setting must become more independent of one another.*[11]

Of course, Brecht's whole point of view depends on his conception of Epic Theater, which aims to make the spectator think the kind of thoughts that will lead to political action. His libretti or plays for use in opera, such as *Mahagonny*, *The Trial of Lucullus*, and the recent *Herr Puntila und sein Knecht Matti*—as was pointed out by Peter Heyworth in *The New York Times* in a review of the last in an East Berlin performance—usually have resulted in restrictions by him or his musical collaborators on the music, to the advantage of the words.[12]

Thus we have two sharply contrasting attitudes about the subject, which actually are very hard to reconcile. However, the influence of the idea of the *Gesamtkunstwerk* is perennial, especially when music, as happens often, becomes itself a kind of signal for certain attitudes of mind rather than dealing in its own kinds of patterning. This signal usage is perhaps clearest in the singing radio or TV commercial and serves, just as Roland Barthes pointed out in Gérard Souzay's singing, as a signal for a certain attitude rather than a presentation of it. Thus there are musical scores whose main intention is to signal that we are in an old-fashioned situation, or a teenage situation, or an avant-garde situation, and this constitutes their main contribution to the spectacle they accompany. Sometimes this spectacle is a concert itself, converted into a theatrical turn with incidental music, much as Paganini and Liszt must at times have engaged in. Whatever goes on, though, any such production almost invariably turns out to be effective only if one of the arts dominates the others, and only if this art is handled in a convincing and imaginative way.

The effect of all this on the actual art of music considered in itself is very evident and widespread, just as is the influence of mathematical "programs"

11. Bertold Brecht, "The Modern Theatre Is the Epic Theatre," in *Brecht on Theatre: The Development of an Aesthetic*, trans. and ed. John Willett (New York: Hill and Wang, 1964), 35–38.

12. This, however, has not occurred in Roger Sessions's setting of *The Trial of Lucullus*.

applied to composition. Both resemble the process expressed in Rimbaud's admonition to poets—"The poet makes himself a visionary through a long, immense, and reasoned derangement of all the senses"—and perhaps even more Paul Valéry's artistic contention that "literature has become an art based on the abuse of language." But for all their faults, these various tendencies do put musical discourse into question and make us reconsider it in a new light. They are often interesting in themselves, too.

Soviet Music
(1967/94)

The roots of advanced or experimental art in Russia seem embedded far more deeply in the nineteenth century than they are in the United States. We have our Whitman, Poe, and Whistler; they have their Dostoevsky and Gogol. And in the early years of the twentieth century, at the actual origins of contemporary art, it is obvious that the Russians with their controversial liveliness and brilliance supplied the modern movement with many important philosophical and aesthetic ideas, as well as the works that embodied them, and that these determined much of the direction of modern music and painting. We all owe a great debt to such composers as Scriabin, Prokofiev, and especially the perennial and remarkable Stravinsky; to such painters as Lissitzky, Malevitch, and Kandinsky; and to writers like Bely, Blok, and Balmont. Kandinsky, for instance, was closely connected with the German expressionist movement in painting. The reprint of *Der blaue Reiter* that has recently appeared in Munich serves to remind us that almost half the 100 pages of that famous document were written by Russians. There is an article about Scriabin's *Prométhée* by Leonid Sabaneyev, articles about Russia's "Wild Men," and a great many articles by and about Kandinsky.[1] Also included in *Der blaue Reiter* was Schoenberg's article, "The Relationship to the Text," in which he acknowledged the way in which Kandinsky's ideas about art accorded with his own; we know too from Kandinsky's writings that he admired Schoenberg both as a composer and as a painter. Thus the influence of Russian thought, not only in the primitivist (Stravinsky) and mystical (Scriabin) movements—where it is obvious and easily understood—but also in expressionism, where the connection might at first seem improbable, has been very strong.

The United States, where there has always been a keen interest in Russian art, experienced a constant influx of new works from Russia during the years just before and during the decade after the First World War. The conductors Modest Altschuler and Serge Koussevitzky presented us with the latest works of Scriabin, Prokofiev, and Stravinsky. In the 1920s, we saw the Moscow Art Theatre, the Moscow Opera, and various Russian ballet companies in very "advanced" and striking performances. I remember the Moscow Opera's performance of Bizet's *Carmen*, which had been completely renovated so that it

---

1. *Der blaue Reiter*, new documentary ed. with an introd. by Klaus Lankheit (Munich: R. Piper Verlag, 1965); trans. Henning Falkenstein as *The blaue Reiter Almanac* (New York: Viking, 1974).

looked like a kind of expressionistic movie, called *Carmencita and the Soldier*. It was a very rapid, exciting, and passionate production, one of the most remarkable I have ever seen in my life, such as one would seldom have expected, then or now, from the Metropolitan Opera.

Around that time, it is true, the Met kept Stravinsky's *Petrouchka*, John Alden Carpenter's *Skyscrapers*, and De Falla's *Vida Breve* in its repertory for a while—but more adventurously, the League of Composers gave as part of its modern music season occasional evenings at the (sold-out) Opera House. It presented *Wozzeck*, Stravinsky's *Oedipus Rex* with the remarkable, gigantic puppets of Remo Buffano, sets by Norman Bel Geddes, and the Harvard Glee Club (in which I sang)—and Prokofiev's *Pas d'acier*, a ballet which concluded with all the dancers waving red hammer-and-sickle flags, filling the stage with them.

Certain places and people in and around New York still recall this very early period, such as the museum on Riverside Drive at 103rd Street devoted to the paintings of Nikolai Roerich, who designed the original sets for Stravinsky's *Le Sacre* and is said still to live in the city—as also did, until very recently, the sculptor Alexander Archipenko and the painter David Burliuk, whose work continued to carry on the expressionist ideas of that early time. But of course it is Stravinsky who, with the constant stream of outstanding and marvelous works he has produced in our country, has done the most to maintain our awareness of how valuable Russian art is to us.

During the 1920s and early '30s, many young composers in the United States—including myself—were interested in the latest developments in the Soviet Union. We kept up with the publication of scores by composers like Nikolai Roslavets, Samuel Feinberg, and Sergei Protopopov, as well as others who were following the implications of Scriabin's ideas and developing them further. At the same time we were very impressed by some of the early works of Dmitri Shostakovich, particularly his very lively and amusing opera *The Nose*, and his Second and Third Symphonies, "Offering to October" and "The First of May"—which although influenced, as were many of our own works, by much Western progressive music from Milhaud to Berg, made a deep impression for their vigorous individual expression. My early enthusiasm for *The Nose* was corroborated at a performance of this broadly comic work that I saw a few years ago at the Maggio Fiorentino. It lived up to all my expectations: it is one of the funniest operas I have ever seen in my life—like an old Max Sennett comedy—and of a musical brilliance which perhaps makes it difficult for the typical opera house to produce.

During this same period, outside of Russia, the remarkable, often fantastic talents of émigrés living in Europe attested to the importance of the Russian heritage. There was the strange, mystical composer Nikolai Oboukhov, who periodically performed fragments of his *Le Livre de la vie*, apparently never finishing it but continuing from year to year. There was also Ivan Vyshnegradsky's highly original development of a microtonal system—and, in the United States, Joseph Schillinger, who arrived here in the 1920s and brought numerical ideas about the organization of music which were novel and shocking for the time, but which were apparently influential upon composers such as George Gershwin and others whom he taught. It is a curious turn of history that ideas very clearly and closely related to Schillinger's have now become important to the Darmstadt School, as if Russian ideas had ended up in Europe by way of the United States. To complete the circle, some of the younger Russian composers whose work we will hear tonight have rekindled certain traditions of the Darmstadt School; thus they are in a sense heirs to ideas that came originally from their own country, but by a very roundabout route.[2]

Although on a lesser scale than Russia, the United States during this same period experienced a significant burst of avant-garde activity in the works of Varèse, Ruggles, Ives, Cowell, Riegger, and a few others. And each of these composers, in a less severe way than their counterparts in Russia, suffered from the wave of artistic reaction that in the United States accompanied the Great Depression and the great social changes that followed from it.

Soviet composers of the present day are not, as yet, widely known anywhere, not even in their own country, because after years of determined opposition to any form of music which did not reflect the artistic directive of socialist realism aimed at glorifying the Soviet regime, Russians have been isolated from developments in the West and thus poorly prepared to break away from this limiting attitude. Stalin's shocking suppression of Shostakovich's *Lady Macbeth of Mtsensk* in 1936 was only a particularly visible manifestation of a trend that had been gathering force for some time. The directive of artistic socialist realism, imposed that same year after much discussion within the Soviet Composers' Union, was intended to produce music that would be immediately accessible to the masses. What actually resulted was music of a manufactured optimism and a false simplicity. Many of the most talented Russian composers, like Shostakovich and Prokofiev, had to give up their "advanced" styles at the risk of incurring utter ostracism from the society, if not worse.

This drastic repression had a strange and disturbing parallel in a trend which became increasingly evident in the capitalist cultural marketplace of the West. For the American public, after being shocked by the new avant-garde works of the 1920s, was by the '30s beginning to revolt against musical modernism and to discourage performances of works in this style—an attitude which still dominates in many places here. Ironically, the musical, and by and large political, conservatives whose tastes began to prevail during those years had to turn to the music of Russian "socialist realism" for new repertory, since very few works of this sort were being written in the United States. The great many rather long, epigonous Russian symphonies that began to make their way here became very popular with the bourgeois public, who found that these pieces could be relied upon for a steady supply of the traditional, old-fashioned concert-hall sounds that they were used to, and that orchestras here were accustomed to playing.

2. The concert program of 24 May 1967 consisted of the following works: Valentin Silvestrov, Trio (1962); Andrei Volkonsky, *Lamentations of Shchaza* (1963), for soprano and five players; Vladimir Zagortsev, *Dimensions* (1965); and Edison Denisov, Cantata, *"Sun of the Incas"* (1964), for soprano and ten players. [B]

Of course, these reactionary works were successful in the United States for other reasons, too: many were, after all, written by composers whose great talents could be observed even though bridled by the political directives under which they worked. It is also true that during the years 1933–48 many of the most characteristic works of Bartók, Schoenberg, Hindemith, Stravinsky, Milhaud, and others were written here, and that most of these composers were somehow able to get along—except for the extremely shy Bartók, who had a difficult time, partly because of his retiring nature and partly because he was reluctant to teach, which has been the American composer's burden. But even if there has never been any real musical censorship in the United States— only the *de facto* variety resulting from neglect—neither have there been any rewards for serious composers commensurate with those showered on Soviet composers by the Soviet Composers' Union if they conformed. The pressure to write for the large public here, while never very strong, has at times meant the difference between utter destitution and a very marginal existence. Thus for different reasons advanced contemporary music in Russia and in the United States either went underground or ceased to be composed altogether from about 1935 to 1950. The almost total eclipse of Schoenberg, Bartók, Varèse, Ruggles, Wolpe, and others in the United States during these years does not match the violent measures taken in Russia during this time, but it had much the same effect, at least in the short run.

At the end of the Second World War, a reemergence of interest in the American progressive composers began to take place. In Europe, where indigenous avant-garde musical organizations had been very much more submerged, especially in Germany, there was a great resurgence of the progressive movement that had begun in the 1920s—and in Poland, the annual Warsaw Autumn has been for the past eleven years one of the important events.[3] During this same period, many early avant-garde works, such as Stravinsky's *Le Sacre*, *Les Noces*, and *L'Histoire du soldat*, and the Bartók quartets, concerti, and symphonic works, have become part of the standard repertory, pushing out many of the less convincing works of the previous period that have not worn well.

In the course of time, it was only natural that the Soviet Union, under the influence of a greater relaxation of the artistic climate, should start to pick up the broken threads of its older progressive artistic developments. We are already familiar with much of the literature that has emerged—but music, requiring more special experience and contact with public performance, has been slower to develop: from what I hear, very little progressive contemporary music has been played, until very recently, in the Soviet Union.[4]

3. In fact, one now sees progressive musical activity all over Eastern Europe, as I was able to notice in the Warsaw Festival of 1965: in Rumania with Aurel Stroe, Stefan Nicolescu, and Tiberiu Olah; in Estonia with Arvo Pärt; and in Yugoslavia, Hungary, Czechoslovakia, and elsewhere.

4. I have been invited by the U.S. State Department to go to the Soviet Union on two different occasions. Both times I refused to do so when I learned that not one performance of a work of mine could be scheduled while I was there. Remembering, by contrast, how when Soviet composers come here they are played right and left, I felt this to be unfair representation.

The first glimmering of the new movement came to me, I think, in 1962 at Warsaw, when I met Edison Denisov. He pointed out to me that his first name was an anagram of (all but the last letter of) his last name, and that he also wrote twelve-tone music, which seemed somehow appropriate in light of this. He took me off to a room in the Composers' Union in Warsaw and played me some of his work, which I found impressive. I gave him a score and recording of my Double Concerto and later wrote the Composers' Union in Moscow for his works, which they sent to me. At the 1961 festival, I also heard a number of other Soviet composers of quite a different stamp from the ones we had heard here up to that time. Since then more and more interesting Soviet music has come my way by tapes and by performances over European radio stations. The works of Denisov, Andrei Volkonsky, Valentin Silvestrov, and Alfred Schnittke, among a number of others, show great interest and promise.

The Russians have something vital to contribute, it has always seemed to me, in the musical field: they have a kind of liveliness, a fantasy and vigor which is very special and attractive, and in the best works of their younger composers these qualities are quite evident. It is heartening indeed to see these composers picking up again where the Stalin period cut them off, rediscovering the long Russian tradition and the really interesting musical developments of the early Soviet period, all of which have become so important to Western culture. In America, we all hope that this movement will have the opportunity to grow, that Russian composers will be able to continue writing music as they wish and become once again important to the development of new music.

Music Criticism
(1972)

The interplay between words about musical compositions and compositions themselves is very interesting to speculate about. Yet what impresses a composer about any attempt to verbalize about musical composition is the inadequacy of words to grasp something which is far more real to him in many important respects than words can be. Musical sounds are notoriously resistant to description, and so, to a composer, any attempt to discuss them always tends to be a matter of "flawed words and stubborn sounds"—the line from Wallace Stevens I used as the title of a recent book of conversations between Mr. Allen Edwards and myself.[1]

Beethoven's answer to someone who asked questions about some music he had just played was to play it over again. This is, of course, the composer's true response about his own work.

Yet writing about music—music criticism—does play an important part in musical life, and in one way or another affects the musical public, performers, and even composers. In cases where society gives fairly clear directives as to what music shall be—as in most periods of the past before the Romantic, or

---

1. Allen Edwards, *Flawed Words and Stubborn Sounds: A Conversation with Elliott Carter* (New York: W. W. Norton & Co., 1971). [S]

in socially conscious societies like that of the United States in the 1930s or that of the Soviet Union for most of its existence—the influence of dominant ideas and procedures as expressed in musical criticism is very powerful and pervasive. In our present Western society, such social directives are not clearly defined, so that a wide range of different methods and aesthetics, originated by composers and their critics, admits different attitudes, none of them binding. Works of great quality elicit very different criticism from one cultural milieu and period to another, and seem to change their meaning and character, and therefore their influence, for one place and time to another. Even so perceptive a critic as the American Paul Rosenfeld changed his mind about Schoenberg's music between 1920 and 1923. At first he described the Viennese composer as

> the great troubling presence of modern music. His vast, sallow skull lowers over it like a sort of North Cape. For with him, with the famous cruel five orchestral and nine piano pieces, we seem to be entering the arctic zone of musical art.[2]

Later, in 1923, after hearing *Pierrot lunaire*, Rosenfeld wrote:

> The human torso of this time is in the music of Schoenberg. He is the thing without arms, without legs, without organs of communication, without a phallus. He is the helpless quivering pulp; blindly stirring, groping, stretching . . . Anguish speaks out of the sweetest dreams. "Eine blasse Wäscherin" is like a cool hand upon a pain-rent head; like the cool linens that release the body after states of exhaustion. It is out of some starvation-pit that the Pierrot yearns for Columbine. She is the drink of water to a black and leathern mouth.[3]

This description seems preposterous if considered out of the context of its time, and when compared to what Pierre Boulez says of the work in 1961:

> The aesthetic of *Pierrot lunaire* is not so distant—disregarding questions of temperament and of musical characterization—from certain works of Debussy, like the Sonata for Cello and Piano. . . . As far as the instrumental writing goes, Schoenberg is at the height of his invention and originality: using a free language, he organizes it into sonorous shapes with more or less thematic tendencies, occasionally using the strictest forms of counterpoint. Oddly enough, it is the use of these forms which struck the earliest listeners, or at least the earliest chronicle writers and reviewers . . . even though these are far from being predominant.[4]

Schoenberg himself described the work in a letter of 1940, written about a performance he was to give and record in New York:

2. Paul Rosenfeld, *Musical Portraits* (New York: Harcourt, Brace & Co., 1920), 233.

3. Paul Rosenfeld, *Musical Chronicle* (New York: Harcourt, Brace & Co., 1923), 304–5.

4. Pierre Boulez, *Relevés d'apprenti*, textes réunis et présentés par Paule Thévenin (Paris: Editions du Seuil, 1966), 356–57; my translation. The quotation is from an article on Schoenberg that Boulez wrote for the *Encyclopédie de la Musique* (Paris: Fasquelle, 1961).

This time I intend to catch perfectly the light, ironical, satirical tone in which the piece was actually conceived. Then, too, times and ideas have changed a lot, so that what might have sounded Wagnerian or at worst Tchaikovskian to us then would remind us of Puccini, Léhar or worse, today.[5]

It is obvious that each of these writings about the same piece has some relevance to the music, yet is even more revealing about its time and milieu. Schoenberg, himself, points out how tastes and even perceptions change from period to period. In rereading the criticism of Paul Rosenfeld today, it is hard for me to remember why it was that they stimulated such a great interest in the work he described and led me to it. Now, of course, the descriptions seem almost totally irrelevant, as the music itself has become a primary consideration.

For the importance of critiques and descriptions of music in drawing listeners' attention to certain qualities and procedures and leading them to grasp things that would have otherwise escaped their attention, is certainly very great. When listeners not accustomed to hearing Western music first encounter polyphony, they hardly notice what is happening unless it is pointed out to them, just as those unfamiliar with East Indian music have difficulty hearing the characteristic inflections of pitch and attack. It is entirely possible that many developments in the arts would never have taken place if there had not been critics to explain to listeners what they were hearing and to develop their judgment by drawing attention to qualities, subtleties—and faults. The very elementary descriptions of the differences between consonances and dissonances by the early Western theorists were a way of making listeners conscious of what they were hearing as well as a way to teach musicians how to produce these effects. How serious music would have developed without its accompaniment of verbiage is hard to imagine, and it seems that in most cases it was the composer who led the way with new ideas and approaches, such as those of Haydn, Beethoven, or Wagner, and that these in turn have given rise to the vast cloud of words that occasionally confounds us.

Yet it is not only words that serve to define and clarify the new in music, it is also previous works themselves. Just as any new composition can be considered as a criticism of the past, throwing into question some of the assumptions it was based on, and making us hear it in a different perspective, so a knowledge of older works makes us hear new ones differently. The effect of Stravinsky's neoclassic music, with its motoric vigor, was to force us to hear the rhythm of Baroque music in a new way, just as much music of the 1950s and '60s makes us understand much more vividly the hocketing of thirteenth- and fourteenth-century music. Constant expansion of our horizon through familiarity with the sound of many kinds of old and new Western and non-Western music on recordings has changed the orientation of listeners and indeed all interested musicians in a way that is still hard to describe.

5. Arnold Schoenberg, letter to Fritz Stiedry, 31 August 1940, in Josef Rufer, *The Works of Arnold Schoenberg: A Catalogue of His Compositions, Writings, and Paintings* (London: Faber & Faber, 1962), 40.

In the midst of changes and historical developments, composers them-selves, naturally, are always considering and reconsidering their musical expe-riences; these are expressed in their music, and sometimes also verbally. Usu-ally, in his writings, the composer-critic is trying to clarify or change his attitudes and feelings about certain elements of his own style by discussing other related things. Wagner, for instance, whose early music was much influ-enced by Meyerbeer, gradually rid himself of this dependence by attacking Meyerbeer's music on extra-musical grounds. The same pattern can be seen on a less dramatic scale in Charles Ives, who in his *Essays Before a Sonata* re-veals an extensive knowledge of his immediate European predecessors and contemporaries. He tells of his admiration for Brahms, Elgar, Franck, D'Indy, his contempt for Wagner and Strauss, and his uncertainty about Reger and Mahler. His criticism, like that of many Romantic composers, is usually on moral or aesthetic grounds, as this, for instance:

> We might offer the suggestion that Debussy's content would have been worthier his manner if he had hoed corn. . . . Or we might say that his substance would have been worthier if his adoration or contemplation of Nature—which is often a part of it, and which rises to great heights, as is felt, for example, in *La Mer*—had been more the quality of Thoreau's. Debussy's attitude toward Nature seems to have a kind of sensual sensuousness underlying it, while Thoreau's is a kind of spiritual sensuousness.[6]

The criticism of Debussy is made even more direct in Ives's setting of Ru-pert Brooks's *Grantchester*, in which Brooks's line "Clever modern men have seen a Faun peeping through the green" is accompanied by a quotation from Debussy's *L'Après-midi d'un faune*. In all of this, Ives, like every composer, is seeking his place and his own style in relationship to other music as he hears and experiences it, and this is as true of his discussions of old music as it is of his criticism of Stravinsky's *Firebird*, which he heard in 1919 or 1920 when he wrote, "I thought it was morbid and monotonous. The idea of a phrase, usually a small one, was good enough, and interesting in itself, but he kept it going over and over and it got tiresome."[7] Underneath these criticisms, how-ever, there is a clear note of respect for what Ives calls the "manner," and an evident awareness of much that was going on. He was far from being the recluse that some have pictured.

Similar things can be found in almost any composer, in Mozart, for in-stance, whose letters contain many fascinating remarks, criticisms, and de-scriptions of other music. These, too, show him revolving and reorienting his thoughts. Perhaps the most crucial reorientation is described in the let-ters of March and April 1782, when he was twenty-six, at the time when he married Constanze Weber, and at the time when he first had extensive contact

6. Charles Ives, *Essays Before a Sonata, The Majority and Other Writings*, ed. Howard Boatwright (New York: W. W. Norton & Co., 1962), 82.

7. Charles Ives, *Memos*, ed. John Kirkpatrick (New York: W. W. Norton & Co., 1972), 138.

with the music of Handel and J. S. Bach. He first gives an indication of his new interest in a letter to his father, when he says he is collecting the fugues of J. S. Bach as well as those of his sons. Further evidences of this are the arrangements for string trio and string quartet that he made of many fugues from the *Well-Tempered Clavier*. In a letter to his sister just after his marriage to Constanze he says:

> My dear Constanze is really the cause of this fugue's coming into the world. Baron von Swieten, to whom I go every Sunday, gave me all the works of Handel and Sebastian Bach to take home with me (after I had played them to him). When Constanze heard the fugues, she absolutely fell in love with them. Now she will listen to nothing but fugues, and particularly (in this kind of composition) the works of Handel and Bach. Well, as she had often heard me play fugues out of my head, she asked me if I had ever written any down, and when I said I had not, she scolded me roundly for not recording some of my compositions in this most artistic and beautiful of all musical forms, and never ceased to entreat me until I wrote down a fugue for her. So this is its origin. I have purposely written above it *Andante maestoso*, as it must not be played too fast. . . .[8]

Mozart is referring to his fugue in C major (K. 394), seemingly patterned on that in C minor from the first book of the *Well-Tempered Clavier*. Contact with Bach developed Mozart's taste for counterpoint a great deal, for in the same letter he dismisses the work of a contemporary as not worthy to stand by Handel and Bach. This contact was, as everybody knows, to have far-reaching effects on Mozart's use of counterpoint, which up to that time had been derived from the academic precepts of Padre Martini. Alfred Einstein, in his book *Mozart*, discussing the impact of Bach, says:

> Mozart was too great and fine a musician not to feel deeply and painfully the conflict produced when his habit of thinking in terms of *galant* and "learned" music was shaken by the encounter with a living polyphonic style. . . . Mozart was never completely finished with the experience, but it enriched his imagination and resulted in more and more perfect works.[9]

Cases of the critical impact of one composer on another, with the latter assimilating the former into his own world of self-criticism, could be multiplied. Debussy's attitude about thematic development as derived from Beethoven and taught at the Conservatoire is well known. Whether Debussy's ideas were derived from those of Satie on the same subject is not clear, but such ideas did exert great influence on Stravinsky, who adhered to them from the time of *Le Sacre* on. It is also because of such avoidance of thematic development that the Schoenberg school looked so askance at Debussy and Stravinsky. This division of opinion is at the basis of Theodor Adorno's attack on Stravinsky

8. Mozart, 20 April 1782, in *The Letters of Mozart and His Family*, trans. and ed. Emily Anderson, 3 vols. (London: MacMillan and Co., Ltd., 1938), 3:1194. [B]

9. Alfred Einstein, *Mozart* (New York: Oxford University Press, 1945), 153.

and his praise of the Second Viennese school in his *Philosophie der neuen Musik*.[10]

The role of critics like Adorno, in directing the course of history, seems to be a relatively new one, and perhaps inevitable. For although critics do tend to try to be fair to new music, and try to separate the good from the bad, still they, like composers themselves, cannot fail to have their own preferences and their own picture of what the future has in store for us. Unlike the composer, though, the critic cannot *make* the future, although he can try to prepare a way, even if it is not the way that the future finally takes. Yet in the twentieth century with its very wide variety of aesthetics and supporting arguments, each exemplified in results of vastly different qualities, it often happens that critics, or art historians, have a better grasp of the complex ferment of points of view in the recent past and present than most working artists can have and so seem to be in a better position than they to indicate where the next step lies. Everybody knows the fable of the art critic who knew so much more about art movements in our time than any artist, and who was able, therefore, to go from city to city in his country and invent a special new movement with an aesthetic and supporting ideology for each city and thereby convince local artists in each place to follow his suggestion, pointing out, too, how they would not be repeating their colleagues in the next city. Being also influential as a critic and curator of exhibitions, he later made a harvest of works for a big annual exhibition, and could point out the unusual variety of the works and their excellences, and award prizes.

In America such a role often seems to be played by art and music departments in universities, bent on extrapolating what the next step in their fields will be. After all, one could extrapolate a program for what some consider avant-garde music very easily. Since repetition of a short stretch of music about ten times produced a scandal in the early 1920s, but no longer does, the number must be increased. We have reached well above a hundred now. Likewise, the hushed and almost noteless silences found at the end of the last Mahler works were a great surprise in their day but now are accepted, so we must have softer music, fewer notes, and more silence. The progress from the delicate click of the typewriter in the scoring of Satie's *Parade* to airplane propellers has recently reached the highly amplified scraping of metal on glass. Or, consider the composer: can he be replaced by a machine or by improvisation? Is the player piano or the electronic playback a substitute for the performer? How about giving the listener sounds and theatrical situations he cannot pay attention to in the usual way! However, just as we have seen Schoenberg noticing the change in listening habits from one period to another, it is now clear that the joke of one period can become the serious effort of the next. And vice versa—even without the assistance of the critics and educators.

---

10. Theodor W. Adorno, *Philosophie der neuen Musik* (Tübingen, 1949); trans. Anne G. Mitchell and Wesley V. Blomster as *Philosophy of Modern Music* (New York: Seabury Press, 1980). [S,B]

Journalist-critics are naturally very concerned with such matters as news-producing scandals, oddities that give them scope to write entertainingly, as well as predictions and efforts to force the hand of history even when it involves distorting facts. How else could one explain the following, which is the opening of an article intended to show that there is to be as drastic a change in contemporary music as there was between the Baroque and Classical periods:

> Can we even imagine what their music might have been like if Schoenberg had grown up not knowing the works of Wagner and if Stravinsky had known nothing of Rimsky-Korsakov? Except possibly for Ives, it is hard to find such innocence and insularity in our century. And yet that is what happened to Mozart, he knew the music of Bach's sons intimately, but not that of the father, who stood for everything Mozart's own idols found repellent in the Baroque. . . .

This appeared in July 1972, in the *New York Times,* the only New York paper in these years which reviews the musical scene. Like others that used to but failed, the *Times* may be fighting for its life, so that inaccuracy and sensationalism must inevitably permeate even its music reviews. This, on the part of a paper which is read throughout the United States, is profoundly distressing for an American musician, and appears to be in very great contrast to the literate kind of music writing found in English newspapers and periodicals. Our American weekly and monthly magazines devoted to music, too, are nowhere near the caliber of English ones. We do not understand why this is so, for certainly there are as many literate music-listeners in America as in England. A number of periodicals have been launched in the past twenty years in America—only to fail. On the other hand, academic periodicals supported by private individuals or university music departments, which deal with music in a theoretical way for specialists, seem to have a longer life. Thus there is almost no corrective for the musical journalism which, by necessity, has to be more responsible toward selling the papers than toward music. It is hard to gauge how much good composers derive from reviews in these papers, how much they help in getting their works considered by the lay public.

Within the confines of his own development the composer really has only two critics, in our situation: his own works and his alter ego—his self-critical activity. His works, as they mount up, each tend to suggest new paths of development, or, having fulfilled their particular vein, bring it to a halt. It is quite a common pattern for composers to write successive works exploring opposing areas of experience or technique—the comparison of Beethoven's Eighth and Ninth Symphonies shows this, as do the like-numbered ones of Mahler, as indeed do the three symphonies Mozart wrote in 1788. The carrying out of a general tendency from work to work, such as, for instance, the reduction to essential brief elements found in the series of works Webern wrote up to op. 11, or a similar pattern of reducing rhythm, tempi, and texture to their simplest expression in his last series of works, represents, of course, the opposite tendency.

The development of the self-critical power which leads a composer to try to write the work he would most like to hear—or perhaps what he would like others to hear—involves his commitment to society, to art, as well as to the materials of music. That Ives in the setting of Rupert Brooks's *Grantchester*, mentioned above, chose to illustrate some words about "clever modern men" with a quotation from Debussy, a method quite characteristic of him, indicates that he could not, so to speak, assume the role of a clever modern man and present it out of his own experience. The lapse in style shows that Ives's inner self-criticism did not extend to include the very basic lesson learnable from all art works of any importance, which takes as a fundamental that every part should be marked with the artist's vision, with the corollary that what falls out of the frame falls out because it has not been assimilated.

Thus the inner criticism, or self-criticism, of a composer becomes a demonstration of his relationship with his society, embodying as it does his courtesy to his listeners and performers, by first inducing him to find visions or messages which seem important to communicate, and then communicating them in a way that can eventually lead to understanding. This self-criticism cannot come from without, although acceptance or rejection of a work may reinforce the composer's inner conviction or change its direction.

Appendix 1

Notes on Sources

I. Surveying the Compositional Scene

"The Composer's Viewpoint." First published in *National Music Council Bulletin* 7, no. 1 (September 1946): 10–11.

"A Further Step." First published, in Spanish, as "Un paso adelante," *Buenos Aires Musical* 14, special number (December 1959); published in the original English in *The American Composer Speaks—1770–1965*, ed. Gilbert Chase (Baton Rouge: Louisiana State University Press, 1966), 245–54.

"The Challenge of the New." Previously unpublished. This lecture was given originally under the title "The Challenge of Electronic Music" (paired with a talk by Vladimir Ussachevsky) on 17 June 1960 at a meeting of the American Symphony Orchestra League in St. Louis. Subsequently, an editor at *Hi-Fi/Stereo Review* asked Carter to develop a publishable essay from this lecture, which was tentatively given the title "Orchestra Composing Today." This editor's demands, however, for a substantial revision in tone and emphasis apparently did not sit well with Carter, and after some work on the part of both author and editor toward arriving at a text that would be mutually acceptable, the effort was finally abandoned in 1962. The present edition of this lecture follows the original text for the most part, with some insertion and revision of material based on later versions.

"Fallacy of the Mechanistic Approach." First published in *Modern Music* 23, no. 3 (Summer 1946): 228–30.

"'La Musique sérielle aujourd'hui.'" Previously uncollected. This text, in its original form, was first published, in French, as part of a symposium of brief articles by several authors under the title of the first (and principal) text by André Boucourechliev, "La Musique sérielle aujourd'hui" (*Preuves* 177 [November 1965], 21–38). Carter's contribution, under the subhead (supplied, one would surmise, by the editor) "Le produit authentique d'aujourd'hui est l'oeuvre expérimentale," appeared on pp. 32–33. The original English text, with one page missing and dated 1 August 1965, resides in the Carter Collection of the Sacher Foundation. The version given here restores the missing text through re-translation; the author has also made a few additional revisions for this edition. (See also p. 17n.)

"ISCM Festival, Rome." First published under the title "Current Chronicle: Italy" in *Musical Quarterly* 45, no. 4 (October 1959): 530–41.

"*Rasputin's End* and *Lady Macbeth of Mtsensk*." First published under the title "Current Chronicle: Germany" in *Musical Quarterly* 46, no. 3 (July 1960): 367–71.

"Letter from Europe." First published in *Perspectives of New Music* 1, no. 2 (Spring
1963): 195–205.

"ISCM Festival, Amsterdam." Previously unpublished. This may originally have been
intended as part of "Letter from Rome," which was published under the title "Letter from Europe" (see above). It now stands as a separate report on Carter's experience as a juror for ISCM-Amsterdam and as such is a good deal more informative
(and candid) than "Sixty Staves to Read," the article he wrote for the *New York
Times* in 1960 recounting his experience as an ISCM juror (in Cologne) that year,
which has been omitted from the present collection (see Appendix 2).

II. American Music

"Once Again Swing; Also 'American Music.'" First published in *Modern Music* 16,
no. 2 (January 1939): 99–103. The final two paragraphs, which deal with miscella-
neous incidental items, have been omitted from the present collection.

"American Music in the New York Scene." First published in *Modern Music* 17, no. 2
(January–February 1940): 93–101.

"The Agony of Modern Music in America, 1955." Previously unpublished. This report, written by Carter in early 1955, when he was one of the vice-presidents of the
International Society for Contemporary Music (ISCM), and probably intended for
delivery to the meeting of that organization in Baden-Baden that year, deals with
two principal topics of considerable historical interest: Carter's opinions about
Henry Pleasants's then brand-new book, *The Agony of Modern Music*, and its reception among other American composers; and the artistic and political tensions
surrounding the just-accomplished merger of the US Section of ISCM and the
(much more conservative) League of Composers.

"The Rhythmic Basis of American Music." First published in *The Score and I.M.A.
Magazine* 12 (June 1955): 27–32.

"The European Roots of American Musical Culture." Previously unpublished. This
was written as a radio address, under commission by the North German (Hamburg) Radio in September 1961. No record has survived with the manuscript indicating whether this address was ever broadcast, and if so whether this was done in
German translation. Carter submitted this text to *Perspectives of New Music*; it
was accepted for that journal's very first issue (Fall 1962), but only a severe abridgment of the last few pages was published, under a different title ("The Milieu of the
American Composer"; see Appendix 2) made necessary, one would guess, by the
editor's excision of almost all of the material that had suggested the original title. In
Writings, only this abridgment was reprinted; in the present collection, the original
text has been restored.

"Expressionism and American Music." This text originated as a paper given at the
Convegno Internazionale di Studi sull'Espressionismo at the Maggio Fiorentino
in 1964. Subsequently it was published in *Perspectives of New Music* 4, no. 1
(Fall–Winter 1965): 1–13, then revised for republication in *Perspectives on American Composers*, ed. Benjamin Boretz and Edward T. Cone (New York: W. W.
Norton & Co., 1971), 217–29. The present collection reprints this revised version, with a further revised set of notes.

"'The Composer Is a University Commodity.'" First published in *College Music Symposium* 10 (Fall 1970): 68–70, as an answer to a questionnaire: "The Composer in Academia: Reflections on a Theme of Stravinsky." In *Writings*, the Stones commented: "The Symposium . . . posed as its theme a quotation from *Conversations with Igor Stravinsky*, by Stravinsky and Robert Craft (Garden City, N.Y.: Doubleday & Co., 1959, 153–54). In it, Stravinsky maintains that 'a composer is or isn't; he cannot learn to acquire the gift that makes him one.' He also 'warns young composers . . . against university teaching' because 'teaching is academic,' it conforms to conventional rules, and it may therefore 'not be the right contrast for a composer's non-composing time.'"

III. Charles Ives

"The Case of Mr. Ives." First published in *Modern Music* 16, no. 3 (March 1939): 172–76.

"Ives Today: His Vision and Challenge." First published in *Modern Music* 21, no. 4 (May–June 1944): 199–202.

"An American Destiny." First published in *Listen* 9, no. 1 (November 1946): 4–7.

"Charles Ives Remembered." First published in *Charles Ives Remembered: An Oral History*, ed. Vivian Perlis (New Haven: Yale University Press, 1974), 131–45. In a note to their reprinting of this article in *Writings*, the Stones pointed out, usefully: "This article was written by Carter *after* his interview with Vivian Perlis, i.e., as a result of the interview; it is not a transcript of the interview itself, as the term *oral history* might suggest."

"Documents of a Friendship with Ives." First published in *Parnassus* 3, no. 2 (Summer 1975), 300–15; reprinted in *Tempo* 117 (June 1976): 2–10.

IV. Some Other Composers

"Gabriel Fauré." First published in *Listen* 6, no. 1 (May 1945): 8–10. The brief discography at the end of this article ("Fauré's Music on Records"), omitted in *Writings*, is likewise omitted in this collection.

"The Three Late Sonatas of Debussy." Previously unpublished. This text originated as a lecture, delivered at Princeton University in 1959. It actually deals as much with Debussy in general—his cultural milieu, his compositional history, the significance of his work for the subsequent development of twentieth-century music—as it does with his three last works. The manuscript exists as one continuous draft accompanied by a great deal of more fragmentary, perhaps previously written matterial, much of which is essential to the argument and which in this edition has been incorporated where possible.

"American Figure, with Landscape." First published in *Modern Music* 20, no. 4 (May–June 1943): 219–25.

"Stravinsky in 1940." First published as part of "Stravinsky and Other Moderns in 1940," *Modern Music* 17, no. 3 (March–April 1940): 164–70. In the present collection, the section on "other moderns" has been omitted (see Appendix 2).

"Igor Stravinsky: Two Tributes." Comprises "Igor Stravinsky, 1882–1971," first published in *Perspectives of New Music* 9, no. 2, and 10, no. 1 (double issue, 1971): 1–6; and "Igor Stravinsky, 1882–1971," the text of a eulogy delivered 10 December 1971, first published in *Proceedings of the American Academy of Arts and Letters and the National Institute of Arts and Letters*, second series, no. 22 (1972): 84–86.

"On Edgard Varèse." Previously uncollected. This essay first appeared in *The New Worlds of Edgard Varèse: A Symposium*, ed. Sherman Van Solkema (Brooklyn, N.Y.: Institute for Studies in American Music, 1979), 1–7. It is a revision of an earlier text; see Carter's own note (p. 146).

"Edward Steuermann." First published under the title "Current Chronicle: New York," *Musical Quarterly* 52, no. 1 (January 1966): 93–101.

"Walter Piston." First published in *Musical Quarterly* 32, no. 3 (July 1946): 354–75. The list of Piston's works at the end of this article, omitted in its reprinting in *Writings*, has also been omitted in the present collection.

"Roger Sessions: Violin Concerto." First published under the title "Current Chronicle: New York," *Musical Quarterly* 45, no. 3 (July 1959): 375–81.

"In Memoriam: Roger Sessions, 1896–1985." Previously unpublished in this form. The author and editor collaborated in conflating two previously published (and uncollected) essays for this edition: "Roger Sessions Admired," *Perspectives of New Music* 23, no. 2 (Spring–Summer 1985): 120–22; and "Roger Sessions, 1896–1985," *Proceedings of the American Academy of Arts and Letters and the National Institute of Arts and Letters*, second series, no. 36 (1985): 57–62.

"In Memoriam: Stefan Wolpe, 1902–1972." First published in *Perspectives of New Music* 11, no. 1 (Fall–Winter 1972): 3–5.

"Goffredo Petrassi: Two Essays." "The Recent Works of Goffredo Petrassi," written at Luciano Berio's request for a projected new periodical that never came into being, is a relatively short yet pithy survey of Petrassi's compositions of the 1950s that has remained unpublished up to now. The later, previously uncollected "Some Reflections on *Tre per sette*" was first published in Italian in *Petrassi*, ed. Enzo Restagno (Turin: Edizioni di Torino, 1986), 310–12 (issued in commemoration of the Petrassi festival held in Turin that year), without the musical examples that have been added for this collection.

"To Think of Milton Babbitt." Previously uncollected. First published in *Perspectives of New Music* 14, no. 2, and 15, no. 1 (double issue, 1976): 29–31.

"For Pierre Boulez on His Sixtieth." Previously uncollected. First published in *Pierre Boulez: Eine Festschrift zum 60. Geburtstag am 26. März 1985*, ed. Josef Häusler (Vienna: Universal, 1985), 12–13.

V. Life and Work

"To Be a Composer in America." Previously unpublished. Delivered (under an unknown title) on 27 March 1953 at the University of Illinois, this substantial text touches on numerous matters, including Carter's own music and Western music of the twentieth century in general, but principally it addresses the experience of being an American composer and the ways in which that experience had changed over the past twenty years.

"The Composer's Choices." This text was commissioned by the Fromm Foundation and delivered as a radio lecture with recorded musical examples, probably in about 1960; it was first published in *Writings*, 192–97.

"Shop Talk by an American Composer." First published in *Musical Quarterly* 46, no. 2 (April 1960): 189–201. In *Writings*, the Stones supplied this comment: "Carter wrote the following after a symposium at Princeton University, in an attempt to present a concentrated version of his ideas and the students' reactions and questions."

"The Time Dimension in Music." Given originally as a lecture at Bowdoin College, 21 August 1965; subsequently published in *Music Journal* 23, no. 8 (November 1965): 29–30.

"Two Sonatas, 1948 and 1952." First published as sleeve notes for recording of the Sonata for Cello and Piano and the Sonata for Flute, Oboe, Cello, and Harpsichord, Nonesuch Records H–71234 (1969).

"String Quartets Nos. 1, 1951, and 2, 1959." First published as sleeve notes for a recording by the Composers String Quartet, Nonesuch Records H–71249 (1970).

"The Orchestral Composer's Point of View." First published in *The Orchestral Composer's Point of View: Essays on Twentieth-Century Music by Those Who Wrote It*, ed. Robert Stephan Hines (Norman: University of Oklahoma Press, 1970), 39–61.

"On Saint-John Perse and the Concerto for Orchestra." Previously unpublished. The manuscript for this talk, given on 5 February 1974 at one of the "Informal Evenings" arranged by Pierre Boulez during his tenure as Director of the New York Philharmonic, exists largely as a collection of fragments, which for this edition have been assembled into a coherent essay. Here is documented the way in which Carter's encounter with Perse's epic poem *Vents* influenced his work on one of his most important orchestral pieces. For the present collection, the author has also supplied a new introductory note.

"Brass Quintet." Given originally as an introductory talk for the premiere of this work over the BBC, 20 October 1974; first published in *Writings*, 322–25.

"Double Concerto, 1961, and Duo, 1974." First published as sleeve notes for recording of these works, Nonesuch Records H–71314 (1975). In their edition of these notes for *Writings*, the Stones inserted some material from an unidentified, earlier program note by Carter on the Double Concerto, consisting principally of two quotations from Pope's *Dunciad*, which has been carried over to the present collection.

"Music and the Time Screen." First published in *Current Thought in Musicology*, ed. John W. Grubbs (Austin: University of Texas Press, 1976), 63–88.

"'Elle est la musique en personne': A Reminiscence of Nadia Boulanger." Previously unpublished. The genesis of this essay was an oral reminiscence tape-recorded sometime during the mid-1980s, subsequently transcribed, then worked on in its written form by Carter himself. This edition is a further, thoroughgoing revision that eliminates as far as possible the inevitable repetitious and disorderly aspects of such reminiscences. It is one of the very few published accounts—Aaron Copland's, in *Copland: 1900 through 1942*, is one other notable example—that reveals in any appreciable detail what actually went on in Boulanger's classes and lessons. (See also p. 281, n1.)

"Reminiscence of Italy." Previously uncollected. This short text was written in May 1988 and first published, in Italian, as "Ricordo dell'Italia," one of the "Scritti di Elliott Carter" included in the same volume with the Italian translation of David Schiff, *The Music of Elliott Carter*, expanded version (Naples and Rome: Edizione scientifiche italiane, 1990), 567–70. (See also p. 294, n2.)

VI. Philosophy, Criticism, and the Other Arts

"More about Balanchine." First published in *Modern Music* 14, no. 4 (May–June 1937): 237–39.

"With the Dancers." First published in *Modern Music* 15, no. 2 (January–February 1938): 118–22.

"Remembering Balanchine." Previously uncollected. This text originated in an oral reminiscence, transcribed from tape and published in *I Remember Balanchine: Recollections of the Ballet Master by Those Who Knew Him*, ed. Francis Mason (New York: Doubleday, 1991), 163–69. The version published in the present collection represents a thorough revision, with some new material added by the author.

"Theatre and Films." First published in *Modern Music* 21, no. 1 (November–December 1943): 50–53; the slight abridgments of the article as reprinted in *Writings* have been carried over to the present collection. (The Stones commented: "The cut material consists of a review of *The Merry Widow*, an announcement of the impending premier performance of *Carmen Jones*, and reviews of three motion pictures: *We Will Come Back*, *The Constant Nymph*, and *The Great Mr. Handel*.")

"The Genial Sage." Previously uncollected. This remembrance of the critic Paul Rosenfeld was first published in *Paul Rosenfeld: Voyager in the Arts*, ed. Jerome Mellquist and Lucie Wiese (New York: Creative Age Press, 1948), 163–65. For the present collection, the author has supplied an introductory note.

"Introduction to a Poetry Reading by W. H. Auden." Originally delivered at the Hunter College Playhouse, New York, January 1969; first published in *Writings*, 256–57. A set of notes has been added for the present collection.

"Music as a Liberal Art." First published in *Modern Music* 22, no. 1 (November 1944): 12–16. A set of notes has been added for the present collection.

"Time Lecture." Previously unpublished. Given at Harvard University in 1965, this text bears an obvious relationship to certain later writings, notably "Music and the Time Screen" and "The Time Dimension in Music"; but unlike those two previously published essays, the "Time Lecture" foregoes a focus on Carter's own music in favor of a more general inquiry into the nature of musical time.

"The *Gesamtkunstwerk*." Previously unpublished. This text originated as a lecture given during Carter's semester as Visiting Professor at the Massachusetts Institute of Technology (Fall 1966); it may well have been revised subsequently for other occasions. Far from treating Wagner's ideas exclusively, it deals with many different approaches to the "unified artwork" in which music plays a role: besides Wagner, the reader will find Barthes, Verdi, Edmund Wilson, Poe, Kandinsky, Eisenstein, Artaud, Brecht, and Rimbaud quoted in various contexts.

"Soviet Music." Previously unpublished. Written for a symposium at Sarah Lawrence College on the modern Soviet Union and delivered there on 24 May 1967, this lecture draws some interesting (and occasionally disturbing) parallels between the musical climate in the Soviet Union and that of the United States from the 1920s on. It exists in two forms in the Carter Collection at the Sacher Foundation: a tape recording of the "live" event, the first portion of which was later re-dubbed; and a typescript which corresponds only loosely to the recording. For this edition, a composite version has been made from these sources.

"Music Criticism." Originally written for broadcast over the BBC in August 1972, as part of a series on "Composers and Criticism," ed. Elaine Padmore; first published in *Writings*, 310–18.

Appendix 2

Published Writings by Carter
Not Included in This Collection

NOTE: An asterisk (*) preceding an entry signifies that the article was collected in *The Writings of Elliott Carter*. Page numbers in that book are given in square brackets.

* "The New York Season." *Modern Music* 14, no. 2 (January–February 1937): 90–92. [3–5]

* "Late Winter, New York." *Modern Music* 14, no. 3 (March–April 1937): 147–54. [5–10]

* "The Sleeping Beauty." *Modern Music* 14, no. 3 (March–April 1937): 175–76. [10–11]

* "Season's End in New York." *Modern Music* 14, no. 4 (May–June 1937): 215–17. [11–13]

* "Opening Notes, New York." *Modern Music* 15, no. 1 (November–December 1937): 36–37. [16–17]

* "In the Theatre." *Modern Music* 15, no. 1 (November–December 1937): 51–53. [17–19]

* "With the Dancers." *Modern Music* 15, no. 1 (November–December 1937): 55–56. [19–20]

* "Homage to Ravel, 1875–1937/Vacation Novelties, New York." *Modern Music* 15, no. 2 (January–February 1938): 96–103. [21–22, abridged]

* "Musical Reactions—Bold and Otherwise." *Modern Music* 15, no. 3 (March–April 1938): 199. [27]

* "Orchestras and Audiences; Winter, 1938." *Modern Music* 15, no. 3 (March–April 1938): 167–71. [28–31]

* "Recent Festival in Rochester." *Modern Music* 15, no. 4 (May–June 1938): 241–43. [31–33]

* "Season's End, New York." *Modern Music* 15, no. 4 (May–June 1938): 228–33. [34–38]

* "Coolidge Crusade; WPA; New York Season." *Modern Music* 16, no. 1 (November–December 1938): 33–38. [39–43]

* "Further Notes on the Winter Season." *Modern Music* 16, no. 3 (March 1939): 176–79. [51–54]

* "O Fair World of Music!" *Modern Music* 16, no. 4 (May–June 1939): 238–43. [55–59]

* "Season of Hindemith and Americans." *Modern Music* 16/4 (May–June 1939): 249–54. [60–63]

* "The New York Season Opens." *Modern Music* 17, no. 1 (October–November 1939): 34–38. [64–68]

* "Stravinsky and Other Moderns in 1940" [only section on "other moderns" not reprinted]. *Modern Music* 17, no. 3 (March–April 1940): 167–70. [77–81]

* "The Changing Scene, New York." *Modern Music* 17, no. 4 (May–June 1940): 237–41. [81–85]

"Composers by the Alphabet." *Modern Music* 19, no. 1 (November–December 1941): 70–71.

* "Films and Theatre." *Modern Music* 20, no. 3 (March–April 1943): 205–7. [86–87]

* "Theatre and Films." *Modern Music* 20, no. 4 (May–June 1943): 282–84. [93–95] This text is unrelated to the identically titled "Theatre and Films" that is included in section VI of the present collection.

"The New Compositions." *Saturday Review* 27, no. 4 (22 January 1944): 32–33.

"What's New in Music." *Saturday Review* 28, no. 3 (20 January 1945): 13–14, 34.

* "New Publications of Music." *Saturday Review* 29, no. 4 (26 January 1946): 34–38. [111–16]

* "Scores for Graham; Festival at Columbia." *Modern Music* 23, no. 1 (Winter 1946): 53–55. [116–18]

"Ben Weber and Virgil Thomson Questioned by Eight Composers." *Possibilities* 1 (Winter, 1947): 18–24. Questions by Elliott Carter, 19, 21–22.

* "The Function of the Composer." *Bulletin of the Society for Music in the Liberal Arts College* 3, no. 1, suppl. 3 (1952): 1–7. [150–58]

* "Wallingford Riegger." *American Composers Alliance Bulletin* 2, no. 1 (February 1952): 3. [158–59]

"Illinois Festival—Enormous and Active." *New York Herald Tribune*, 5 April 1953: 17.

"Music of the Twentieth Century." *Encyclopaedia Britannica* (1953), 16: 16–18.

"La Musique aux Etats-Unis." *Synthèses* 9, no. 96 (May 1954): 206–11.

Autobiographical Sketch. In *Twenty-Fifth Anniversary Report of the Harvard Class of 1930* (Cambridge: Harvard University Press, 1955), 165–69.

* "Sixty Staves to Read." *New York Times*, 24 January 1960, 2:9. [197–99]

* "The Milieu of the American Composer." *Perspectives of New Music* 1, no. 1 (1962): 149–51. [216–18] (See note on "The European Roots of American Musical Culture" in Appendix 1, above.)

Letter to the Editor [reply to Gardner Read concerning notation], *Journal of Music Theory* 7, no. 2 (Winter 1963): 270–73.

"Elliott Carter Objects." *New York Times*, 20 October 1968, 2:20.

* "String Quartet No. 2 (1959)." [Program note, 1970.] [273–74]

* "Variations for Orchestra (1955)." [Program note, 1972.] [308–10]

Acceptance by Elliott Carter of Gold Medal for Music, *Proceedings of the American Academy of Arts and Letters and the National Institute of Arts and Letters*, second series, no. 22 (1972): 34.

* "String Quartet No. 3 (1971)." [Program note, 1974.] [320–22]

Foreword to *Sonic Design*, by Robert Cogan and Pozzi Escot (Englewood Cliffs, N.J.: Prentice-Hall, 1976), ix.

"What Is American Music?/Was ist amerikanische Musik?" *Österreichische Musikzeitschrift* 31, no. 10, special bilingual issue (1976): 468–70.

* "A Symphony of Three Orchestras (1976)." [Program note, 1977.] [366–67]

"Concerto for Orchestra" and "Variations for Orchestra." [Program notes.] In Edward Downes, *The New York Philharmonic Guide to the Symphony* (New York: Walker & Co., 1976), 246–47, 250–51.

"France Amérique Ltd." In *Paris—New York* (Paris: Centre national d'art et de culture Georges Pompidou/Musée national d'art moderne, 1977), 7–11.

"Dankesworte von Elliott Carter." In *Ernst-von-Siemens Musikpreis 1981* [booklet issued on the occasion of the award of this prize to Carter] (Zug, Switzerland: Ernst von Siemens Stiftung, 1981), 19–22.

"A Tribute to Paul Jacobs." [Program note, 1983.]

Introduction to *Mademoiselle: Conversations with Nadia Boulanger*, by Bruno Monsaingeon (Manchester: Carcanet Press, 1985), 12–13.

"A Commemorative Tribute to Roger Sessions." *ArtScape* [WGUC FM, Cincinnati] 1, no. 12 (1986): 16–17.

"Mozart's Human Touch." *Musical Times* 132 (November 1991): 549.

Also omitted are numerous short program notes for works that Carter has written since 1977, as well as the many interviews he has given since 1970.

Index

Messiaen, Olivier, 17n, 18, 41, 149, 215, 265; *Oiseaux exotiques*, 21, 24, 28
Metropolitan Opera (New York), 64–65, 67, 73, 138, 293, 300, 306, 332
Meyer, Felix, xn, xii
Meyer, Krzysztof, 153
Meyerbeer, Giacomo, 338
Microtones, 32, 73
Mihailovici, Marcel, 41
Milan electronic music studio, 222
Milhaud, Darius, 108, 119, 208, 332, 334; *Les Choéphores*, 148; *Le Mort d'un tyran*, 151
Mitropoulos, Dimitri, 53, 198, 213
Mittner, L., 75n, 78–79, 80, 82
Modern Dance, 295, 296, 297–99
Modern Music (periodical), vii, viii, x, 52, 100, 104, 111, 112, 163, 204, 222
Monet, Claude, 124
Monod, Jacques-Louis, 198, 213
Monteux, Pierre, 141, 160
Monteverdi, Claudio, 287, 289, 322; madrigals, 285
Moore, Douglas, 113
Moore, Marianne, 306
Morley, Thomas, 310; *A Plaine and Easie Introduction to Practicall Musicke*, 310n
Moscow Art Theatre, 331
Moscow Opera, 331
Mozart, Wolfgang Amadeus, 54, 55, 124, 131, 161, 173, 208, 257, 266, 283, 287, 312, 316, 317, 318, 323, 338–39, 341; *Don Giovanni*, 273, 316, 321; Fugue in C Major (K. 394), 339; *Idomeneo* ("Placido il mar"), 288; Letters, 338–39; *The Magic Flute*, 142
Muck, Karl, 160
Museum of Modern Art (New York), 306
Musical Art Quartet, 46, 47
Musikalisches Würfelspiel, 34
Mussorgsky, Modest, 29, 46, 48, 136, 137, 257, 303; *Night on Bald Mountain*, 138
"My Country 'Tis of Thee," 87
Myrick, Julian. *See* Ives & Myrick
Nabokov, Nicolas, 294, 301, 303; *The Holy Devil*, 29; *Old Friends and New Music*, 142; *Rasputin's End*, 28, 29–31
Nancarrow, Conlon, 61, 62, 266; *Rhythm Study No. 1*, 61–62, 233
Nason, Kathryn, 161
National Institute of Arts and Letters, 182
Nationalism, in music, 66, 159
Neher, Caspar, 28

Neoclassicism, 20, 56, 58, 74, 133, 134, 139, 145, 188, 194, 202, 215, 229
New England Conservatory, 136
New Music Edition, 4, 74, 75, 88, 99, 101, 103, 109, 197; subsidy by Charles Ives of, 109
New Music Quarterly, 109, 110
New School (New York), 151
New York City Ballet, 300
New York City High School of Music and Art, 47
New York Herald Tribune, 46
New York Philharmonic, 52, 53, 141, 180, 186, 213, 250, 251, 252; Informal Evenings, 250, 347; Prospective Encounters, 262
New York Times, 46, 341, 344
Nicolescu, Stefan, 334n
Nicolov, Lazar, 38
Nietzsche, Friedrich, 324
Nijinska, Bronislava, 296
Nilsson, Bo: *Ein irrender Sohn*, 24, 26, 27
Noh dramas, 319
Nono, Luigi, 21; *Il canto sospeso*, 17, 36; *Incontri*, 21, 24
North German Radio, 344
Nutida Musik (periodical), 21

O'Neill, Eugene, Jr., 98, 99
Oboukhov, Nikolai, 146; *Le Livre de la vie*, 332
Offenbach, Jacques, 29; *Tales of Hoffmann*, 327
Office of War Information, vii
Olah, Tiberiu, 334n
Ornstein, Leo, 74, 80, 81, 146, 306
Otto, Teo, 28
Ouspensky, Victor: *Tertium Organum*, 109
Oustvolska, Halina, 38

Paderewski, Ignace, 285
Padmore, Elaine, 349
Paganini, Nicolò, 323–24, 330
Pagano, Carl, 116
Paine, John Knowles, 136
Painting, modern, 18, 23, 82, 91; and spatial analogy to musical time, 262–63
Palermo Festival, 31, 35
Palladio, Andrea, 310
Parker, Horatio, 97, 100
Pärt, Arvo, 334n
Pascal, Blaise, 78; *Pensées*, 282
Pasternak, Boris: *Dr. Zhivago*, 29
Pater, Walter, 76

Stalin, Josef, 333
Stavisky affair, 211, 286–87
Stein, Erwin, 240
Stein, Gertrude, 286, 306
Steiner, Rudolf, 99
Steuermann, Edward, 55, 151–58, 198;
    arrangement of *Wohin* (Schubert), 153;
    Cantata, 151; *Drei Chöre*, 153; Suite,
    piano, 153; *Suite for Chamber
    Orchestra*, 153, 154–56
Stevens, Wallace, 335; *Esthétique du mal*, 228
Stieglitz, Alfred, 306
Stochastic music, 36
Stockhausen, Karlheinz, 41, 100, 148, 265;
    Klavierstück XI, 35
Stokowski, Leopold, 73, 105, 151, 157
Stone, Else and Kurt, ix, x, xii
Strang, Gerald, 74
Strauss, Johann, 54, 281n
Strauss, Richard, 53, 55, 121, 207, 208, 221,
    240, 281n, 338; *Capriccio*, 322; *Elektra*,
    182; *Salome*, 283–84
Stravinsky, Igor, 8, 9, 21, 38, 54, 56, 57, 68,
    74, 83, 87, 101, 119, 122, 125, 131,
    133, 138- 46, 169, 178, 179, 181, 183,
    184, 192, 202, 204, 221, 229, 240, 266,
    270, 281n, 283, 285, 287, 293, 303,
    312, 315, 318, 331, 332, 334, 337, 339,
    341; and Classical forms, 123, 124; and
    discontinuity, 142–44; and neoclassicism,
    139, 145; as pianist, 141; and rhythm,
    58, 147; and serialism, 145; sketching
    methods of, 142; and time, 315
    Compositions:
    Abraham and Isaac, 141; *Agon*, 7, 21,
    141, 241; *Apollon musagète (Apollo)*,
    139, 140, 141, 296; *Le Baiser de la fée*,
    140, 295, 300; *Cantata*, 141, 205;
    Canticum sacrum, 7; *Capriccio*, 139,
    141; *Le Chant du rossignol*, 142;
    Concerto, piano, 123; Concerto, violin,
    140; *Concerto for Two Solo Pianos*,
    140; *Danses concertantes*, 300;
    Dumbarton Oaks Concerto, 138, 140;
    Duo concertant, 287; *The Firebird*, 108,
    139, 145, 338; *Fireworks*, 141; *The
    Flood*, 142; *L'Histoire du soldat*, 138,
    140, 143, 198, 202, 334; *Jeu de cartes*,
    139, 141, 296, 300; *Mass*, 141; *Les
    Noces*, 139, 334; *Octuor*, 140; *Oedipus
    Rex*, 332; *Orpheus*, 141, 142; *The Owl
    and the Pussycat*, 141, 146; *Perséphone*,

141, 143, 286, 287, 291; *Petrouchka*,
53, 73, 108, 139, 144, 145, 148, 306,
332; *Pribaoutki*, 144; *Pulcinella*, 140;
Ragtime, 108; *The Rake's Progress*, 205,
208, 308; *Renard*, 143; *Requiem
Canticles*, 141, 146; *Le Rossignol*, 73,
144, 306; *Le Sacre du printemps*, 37,
74n, 87, 100, 139, 141, 144, 145, 148,
202, 225, 284, 306, 332, 334, 339; *A
Sermon, a Narrative, and a Prayer*, 40;
Sonata, piano, 123; *Symphonie de
psaumes*, 54, 139, 141, 174–75, 291;
Symphonies of Wind Instruments, 6,
142, 188; *Symphony in Three Move-
ments*, 6, 141, 175, 188; *Three Songs
from William Shakespeare*, 55; *Threni*,
21, 141; Variations (Aldous Huxley in
memoriam), 241
Writings:
Autobiography, 315; *Conversations
with Stravinsky* (Robert Craft), 345; *La
Poétique musicale*, 266
Stream of consciousness, 126, 131, 233
Strobel, Heinrich, 19, 105
Stroe, Aurel, 38, 334n
Stuckenschmidt, H. H., 75, 75n
Stupinigi, 303
Suvchinsky, Pierre, 263, 266, 314
Swinburne, Charles, 297
Swing (musical style), 45–46, 88
Szymanowski, Karol, 39

Tala, 228
Tamiris, 297
Tansman, Alexandre, 304; *Flesh and Fantasy*
    (film score), 305; *Triptyque*, 305
Taras, John, 301
Tchaikovsky, Peter Ilich, 29, 54, 138, 139,
    295, 303, 315, 337; *Mozartiana*, 129
Tchelitchew, Pavel, 45, 300, 301, 303, 304
Tcherepnin, Alexander: Symphony No. 1, 148
Theatre Arts Committee (New York), 53
Theosophy, 78, 99
Thompson, Randall, 203–4; *Americana*, 51;
    The Peaceable Kingdom, 51; Symphony
    No. 2, 51
Thomson, Virgil, 161, 203, 322; *Filling
    Station*, 299
Thoreau, Henry David, 93, 95, 338
Time: chronometric, 230, 263, 266, 314, 316;
    chronoametric, 266; clock, 263, 264,
    266, 273; empirical, 315; experienced,

Printed in the United States
23755LVS00004B/40-102